PRECEPTS FOR

A HANDY SCRIPTURAL REFERENCE GUIDE

LEAH YEHUDAH

Publisher: Through The Fire Press

Cover Art: Leah Yehudah-Chokmah

Copyright © 2020, Leah Yehudah-Chokmah

All rights reserved. No part of this publication may be reproduced, distributed or transmitted in any form or by any means, including photocopying, recording, or other electronic or mechanical methods, without the prior written permission of the publisher, except in the case of brief quotations embodied in critical reviews and certain other noncommercial uses permitted by copyright law.

1st Edition, 2020

ISBN-13: 978-0-578-66994-6

Unless stated otherwise, Bible verses and Apocrypha are from The King James Bible.

Dedicated to Judah, my best friend & husband

Condensed Table Of Contents

Foreword—pg. 11
Preface—pg. 12
How To Use This Book—pg. 16
Abbreviations—pg. 18
History and Prophecy for Romans—pg.19
    One People, Two Nations—pg. 20
    Gentiles & Greeks—pg. 27
    Reconciliation: The Two Sticks—pg. 45
Prologue To Romans—pg. 51
    Paul, A Hebrew of Hebrews—pg. 52
    The People Of Romans—pg. 53
    Parable Of The Prodigal Son—pg. 65
Romans Precepts & Commentary—pg. 67
    Romans Chapter 1—pg. 70
    Romans Chapter 2—pg. 120
    Romans Chapter 3—pg. 134
    Romans Chapter 4—pg. 146
    Romans Chapter 5—pg. 160
    Romans Chapter 6—pg. 171
    Romans Chapter 7—pg. 179
    Romans Chapter 8—pg. 193
    Romans Chapter 9—pg. 224
    Romans Chapter 10—pg. 262
    Romans Chapter 11—pg. 289
    Romans Chapter 12—pg. 350
    Romans Chapter 13—pg. 362
    Romans Chapter 14—pg. 369
    Romans Chapter 15—pg. 384
    Romans Chapter 16—pg. 402
APPENDIX 1: Definitions—pg. 412
APPENDIX 2: 'Enemies And All That Hate Us'—pg. 419
APPENDIX 3: The Strangers Among Us—pg. 426
BIBLIOGRAPHY—pg. 439

Expanded Table Of Contents

Foreword—11
Preface—12
How To Use This Book—16
Abbreviations—18
History and Prophecy for Romans—pg. 19
    One People, Two Nations—pg. 20
    Gentiles & Greeks—pg. 27
    Reconciliation: The Two Sticks—pg. 45
Prologue To Romans—pg. 51
    Paul, A Hebrew of Hebrews—pg. 52
    The People Of Romans—pg. 53
    Parable Of The Prodigal Son—pg. 65
Romans Precepts & Commentary—pg. 67
    Romans Chapter 1—pg. 70
- Romans 1:1—pg. 70
- Romans 1:2—pgs. 74-78
- Romans 1:3—pgs. 78-80
- Romans 1:4—pgs. 80-82
- Romans 1:5—pgs. 82-84
- Romans 1:6—pg. 84
- Romans 1:7—pgs. 85-89
- Romans 1:8—pg. 89
- Romans 1:9—pg. 90
- Romans 1:10-12—pg. 93
- Romans 1:13—pg. 94
- Romans 1:14—pg. 95
- Romans 1:15—pg. 96
- Romans 1:16—pgs. 98-103

- Romans 1:17—pg. 103
- Romans 1:18—pg. 105
- Romans 1:19-20—pg. 105
- Romans 1:21—pgs. 106-109
- Romans 1:22-23—pg. 109
- Romans 1:24—pg. 110
- Romans 1:25—pgs. 112-113
- Romans 1:26-27—pg. 114
- Romans 1:28—pgs. 114-116
- Romans 1:29-31—pg. 116
- Romans 1:32—pg. 118

Romans Chapter 2—pg. 120
- Romans 2:1—pg. 120
- Romans 2:2-4—pg. 121
- Romans 2:5-6—pg. 122
- Romans 2:7-8—pg. 122
- Romans 2:9-11—pg. 123
- Romans 2:12-13—pg. 124
- Romans 2:14-15—pg. 126
- Romans 2:16—pg. 127
- Romans 2:17-18—pg. 128
- Romans 2:19-23—pg. 129
- Romans 2:24-26—pg. 131
- Romans 2:27-29—pg. 132

Romans Chapter 3—pg. 134
- Romans 3:1-2—pg. 134
- Romans 3:3-4—pg. 136
- Romans 3:5-8—pg. 136
- Romans 3:9—pg. 137
- Romans 3:10-12—pg. 138
- Romans 3:13-18—pg. 138
- Romans 3:19-20—pg. 139
- Romans 3:21-22—pg. 140

- Romans 3:23—pg. 141
- Romans 3:24—pg. 141
- Romans 3:25—pg. 142
- Romans 3:26-27—pg. 142
- Romans 3:28—pg. 143
- Romans 3:29-30—pg. 143
- Romans 3:31—pg. 144

Romans Chapter 4—pg. 146
- Romans 4:1-3—pg. 146
- Romans 4:4-5—pg. 148
- Romans 4:6-8—pg. 149
- Romans 4:9-10—pg. 150
- Romans 4:11—pg. 150
- Romans 4:12-13—pg. 151
- Romans 4:14-15—pg. 152
- Romans 4:16-18—pg. 154
- Romans 4:19-20—pg. 156
- Romans 4:21-22—pg. 156
- Romans 4:23-24—pg. 157
- Romans 4:25—pg. 157

Romans Chapter 5—pg. 160
- Romans 5:1-2—pg. 160
- Romans 5:3-4—pg. 160
- Romans 5:5—pg. 161
- Romans 5:6-8—pg. 162
- Romans 5:9—pg. 163
- Romans 5:10—pg. 164
- Romans 5:11-13—pg. 165
- Romans 5:14—pg. 167
- Romans 5:15-16—pg. 167
- Romans 5:17—pg. 168
- Romans 5:18-19—pg. 169
- Romans 5:20-21—pg. 170

Romans Chapter 6—pg. 171
- Romans 6:1-3—pg. 171
- Romans 6:4-5—pg. 172
- Romans 6:6-7—pg. 173
- Romans 6:8-10—pg. 173
- Romans 6:11-12—pg. 174
- Romans 6:13-14—pg. 175
- Romans 6:15-16—pg. 176
- Romans 6:17-18—pg. 176
- Romans 6:19—pg. 177
- Romans 6:20-21—pg. 177
- Romans 6:22-23—pg. 178

Romans Chapter 7—pg. 179
- Romans 7:1-3—pg. 179
- Romans 7:4—pg. 180
- Romans 7:5—pg. 181
- Romans 7:6—pg. 182
- Romans 7:7-8—pg. 184
- Romans 7:9-10—pg. 185
- Romans 7:11—pg. 187
- Romans 7:12—pg. 188
- Romans 7:13—pg. 188
- Romans 7:14-15—pg. 188
- Romans 7:16-20—pg. 189
- Romans 7:21-23—pg. 190
- Romans 7:24-25—pg. 191

Romans Chapter 8—pg. 193
- Romans 8:1—pg. 193
- Romans 8:2-3—pg. 193
- Romans 8:4—pg. 195
- Romans 8:5-8—pg. 195
- Romans 8:9—pg. 197
- Romans 8:10-11—pg. 197

- Romans 8:12-13—pg. 200
- Romans 8:14—pgs. 201-202
- Romans 8:15—pgs. 202-203
- Romans 8:16-17—pg. 204
- Romans 8:18—pg. 204
- Romans 8:19—pg. 206
- Romans 8:20-22—pg. 208
- Romans 8:23—pg. 208
- Romans 8:24-25—pg. 209
- Romans 8:26-27—pg. 211
- Romans 8:28—pg. 211
- Romans 8:29—pg. 212
- Romans 8:30—pgs. 213-215
- Romans 8:31—pg. 215
- Romans 8:32—pg. 217
- Romans 8:33—pgs. 218-220
- Romans 8:34—pg. 220
- Romans 8:35-36—pg. 221
- Romans 8:37-39—pg. 221

Romans Chapter 9—pg. 224
- Romans 9:1-2—pg. 224
- Romans 9:3-4—pg. 224
- Romans 9:4—pgs. 225-236
- Romans 9:5—pgs. 236-241
- Romans 9:6—pg. 241
- Romans 9:7-9—pg. 244
- Romans 9:10-11—pg. 245
- Romans 9:12—pg. 247
- Romans 9:13—pg. 247
- Romans 9:14-16—pg. 252
- Romans 9:17-18—pg. 252
- Romans 9:19-21—pg. 253
- Romans 9:22—pg. 254

- Romans 9:23-24—pg. 255
- Romans 9:25-26—pg. 256
- Romans 9:27—pg. 256
- Romans 9:28-29—pg. 257
- Romans 9:30—pg. 258
- Romans 9:31—pg. 258
- Romans 9:32-33—pg. 260

Romans Chapter 10—pg. 262
- Romans 10:1—pgs. 262-265
- Romans 10:2—pg. 265
- Romans 10:3—pg. 266
- Romans 10:4—pg. 267
- Romans 10:5—pg. 268
- Romans 10:6-8—pg. 269
- Romans 10:9-10—pg. 270
- Romans 10:11—pg. 271
- Romans 10:12—pgs. 271-276
- Romans 10:13—pg. 276
- Romans 10:14-15—pg. 277
- Romans 10:16-17—pg. 278
- Romans 10:18—pg. 279
- Romans 10:19—pgs. 279-287
- Romans 10:20-21—pg. 288

Romans Chapter 11—pg. 289
- Romans 11:1—pgs. 289-291
- Romans 11:2-4—pgs. 291-293
- Romans 11:5—pgs. 293-294
- Romans 11:6—pg. 294
- Romans 11:7—pgs. 294-297
- Romans 11:8—pg. 297
- Romans 11:9—pgs. 298-299
- Romans 11:10—pg. 299
- Romans 11:11—pgs. 299-302

- Romans 11:12—pgs. 303-312
- Romans 11:13—pg. 313
- Romans 11:14—pgs. 313-319
- Romans 11:15—pgs. 319-324
- Romans 11:16—pg. 325
- Romans 11:17—pgs. 326-332
- Romans 11:18—pg. 332
- Romans 11:19-21—pg. 332
- Romans 11:22—pg. 334
- Romans 11:23—pg. 334
- Romans 11:24—pg. 335
- Romans 11:25—pgs. 336-340
- Romans 11:26—pg. 341
- Romans 11:27—pg. 341
- Romans 11:28—pgs. 342-345
- Romans 11:29—pg. 345
- Romans 11:30-31—pg. 346
- Romans 11:32—pgs. 347-348
- Romans 11:33—pg. 348
- Romans 11:34—pg. 348
- Romans 11:35-36—pg. 349

Romans Chapter 12—pg. 350
- Romans 12:1—pg. 350
- Romans 12:2—pg. 351
- Romans 12:3—pg. 352
- Romans 12:4-5—pg. 353
- Romans 12:6-8—pg. 354
- Romans 12:9—pg. 355
- Romans 12:10—pg. 355
- Romans 12:11—pg. 356
- Romans 12:12—pg. 357
- Romans 12:13-14—pg. 358
- Romans 12:15-16—pg. 359

- Romans 12:17-18—pg. 359
- Romans 12:19—pg. 360
- Romans 12:20-21—pg. 360

Romans Chapter 13—pg. 362
- Romans 13:1—pg. 362
- Romans 13:2-3—pg. 362
- Romans 13:4-5—pg. 363
- Romans 13:6-7—pg. 363
- Romans 13:8—pg. 365
- Romans 13:9-10—pg. 365
- Romans 13:11-12—pg. 366
- Romans 13:13-14—pg. 367

Romans Chapter 14—pg. 369
- Romans 14:1—pg. 369
- Romans 14:2—pgs. 370-373
- Romans 14:3—pg. 373
- Romans 14:4—pg. 374
- Romans 14:5-6—pg. 374
- Romans 14:7-9—pg. 376
- Romans 14:10—pg. 377
- Romans 14:11—pg. 377
- Romans 14:12—pg. 377
- Romans 14:13—pg. 378
- Romans 14:14—pg. 379
- Romans 14:15-16—pg. 381
- Romans 14:17-19—pg. 382
- Romans 14:20-21—pg. 382
- Romans 14:22—pg. 383
- Romans 14:23—pg. 383

Romans Chapter 15—pg. 384
- Romans 15:1-2—pg. 384
- Romans 15:3—pg. 385
- Romans 15:4—pg. 386

- Romans 15:5-7—pg. 387
- Romans 15:8—pg. 387
- Romans 15:9—pg. 388
- Romans 15:10—pg. 389
- Romans 15:11—pg. 391
- Romans 15:12—pg. 391
- Romans 15:13-14—pg. 392
- Romans 15:15—pg. 393
- Romans 15:16—pg. 393-397
- Romans 15:17-19—pg. 397
- Romans 15:20-21—pg. 397
- Romans 15:22-25—pg. 398
- Romans 15:26-29—pg. 399
- Romans 15:30-32—pg. 400

Romans Chapter 16—pg. 402

- Romans 16:1-4—pg. 402
- Romans 16:5-9—pg. 402
- Romans 16:10-16—pg. 403
- Romans 16:17—pg. 404
- Romans 16:18—pg. 404
- Romans 16:19-20—pg. 406
- Romans 16:21—pg. 407
- Romans 16:22-23—pg. 408
- Romans 16:24-25—pg. 409
- Romans 16:26—pg. 410
- Romans 16:27—pg. 411

APPENDIX 1: Definitions—pg. 412
APPENDIX 2: 'Enemies And All That Hate Us'—pg. 419
APPENDIX 3: The Strangers Among Us—pg. 426
BIBLIOGRAPHY—pg. 439

FOREWORD

Today we live as the Diaspora on a journey of conflict and discernment. Our challenge is to endure and overcome the constant battle between flesh and spirit, while struggling to understand what the bible actually teaches. Leah's first book, "*For A Sign and A Wonder*" helped us separate scriptural truth from the theological and cultural conditioning of contemporary Christian doctrine.

"*Precepts For Romans*" builds on and extends the effectiveness of that tool. First, by identifying the attributes that give context to our natural and supernatural conflict. And second, by clarifying (through prophetic and historical references) the distinction between Israelite Gentiles, for whom the Apostle Paul was called to minister to, and Non-Israelite Gentiles. We pray this tool not only helps you in your daily walk of faith, but also, that you're able to use it to edify others.

The journey and the struggle continue.

—Judah Chokmah

Preface

> And it came to pass, that when he was returned, having received the kingdom, then he commanded these servants to be called unto him, to whom he had given the money, that he might know how much every man had gained by trading.
> —Luke 19:15

Last year a brother I follow on Twitter suggested that *somebody* needed to **write** a breakdown on the true identity of the New Testament (NT) Greeks and Gentiles. He tagged me specifically and a few others. From the frustrated tone of his tweet, I figured he'd run into some brethren still grappling with this issue. Not surprising. This is a major stumbling block for our people...and the Christian world at large.

Since I'd had my share of back and forths about the subject, the brother had my sympathy. Even so, I declined the challenge. I like to stay away from problematic topics. In fact, I usually avoid the Gentile/Greek issue like root canal because to me, it's a headache waiting to happen.

So how the heck did I end up here? Publishing a breakdown on a Pauline epistle that's at the center of the Gentile/Greek debate? Well, I guess I got here the same way I was led to write **For A Sign And A Wonder**.

Necessity and The Most High. (TMH)

That I didn't want to deal with this issue, let alone write a precept book on *Romans*, yet begrudgingly ended up doing both anyway, says a lot. In my experience, whenever I tackle something challenging like this, TMH's prodding is usually the catalyst. In my case, I kept getting constant reminders of the parable of the talents, and what the Master did to the wicked servant who buried his—*the one He called lazy.* ☺

I also kept running into people who had random questions about the NT Greeks, Gentiles, and the grafting-in controversy. Add to this a number of weird coincidences and spiritual nudgings that started piling up. Things that, try as I might, could no longer be ignored.

Again, I didn't want to deal with this subject—at all—but this wasn't about me, or what I wanted. So I got busy.

Every serious biblical swordsman knows Paul's writings can be a virtual quagmire—this due to the level of Mosaic scholarship he brings. That's why there are so many ways to go wrong with his epistles, especially *Romans*, because he pulls from numerous sources within the Old Testament (OT), *Apocrypha*, and *Pseudepigrapha*. And *this* is what people have a tendency to forget: that his epistles are scholarly summaries or 'cliffs notes' on the *meat* of the Law and the prophets.

I found myself trying to explain this to a relative, who, at the time, didn't get why she couldn't understand "the Gentile thing" without having to read the books that preceded the NT. To make my point, I gave her a secular example that went something like this:

ME: Have you ever seen *Citizen Kane*?

HER: No, what's that?

ME: An academy-award-winning black & white film starring Orson Welles (1941). It opens with the camera fixed on a spooky old mansion blanketed in fog. Creepy music plays as the picture fades from one exterior shot to the next, until we're transitioned into an interior room where a man lies on his deathbed. A blinding snowstorm flashes on the screen. This slowly morphs to reveal a winter cabin embedded inside a snow globe that lies within the man's open palm. The next shot is a close-up of the man's mustached mouth. After he whispers, "Rosebud," the camera pans back to the snow globe as it rolls from his lifeless hand and crashes to the floor.

HER: (A few moments of silence later...) *Ooookay*. Your point?

ME: What's 'Rosebud'?

HER: Huh?

ME: His last word was 'Rosebud.' What does it mean?

HER: How should I know??? I haven't seen the movie.

ME: *Exactly*. From my brief description, you're left to wonder if he meant an actual rosebud, or maybe he named the broken snow globe 'Rosebud' or perhaps there's something deeper still. Either way, you don't know, which is why you have to watch the movie, correct?

HER: Oh. Well, yeah.

ME: But that's not all. In this particular film, Rosebud's identity is revealed in the very last scene; HOWEVER even then, if you don't watch the whole movie you won't understand Rosebud's history, or its psychological and emotional meaning. That's because these clues are interwoven within the fabric of the entire movie. In short, anyone curious can just watch the opening and closing scenes to discover what the physical Rosebud really was, but they won't understand its <u>intended and spiritual</u> significance without viewing *Citizen Kane* in its entirety.

It's the same with words, symbols, and themes in the Bible. Context, prophecy, and history inform everything. You need a complete picture because not all words have conventional meanings. That's why you can't isolate the last 300 and some odd pages (NT) of a 1700+page book (The Bible) and expect to understand it.

That's just absurd.

Yet this is what contemporary Christianity has done by isolating the NT and pouring its own meanings into words with doctrines that ignore prophetic and historical precedent. They've even published the NT by itself, claiming that it and the OT are mutually exclusive when the truth is, no one can understand the NT without an OT and apocryphal lens.

As a result, *The Book of Romans* (along with most of Paul's epistles) has been twisted and misunderstood by all of Christendom. This is why the vast majority of apologetic books and Christian arguments against Israel's spiritual awakening, are mostly full of misapplied NT scriptures. What they fail to realize is that the very OT scriptures they avoid define the NT scriptures they run to.

At the end of the day, we must ask ourselves why did Christendom teach our people that the OT had little relevance? Why do they continue to publish the NT alone? And why do they try to discredit the *Apocrypha*, calling it heretical, when it was originally part of the 1611 *King James*? To those crying about apocryphal 'errors,' 'contradictions,' and such, you do know there are just as many, if not more of these...*difficulties* in the Old and New testaments, right? So please, miss me with that argument.

I submit that they removed the *Apocrypha* because they had to. How else could they push the warped doctrines that plague Christian churches today? There's been one misconception after another about the NT Greeks and Gentiles, as well as who's getting grafted in, and other related questions. This great ball of confusion lives on because people fail to connect the dots.

And because they removed the *Apocrypha*.

One **cannot understand** *The Book Of Romans* without understanding and *applying* prophecy, biblical history, the *Apocrypha*, OT similes and metaphors, *and* the deeper meanings embedded within NT parables.

Messiah promised His Spirit would teach us all things—us, meaning His people, the Israelites. If this weren't the case, then why did we not have an identity until the children of Israel started waking up? Now we're preaching on the highways and byways, witnessing to friends and family, publishing books, and churning out countless teaching videos, documentaries, and feature length films. We're congregating in assemblies, our homes, over the phone, and online—across the country and around the world. This truth is spreading like wildfire. All praises to TMH!

The Bible tells the story of our family's many failings, heartaches, tragedies, feuds, triumphs, wars, punishments, and ultimate redemption. The moment we forget this, we stumble. Non-Israelite nations are *supporting characters* in this epic historical narrative. I say this boldly, unashamedly, and without blinking. This doesn't mean <u>sincerely</u> repentant non-Israelites have no hope, because they do. *(See The Strangers Among Us, pg.426)* However when it comes to the story of the scriptures, it truly is ALL ABOUT ISRAEL.

So, like I said, I really, *really*, didn't want to write this book.

Nevertheless, I had to.

How To Use This Book

Precepts For Romans was written to help awakened Israelites share the truth with the scattered sheep of the diaspora. This handy reference guide examines Paul's epistle to the Romans through an historical and prophetic lens via OT, *Apocrypha*, NT and *Pseudepigrapha* scriptures as well as supporting reference material.

The first two sections include historical milestones, and prophecies about the children of Israel's fall and rise, as well as applicable word studies. This information is essential for understanding word usage, citations, and Hebraic concepts within Paul's epistle.

The precept section provides chapter-by-chapter and verse-by-verse breakdowns of *The Book of Romans* as shown below:

ROMANS 1:6
Among whom are ye also <u>the called</u> of Jesus Christ.

ISAIAH 48:12—Hearken unto me, O Jacob and Israel, my called; I am he; I am the first, I also am the last.

HOSEA 11:1—When Israel was a child, then I loved him, and called my son out of Egypt.

ISAIAH 45:3-4—(3) And I will give thee the treasures of darkness, and hidden riches of secret places, that thou mayest know that I, the Lord, which call thee by thy name, am the God of Israel. (4) For Jacob my servant's sake, and Israel mine elect, I have even called thee by thy name: I have surnamed thee, though thou hast not known me.

Many precept sections include in-depth commentary. In some instances, you'll find multiple breakdowns of the same verse, highlighting key words or phrases.

Topical scripture listings (ordered according to relevance) include related biblical, apocryphal, pseudepigraphal, and other applicable historical citations. Extra-biblical references provided either agree with, complement, or expound upon scripture.

What's a 'Precept'?

STRONG'S #H6490: 'precept'—*piqquwd (פִּקּוּדִים)*
Definition: law, statute, commandment

For the purposes of this book, precepts are scriptural precedents used as authoritative and trustworthy sources. These rules, or guidelines help us define and understand context and intent. This principle is based upon the laws, statutes, and commandments as revealed in the Holy Bible. Therefore, precepts can be seen as divine data points that assist us in rightly dividing TMH's word.

Since the Apostle Paul delivers a master class on the Law and the prophets in *The Book Of Romans*, using supporting scripture as an aid in understanding his exegesis is essential. Without a complete OT perspective, his epistles (letters) can only be seen through a glass darkly.

The apostles, disciples, and the Messiah Himself frequently quoted from the OT, so it's essential that we do likewise when studying these letters, which are just summaries of the OT and Apocrypha. This is why it's important to remember that while context is key, past *is* prologue.

PRECEPTS FOR ROMANS
is specifically for awakened Israelites who believe:

—the *Old* and *New Testaments* and the *Apocrypha* are the inspired word of TMH.

—the King of Kings whom the world calls "Jesus" (AKA Yahawashi, Y'shua, Yahoshua, Yashayah, Yahushua, Yahusha, Yahayah, Yeshua, Yahshua, Yashua, Iesous, Iesus and any other names not mentioned) is The Messiah. *

—the *Book of Romans* was written to Israel, by Israel, and for Israel.

DISCLAIMER: *Precepts For Romans* isn't exhaustive. It would be impossible to include every scripture or scriptural breakdown for each verse; however, there are enough precepts here to get you started.

---

* *The arguments concerning The Messiah's true name are too numerous to address in the volume of this book. Therefore, the name "Jesus" as it appears in The King James will be seen in all scriptural quotations, and occasionally within commentary where appropriate, while the title Messiah is used elsewhere.*

ABBREVIATIONS

AKJV—American King James Version
ASV—American Standard Version
BAUER'S—Greek-English Lexicon of the New Testament
BDB—The Brown-Driver-Briggs Hebrew-English Lexicon, Francis Brown, R. Driver, and Charles Briggs
BLB—Berean Literal Bible
BSB—Berean Study Bible
BST—Brenton Septuagint Translation
CSB—Christian Standard Bible
DBT—Darby Bible Translation
DRB—Douay-Rheims Bible
ERV—English Revised Version
ESV—English Standard Version
GNT—Good News Translation
GWT—God's Word Translation
HCSB—Holman Christian Standard Bible
ISV—International Standard Version
JPST—JPS Tanakh
JB2000—Jubilee Bible 2000
KJB— King James Bible
KJ2000—King James 2000 Bible
NASB—New American Standard Bible
NAS77—New American Standard 1977
NB—Net Bible
NHEB—New Heart English Bible
NIV—New International Version
NK—Northern Kingdom
NKJV—New King James Version
NLT—New Living Translation
NT—New Testament
OT—Old Testament
SK—Southern Kingdom
STRONG'S—Strong's Exhaustive Concordance of the Bible
THAYER'S—Thayer's Greek-English Lexicon of the New Testament
TMH—The Most High
WBT—Webster's Bible Translation
WEB—World English Bible
WNT—Weymouth New Testament
YLT—Young's Literal Translation

History and Prophecy For

Through thy precepts I get understanding: therefore I hate every false way. Thy word is a lamp unto my feet, and a light unto my path.
—Psalms 119:104-105

One People, Two Nations

Woe to the rebellious children, saith the Lord, that take counsel, but not of me; and that cover with a covering, but not of my spirit, that they may add sin to sin.
—Isaiah 30:1

In order to identify the audience Paul is writing to in his epistles, it's important to understand the historical basis for the split and ultimate regathering of the children of Israel. This is the crux of *The Book of Romans*: the reconciliation and redemption of both houses of TMH God.

So let's begin at the point where the twelve tribes are just entering the Promised Land after 40 years in the wilderness. Though our ancestors overcame a perilous journey, their struggle to become a sanctified and righteous people was far from over.

THE JUDGES

After the Israelites entered the Promised Land, they were tasked to displace the heathen nations. They were largely successful—when they obeyed TMH, that is. Unfortunately, things deteriorated just *one* generation after Joshua's death when the tribes fell into idolatry and forsook TMH *(Judges 2:10-14, Isaiah 43:22-28; Jeremiah 2:23-37)*

Ever faithful, TMH continued to work with them:

JUDGES 2:16-19, 23—(16) Nevertheless the Lord raised up judges, which delivered them out of the hand of those that spoiled them. (17) And yet they would not hearken unto their judges, but they went a whoring after other gods, and bowed themselves unto them: they turned quickly out of the way which their fathers walked in, obeying the commandments of the LORD; but they did not so. (18) And when the LORD raised them up judges, then the LORD was with the judge, and delivered them out of the hand of their enemies all the days of the judge: for it repented the LORD because of their groanings by reason of them that oppressed them and vexed them. (19) And it came to pass, when the judge was dead, that they returned, and corrupted themselves more than their fathers, in following other gods to serve them, and to bow down unto them; they ceased not from their own doings, nor from their stubborn way...(23)

Therefore the LORD left those nations, without driving them out hastily; neither delivered he them into the hand of Joshua.

Because of Israel's chronic disobedience, TMH didn't help them drive out the residue of the heathen. Instead, He left the nations there to chastise and test His people, while he continued to raise up judges:

Othniel *(Judges 3:9-10)*; Ehud *(Judges 3:15-30)*; Deborah and Barak *(Judges 4:4-16; Judges 5)*; Gideon *(Judges 6:13-40)*; Gibeon *(Judges 7 and 8)*; Abimelech *(Judges 9:1-57, 2 Samuel 11:21)*; Tola *(Judges 10:1-2)*; Jair *(Judges 10:3-5)*; Jephthah *(Judges 11 &12)*; Ibzan *(Judges 12:8-10)*; Elon *(Judges 12:11-12)*; Abdon *(Judges 12:13-15)*; Samson *(Judges 13 & 16)*; Eli *(1 Samuel 1-4)* and finally, Samuel *(1 Samuel 2:18 – 1 Samuel 4-7)* along with his evil sons Joel and Abijah *(1 Samuel 8:1-2)*

THE KINGS

The people eventually got tired of being ruled by judges, so they demanded a king—all because they wanted to be like the other nations. *(1 Samuel 8:4-5)* This vexed the prophet Samuel since he, as their longtime judge, felt rejected, but TMH clarified things. The children of Israel hadn't rejected Samuel, TMH told him. *They'd actually rejected TMH Himself. (1 Samuel 8:7-9)*

As a consequence, before the first king was even named, Samuel warned Israel, via revelation from TMH, that a mortal king would eventually prove disastrous for the nation.

Consequences And Repercussions...

1 SAMUEL 8:11-17—(11) And he said, This will be the manner of the king that shall reign over you: He will take your sons, and appoint them for himself, for his chariots, and to be his horsemen; and some shall run before his chariots. (12) And he will appoint him captains over thousands, and captains over fifties; and will set them to ear his ground, and to reap his harvest, and to make his instruments of war, and instruments of his chariots. (13) And he will take your daughters to be confectionaries, and to be cooks, and to be bakers. (14) And he will take your fields, and your vineyards, and your olive yards, even the best of them, and give them to his servants. (15) And he will take the tenth of your seed, and of your vineyards, and give to his officers, and to his servants. (16) And he will take your menservants, and your maidservants, and your goodliest young men, and your asses, and put them to his work. (17) He will take the tenth of your sheep: and ye shall be his servants.

Even after hearing all this, the people still wanted a king. So Samuel prophesied that they'd eventually get weary of their king's oppression, and when they begged for relief, TMH would ignore them:

> **1 SAMUEL 8:18-22**—(18) And ye shall cry out in that day because of your king, which ye shall have chosen you; and the LORD will not hear you in that day. (19) Nevertheless the people refused to obey the voice of Samuel; and they said, Nay; but we will have a king over us; (20) That we also may be like all the nations; and that our king may judge us, and go out before us, and fight our battles. (21) And Samuel heard all the words of the people, and he rehearsed them in the ears of the LORD. (22) And the LORD said to Samuel, Hearken unto their voice, and make them a king. And Samuel said unto the men of Israel, Go ye every man unto his city.

King #1: Saul

Israel's first king, Saul, was a mighty Israelite from the tribe of Benjamin. Said to be a *"choice young man"* who stood out so much that *"there was not among the children of Israel a goodlier person than he: from his shoulders and upward, he was higher than any of the people."* (1 Samuel 9:2)

So Saul was tall, dark and handsome, a real looker, which likely satisfied the people immensely as he fit the outward image they craved. However, TMH isn't concerned about outward appearances. He looks inward, and as it turns out, Saul was a faithless man with a wicked heart.

> **1 SAMUEL 13:8-14**—(8) And he tarried seven days, according to the set time that Samuel had appointed: but Samuel came not to Gilgal; and the people were scattered from him. (9) And Saul said, Bring hither a burnt offering to me, and peace offerings. And he offered the burnt offering. (10) And it came to pass, that as soon as he had made an end of offering the burnt offering, behold, Samuel came; and Saul went out to meet him, that he might salute him. (11) And Samuel said, What hast thou done? And Saul said, Because I saw that the people were scattered from me, and that thou camest not within the days appointed, and that the Philistines gathered themselves together at Michmash; (12) Therefore said I, The Philistines will come down now upon me to Gilgal, and I have not made supplication unto the LORD: I forced myself therefore, and offered a burnt offering. (13) And Samuel said to Saul, Thou hast done foolishly: thou hast not kept the commandment of the LORD thy God, which he commanded thee: for now would the LORD have established thy

kingdom upon Israel forever. (14) But now thy kingdom shall not continue: the LORD hath sought him a man after his own heart, and the LORD hath commanded him to be captain over his people, because thou hast not kept that which the LORD commanded thee.

Saul was also disobedient, *(1 Samuel 15:1-19)* paranoid and envious, *(1 Samuel 18:5-16, 19:8-10, 23:15-29)* and worst of all, he practiced divination. *(1 Samuel 28:7-19)* He also spent much of his kingly life envious of David, his successor, and made many attempts to kill him. *(1 Samuel 18:11, 17, 21, 19:1-22, 23:15k 26:2)* Yet when given the opportunity to do likewise, David, fearing TMH, repeatedly spared Saul. *(1 Samuel 24:1-15, 1 Samuel 26:5-25)*

King #2: David

Israel's second king hailed from the tribe of Judah. While he wasn't as tall and formidable as Saul, presence-wise, he had just what TMH was looking for. *(1 Samuel 16:1-13)* He was a man after the Creator's own heart *(Acts 13:22)* and he pursued TMH relentlessly through prayer, fasting, and psalms. However, he wasn't without sin. *(2 Samuel 11 & 12)*

Even so, TMH loved him through it all and promised to bless his seed:

2 SAMUEL 7:12-16—(12) And when thy days be fulfilled, and thou shalt sleep with thy fathers, I will set up thy seed after thee, which shall proceed out of thy bowels, and I will establish his kingdom. (13) He shall build an house for my name, and I will stablish the throne of his kingdom for ever. (14) I will be his father, and he shall be my son. If he commit iniquity, I will chasten him with the rod of men, and with the stripes of the children of men: (15) But my mercy shall not depart away from him, as I took it from Saul, whom I put away before thee. (16) And thine house and thy kingdom shall be established forever before thee: thy throne shall be established forever.

King #3: Solomon

Solomon, David's son is known for his unmatched discernment. When he was first crowned, he humbly asked TMH to give him wisdom and understanding since he knew he'd need it to rule the people. Impressed by his humility and unselfishness, TMH blessed him with more than wisdom:

1 KINGS 3:12-14—(12) Behold, I have done according to thy words: lo, I have given thee a wise and an understanding heart; so that there was none like thee before thee, neither after thee shall any arise like unto thee. (13) And I have also given thee that which thou hast not asked, both riches, and honour: so that there shall not be any among the kings like unto thee all thy days. (14) And if thou wilt walk in my ways, to keep my statutes and my commandments, as thy father David did walk, then I will lengthen thy days.

Unfortunately, Solomon didn't continue walking in TMH's ways. He racked up wealth, married and collected hundreds of women, many of them strange, *(1 Kings 11:1-8)* women who, in his old age, turned him away from serving TMH. These are the very things TMH forbade a king to do.

DEUTERONOMY 17:16-20—(16) But he shall not multiply horses to himself, nor cause the people to return to Egypt, to the end that he should multiply horses: forasmuch as the LORD hath said unto you, Ye shall henceforth return no more that way. (17) Neither shall he multiply wives to himself, that his heart turn not away: neither shall he greatly multiply to himself silver and gold. (18) And it shall be, when he sitteth upon the throne of his kingdom, that he shall write him a copy of this law in a book out of that which is before the priests the Levites: (19) And it shall be with him, and he shall read therein all the days of his life: that he may learn to fear the LORD his God, to keep all the words of this law and these statutes, to do them: (20) That his heart be not lifted up above his brethren, and that he turn not aside from the commandment, to the right hand, or to the left: to the end that he may prolong his days in his kingdom, he, and his children, in the midst of Israel.

Solomon eventually turned to idol worship and making sacrifices to Molech. Consequently, TMH decreed that the Kingdom of Israel would be split in two: The Southern Kingdom/The House of Judah (Judah, Benjamin & Levi) and The Northern Kingdom/The House of Israel (Reuben, Issachar, Zebulon, Joseph [Ephraim &Manasseh] Gad, Dan, Simeon, Naphtali, Asher.) As an aside, The Northern Kingdom is also known as *Ephraim* as well.

TMH Vows To Split Israel Into Two Kingdoms & Give One Kingdom To Solomon's Servant

1 KINGS 11:5-12—(5) For Solomon went after Ashtoreth the goddess of the Zidonians, and after Milcom the abomination of the Ammonites. (6) And Solomon did evil in the sight of the LORD, and went not fully after the LORD, as did David his father. (7) Then did Solomon build an high place for Chemosh, the abomination of Moab, in the hill that is before Jerusalem, and for Molech, the abomination of the children of Ammon. (8) And likewise did he for all his strange wives, which burnt incense and sacrificed unto their gods. (9) And the LORD was angry with Solomon, because his heart was turned from the LORD God of Israel, which had appeared unto him twice, (10) And had commanded him concerning this thing, that he should not go after other gods: but he kept not that which the LORD commanded. (11) Wherefore the LORD said unto Solomon, Forasmuch as this is done of thee, and thou hast not kept my covenant and my statutes, which I have commanded thee, I will surely rend the kingdom from thee, and will give it to thy servant. (12) Notwithstanding in thy days I will not do it for David thy father's sake: but I will rend it out of the hand of thy son.

Jeroboam, The Servant Who Would Be King

1 KINGS 11:26-28—(26) And Jeroboam the son of Nebat, an Ephrathite of Zereda, Solomon's servant, whose mother's name was Zeruah, a widow woman, even he lifted up his hand against the king. (27) And this was the cause that he lifted up his hand against the king: Solomon built Millo, and repaired the breaches of the city of David his father. (28) And the man Jeroboam was a mighty man of valor: and Solomon seeing the young man that he was industrious, he made him ruler over all the charge of the house of Joseph.

The Great Divide

Because of King Solomon's lavish lifestyle, extravagant spending and never-ending building projects, Israel *and* strangers dwelling with Israel were burdened with hard labor. *(1 Kings 4:1-19, 5:13-15, 9:23)* While he 'technically' didn't put his own people into slavery, it resembled the same arduous work forced upon the Israelites in *Exodus 1:11*. This was the spark that compelled The Northern Kingdom (the other ten tribes) to demand independence.

Rehoboam (Solomon's son and heir) wasted no time in establishing himself as king after his father's death. He did what was evil in the sight of TMH, *(2 Chronicles 12:14)* starting with his coronation in Shechem. *(1 Kings 12:1-15)* When all Israel (10 tribes) asked him to lighten the labor load his father Solomon had placed on them, King Rehoboam sought advice from two sources:

Source #1: Advice From The Elders

1 KINGS 12:6-7—(6) And king Rehoboam consulted with the old men, that stood before Solomon his father while he yet lived, and said, How do ye advise that I may answer this people? (7) And they spake unto him, saying, If thou wilt be a servant unto this people this day, and wilt serve them, and answer them, and speak good words to them, then they will be thy servants forever.

Source #2: Advice From Rehoboam's Peers

1 KINGS 12:8-11—(8) But he forsook the counsel of the old men, which they had given him, and consulted with the young men that were grown up with him, and which stood before him: (9) And he said unto them, What counsel give ye that we may answer this people, who have spoken to me, saying, Make the yoke which thy father did put upon us lighter? (10) And the young men that were grown up with him spake unto him, saying, Thus shalt thou speak unto this people that spake unto thee, saying, Thy father made our yoke heavy, but make thou it lighter unto us; thus shalt thou say unto them, My little finger shall be thicker than my father's loins. (11) And now whereas my father did lade you with a heavy yoke, I will add to your yoke: my father hath chastised you with whips, but I will chastise you with scorpions.

TMH doesn't call our people "sottish" and "stiff-necked" for nothing. *(Deuteronomy 9:6, Jeremiah 4:22)*

A Fateful Choice That Divided A Kingdom

1 KINGS 12:13-17—(13) And the king answered the people roughly, and forsook the old men's counsel that they gave him; (14) And spake to them after the counsel of the young men, saying, My father made your yoke heavy, and I will add to your yoke: my father also chastised you with whips, but I will chastise you with scorpions. (15) Wherefore the king hearkened not unto the people; for the cause was from the LORD, that he might perform his saying, which the LORD spake by Ahijah the Shilonite unto Jeroboam the son of Nebat. (16) So when all Israel saw that the king hearkened not unto them, the people answered the king, saying, What portion have we in David? Neither have we inheritance in the son of Jesse: to your tents, O Israel: now see to thine own house, David. So Israel departed unto their tents. (17) But as for the children of Israel, which dwelt in the cities of Judah, Rehoboam reigned over them.

Because the young King chose unwisely, the Northern ten tribes broke away from the Southern Kingdom of Judah. In rejecting Rehoboam's leadership, they fulfilled TMH's prophecy by choosing Jeroboam (Solomon's servant) of the Tribe of Ephraim as their new king.

1 KINGS 12-19-20—(19) So Israel rebelled against the house of David unto this day. (20) And it came to pass, when all Israel heard that Jeroboam was come again, that they sent and called him unto the congregation, and made him king over all Israel: there was none that followed the house of David, but the tribe of Judah only.

Gentiles & Greeks

A man had two sons. The younger of them said to his father, 'Father, give me the share of the estate that falls to me.' So he divided his wealth between them.
—Luke 15:11-12

THE NORTHERN KINGDOM

Following the split of the Northern and Southern kingdoms, The Northern Kingdom tribes chose Jeroboam as their new king. This fateful move led to their downfall for Jeroboam's first and gravest mistake was to reject the Levitical priesthood. *(1 Kings 12:27-31, 2 Chronicles 11:13-17)*

Instead, he chose idolatry and pagan worship, and the people who remained in the land followed his wicked lead.

1 KINGS 14:7-15—(7) Go, tell Jeroboam, Thus saith the LORD God of Israel, Forasmuch as I exalted thee from among the people, and made thee prince over my people Israel, (8) and rent the kingdom away from the house of David, and gave it thee: and yet thou hast not been as my servant David, who kept my commandments, and who followed me with all his heart, to do that only which was right in mine eyes; (9) but hast done evil above all that were before thee: for thou hast gone and made thee other gods, and molten images, to provoke me to anger, and hast cast me behind thy back: (10) Therefore, behold, I will bring evil upon the house of Jeroboam, and will cut off from Jeroboam him that pisseth against the wall, and him that is shut up and left in Israel, and will take away the remnant of the house of Jeroboam, as a man taketh away dung, till it be all gone. (11) Him that dieth of Jeroboam in the city shall the dogs eat; and him that dieth in the field shall the fowls of the air eat: for the LORD hath spoken it. (12) Arise thou therefore, get thee to thine own house: and when thy feet enter into the city, the child shall die. (13) And all Israel shall mourn for him, and bury him: for he only of Jeroboam shall come to the grave, because in him there is found some good thing toward the LORD God of Israel in the house of Jeroboam. (14) Moreover the LORD shall raise him up a king over Israel, who shall cut off the house of Jeroboam that day: but what? Even now. (15) For the LORD shall smite Israel, as a reed is shaken in the water, and he shall root up Israel out of this good land, which he gave to their fathers, and shall scatter them beyond the river, because they have made their groves, provoking the LORD to anger.

Many Levites left at that point and rejoined the Southern Kingdom tribes *(2 Chronicles 11:13-14)*. The faithful within some of the other Northern Kingdom tribes rejoined the Southern Kingdom as well *(2 Chronicles 11:16-17)*. Some time later under Judah's righteous King Asa's reign, a few more northern kingdomers came back as well. However, the majority stayed and continued in idolatry.

The Northern Kingdom In Prophecy

Before all this, TMH warned our people that if they fell into sin they would face captivity, and would be scattered. *(Leviticus 18:3, 26:33; Deuteronomy 18:9-14, 29:26-29, 32:16-17)*. The Northern Kingdom was the first to fully experience this curse:

EZEKIEL 39:22-24—(22) So the house of Israel shall know that I am the LORD their God from that day and forward. (23) And the heathen shall know that the house of Israel went into captivity for their iniquity: because they trespassed against me, therefore hid I my face from them, and gave them into the hand of their enemies: so fell they all by the sword. (24) According to their uncleanness and according to their transgressions have I done unto them, and hid my face from them.

NEHEMIAH 1:8—Remember, I beseech thee, the word that thou commandedst thy servant Moses, saying, *If* ye transgress, I will scatter you abroad among the nations...

As a result of their wickedness, TMH delivered the Northern Kingdom to the Assyrians who <u>carried them away</u> into captivity, scattering them throughout Assyria and its territories. The first Assyrian invasion of the Northern Kingdom is recorded in *2 Kings and 1 Chronicles*:

2 KINGS 15:27-29—(27) In the two and fiftieth year of Azariah king of Judah, Pekah the son of Remaliah began to reign over Israel in Samaria, and reigned twenty years. (28) And he did that which was evil in the sight of the LORD: he departed not from the sins of Jeroboam the son of Nebat, who made Israel to sin. (29) In the days of Pekah king of Israel came Tiglathpileser king of Assyria, and took Ijon, and Abelbethmaachah, and Janoah, and Kedesh, and Hazor, and Gilead, and Galilee, all the land of Naphtali, and carried them captive to Assyria.

1 CHRONICLES 5:25-26—(25) And they transgressed against the God of their fathers, and went a whoring after the gods of the people of the land, whom God destroyed before them. (26) And the God of Israel stirred up the spirit of Pul king of Assyria, and the spirit of Tilgathpilneser king of Assyria, and he carried them away, even the Reubenites, and the Gadites, and the half tribe of Manasseh, and brought them unto Halah, and Habor, and Hara, and to the river Gozan, unto this day.

2 KINGS 17:1-8—(1) In the twelfth year of Ahaz king of Judah began Hoshea the son of Elah to reign in Samaria over Israel nine years. (2) And he did that which was evil in the sight of the LORD, but not as the kings of Israel that were before him. (3) Against him came up Shalmaneser king of Assyria; and Hoshea became his servant, and gave him presents. (4) And the king of Assyria found conspiracy in Hoshea: for he had sent messengers to So king of Egypt, and brought no present to the king of Assyria, as he had done year by year: therefore the king of Assyria shut him up, and bound him in prison. (5) Then the king of Assyria came up throughout all the land, and went up to Samaria, and besieged it three years. (6) In the ninth year of Hoshea the king of Assyria took Samaria, and carried Israel away into Assyria, and placed them in Halah and in Habor by the river of Gozan, and in the cities of the Medes. (7) For so it was, that the children of Israel had sinned against the LORD their God, which had brought them up out of the land of Egypt, from under the hand of Pharaoh king of Egypt, and had feared other gods, (8) And walked in the statutes of the heathen, whom the LORD cast out from before the children of Israel, and of the kings of Israel, which they had made.

2 KINGS 17:18-24—(18) Therefore, the LORD was very angry with Israel and removed them out of his sight: there was none left but the tribe of Judah only. (19) Also Judah kept not the commandments of the LORD their God, but walked in the statutes of Israel, which they made. (20) And the LORD rejected all the seed of Israel, and afflicted them, and delivered them into the hand of spoilers, until he had cast them out of his sight. (21) For he rent Israel from the house of David; and they made Jeroboam the son of Nebat king: and Jeroboam drave Israel from following the LORD, and made them sin a great sin. (22) For the children of Israel walked in all the sins of Jeroboam, which he did; they departed not from them; (23) Until the LORD removed Israel out of his sight, as he had said by all his servants the prophets. So was Israel carried away out of their own land to Assyria unto this day. (24) And the king of Assyria brought men from Babylon, and from Cuthah, and from Ava, and from Hamath, and from Sepharvaim, and placed them in the cities of Samaria instead of the children of Israel: and they possessed Samaria, and dwelt in the cities thereof.

Not everyone got carried away. A few northern kingdomers escaped to Judah and elsewhere, and still, a small remnant remained in the land. Assyrian King Sargon II documented how he took some—not all—of the Northern Kingdom Israelites from Samaria.

I besieged and occupied the town of Samaria and took 27,280 of its inhabitants captive. I took from them 50 chariots, but left them the rest of their belongings. I placed my lieutenants over them; I renewed the obligation imposed upon them by one of the kings who preceded me.

MS2368, Royal Inscription Of Sargon II of Assyria,
Nimrod (722-705 BC) — Palace of Khorasbad

This is when the Northern Kingdom completely lost control of their land since Assyria made a habit of dispossessing the people they conquered and repopulating the land with other nations. *(2 Kings 17:24)* This is how Samaria became overrun with foreigners. Yet, again, an Israelite remnant remained even unto the Roman occupation as seen in the Gospel of John during Messiah's conversation with the woman at the well.

JOHN 4:5-15—(5) Then cometh he to a city of Samaria, which is called Sychar, near to the parcel of ground that Jacob gave to his son Joseph. (6) Now Jacob's well was there. Jesus therefore, being wearied with his journey, sat thus on the well: and it was about the sixth hour. (7) There cometh a woman of Samaria to draw water: Jesus saith unto her, Give me to drink. (8) (For his disciples were gone away unto the city to buy meat.) (9) Then saith the woman of Samaria unto him, How is it that thou, being a Jew, askest drink of me, which am a woman of Samaria? For the Jews have no dealings with the Samaritans. (10) Jesus answered and said unto her, If thou knewest the gift of God, and who it is that saith to thee, Give me to drink; thou wouldest have asked of him, and he would have given thee living water. (11) The woman saith unto him, Sir, thou hast nothing to draw with, and the well is deep: from whence then hast thou that living water? (12) <u>Art thou greater than our father Jacob, which gave us the well, and drank thereof himself, and his children, and his cattle?</u> (13) Jesus answered and said unto her, Whosoever drinketh of this water shall thirst again: (14) But whosoever drinketh of the water that I shall give him shall never thirst; but the water that I shall give him shall be in him a well of water springing up into everlasting life. (15) The woman saith unto him, Sir, give me this water, that I thirst not, neither come hither to draw.

Still, the Assyrians *did* carry many northern kingdomers away, scattering them throughout Asia Minor and beyond. *(2 Kings 15:18-19, 29; 1 Chronicles 5:26; Nehemiah 9:32; Jeremiah 50:17, Acts 2:5-9, Acts 19:10).* This is how they became 'not a people' (per prophecy) since they tossed their heritage away and assimilated into other nations, taking on heathen customs and cultures as their own, much as the so-called Negro has done in America and elsewhere.

ISAIAH 7:8-9—(8) For the head of Syria is Damascus, and the head of Damascus is Rezin; and within threescore and five years shall Ephraim be broken, that it be not a people. (9) And the head of Ephraim is Samaria, and the head of Samaria is Remaliah's son. If ye will not believe, surely ye shall not be established.

After the final Assyrian assault, Judah remained in its land, along with some of Levi, Benjamin and a remnant from the other tribes that managed to escape. However, Judah did fall into idolatry off and on.

The carrying away of the Northern Kingdom was both physical and spiritual. While the Assyrians took them from their lands and scattered them throughout enemy territories, the righteous heritage forged by faith in TMH God of Israel had already started eroding in these tribes even before the captivity as they'd already fallen into idolatry. Once outside the confines of the Promised Land, the separation was complete. They continued in idolatry, rejecting their own heritage by living as Gentiles.

Hosea 7:8 shows us that Ephraim (a representation of all ten Northern Kingdom tribes) "mixed himself" with the other nations, while *Hosea 8:8-11* goes even further:

HOSEA 8:8-11—(8) Israel is swallowed up: now shall they be among the Gentiles as a vessel wherein is no pleasure. (9) For they are gone up to Assyria, a wild ass alone by himself: Ephraim hath hired lovers. (10) Yea, though they have hired among the nations, now will I gather them, and they shall sorrow a little for the burden of the king of princes. (11) Because Ephraim hath made many altars to sin, altars shall be unto him to sin.

The ten tribes are often referred to as Ephraim, Israel, or The House of Israel. In the above scripture, it's stated that Israel (the 10 tribes) has been 'swallowed up.' To swallow up, in this context, means to engulf or overwhelm, which is exactly what happened. The Northern Kingdom was engulfed with the heathen nations by mixing with them. This is how they became Gentiles.

Unfortunately, the falling away was bound to continue since Assyria filled the land with non-Israelites when much of Ephraim was carried away. Those that remained intermingled with Gentiles and lived like them. However, about a century after the Assyrian invasion, Judah's King Josiah tried to bring the Northern Kingdom back into the holy covenant:

2 CHRONICLES 34:5-9—(5) And he burnt the bones of the priests upon their altars, and cleansed Judah and Jerusalem. (6) <u>And so did he in the cities of Manasseh, and Ephraim, and Simeon, even unto Naphtali, with their mattocks round about.</u> (7) And when he had broken down the altars and the groves, and had beaten the graven images into powder, and cut down all the idols throughout all the land of Israel, he returned to Jerusalem. (8) Now in the eighteenth year of his reign, when he had purged the land, and the house, he sent Shaphan the son of Azaliah, and Maaseiah the governor of the city, and Joah the son of Joahaz the recorder, to repair the house of the LORD his God. (9) And when they came to Hilkiah the high priest, <u>they delivered the money that was brought into the house of God, which the Levites that kept the doors had gathered of the hand of Manasseh and Ephraim, and of all the remnant of Israel, and of all Judah and Benjamin</u>; and they returned to Jerusalem.

Although King Josiah made a valiant effort, eventually the Northern Kingdom remnant still living in Ephraim's land fell away. So they and the scattered were separated from the light of TMH to live in outer darkness. The evidence of this is demonstrated much later in *Matthew 4:15-16* where two Northern Kingdom tribes are mentioned:

MATTHEW 4:15-16—(15) The land of Zebulun, and the land of Nephthalim, by the way of the sea, beyond Jordan, Galilee of the Gentiles; (16) The people which sat in darkness saw great light; and to them which sat in the region and shadow of death light is sprung up.

These scriptures connect directly with *Isaiah 9:1-4*:

ISAIAH 9:1-4—(1) Nevertheless the dimness shall not be such as was in her vexation, when at the first he lightly afflicted the land of Zebulun and the land of Naphtali, and afterward did more grievously afflict her by the way of the sea, beyond Jordan, in Galilee of the nations. (2) The people that walked in darkness have seen a great light: they that dwell in the land of the shadow of death, upon them hath the light shined. (3) Thou hast multiplied the nation, and not increased the joy: they joy before thee according to the joy in harvest, and as men rejoice when they divide the spoil. (4) For thou hast broken the yoke of his burden, and the staff of his shoulder, the rod of his oppressor, as in the day of Midian.

Isaiah 9:1-4's 'Galilee of the nations' (gentiles) refers to Zebulun and Naphtali, two Northern Kingdom tribes who would become Gentiles. In Galilee they dwelled among the heathen and lived just like them. Since Nazareth, a northern part of Israel, was in the province of Galilee, the Kingdom of Judah looked down on its inhabitants. This is why, in *John 1:46*, Nathaniel says, "Can there any good thing come out of Nazareth?" This disdain is reiterated in *John 7:34-35*:

JOHN 7:34-35—(34) Ye shall seek me, and shall not find me: and where I am, thither ye cannot come. (35) Then said the Jews among themselves, Whither will he go, that we shall not find him? Will he go unto the dispersed among the Gentiles, and teach the Gentiles?

Here we see the disciples referring to the dispersion Israelites as Gentiles. In *"Will he go to **the dispersed** AMONG the gentiles"* the subject is the dispersed. While the 'go unto the dispersed" is the action. These two definitive statements tell us whom the latter portion of the sentence addresses. The dispersed AMONG the Gentiles are the Israelite Gentiles who would be taught. At the time of this scripture, the bulk of Judah wasn't part of the dispersion. For the most part, they remained the faithful son, staying home with the 'Father,' while the younger, 'prodigal' one—Ephraim—strayed and fell away.

The Northern Kingdom and some of the House of Judah of the dispersion, resided in Greek-speaking territories throughout Asia Minor, living as Gentiles. So there were Greek-speaking Israelites, as well as Israelites who considered themselves Greek. This is much in the same way as there are English speaking Chinese people who consider themselves American, French-speaking Spaniards who consider themselves French, or English speaking Africans who consider themselves British, etc.

THE SOUTHERN KINGDOM

Babylonian Captivity

Years after the Northern Kingdom was carried away by Assyria into captivity, the Southern Kingdom would drink from the same cup of TMH's wrath. Because of sin and idolatry, Judah, like Ephraim, would go into captivity, this time to Nebuchadnezzar, king of Babylon:

JEREMIAH 27:1-8—(1) In the beginning of the reign of Jehoiakim the son of Josiah king of Judah came this word unto Jeremiah from the LORD, saying, (2) Thus saith the LORD to me; Make thee bonds and yokes, and put them upon thy neck, (3) and send them to the king of Edom, and to the king of Moab, and to the king of the Ammonites, and to the king of Tyrus, and to the king of Zidon, by the hand of the messengers which come to Jerusalem unto Zedekiah king of Judah; (4) And command them to say unto their masters, Thus saith the LORD of hosts, the God of Israel; Thus shall ye say unto your masters; (5) I have made the earth, the man and the beast that are upon the ground, by my great power and by my outstretched arm, and have given it unto whom it seemed meet unto me. (6) And now have I given all these lands into the hand of Nebuchadnezzar the king of Babylon, my servant; and the beasts of the field have I given him also to serve him. (7) And all nations shall serve him, and his son, and his son's son, until the very time of his land come: and then many nations and great kings shall serve themselves of him. (8) And it shall come to pass, that the nation and kingdom which will not serve the same Nebuchadnezzar the king of Babylon, and that will not put their neck under the yoke of the king of Babylon, that nation will I punish, saith the LORD, with the sword, and with the famine, and with the pestilence, until I have consumed them by his hand.

King Jehoiakim of Judah didn't hearken to TMH and rebelled against King Nebuchadnezzar, so he was bound "in fetters" and carried off to Babylon along with many prized temple vessels. *(2 Chronicles 36:6-7)* The next Judean king didn't fare much better. At eight years old, Johoiachin also did wickedness in the sight of TMH by rebelling against Nebuchadnezzar, so he too got carried off. After this, Johoiachin's 21-year-old brother, Zedekiah took over, and reigned 11 years, but he too did what was evil in the eyes of TMH. He also ignored the prophet Jeremiah's warnings.

2 CHRONICLES 36:14-21—(14) Moreover all the chief of the priests, and the people, transgressed very much after all the abominations of the heathen; and polluted the house of the LORD which he had hallowed in Jerusalem. (15) And the LORD God of their fathers sent to them by his messengers, rising up betimes, and sending; because he had compassion on his people, and on his dwelling place: (16) But they mocked the messengers of God, and despised his words, and misused his prophets, until the wrath of the LORD arose against his people, till there was no remedy. (17) Therefore he brought upon them the king of the Chaldees, who slew their young men with the sword in the house of their sanctuary, and had no compassion upon young man or maiden, old man, or him that stooped for age: he gave them all into his hand. (18) And all the vessels of the house of God, great and small, and the treasures of the house of the LORD, and the treasures of the king, and of his princes; all these he brought to Babylon. (19) And they burnt the house of God, and brake down the wall of Jerusalem, and burnt all the palaces thereof with fire, and destroyed all the goodly vessels thereof. (20) And them that had escaped from the sword carried he away to Babylon; where they were servants to him and his sons until the reign of the kingdom of Persia: (21) To fulfill the word of the LORD by the mouth of Jeremiah, until the land had enjoyed her sabbaths: for as long as she lay desolate she kept Sabbath, to fulfill threescore and ten years.

After Judah served their time under Nebuchadnezzar, Cyrus The Great of Persia, who'd conquered Babylon, allowed the Israelites to go back and rebuild.

Ezra 1:1-5—(1) Now in the first year of Cyrus king of Persia, that the word of the LORD by the mouth of Jeremiah might be fulfilled, the LORD stirred up the spirit of Cyrus king of Persia, that he made a proclamation throughout all his kingdom, and put it also in writing, saying, (2) Thus saith Cyrus king of Persia, The LORD God of heaven hath given me all the kingdoms of the earth; and he hath charged me to build him an house at Jerusalem, which is in Judah. (3) Who is there among you of all his people? His God be with him, and let him go up to Jerusalem, which is in

Judah, and build the house of the LORD God of Israel, (he is the God,) which is in Jerusalem. (4) And whosoever remaineth in any place where he sojourneth, let the men of his place help him with silver, and with gold, and with goods, and with beasts, beside the freewill offering for the house of God that is in Jerusalem. (5) Then rose up the chief of the fathers of Judah and Benjamin, and the priests, and the Levites, with all them whose spirit God had raised, to go up to build the house of the LORD which is in Jerusalem.

A remnant of Benjamin and Levi that left the Northern Kingdom under Jeroboam *(2 Chronicles 2:1-17)* stayed with Judah in Babylon, and throughout Persia's rulership. However, many of the people who were carried away by Nebuchadnezzar, remained in the Mesopotamian region even after Cyrus The Great's reign.

Greek Captivity

The Southern Kingdom's next captivity came after Alexander the Great conquered the Persians. During the Greek captivity, some within Judah and remnants of the other tribes who remained within the kingdom fell away from TMH—some by force and others purely by choice, wherein they started living as heathens.

The first book of Maccabees lays out how it all began:

1 MACCABEES 1:7-15—(7) So Alexander reigned twelve years, and then died. (8) and his servants bare rule every one in his place. (9) And after his death they all put crowns upon themselves; so did their sons after them many years: and evils were multiplied in the earth. (10) And there came out of them a wicked root Antiochus surnamed Epiphanes, son of Antiochus the king, who had been an hostage at Rome, and he reigned in the hundred and thirty and seventh year of the kingdom of the Greeks. (11) In those days went there out of Israel wicked men, who persuaded many, saying, Let us go and make a covenant with the heathen that are round about us: for since we departed from them we have had much sorrow. (12) So this device pleased them well. (13) Then certain of the people were so forward herein, that they went to the king, who gave them license to do after the ordinances of the heathen: (14) Whereupon they built a place of exercise at Jerusalem according to the customs of the heathen: (15) And made themselves uncircumcised, and forsook the holy covenant, and joined themselves to the heathen, and were sold to do mischief.

Since circumcision was an outward sign of a divine covenant, becoming uncircumcised had both physical and spiritual implications. By *desiring* the unholy ways of the heathen, their hearts became uncircumcised the moment desire gave birth to sin. *(James 1:14-15)*

> **PROVERBS 3:31-35**—(31) Envy thou not the oppressor, and choose none of his ways. (32) For the froward is abomination to the LORD: but his secret is with the righteous. (33) The curse of the LORD is in the house of the wicked: but he blesseth the habitation of the just. (34) Surely he scorneth the scorners: but he giveth grace unto the lowly. (35) The wise shall inherit glory: but shame shall be the promotion of fools.

Josephus also documents how Israelites altered their private parts to make themselves appear Greek. This procedure was especially important to those who frequented the Greek-style gymnasium they built in Jerusalem, since nakedness was the norm for all attendees.

> ...Menelaus and the sons of Tobias were distressed, and retired to Antiochus, and informed him that they were desirous to leave the laws of their country, and the Jewish way of living according to them, and to follow the king's laws, and the Grecian way of living. Wherefore they desired his permission to build them a Gymnasium at Jerusalem. And when he had given them leave, they also hid the circumcision of their genitals, **that even when they were naked they might appear to be Greeks. Accordingly, they left off all the customs that belonged to their own country, and imitated the practices of the other nations.**
> *Josephus, "Antiquities of the Jews - Book XII, chapter 5, paragraph 1*

This falling away from the covenant is further described in *2 Maccabees*:

> **2 MACCABEES 4:7-15**—(7) But after the death of Seleucus, when Antiochus, called Epiphanes, took the kingdom, Jason the brother of Onias labored underhand to be high priest, (8) Promising unto the king by intercession three hundred and threescore talents of silver, and of another revenue eighty talents: (9) Beside this, he promised to assign an hundred and fifty more, if he might have license to set him up a place for exercise, and for the training up of youth in the fashions of the heathen, and to write them of Jerusalem by the name of Antiochians. (10) Which when the king had granted, and he had gotten into his hand the rule he forthwith brought his own nation to Greekish fashion. (11) And the royal privileges granted of special favor to the Jews by the means of John the father of Eupolemus, who went ambassador to Rome for amity and aid, he took away; and putting down the governments which were according to the law, he brought up new customs against the law: (12) For he built gladly a place of exercise under the tower itself, and brought the chief young men under his subjection, and made them wear a hat. (13) Now such was the height of Greek fashions, and increase of heathenish

manners, through the exceeding profaneness of Jason, that ungodly wretch, and no high priest; (14) That the priests had no courage to serve any more at the altar, but despising the temple, and neglecting the sacrifices, hastened to be partakers of the unlawful allowance in the place of exercise, after the game of Discus called them forth; (15) Not setting by the honors of their fathers, but liking the glory of the Grecians best of all.

In essence, their trust in oppression was so strong, *(Psalms 62:10; Isaiah 30:12-13)* they made a lethal covenant with their enemies.

ISAIAH 28:14-15—(14) Wherefore hear the word of the LORD, ye scornful men, that rule this people which is in Jerusalem. (15) Because ye have said, We have made a covenant with death, and with hell are we at agreement; when the overflowing scourge shall pass through, it shall not come unto us: for we have made lies our refuge, and under falsehood have we hid ourselves.

Although *The Assumption of Moses* was allegedly written in the first century—meaning, they can't prove it—the book contains prophecies Joshua received from Moses that fit what happened during the Greek and Roman captivities as well as what so-called Negroes are experiencing with the spiritual leadership of today:

THE ASSUMPTION OF MOSES 5:4-6—(4) For they shall forsake the truth of God, but there shall be those who shall pollute the altar...even with their gifts, which they offer to the Lord, not being priests, but slaves born of slaves. (5) And those who are their lawgivers, their teachers, in those days shall have respect unto men's persons for reward and receive gifts and pervert justice by receiving bribes. (6) And it shall come to pass that the whole colony and the bounds of their habitations shall be filled with sins and iniquities...their judges shall be those who work unrighteousness against the Lord, and they shall give judgment for money according as each man desireth.

Even with the failure of leadership in Jerusalem at that time, there were many faithful Israelites who refused to voluntarily break covenant with TMH. In response, Greek rulership used a familiar ploy of the wicked:

WISDOM OF SOLOMON 2:10-21—(10) Let us oppress the poor righteous man, let us not spare the widow, nor reverence the ancient gray hairs of the aged. (11) <u>Let our strength be the law of justice: for that which is feeble is found to be nothing worth.</u> (12) Therefore let us lie in wait for the righteous; because he is not for our turn, and he is clean contrary to our doings: he upbraideth us with our offending the law, and objecteth to our infamy the transgressings of our education. (13) He professeth to have the knowledge of God: and he calleth himself the child of the Lord. (14) He was made to reprove our thoughts. (15) He is grievous unto us even to behold: for his life is not like other men's, his ways are of another fashion. (16) We are esteemed of him as counterfeits: he abstaineth from our ways as from filthiness: he pronounceth the end of the just to be blessed, and maketh his boast that God is his father. (17) Let us see if his words be true: and let us prove what shall happen in the end of him. (18) For if the just man be the son of God, he will help him, and deliver him from the hand of his enemies. (19) Let us examine him with despitefulness and torture that we may know his meekness, and prove his patience. (20) Let us condemn him with a shameful death: for by his own saying he shall be respected. (21) Such things they did imagine, and were deceived: for their own wickedness hath blinded them.

Laws of the land made chattel slavery and Jim Crow legal in the U.S., Apartheid legal in South Africa, and Abortion legal practically worldwide. Whenever wicked men want to do wicked deeds they pass laws to justify their wickedness. The rulers of this present fallen world are merely following in the Greek's wicked footsteps:

1 MACCABEES 1:41-43—(41) Moreover king Antiochus wrote to his whole kingdom, that all should be one people, (42) and every one should leave his laws: so all the heathen agreed according to the commandment of the king. (43) Yea, many also of the Israelites consented to his religion, and sacrificed unto idols, and profaned the Sabbath.

The laws, statutes and commandments set Israel apart. They're the wellspring of our heritage, but most importantly, they're what kept our ancestors connected with our Power, which is TMH. The Greeks knew this, which is why they enacted their draconian laws.

1 MACCABEES 1:44-50—(44) For the king had sent letters by messengers unto Jerusalem and the cities of Judah that they should follow the strange laws of the land, (45) and forbid burnt offerings, and sacrifice, and drink offerings, in the temple; and that they should profane the sabbaths and festival days: (46) And pollute the sanctuary and holy people: (47) Set up altars, and groves, and chapels of idols, and sacrifice swine's flesh, and unclean beasts: (48) That they should also leave their children uncircumcised, and make their souls abominable with all manner of uncleanness and profanation: (49) To the end they might forget the law, and change all the ordinances. (50) And whosoever would not do according to the commandment of the king, he said, he should die.

2 MACCABEES 6:1-5—(1) Not long after this the king sent an old man of Athens to compel the Jews to depart from the laws of their fathers, and not to live after the laws of God: (2) And to pollute also the temple in Jerusalem, and to call it the temple of Jupiter Olympius; and that in Garizim, of Jupiter the Defender of strangers, as they did desire that dwelt in the place. (3) The coming in of this mischief was sore and grievous to the people: (4) For the temple was filled with riot and reveling by the Gentiles, who dallied with harlots, and had to do with women within the circuit of the holy places, and besides that brought in things that were not lawful. (5) The altar also was filled with profane things, which the law forbiddeth.

This tragic fall was prophesied in *The Book of Jubilees*:

THE BOOK OF JUBILEES 1:8-9, 13—(8) And they will eat and be satisfied, and they will turn to strange gods, to (gods) which cannot deliver them from aught of their tribulation: and this witness shall be heard for a witness against them. For they will forget all My commandments, (even) all that I command them, and they will walk after the Gentiles, and after their uncleanness, and after their shame, and will serve their gods, and these will prove unto them an offense and a tribulation and an affliction and a snare. (9) And many will perish and they will be taken captive, and will fall into the hands of the enemy, because they have forsaken My ordinances and My commandments, and the festivals of My covenant, and My sabbaths, and My holy place which I have hallowed for Myself in their midst, and My tabernacle, and My sanctuary, which I have hallowed for Myself in the midst of the land, that I should set my name upon it, and that it should dwell there...(13) And they will forget all My law and all My commandments and all My judgments, and will go astray as to new moons, and sabbaths, and festivals, and jubilees, and ordinances.

THE BOOK OF JUBILEES 6:34-38—(34) And all the children of Israel will forget and will not find the path of the years, and will forget the new moons, and seasons, and sabbaths and they will go wrong as to all the order of the years. (35) For I know and from henceforth will I declare it unto thee, and it is not of my own devising; for the book lies written before me, and on the heavenly tablets the division of days is ordained, lest they forget the feasts of the covenant and walk according to the feasts of the Gentiles after their error and after their ignorance. (36) For there will be those who will assuredly make observations of the moon—how it disturbs the seasons and comes in from year to year ten days too soon. (37) For this reason the years will come upon them when they will disturb the order, and make an abominable day the day of testimony, and an unclean day a feast day, and they will confound all the days, the holy with the unclean, and the unclean day with the holy; for they will go wrong as to the months and sabbaths and feasts and jubilees. (38) For this reason I command and testify to thee that thou mayst testify to them; for after thy death thy children will disturb them, so that they will not make the year three hundred and sixty-four days only, and for this reason they will go wrong as to the new moons and seasons and sabbaths and festivals, and they will eat all kinds of blood with all kinds of flesh.

Ezra/Esdras and Daniel mention a "confusion of face" whereby our people either forgot who they were through circumstances they didn't control, or foolishly abandoned the God who loved and delivered them. The end result was an epic descent into darkness, a darkness where confusion thrived:

EZRA 9:7—Since the days of our fathers have we been in a great trespass unto this day; and for our iniquities have we, our kings, and our priests, been delivered into the hand of the kings of the lands, to the sword, to captivity, and to a spoil, and to confusion of face, as it is this day.

DANIEL 9:7-8—(7) O Lord, righteousness belongeth unto thee, but unto us confusion of faces, as at this day; to the men of Judah, and to the inhabitants of Jerusalem, and unto all Israel, that are near, and that are far off, through all the countries whither thou hast driven them, because of their trespass that they have trespassed against thee. (8) O Lord, to us belongeth confusion of face, to our kings, to our princes, and to our fathers, because we have sinned against thee.

It should be noted that many within the Southern Kingdom refused to abandon the holy covenant. The Maccabean Revolt as recorded in *1st and 2nd Maccabees* gives a detailed account of how righteous Israelites fought against Greek tyranny. And the tyranny was horrific:

1 MACCABEES 1:54-64—(54) Now the fifteenth day of the month Casleu, in the hundred forty and fifth year, they set up the abomination of desolation upon the altar, and builded idol altars throughout the cities of Judah on every side; (55) And burnt incense at the doors of their houses, and in the streets. (56) And when they had rent in pieces the books of the law, which they found, they burnt them with fire. (57) And whosoever was found with any the book of the testament, or if any committed to the law, the king's commandment was, that they should put him to death. (58) Thus did they by their authority unto the Israelites every month, to as many as were found in the cities. (59) Now the five and twentieth day of the month they did sacrifice upon the idol altar, which was upon the altar of God. (60) At which time according to the commandment they put to death certain women that had caused their children to be circumcised. (61) And they hanged the infants about their necks, and rifled their houses, and slew them that had circumcised them. (62) Howbeit many in Israel were fully resolved and confirmed in themselves not to eat any unclean thing. (63) Wherefore they rather to die, that they might not be defiled with meats, and that they might not profane the holy covenant: so then they died. (64) And there was very great wrath upon Israel.

Josephus recorded similar atrocities.

Now it came to pass, after two years, in the hundred forty and fifth year, on the twenty-fifth day of that month which is by us called Chasleu, and by the Macedonians Apelleus, in the hundred and fifty-third olympiad, that the king came up to Jerusalem, and, pretending peace, he got possession of the city by treachery; at which time he spared not so much as those that admitted him into it, on account of the riches that lay in the temple; but, led by his covetous inclination, (for he saw there was in it a great deal of gold, and many ornaments that had been dedicated to it of very great value,) and in order to plunder its wealth, he ventured to break the league he had made. So he left the temple bare, and took away the golden candlesticks, and the golden altar of incense, and table of shew-bread, and the altar of burnt-offering; and did not abstain from even the veils, which were made of fine linen and scarlet. He also emptied it of its secret treasures, and left nothing at all remaining; and by this means cast the Jews into great lamentation, for he forbade them to offer those daily sacrifices which they used to offer to God, according to the law. And when he had pillaged the whole city, some of the inhabitants he slew, and some he carried captive, together with their wives and children, so that the multitude of those captives that were taken alive amounted to about ten thousand. He also burnt down the finest buildings; and when he had overthrown the city walls, he built a citadel in the lower part of the city, (17) for the place was high, and overlooked the temple; on which account he fortified it with high walls and towers, and put into it a garrison of Macedonians. However, in that citadel dwelt the impious and wicked part of the [Jewish] multitude, from whom it proved that the citizens suffered many and sore calamities. And when the king had built an idol altar upon God's altar, he slew swine upon it, and so offered a sacrifice neither according to the law, nor the Jewish religious worship in that country. He also compelled them to forsake the worship, which they paid their own God, and to adore those whom he took to be gods; and made them build temples, and raise idol altars in every city and village, and offer swine upon them every day. He also commanded them not to circumcise their sons, and threatened to punish any that should be found to have transgressed his injunction. He also appointed overseers, who should compel them to do what he commanded. And indeed many Jews there were who complied with the king's commands, either voluntarily, or out of fear of the penalty that was denounced. But the best men, and those of the noblest souls, did not regard him, but did pay a greater respect to the customs of their country than concern as to the punishment which he threatened to the disobedient; on which account they every day underwent great miseries and bitter torments; for they were whipped with rods, and their bodies were torn to pieces, and were crucified, while they were still alive, and breathed. They also strangled those women and their sons whom they had circumcised, as the king had appointed, hanging their sons about their necks as they were upon the crosses. And if there were any sacred book of the law found, it was destroyed, and those with whom they were found miserably perished also.

Josephus, "Antiquities of the Jews - Book XII, chapter 5, paragraph 4

This wasn't some random decree. This wicked king knew exactly what he was doing. While it might look like he was just trying to unite his kingdom under one set of laws, the Israelites were his main target—*just as it is today*. Heathen nations always studied the Israelites closely. They did this in order to find out how to gain a foothold. The crafty ones discovered the answer sooner rather than later: Get the children of Israel to sin against TMH and they win. We see a great example of this with Achior the Ammonite in the book of *Judith* where the Assyrians plotted how to take Israel down:

JUDITH 5:20-21—(20) Now therefore, my lord and governor, if there be any error against this people, and they sin against their God, let us consider that this shall be their ruin, and let us go up, and we shall overcome them. (21) But if there be no iniquity in their nation, let my lord now pass by, lest their Lord defend them, and their God be for them, and we become a reproach before all the world.

However, for the Greeks, it wasn't enough to separate the Israelites from their Power; they sought to rob them of their very identity.
Sound familiar?

Consequently, *HERE* ↓ is where the NT Israelite Greeks originated.

2 MACCABEES 6:6-9—(6) Neither was it lawful for a man to keep Sabbath days or ancient fasts, **or to profess himself at all to be a Jew**. (7) And in the day of the king's birth every month they were brought by bitter constraint to eat of the sacrifices; and when the fast of Bacchus was kept, the Jews were compelled to go in procession to Bacchus, carrying ivy. (8) Moreover there went out a decree to the neighbour cities of the heathen, by the suggestion of Ptolemee, against the Jews, that they should observe the same fashions, and be partakers of their sacrifices: (9) And whoso would not conform themselves to the manners of the Gentiles should be put to death. Then might a man have seen the present misery.

—If Israelites were forced to touch and eat abominable meats and participate in idolatrous festivals and sacrifices, what did they become?

Unclean *(Leviticus 5:2-3)*

—If Israelites stopped circumcising their children, what did they become?

Uncircumcised *(Genesis 17:10-14, Leviticus 12:3)*

—If the Greek King decreed that Israelites were to be one with *his* people, and they couldn't—under threat of death—call themselves Israelites anymore, what would they call themselves and what would others call them?

Greeks/GENTILES *(Hosea 1:8-9; 7:8, 13; Isaiah 7:8)*

Other Israelite Gentiles/Greeks During The Greek Captivity

As shown previously, a small remnant of Ephraim and Manasseh remained in their lands and lived as Gentiles up until the time of the Messiah. This was one of the reasons their relationship with the Southern Kingdom (Judah, Benjamin, & Levi) was so toxic. Josephus documents how their strained relations played out during Judah's Greek captivity:

> So when Alexander had thus settled matters at Jerusalem, he led his army into the neighboring cities; and when all the inhabitants to whom he came received him with great kindness, the Samaritans, who had then Shechem for their metropolis, (a city situate at Mount Gerizzim, and inhabited by apostates of the Jewish nation,) seeing that Alexander had so greatly honored the Jews, determined to profess themselves Jews; for such is the disposition of the Samaritans, as we have already elsewhere declared, that when the Jews are in adversity, they deny that they are of kin to them, and then they confess the truth; but when they perceive that some good fortune hath befallen them, they immediately pretend to have communion with them, saying that they belong to them, and derive their genealogy from the posterity of Joseph, Ephraim, and Manasseh.
> *Josephus, "Antiquities of the Jews - Book XI, chapter 8, paragraph 5*

Just as the Southern Kingdom used the Samaritans when it was convenient, Samaritans claimed and disowned Judah when it suited their purposes as well. This was especially true during the dark days of Greek tyranny. The next quote shows how invested many Israelites were in living as Greeks:

When the Samaritans saw the Jews under these sufferings, they no longer confessed that they were of their kindred, nor that the temple on Mount Gerizzim belonged to Almighty God. This was according to their nature, as we have already shown. And they now said that they were a colony of Medes and Persians; and indeed they were a colony of theirs. So they sent ambassadors to Antiochus, and an epistle, whose contents are these: "To king Antiochus the god, Epiphanes, a memorial from the Sidonians, who live at Shechem. Our forefathers, upon certain frequent plagues, and as following a certain ancient superstition, had a custom of observing that day which by the Jews is called the Sabbath. And when they had erected a temple at the mountain called Gerrizzim, though without a name, they offered upon it the proper sacrifices. Now, upon the just treatment of these wicked Jews, those that manage their affairs, supposing that we were of kin to them, and practiced as they do, make us liable to the same accusations, although we be originally Sidonians, as is evident from the public records. We therefore beseech thee, our benefactor and Savior, to give order to Apollonius, the governor of this part of the country, and to Nicanor, the procurator of thy affairs, to give us no disturbance, nor to lay to our charge what the Jews are accused for, since we are aliens from their nation, and from their customs; but let our temple, which at present hath no name at all be named the Temple of Jupiter Hellenius. If this were once done, we should be no longer disturbed, but should be more intent on our own occupation with quietness, and so bring in a greater revenue to thee." When the Samaritans had petitioned for this, the king sent them back the following answer, in an epistle: "King Antiochus to Nicanor. The Sidonians, who live at Shechem, have sent me the memorial enclosed. When therefore we were advising with our friends about it, the messengers sent by them represented to us that they are no way concerned with accusations which belong to the Jews, but choose to live after the customs of the Greeks. Accordingly, we declare them free from such accusations, and order that, agreeable to their petition, their temple be named the Temple of Jupiter Hellenius." He also sent the like epistle to Apollonius, the governor of that part of the country, in the forty-sixth year, and the eighteenth day of the month Hecatorabeom.

Josephus, "Antiquities of the Jews - Book XII, chapter 5, paragraph 5

Remember, not all Samaritans were Israelites. While a remnant were of the seed of Ephraim and Manasseh, just as many were descendants of the people the Assyrians used to repopulate the area when they conquered the Northern Kingdom. However, the animosity and dysfunction between the Northern and Southern kingdoms continued up until the time of the Messiah and is demonstrated throughout the New Testament.

Reconciliation: The Two Sticks

Gather my saints together unto me; those that have made a covenant with me by sacrifice.
—Psalms 50:5

As the saying goes, you've got to break a few eggs to make an omelet, which is what TMH had to do to the children of Israel. He had to destroy His people in order to rebuild and reconcile them to Himself. The purpose of this necessary destruction was to make them unbreakable and everlastingly faithful.

TMH'S JUDGMENT ON HIS TWO REBELLIOUS CHILDREN: JUDAH & THE HOUSE OF ISRAEL/EPHRAIM (Southern & Northern Kingdoms)

HOSEA 5:5-15—(5) And the pride of Israel doth testify to his face: therefore shall Israel and Ephraim fall in their iniquity; Judah also shall fall with them. (6) They shall go with their flocks and with their herds to seek the LORD; but they shall not find him; he hath withdrawn himself from them. (7) They have dealt treacherously against the LORD: for they have begotten strange children: now shall a month devour them with their portions. (8) Blow ye the cornet in Gibeah, and the trumpet in Ramah: cry aloud at Bethaven, after thee, O Benjamin. (9) Ephraim shall be desolate in the day of rebuke: among the tribes of Israel have I made known that which shall surely be. (10) The princes of Judah were like them that remove the bound: therefore I will pour out my wrath upon them like water. (11) Ephraim is oppressed and broken in judgment, because he willingly walked after the commandment. (12) Therefore will I be unto Ephraim as a moth, and to the house of Judah as rottenness. (13) When Ephraim saw his sickness, and Judah saw his wound, then went Ephraim to the Assyrian, and sent to king Jareb: yet could he not heal you, nor cure you of your wound. (14) For I will be unto Ephraim as a lion, and as a young lion to the house of Judah: I, even I, will tear and go away; I will take away, and none shall rescue him. (15) I will go and return to my place, till they acknowledge their offence, and seek my face: in their affliction they will seek me early.

JUDAH & ISRAEL/EPHRAIM: RECONCILING THE TWO HOUSES
Broken Covenant, Broken Sticks

Because of the children of Israel's repeated rebellion, TMH had no choice but to pronounce a great judgment against them, one that would completely change the course of biblical history. Here is a direct prophecy foretelling the divine origin of the Israelite's portentous split:

ZECHARIAH 11:10-14—(10) And I took my staff, even Beauty, and cut it asunder, that I might break my covenant which I had made with all the people. (11) And it was broken in that day: and so the poor of the flock that waited upon me knew that it was the word of the LORD. (12) And I said unto them, If ye think good, give me my price; and if not, forbear. So they weighed for my price thirty pieces of silver. (13) And the LORD said unto me, Cast it unto the potter: a goodly price that I was prized at of them. And I took the thirty pieces of silver, and cast them to the potter in the house of the LORD. (14) <u>Then I cut asunder mine other staff, even Bands, that I might break the brotherhood between Judah and Israel.</u>

Two Sticks To Become One Again: The REAL Meaning Behind 'Grafting In'

Though the split was necessary, it was always TMH's plan to bring Judah and the House of Israel/Ephraim back together again. This was the crux of the Messiah's mission. The Law and the prophets attest to this. As does the NT since the other sheep the Messiah alluded to in *John 10:16* are The Northern Kingdom Israelites who were carried away by the Assyrians. They were subsequently scattered throughout Asia Minor and beyond, however TMH vowed to bring all his people back together again, making them one nation under one God and King.

TMH recognized that this reconciliation wouldn't be possible without first healing the breech between the two houses, which is what Ezekiel prophesied below. Here you'll find a prophetic precursor to the 'Grafting In' doctrine of *Romans*. *Ezekiel* speaks about re-attaching (re-grafting) the two sticks, which represent both houses, together into one:

EZEKIEL 37:19-25—(19) Say unto them, Thus saith the Lord GOD; Behold, <u>I will take the stick of Joseph, which is in the hand of Ephraim, and the tribes of Israel his fellows, and will put them with him, even with the stick of Judah, **and make them one stick, and they shall be one in mine hand.**</u> (20) And the sticks whereon thou writest shall be in thine hand before their eyes. (21) And say unto them, Thus saith the Lord GOD; Behold, <u>I will **take the children of Israel from among the heathen,**</u>

whither they be gone, and will gather them on every side, and bring them into their own land: (22) **And I will make them one nation** in the land upon the mountains of Israel; and one king shall be king to them all: and they shall be no more two nations, **neither shall they be divided into two kingdoms any more** at all: (23) Neither shall they defile themselves any more with their idols, nor with their detestable things, nor with any of their transgressions: but I will save them out of all their dwelling places, wherein they have sinned, and will cleanse them: so shall they be my people, and I will be their God. (24) And David my servant *shall be* king over them; and they all shall have one shepherd: **they shall also walk in my judgments, and observe my statutes, and do them**. (25) And they shall dwell in the land that I have given unto Jacob my servant, wherein your fathers have dwelt; and they shall dwell therein, *even* they, and their children, and their children's children forever: and my servant David *shall be* their prince forever.

EZEKIEL 39:25-29—(25) Therefore thus saith the Lord GOD; Now will I bring again the captivity of Jacob, and have mercy upon the whole house of Israel, and will be jealous for my holy name; (26) After that they have borne their shame, and all their trespasses whereby they have trespassed against me, when they dwelt safely in their land, and none made *them* afraid. (27) **When I have brought them again from the people, and gathered them out of their enemies' lands, and am sanctified in them in the sight of many nations**; (28) Then shall they know that I *am* the LORD their God, which caused them to be led into captivity among the heathen: but I have gathered them unto their own land, and have left none of them any more there. (29) Neither will I hide my face any more from them: for I have poured out my spirit upon the house of Israel, saith the Lord GOD.

ROMANS 11:19-24—(19) Thou wilt say then, The branches were broken off, that I might be graffed in. (20) Well; because of unbelief they were broken off, and thou standest by faith. Be not high-minded, but fear: (21) For if God spared not the natural branches, take heed lest he also spare not thee. (22) Behold therefore the goodness and severity of God: on them which fell, severity; but toward thee, goodness, if thou continue in his goodness: otherwise thou also shalt be cut off. (23) And they also, if they abide not still in unbelief, shall be graffed in: for God is able to graph them in again. (24) For if thou wert cut out of the olive tree which is wild by nature, and wert graffed contrary to nature into a good olive tree: how much more shall these, which be the natural branches, be graffed into their own olive tree?

One Flock Under One Shepherd

JEREMIAH 50:4-7—(4) In those days, and in that time, saith the LORD, **the children of Israel shall come, they and the children of Judah together**, going and weeping: they shall go, and seek the LORD their God. (5) They shall ask the way to Zion with their faces thitherward, saying, Come, and let us join ourselves to the LORD in a perpetual covenant that shall not be forgotten. (6) **My people hath been lost sheep: their shepherds have caused them to go astray**, they have turned them away on the mountains: they have gone from mountain to hill, they have forgotten their resting place. (7) All that found them have devoured them: and their adversaries said, We offend not, because they have sinned against the LORD, the habitation of justice, even the LORD, the hope of their fathers.

JEREMIAH 50:17—**Israel is a scattered sheep**; the lions have driven him away: first the king of Assyria hath devoured him; and last this Nebuchadnezzar king of Babylon hath broken his bones.

EZEKIEL 34:11-31—(11) For thus saith the Lord GOD; Behold, I, even I, will both search my sheep, and seek them out. (12) As a shepherd seeketh out his flock in the day that he is among his sheep that are scattered; so will I seek out my sheep, and will deliver them out of all places where they have been scattered in the cloudy and dark day. (13) And I will bring them out from the people, and gather them from the countries, and will bring them to their own land, and feed them upon the mountains of Israel by the rivers, and in all the inhabited places of the country. (14) I will feed them in a good pasture, and upon the high mountains of Israel shall their fold be: there shall they lie in a good fold, and in a fat pasture shall they feed upon the mountains of Israel. (15) I will feed my flock, and I will cause them to lie down, saith the Lord GOD. (16) I will seek that which was lost, and bring again that which was driven away, and will bind up that which was broken, and will strengthen that which was sick: but I will destroy the fat and the strong; I will feed them with judgment. (17) And as for you, O my flock, thus saith the Lord GOD; Behold, I judge between cattle and cattle, between the rams and the he goats. (18) Seemeth it a small thing unto you to have eaten up the good pasture, but ye must tread down with your feet the residue of your pastures? and to have drunk of the deep waters, but ye must foul the residue with your feet? (19) And as for my flock, they eat that which ye have trodden with your feet; and they drink that which ye have fouled with your feet. (20) Therefore thus saith the Lord GOD unto them; Behold, I, even I, will judge between the fat cattle and between the lean cattle. (21) Because ye have thrust with side and with shoulder, and pushed all the diseased with your horns, till ye have scattered them abroad; (22) **Therefore will I save my flock**, and they shall no more be a prey; and I will judge between cattle and cattle. (23) And I will set up one shepherd over them, and he shall feed them, even my servant David; he shall feed them, and he shall be their shepherd. (24) And I the LORD will be their God, and my servant David a prince among them; I the LORD have spoken it. (25) And I will make with them a covenant of peace, and will cause the evil beasts to cease out of the land: and they shall dwell safely in the wilderness, and sleep in the woods. (26) And I will make them and the places round about my hill a blessing; and I will cause the shower to come down in his season; there shall be showers of blessing. (27) And the tree of the field shall yield her fruit, and the earth shall yield her increase, <u>and they shall be safe in their land, and shall know that I am the LORD, when I have broken the bands of their yoke, and delivered them out of the hand of those that served themselves of them. (28) And they shall no more be a prey to the heathen, neither shall the beast of the land devour them; but they shall dwell safely, and none shall make them afraid</u>. (29) And I will raise up for them a plant of renown, and they shall be no more consumed with hunger in the land, neither bear the shame of the heathen any more. (30) Thus shall they know that I the LORD their God am with them, and that they, even the house of Israel, are my people, saith the Lord GOD. (31) And ye my flock, the flock of my pasture, are men, and I am your God, saith the Lord GOD.

JOHN 10:11-16—(11) I am the good shepherd: the good shepherd giveth his life for the sheep. (12) But he that is an hireling, and not the shepherd, whose own the sheep are not, seeth the wolf coming, and leaveth the sheep, and fleeth: and the wolf catcheth them, and scattereth the sheep. (13) The hireling fleeth, because he is an hireling, and careth not for the sheep. (14) I am the good shepherd, and know my sheep, and am known of mine. (15) As the Father knoweth me, even so know I the Father: and <u>I lay down my life for the sheep. (16) And other sheep I have, which are not of this fold</u>: them also I must bring, and they shall hear my voice; <u>and there shall be one fold, and one shepherd</u>.

LUKE 15:1-6—(1) Then drew near unto him all the publicans and sinners for to hear him. (2) And the Pharisees and scribes murmured, saying, This man receiveth sinners, and eateth with them. (3) And he spake this parable unto them, saying, (4) <u>What man of you, having an hundred sheep, if he lose one of them, doth not leave the ninety and nine in the wilderness, and go after that which is lost, until he find it? (5) And when he hath found it, he layeth it on his shoulders, rejoicing. (6) And when he cometh home, he calleth together his friends and neighbors, saying unto them, Rejoice with me; for I have found my sheep which was lost</u>.

(Jeremiah 12:10-11; 23:1-2; John 10:27-30, Genesis 29:1-8)

A People Gathered From The Four Corners Of The Earth

JEREMIAH 31:8-11—(8) Behold, I will bring them from the north country, and gather them from the coasts of the earth, *and* with them the blind and the lame, the woman with child and her that travaileth with child together: a great company shall return thither. (9) They shall come with weeping, and with supplications will I lead them: I will cause them to walk by the rivers of waters in a straight way, wherein they shall not stumble: for I am a father to Israel, and Ephraim *is* my firstborn. (10) Hear the word of the LORD, O ye nations, and declare *it* in the isles afar off, and say, He that scattered Israel will gather him, and keep him, as a shepherd *doth* his flock. (11) For the LORD hath redeemed Jacob, and ransomed him from the hand of *him that was* stronger than he.

JEREMIAH 33:7—And I will cause the captivity of Judah and the captivity of Israel to return, and will build them, as at the first.

JEREMIAH 46:27—But fear not thou, O my servant Jacob, and be not dismayed, O Israel: for, behold, I will save thee from afar off, and thy seed from the land of their captivity; and Jacob shall return, and be in rest and at ease, and none shall make *him* afraid.

2 MACCABEES 2:17-18—(17) We hope also, that the God, that delivered all his people, and gave them all an heritage, and the kingdom, and the priesthood, and the sanctuary, (18) As he promised in the law, will shortly have mercy upon us, and gather us together out of every land under heaven into the holy place: for he hath delivered us out of great troubles, and hath purified the place.

THE PSALMS OF SOLOMON 8:34-38—(34) Gather together the dispersed of Israel, with mercy and goodness; (35) For Thy faithfulness is with us. And though we have stiffened our neck, yet Thou art our chastener; (36) Overlook us not, O our God, lest the nations swallow us up, as though there were none to deliver. (37) But Thou art our God from the beginning, and upon Thee is our hope (set), O Lord; (38) and we will not depart from Thee, for good are Thy judgments upon us.

THE PSALMS OF SOLOMON 11:1-5—(1) Sound the trumpet in Zion, the signal for the saints! (2) Proclaim in Jerusalem the voice of one bringing good news for God became merciful to Israel in watching over them. (3) Stand on a high place, Jerusalem, and look at your children brought together from the east and the west by the Lord. (4) From the north they come in the joy of their God; from distant islands God has brought them. (5) He lowered high mountains to level ground for them; the hills fled at their coming.

PROLOGUE TO

As also in all his epistles, speaking in them of these things; in which are some things hard to be understood, which they that are unlearned and unstable wrest, as they do also the other scriptures, unto their own destruction.
— *2 Peter 3:16*

Paul, A Hebrew of Hebrews

But the Lord said to him, 'Go your way, for he is my chosen vessel to bear my name before the nations [[ethnōn (ἐθνῶν)] *and kings, and the children of Israel.'*
—Acts 9:15

The apostle Paul was tasked to fulfill a divine mission, which was to bear TMH's name before the nations, including their kings, queens, and magistrates during his ministry to the children of Israel. Repentant non-Israelites who believed in the God of Israel as a result of his outreach to our people were welcomed to worship TMH. This has been the case since the beginning of the nation. *(Exodus 12:38; Leviticus 19:34; Zechariah 8:22-23)*

However, Paul's primary mission, (as with our Messiah & his other disciples) was to reach the lost sheep of the house of Israel.

Born in Tarsus, which was located in Asia Minor, the Apostle Paul described himself as *"circumcised the eighth day, of the stock of Israel, of the tribe of Benjamin, an Hebrew of the Hebrews; as touching the law, a Pharisee."* *(Philippians 3:5)* This last point is very important. He studied under Gamaliel *(Acts 22:3)* a well-respected Pharisaic teacher of his day. *(Acts 5:33-40)* So given his strong theological pedigree, it's not hard to understand why TMH chose Paul. Who but an expert in the Law could effortlessly serve up both spiritual milk and meat to the starving masses?

It must be noted that when Paul composed his epistles, the NT didn't exist. Every letter he wrote contained words, concepts, and oftentimes, whole quotations from the Law (Torah), the prophets (prophecies), the *Psalms* (David, Asaph, Korah and others), the wisdom books (Solomon, Ben Sirach), the *Apocrypha* (hidden books) and the *Pseudepigrapha* (disputed books).

This rich background informed everything he wrote and taught. It cannot be overstated that Paul was a master of the Law, which is why Peter warned that his writings were difficult to understand. So in reading his work, never forget that the books he quoted from throughout his epistles are not there for decoration. They serve many purposes—one being to *unlock the mystery of the Gentiles. (Ephesians 3:6)*

THE PEOPLE OF ROMANS

Moreover, brethren, I would not that ye should be ignorant, how that all our fathers were under the cloud, and all passed through the sea; And were all baptized unto Moses in the cloud and in the sea; And did all eat the same spiritual meat; And did all drink the same spiritual drink: for they drank of that spiritual Rock that followed them: and that Rock was Christ.
—1 Corinthians 1-4

Within The Book Of Romans you'll find two main groups amongst the children of Israel:

THE CIRCUMCISION

These were Torah-observant Israelites from the tribes of Judah, Benjamin, a small remnant from Levi, and an even smaller remnant of the other tribes. While many remained faithful to the Torah, some also followed the traditions taught by the Scribes, Pharisees and Sadducees. Carried over from the Babylonian captivity, these traditions oftentimes contradicted TMH's commandments. (Matthew 23:23-24)

All three tribes within the Circumcision (and the small remnant from the other tribes) fell under the House of Judah and were referred to as Judeans or "Jews." For instance, Paul, who was from the tribe of Benjamin, (Romans 11:1) was a self-described "Jew" (Acts 21:39) and a Pharisee. (Philippians 3:5).

THE UNCIRCUMCISION

Many in the diaspora were named the 'Uncircumcision' because they were living as heathens and pagans, and had therefore, broken covenant with TMH. Kindred in this group included the majority of the ten Northern Kingdom tribes. These Israelites, scattered throughout Asia Minor as well as nations foreign (language-wise) to the Greco-Roman empire, were disdainfully called 'Gentiles'—*Ethnos*—by the Circumcision.

Jews and Northern Kingdom Israelites who embraced Greek culture, customs, identity and language were known as 'Greeks'—*Hellenes*—a demographic the Circumcision considered Gentile as well.

Gentiles/Nations & Greeks

There is a huge misconception about the terms "Gentiles" [*Ethnos*] and "Greeks" [*Hellenes*] in the New Testament. In order to support mainstream Christian doctrines, apologists have alleged that these words refer exclusively to non-Israelites. However, this doesn't fit the context, history, language-usage, or the overall message of the scriptures. In fact, Bible translators and theologians created hundreds of contradictory translations, dictionaries, and thesauruses just to keep this false narrative afloat. Word usage within translations is at the sole discretion of the translator. And if said translator doesn't consider context along with history and prophecy, a sentence, or a passage, if not an entire chapter, can come out meaning something quite different than what was originally intended. How do we know what was originally intended? Biblical prophecy and history make it plain.

First, let's examine the Greek.

Ethnos

Ethnos/Ethnon from *ethō* (Strong's #1484) mainly means **nation**, but gradually (and inaccurately) came to mean Gentile (AKA non-Israelite) exclusively. However, in scripture it can mean: (a) a race (b) a people (c) the nations (d) Israelites (e) non-Israelites (f) the heathen world (g) culture.

Nation: (n) – [1] a race of people; an aggregation of persons of the same ethnic family, and speaking the same language or cognate languages, [2] an organized community within a certain territory.

Definitions [1] and [2] hold equal weight. However, if you combine definition [2] with a portion of [1], you have the essence of America:

> "An organized community within a certain
> territory, speaking the same language."

Keep this definition in mind because it will come into play later.

Now, as I've shown, *Ethnos/Ethnon* doesn't just mean 'Gentile'. It has many nuances. For instance, here are but a few verses where it's translated as "nation" and "people" and applied to the nation of Israel and the house of Judah: *Luke 7:5; 23:2; John 11:48, 50, 52; Acts 10:22, 24:17, 26:4.*

Also, the word 'Gentile' doesn't just mean non-Israelite. This is especially true in the case of NT Israelites since they existed as (1) a race of people, and/or (2) persons of the same ethnic family, and/or (3) persons speaking a certain language, and/or (4) an organized community within a certain territory. To demonstrate this point, let's look at this from a language/cultural angle. A Greek-speaking Israelite born and raised as a Gentile in Athens had more in common (culture and language-wise) with a Non-Israelite Athenian than with a Jew from Bethlehem. Likewise, a native-born Japanese American has more in common with a native-born Korean American than a Japanese Frenchman.

What's more, **Ethnos/Ethnon** is used interchangeably for non-Israelites *and* Israelites in the NT, specifically in *The Book Of Romans*, which you'll see in the Precepts section.

Goy

The Septuagint (the Greek translation of the OT) translates the Hebrew word for nation, which is 'goy,' (Strong's #1471) as *Ethnos* as well. And like *Ethnos*, *'Goy'* is thought to only refer to non-Israelites, but this too is wrong. Again, in scripture, it mainly means 'nation.'

GENESIS 35:10-11—(10) And God said unto him, Thy name is Jacob: thy name shall not be called any more Jacob, but Israel shall be thy name: and he called his name Israel. (11) And God said unto him, I am God Almighty: be fruitful and multiply; a nation [gō-w/**GOY** (גוֹי)] and a company of nations [gō-w-yim/**GOY** (גוֹיִם)] shall be of thee, and kings shall come out of thy loins.

TMH told Jacob He would make him into one nation *(goy)* AND a multitude of nations *(gowyims/goy)*. This was a prophecy of Judah and Ephraim who would later become a multitude or fullness of gentiles/nations. *(Genesis 48:17-20; Romans 11:25)* This is important to remember because each tribe would later come to be considered *its own nation*, namely because of the split.

The word <u>gowyims</u> doesn't just apply to non-Israelites or the sons of Japheth specifically.

Here are a few more places where 'goy' (used as 'nation') is applied to the nation of Israel: *Genesis 12:2* [Strong's #1471: "nation"—*lə-ḡō-w* (לְגוֹי)]; *Genesis 18:18* [Strong's #1471: "nation"—*lə-ḡō-w* (לְגוֹי)]; *Genesis 46:3* [Strong's #1471: "nation"—*lə-ḡō-w* (לְגוֹי)], *Genesis 48:19* [Strong's #1471: "of nations"—*hag-gō-w-yim* (הַגּוֹיִם)]; *Exodus 32:10* [Strong's #1471: "nation"—*lə-ḡō-w* (לְגוֹי)]; *Deuteronomy 26:5* [Strong's #1471: "nation"—*lə-ḡō-w* (לְגוֹי)]; *Ezekiel 37:22* [Strong's #1471: "nation"—*lə-ḡō-w* (לְגוֹי)] and [Strong's #1471: "nations"—*ḡō-w-yim* (גוֹיִם)]; *Micah 4:7* [Strong's #1471: "nation"—*lə-ḡō-w* (לְגוֹי)].

By the way, the Hebrew word *lə-ḡō-w* (לְגוֹי)—"nation" isn't just used for Israelites. It's used for non-Israelites as well: Egypt in *Exodus 9:24* and Ishmael in *Genesis 17:20*. The same holds true for *hag-gō-w-yim*

(הַגּוֹיִם:)—"of nations." It's used in *Genesis 10:5* for the "isles of the Gentiles"/maritime people and for Gentile slaves in *Leviticus 25:44*.

As previously shown, after the two kingdoms split, the House of Judah and the scattered 10 tribes (Ephraim/The House of Israel) were considered two distinct *ḡō-w-yim* (nations), i.e. bloodlines; just as distinct as the many other *ḡō-w-yim* (nations) chronicled in the Bible.

From this split, Ephraim fell into idolatry and became completely heathen before and during the Assyrian captivity *(Hosea 4:17; Ezekiel 20:31-32)* while Judah fell into idolatry *(Jeremiah 3:6-10)* and went into Babylonian captivity *(2 Kings 24:8–16, 25:1-12)*, Medo-Persian rule *(2 Chr. 36:22–23; Ezra 1–2, Esther 3:8–13)*, and then Greco-Roman captivity *(Joel 3:6, 1 & 2 Maccabees; Luke 3:1-2; John 19:15)*. Although many remained loyal within Judah, many others became 'Greeks" AKA, Gentiles. *(1 Maccabees 1:41-43, 48)*

Consequently, in scripture, the Greek "*Ethnos*" and the Hebrew "*Goy*" cannot and do not exclusively pertain to non-Israelites.

Now consider one more example:

ISAIAH 11:10—And in that day there shall be a root of Jesse, which shall stand for an ensign of the people; to it shall the Gentiles [gō-w-yim (גּוֹיִם)] seek: and his rest shall be glorious.

Although the Hebrew word *gō-w-yim* (גּוֹיִם) is used, we just saw the prophecy in *Genesis 35:10-11*. According to verse 11, "a nation [gō-w/**GOY** (גּוֹי)] and a company of nations [gō-w-yim/**GOY** (גּוֹיִם)]" would come out of Jacob. The same Hebrew word used there in *Genesis* is used here in *Isaiah 11:10*: *gō-w-yim* (גּוֹיִם). So let's examine this:

Isaiah 11 begins with the promise of a wise, powerful, and righteous root of Jessie, AKA a messiah who will be an ensign (**leader**, standard bearer) for the people.

QUESTION: The definition of Messiah is deliverer, so who did the Messiah come to deliver and lead? Which people did He die for?

ANSWER: That would be the people of Israel. *(Matthew 1:21, 15:24; Luke 1:76-77)*

Further on we see that the "Gentiles" in *Isaiah 11:10* will **seek** His rest. Similarly, TMH's people were promised to one day receive rest—*His rest*. *(Psalms 95:7-11; Hebrews 3:16-19, 4:1-8)* In fact, this has been a repetitive theme for perpetually oppressed, spoiled, and enslaved Israel throughout biblical history. *(Deuteronomy 25:19, Isaiah 35:4, 41:8-10, 43:1-2, Jeremiah 30:6-8, 50:34, Baruch 4:18, 21-24)* What's more, TMH has said repeatedly, that before He forgives and recovers His people, they must first **seek** Him with all their heart, mind and soul. *(Deuteronomy 4:29; 2 Chronicles 6:36-39; Jeremiah 29:10-14)* Only then will He redeem and heal them. *(2 Chronicles 7:14)*

As we read on, *Isaiah 11:11* foretells Israel's regathering while verse 13 promises a reunion for Ephraim and Judah. These verses point to Israel's awakening and reconciliation. Therefore, the Gentiles in *Isaiah 11:10* are the same scattered Gentile Israelites whom TMH said He would redeem and regather. These are the Gentiles who will seek Him with all their heart, mind, and soul.

> **QUESTION: Are Israelites and non-Israelites seeking the same Messiah?**
>
> **ANSWER: No. The majority of Non-Israelite 'believers' are looking for the Jesus and gospel of contemporary Christianity. Israelites are looking for the Messiah of the Bible who promised to save them from their sins, and deliver them from their haters, oppressors, and enemies.** (*Psalms 14:7; Jeremiah 30:8-24; Ezekiel 20:33-34, 34:11-13; 37:21-25; Isaiah 61, 63, Obadiah, Matthew 24:29-31; Luke 1:67-80, Revelation, etc.*)

Héllēn
Phonetic Spelling: *Hel'-lane*

I've said this a million times already, but it bears repeating. Without historical and prophetic understanding of who the NT Greeks actually are, we end up with Christian doctrine and strong delusion. So let's examine the word *Héllēn* carefully.

First, here's a combined summary definition from *Strong's* and *Bauer's Greek English Lexicon*:

Hellén [Ἕλλην] (Strong's #1672) — a 'Hellen' (Grecian) or resident of Hellas; a person who speaks Greek, someone of Greek language and culture. 2. In general, ALL PEOPLE influenced by Greek, AKA PAGAN CULTURE.

If you look this up in *Strong's Concordance*, you'll see "*especially a non-Jew*," along with the term "*Gentile Greek*" in *Bauer's*.

First of all, how can *Hellén* both mean ALL PEOPLE influenced by Greek culture, along with Greek-speaking people, but then not apply to Greek-speaking Israelites who were born in the land like all the other racial groups there? Nothing in *Hellén's* biblical usage even hints that it excludes Israelite Greeks. The word "*especially*" isn't exclusive. It's used to highlight a certain portion, a word those pushing contemporary Christian doctrine toss out there to muddy the water.

Then there's the '*Gentile Greek*' qualifier in *Bauer's*. The fact that they even use this weakens their argument. Think about it. In order for there to be "Gentile Greeks," there *must* also be non-Gentile Greeks, correct?

That's just common sense. I mean, isn't the term "Gentile Greek" redundant anyway since Greeks (as a racial group) are considered Gentiles?

Now look at this:

> Hellénistés [Ἑλληνιστής] (Strong's #1675) — a Hellenist, a Grecian Jew, a Greek-speaking Jew, a person who speaks only Greek and no Hebrew

Take a look at how this word is defined above. According to Strong's, 'Hellénistés' seems to apply mostly to Greek-speaking "Jews." However, if you look at the various translations for this same word, 'Hellénistés' in Acts 11:20, we encounter a veritable free-for-all:

> Greeks (NIV); Gentiles (NLT); Hellenists (ESV); Greeks (BSB) Greeks (NASB); Hellenists (NKJV); Grecians (KJB); Greeks (CSB); Gentiles (CEV); Greeks (DRB); Greeks (ERV); Greeks (DBT), Gentiles (GNT)

So which is it? Greeks? Grecians? Hellenists? Or Gentiles? Remember what they said about Hellén above (Strong's 1672), how they claimed it 'especially' applied to non-Jews? Our question should be, according to whom? Because as you can see, it mostly depends on the translator.

Even more bizarre: This same word "Hellénistés" [root word: Hellén] is biblically translated as 'Hellenistic Jews,' 'Grecians,' 'Gentiles and Greeks," 'Jews who spoke Greek,' 'Grecian Jews,' 'Greek-speaking Jews' and 'Hellenists' by these same translators in Acts 9:29. Mind you, don't forget about the free-for-all in Acts 11:20 for "Hellénistés as well.

You see the same confusion in Acts 17:12 where some translate Hellēnidōn [Ἑλληνίδων] as 'Greeks,' others use 'Grecians,' while others use 'Gentiles.' Let us not forget that the root word for Hellēnidōn is Hellén also. And if all that isn't bewildering enough, there's this:

According to Zondervan's Compact Bible Dictionary, the words 'Greeks' and 'Grecians' must 'be distinguished' from each other. They claim 'Greeks' belong to 'the Hellenistic race,' but the term 'Grecian' is specific to Israelites of the diaspora. This is an interesting supposition in light of the King James' translation in Joel 3:6:

> **JOEL 3:6**—The children also of Judah and the children of Jerusalem have ye sold unto **the Grecians**, that ye might remove them far from their border.

See what I mean? Confusion. Joel 3:6 documents when the Israelites went into Greek captivity and *became* 'Grecians,' a word the aforementioned scholars claim specifically applies to Israelites.

Did they sell themselves to themselves?

For what it's worth, *The Jubilee Bible 2000*, the *American King James*, the *American Standard Version*, the *English Revised Version*, and *Webster's Bible Translation* also translated this verse the same way— Grecians. However, the word rendered as 'Grecians' (*Hellēnōn* [Ἑλλήνων]) by the above referenced translators is translated as 'Greeks' by the Septuagint in *Joel 3:6*. The Septuagint renders the same word (*Hellēnōn* [Ἑλλήνων]) in *Daniel 11:2* as 'Greeks' also, with other bible versions translating it as 'Grecian,' 'Grecia,' and 'Greece.'

We see a similar issue in *The Apocrypha*. *2 Maccabees 4:13-15* details how Judah became 'Greek' during the Greek captivity. Considering what the scholars said about the word 'Grecian' it's not hard to understand why they removed *The Apocrypha*:

> **2 MACCABEES 4:13-15**—(13) Now such was the height of Greek fashions, and increase of heathenish manners, through the exceeding profaneness of Jason, that ungodly wretch, and no high priest; (14) That the priests had no courage to serve any more at the altar, but despising the temple, and neglecting the sacrifices, hastened to be partakers of the unlawful allowance in the place of exercise, after the game of Discus called them forth; (15) <u>Not setting by the honors of their fathers, but **liking the glory of the Grecians best of all**</u>. (Translated as 'Grecians' by KJB & DRB. Other translations use 'Greeks')

If Judah liked the glory of the Grecians most of all, how then can the term Grecians refer exclusively to Judah? See, TMH is *not* the author of confusion, and this most certainly is confusion. These so-called scholars and Bible dictionary writers translate and redefine words according to their theological biases—the truth be damned.

Obviously, there isn't a *specific* word for Hellenized Israelites. Sure, they try to designate 'Grecian' as the go-to definition, but as demonstrated, the words 'Grecian,' 'Greek,' and 'Gentile' don't have exclusive meanings. Used interchangeably, they can apply to both non-Israelite Gentiles and Israelite Gentiles alike. Hellenization took place throughout the colonized world. *All* people within the conquered territories were subject to it, not just Israel. However, translators deliberately ignored context, biblical history, and prophecy in order to promote false doctrine.

So let's get some clarity.

2 Maccabees 6:6 and *1 Maccabees 1:41-42* reveal why Israelites would not only speak Greek, but would abandon their heritage and, as a result, would be referred to as 'GREEKS' and 'GENTILES' in the New Testament.

2 MACCABEES 6:6—**Neither was it lawful for a man** to keep Sabbath days or ancient fasts, or **to profess himself at all to be a Jew**.

So. Logically speaking, if Judeans living under totalitarian Greek captivity weren't allowed to call themselves "Jews" anymore, what would they be called?

GREEKS!

If you're still in doubt, *1 Maccabees 1:41-42* drives the point home:

1 MACCABEES 1:41-42—Moreover king Antiochus wrote to **his whole kingdom, that all should be one people**, and **every one should leave his laws**: so all the heathen agreed according to the commandment of the king.

Now remember that definition I told you to keep in mind at the beginning of this essay? Well, King Antiochus' proclamation made the Greek kingdom:

"An organized community within a certain territory,
speaking the same language."

Just like America. Just like Britain. Just like France. Just like most European countries today. Regardless of a person's race, the citizens in these countries consider themselves one people, speaking the same language, under ONE name.

During Israel's Greek, and later, Greco-Roman captivities, national *citizenship* was the name of the game. Hellenists were people from all walks of life who lived as Greeks in the colonized territories. Their former allegiances, ethnicities, creeds and religions were secondary, if not non-existent. Hellenization erased these distinctions through war, murder, oppression, assimilation and colonization.

Therefore, to call someone a Greek during NT times was to merely recognize their (1) citizenship (being a citizen member of Greece and its former territories), and/or (2) ethnicity (Greek language and cultural identity), and/or (3) actual bloodline [racial identity]. This was across the board for all peoples, which is why the word 'Greek' is used so liberally in the NT epistles.

While Hellenization couldn't wipe away a person's race, it acted as a sort of virus, infecting everything it touched, replicating itself and replacing what came before it, doing away with national identities, as well as individual heritages, cultures and languages. Now let's look at another derivative of *Hellén*.

Hellēnis (Ἑλληνίς)

Hellēnis (Ἑλληνίς)—Strong's #1674: (1) a Greek woman. (2) a Gentile woman and not a Jewess

As we can see, **Hellēnis** has the same root word, which is **Héllēn** (Ἕλλην Strong's #1672) — a 'Hellen' **(Grecian)** or resident of Hellas; a person who speaks Greek, someone of Greek language and culture. 2. In general, ALL PEOPLE influenced by Greek, AKA PAGAN CULTURE.

The Syrophenician Woman

Now read this scripture carefully:

MARK 7:25-26—(25) For a certain woman, whose young daughter had an unclean spirit, heard of him, and came and fell at his feet: (26) The woman was a Greek **[Hellēnis** (Ἑλληνίς)**]**, a Syrophenician by nation; and she besought him that he would cast forth the devil out of her daughter. (KJB)

Other translations render this woman as:

Greek, but born in Syrian Phoenicia— NIV
Gentile, Syrophenician by nation—WNT
Gentile born in Syrian Phoenicia—NLT,
Gentile and Syrophenician by birth—ESV, CSB
Greek and Syrophenician by birth—HCSB,
Greek and born in Phoenicia in Syria—ISV, GWT,
Greek and Syrophenician by nation—NKJV, JB2000, AKJV, YLT
Greek of Syrophenician origin—BSB, NET Bible,
Gentile and Syrophenician by race— BLB, NASB, NAS77:
Greek, Syrophenician by race—ASV, DBT, NHEB, ERV, WEB

Now remember that passage from *Zondervan's Compact Bible Dictionary*? Where it said 'Greeks' and 'Grecians' must 'be distinguished' from each other? That the word 'Greek' belongs to 'the Hellenistic race,' but 'Grecian' is specific to Israelites of the diaspora?

Well, this woman wasn't *Greek by race*. She was Syrophenician. Yet, the apostle Mark called her a Greek. Not only that, she was identified as a *Canaanite* (a descendant of Ham) in *Matthew 15:21-28's* version of this same encounter. This is a clear example of duel identity: A non-Greek person (racially speaking) referred to as a Greek. Most likely, she was culturally Greek—speaking the Greek language and following its traditions, and customs.

It was the same for NT Greek Israelites: racially speaking, they were Israelites, but culturally, socially, and language-wise, etc., they identified as Greeks. Some were raised as Greeks and/or lived in Greece and its former territories. Others were raised as Gentiles and lived in other countries, like the Scythians and Barbarians.

So if a Canaanite woman can be called a Greek, it's not a stretch for an Israelite man, whose identity was ripped from him and replaced with Greek EVERYTHING, to identify as Greek too. Just look at the apostle Paul for example. He was an Israelite, yet he referred to himself as Roman. *(Acts 22:25, 27) And* he was called a Roman by others. *(Acts 22:26, 23:27)*

Why? Because he was a Roman citizen.

We see the same thing today in the U.S., the self-described 'melting pot' of the world. Regardless of their racial background, citizens of this country are called Americans, whether native born or naturalized. Within this same handful of citizens, we have Chinese-Americans, Italian-Americans, Mexican-Americans, etc. While they're still American, and have maintained their individual cultures, religious-leanings, and languages, they're *strongly* encouraged to assimilate into the dominant society. As such, all are expected to observe the same national holidays, speak the same language, spend the same money, salute the same flag, follow the same laws, and are ruled by the same government.

Today, contemporary Israelites are still Israelites by blood, but through sin, ignorance, and brainwashing, we became Canadians, Haitians, Americans, French, British, Jamaicans...etc.—Gentiles in the flesh *(Ephesians 2:11)* who, as a consequence of breaking our holy covenant, forgot our heritage, history, and God.

Likewise, Israelites of the NT diaspora were called Greeks, Grecians, and Gentiles for the same reasons. Some identified as Greek nationally because they were citizens of Greece and Greco-Roman territories. They also identified as *ethnically* Greek because of the culture, language, and pagan religious practices they grew up with.

Contemporary Christianity conveniently forgets the multitude of prophetic promises concerning the redemption and reconciliation of the estranged Northern and Southern kingdoms. That the NT is mostly about TMH fulfilling these promises—to Israel—seems to have escaped their notice.

With these points in mind, let's identify the key NT Israelite players:

[1] Northern Kingdom Israelites of the diaspora called 'Gentiles' *(Matthew 4:15; John 4:12; 7:35)*, [2] believing Greek Jews *(Acts 6:1)*; [3] Non-

believing Greek Jews *(Acts 9:29)*, [4] Non-believing Jews of the Circumcision *(John 19:12)*, [5] devout Jews of the diaspora who spoke languages other than Hebrew and Greek *(Acts 2:5)*, and [6] believing Jews of the Circumcision. *(The apostle Paul et al.)*

These Israelite saints *(Psalms 50:5, 148:14)* are the 'Greeks,' 'Jews,' and 'Gentiles' that the apostles sought, which is why Paul targeted Israelite places of worship in his ministry:

1. The synagogue at Antioch—*Acts 13:42*
2. The synagogue at Iconium—*Acts 14:1*
3. The synagogue at Thessalonica—*Acts 17:1-4; 1 & 2 Thessalonians*
4. The synagogue at Berea—*Acts 17:10-13*
5. The synagogue at Corinth—*Acts 18:4-8; 1 & 2 Corinthians*
6. The synagogue at Ephesus—*Acts 18:19-26, 19:1-8; The Book of Ephesians*
7. Just like Thessalonica, Corinth, and Ephesus, the Galatia of *Acts 18:22-23* is the same Galatia of Paul's epistle. These are the same people the apostle Peter referred to as *"the strangers scattered throughout Pontus, Galatia, Cappadocia, Asia, and Bithynia,* **elect** *according to the foreknowledge of God the Father, through sanctification of the Spirit."*

These 'Elect,' scattered strangers were Israelites, TMH's chosen people as referenced in *Genesis 15:13; Obadiah 1:10-14; Matthew 25:41-46; The Ladder of Jacob 6 (Rec 1); Isaiah 65:22, Sirach 46:1; 47:22, Psalms 44:11, 155:21; Deuteronomy 28:63-64, 32:26; Ezekiel 20:23-24, 22:15; Jeremiah 9:16;* and *Micah 5:7-8.*

Paul's ministry wasn't limited to synagogues. Since Israelites were scattered among the heathen, worshipping their dumb idols, he traveled throughout Asia Minor to reach them. *(Acts 28:1-9)* His extraordinary testimony on Mars Hill in Athens is an expert example of how to teach unlearned idolaters, using concepts familiar to them. *(Acts 17:18-34)*

THE BOTTOM LINE

As I've said before, so now I say again, to properly understand the NT, we must read each verse through an historical, prophetic, and contextual lens. We do this by rightly dividing the truth using applicable precepts. Prophecy and history inform context, which in turn determines how to correctly translate words and interpret scriptures. Any methodology that ignores these key elements will result in confusion, twisted scriptures, false doctrine, and strong delusion, i.e. contemporary Christian theology.

For *The Book Of Romans*, it all boils down to how we differentiate Israelite Gentiles from Non-Israelite Gentiles. So when we're reading *Romans* we must **constantly** remind ourselves of some foundational and irreversible truths.

Who are TMH's chosen people? Israel. *(Leviticus 20:26; Isaiah 14:1)* Who did Messiah come for? Israel. *(Matthew 15:24)* Whose sins did Messiah die for? Israel. *(Luke 1:77)* Who does the adoption, the glory, the covenants, the giving of the law, and the service of TMH belong to? Israel. *(Romans 9:4-5)* Who did TMH make the Old and New covenants with?

That would be Israel again.

HEBREWS 8:8-13—(8) For finding fault with them, he saith, Behold, the days come, saith the Lord, when I will make a new covenant with the house of Israel and with the house of Judah: (9) Not according to the covenant that I made with their fathers in the day when I took them by the hand to lead them out of the land of Egypt; because they continued not in my covenant, and I regarded them not, saith the Lord. (10) For this [is] the covenant that I will make with the house of Israel after those days, saith the Lord; I will put my laws into their mind, and write them in their hearts: and I will be to them a God, and they shall be to me a people: (11) And they shall not teach every man his neighbour, and every man his brother, saying, Know the Lord: for all shall know me, from the least to the greatest. (12) For I will be merciful to their unrighteousness, and their sins and their iniquities will I remember no more. (13) In that he saith, A new [covenant], he hath made the first old. Now that which decayeth and waxeth old [is] ready to vanish away.

Parable Of The Prodigal Son

A certain man had two sons: and the younger of them said to his father, "Father, give me the portion of goods that falleth to me."

And he divided unto them his living. And not many days after the younger son gathered all together, and took his journey into a far country, and there wasted his substance with riotous living.

And when he had spent all, there arose a mighty famine in that land; and he began to be in want. And he went and joined himself to a citizen of that country; and he sent him into his fields to feed swine. And he would fain have filled his belly with the husks that the swine did eat: and no man gave unto him.

And when he came to himself, he said, "How many hired servants of my father's have bread enough and to spare, and I perish with hunger! I will arise and go to my father, and will say unto him, 'Father, I have sinned against heaven, and before thee, and am no more worthy to be called thy son: make me as one of thy hired servants.'"

And he arose, and came to his father. But when he was yet a great way off, his father saw him, and had compassion, and ran, and fell on his neck, and kissed him. And the son said unto him, Father, I have sinned against heaven, and in thy sight, and am no more worthy to be called thy son.

But the father said to his servants, "Bring forth the best robe, and put it on him; and put a ring on his hand, and shoes on his feet: And bring hither the fatted calf, and kill it; and let us eat, and be merry: For this my son was dead, and is alive again; he was lost, and is found."

And they began to be merry.

Now his elder son was in the field: and as he came and drew nigh to the house, he heard music and dancing. And he called one of the servants, and asked what these things meant.

And he said unto him, "Thy brother is come; and thy father hath killed the fatted calf, because he hath received him safe and sound."

And he was angry, and would not go in: therefore came his father out, and entreated him.

And he answering said to his father, "Lo, these many years do I serve thee, neither transgressed I at any time thy commandment: and yet thou never gavest me a kid, that I might make merry with my friends: But as soon as this thy son was come, which hath devoured thy living with harlots, thou hast killed for him the fatted calf."

And he said unto him, "Son, thou art ever with me, and all that I have is thine. It was meet that we should make merry, and be glad: for this thy brother was dead, and is alive again; and was lost, and is found."

—LUKE 15:11-32

Precepts
&
Commentary

Who are Israelites; to whom pertaineth the adoption, and the glory, and the covenants, and the giving of the law, and the service of God, and the promises; whose are the fathers, and of whom as concerning the flesh Christ came, who is over all, God blessed for ever. Amen.
—Romans 9:4-5

What follows is a scripture-by-scripture examination of *The Book of Romans*. Some sections include biblical precepts alone (e.g. a list of relevant scriptures for the reader to explore independently), while others feature precepts, commentary, word studies, definitions, and/or excerpts from other source material. In some instances, however, you'll find multiple breakdowns of the same verse (e.g. [a] [b] [c] ... etc.) that include separate analyses of underlined words, phrases, and concepts.

ROMANS 1

ROMANS 1:1
Paul, a servant of Jesus Christ, called to be an apostle separated unto the gospel [euaggelion (εὐαγγέλιον)] of God

STRONG'S #2098: "Gospel"—*euaggelion* (εὐαγγέλιον)
USAGE: the good news of the coming of the Messiah, the gospel; the gen. after it expresses sometimes the giver (God), sometimes the subject (the Messiah, etc.), sometimes the human transmitter (an apostle)

TIDING: (ti'ding), The announcement of an event or occurrence not previously known; a piece of news; hence, in the plural, News; information. *The Century Dictionary And Cyclopedia, Vol. VIII, pg. 6331*

QUESTION: Where can we find one of the first mentions of the gospel/good tidings for the children of Israel?

ANSWER: See *Isaiah 61:1-11*.

ISAIAH 61:1-11—(1) The Spirit of the Lord GOD is upon me; because the LORD hath anointed me **to preach good tidings** unto the meek; he hath sent me to bind up the brokenhearted, to proclaim liberty to the captives, and the opening of the prison to them that are bound; (2) To proclaim the acceptable year of the LORD, and the day of vengeance of our God; to comfort all that mourn; (3) To appoint unto them that mourn in Zion, to give unto them beauty for ashes, the oil of joy for mourning, the garment of praise for the spirit of heaviness; that they might be called trees of righteousness, the planting of the LORD, that he might be glorified. (4) And they shall build the old wastes, they shall raise up the former desolations, and they shall repair the waste cities, the desolations of many generations. (5) And strangers shall stand and feed your flocks, and the sons of the alien shall be your plowmen and your vinedressers. (6) But ye shall be named the Priests of the LORD: men shall call you the Ministers of our God: ye shall eat the riches of the Gentiles, and in their glory shall ye boast yourselves. (7) For your shame ye shall have double; and for confusion they shall rejoice in their portion: therefore in their land they shall possess the double: everlasting joy shall be unto them. (8) For I the LORD love judgment, I hate robbery for burnt offering; and I will direct their work in truth, and I will make an everlasting covenant with them. (9)

And their seed shall be known among the Gentiles, and their offspring among the people: all that see them shall acknowledge them that they are the seed, which the LORD hath blessed. (10) I will greatly rejoice in the LORD, my soul shall be joyful in my God; for he hath clothed me with the garments of salvation, he hath covered me with the robe of righteousness, as a bridegroom decketh himself with ornaments, and as a bride adorneth herself with her jewels. (11) For as the earth bringeth forth her bud, and as the garden causeth the things that are sown in it to spring forth; so the Lord GOD will cause righteousness and praise to spring forth before all the nations.

Now let's look at a breakdown of *Isaiah 61's 'Good Tidings':*

EXCERPT FROM: For A Sign And A Wonder:

As it is written, "no prophecy of the scripture is of any private interpretation." *(2 Peter 1:20)* Meaning, it must be interpreted line upon line, and precept upon precept. In other words, scripture explains scripture. *(Isaiah 28:10)* With this in mind, let's analyze *Isaiah 61,* verse-by-verse.

VERSE 1

■ What people constitute the meek? Hint: *Psalms 37:11* states the meek will inherit the earth; *Daniel 7:18* says the saints will possess the kingdom; *Psalms 148:14* identifies the saints as the children of Israel. (See also: *Psalms 37:11; 1 Corinthians 6:2; Revelation 2:15-27; Wisdom of Solomon 3:8*)

■ What people have spent the majority of their existence in captivity? And what people went into captivity as a curse? *(See: Deuteronomy 28:41; 2 Chronicles 6:37-38; Luke 1:71, 74, 79)*

■ Who are the bound prisoners? *(See Isaiah 42:22)*

VERSE 2

■ Whom will God avenge? *(See: Psalms 149:4-9; Deuteronomy 32:43)*

VERSE 3

■ Who is in mourning? *(See Jeremiah 14:2, 31:1-14; Zephaniah 3:18-20; Baruch 4:10)*

VERSE 4

■ What "waste cities" does this verse refer to? *(Ezekiel 36:38; Amos 9:14)*

VERSE 5

■ Who are the strangers in this verse? *(See Isaiah 14:1-3)*

■ Whose flocks will the strangers feed? *(See: Psalms 18:43-48; Isaiah 60:10)*

> **VERSE 6**
> - What people were elected to be "Priests of the Lord"? *(See Exodus 19:5-6; Revelation 1:6, 5:10, 20:6)*
> - Will the Gentiles eat the riches of the Gentiles, or will Israel eat the riches of the Gentiles? *(See Isaiah 60:16)*
>
> **VERSE 7**
> - What people suffered shame, and who shamed them? *(See Isaiah 54:3-17; Ezekiel 34:29-30; Zephaniah 3:18-20)*
> - What land does this verse refer to and to whom does it belong? *(See Genesis 13:14-15; Deuteronomy 25:19; Jeremiah 3:17-18)*
>
> **VERSE 8**
> - With whom will God make an everlasting covenant? HINT: The same people of the first covenant. *(See Exodus 24:8; Psalms 50:5; Ezekiel chapter 37; Luke 1:73, 77; Romans 9:4)*
>
> **VERSE 9**
> - Who is the seed The Most High will bless in front of the Gentiles? *(See Isaiah 62:2-4; Ezekiel 28:25, Luke 1:74-75)*
>
> **VERSE 10**
> - Who is the bride? *(See Jeremiah 3:14; Hosea 2:14-20; Revelation 19:7-9)*
>
> **VERSE 11**
> - How will The Most High spring forth righteousness "before" all nations?
>
> BEFORE: 1a (1) forward of; in front of; stood before the fire (2) in the presence of; speaking before the conference
>
> **HINT:** The answer is in Verse 9 above. *(See also Isaiah 62:2-4; The Wisdom of Solomon 5:1-11)* This is the kingdom our ancestors were looking for. This is the kingdom The Most High promised to give us, His chosen, IF we obey Him.

—END EXCERPT—

If we dig deeper into Paul's reference of the 'gospel' in **Romans 1:1**, and its relation to the 'good tidings' of *Isaiah 61*, we find they correlate with a prophecy in *The Book Of Luke* that outlines why this 'good news' is specific to the children of Israel:

LUKE 1:68-79—(68) Blessed be the Lord God of Israel; <u>for he hath visited and redeemed his people</u>, (69) And hath raised up an horn of salvation for us in the house of his servant David; (70) As he spake by the mouth of his holy prophets, which have been since the world began: (71) <u>That we should be saved from our enemies, and from the hand of all that hate us; (72) To perform the mercy promised to our fathers, and to remember his holy covenant; (73) The oath which he sware to our father Abraham, (74) That he would grant unto us, that we being delivered out of the hand of our enemies might serve him without fear, (75) In holiness and righteousness before him, all the days of our life. (76) And thou, child, shalt be called the prophet of the Highest: for thou shalt go before the face of the Lord to prepare his ways; (77) To give knowledge of salvation unto his people by the remission of their sins, (78) Through the tender mercy of our God; whereby the dayspring from on high hath visited us, (79) To give light to them that sit in darkness and in the shadow of death, to guide our feet into the way of peace.</u>

This is the essence of TMH's covenant with Israel as foretold by Jeremiah and the other prophets.

JEREMIAH 31:31—Behold, the days come, saith the LORD, that I will make <u>a new covenant with the house of Israel, and with the house of Judah.</u>

Therefore, it is through *this* lens that we must view the NT gospels and *Romans* specifically. The New Covenant is the Gospel/Good News/Tidings for the children of Israel:

LUKE 22:14-20—(14) When the hour had come, Jesus reclined at the table with His apostles. (15) And He said to them, "I have eagerly desired to eat this Passover with you before My suffering. (16) For I tell you that I will not eat it again until it is fulfilled in the kingdom of God." (17) After taking the cup, He gave thanks and said, Take this and divide it among yourselves. (18) For I tell you that I will not drink of the fruit of the vine from now on until the kingdom of God comes. <u>(19) And He took the bread, gave thanks and broke it, and gave it to them, saying, "This is My body, given for you; do this in remembrance of Me." (20) In the same way, after supper He took the cup, saying, "This cup is the new covenant in My blood, which is poured out for you.</u>

MATTHEW 1:21—And she shall bring forth a son, and thou shalt call his name JESUS: for <u>he shall save his people from their sins.</u>

1 CORINTHIANS 15:1-4—(1) Moreover, brethren, <u>I declare unto you the gospel</u> which I preached unto you, which also ye have received, and wherein ye stand; (2) <u>by which also ye are saved,</u> if ye keep in memory what I preached unto you, unless ye have believed in vain. (3) For I delivered unto you first of all that which I also received, how that <u>Christ died for our sins according to the scriptures; (4) And that he was buried, and that he rose again the third day according to the scriptures...

JOHN 11:49-52—(49) And one of them, named Caiaphas, being the high priest that same year, said unto them, Ye know nothing at all, (50) Nor consider that it is expedient for us, that one man should die for the people, and that the whole nation perish not. (51) And this spake he not of himself: but being high priest that year, he prophesied that Jesus should die for that nation; (52) And not for that nation only, but that also he should gather together in one the children of God that were scattered abroad.

JAMES 1:1—James, a servant of God and of the Lord Jesus Christ, to the twelve tribes, which are scattered abroad, greeting.

ROMANS 9:4-5—(4) Who are Israelites; to whom pertaineth the adoption, and the glory, and the covenants, and the giving of the law, and the service *of God*, and the promises; (5) whose are the fathers, and of whom as concerning the flesh Christ came, who is over all, God blessed forever. Amen.

THE PSALMS OF SOLOMON 10:8—For good and merciful is God forever, and the assemblies of Israel shall glorify the name of the Lord. The salvation of the Lord be upon the house of Israel unto everlasting gladness!

(Genesis 22:8, Isaiah 9:6, Acts 9:3-6, 15-16, 13:2, 22:6-11; 1 Timothy 1:11; Galatians 1:1, 15)

ROMANS 1:2 [a]
(which he had promised afore by his prophets in the Holy Scriptures)

Renewed Covenant & Gospel Promised 'Afore'

JEREMIAH 31:31-34—(31) Behold, the days come, saith the LORD, that I will make a new covenant with the house of Israel, and with the house of Judah: (32) Not according to the covenant that I made with their fathers in the day that I took them by the hand to bring them out of the land of Egypt; which my covenant they brake, although I was an husband unto them, saith the LORD: (33) But this shall be the covenant that I will make with the house of Israel; After those days, saith the LORD, I will put my law in their inward parts, and write it in their hearts; and will be their God, and they shall be my people. (34) And they shall teach no more every man his neighbour, and every man his brother, saying, Know the LORD: for they shall all know me, from the least of them unto the greatest of them, saith the LORD: for I will forgive their iniquity, and I will remember their sin no more.

ISAIAH 36:22-28—(22) Therefore say unto the house of Israel, Thus saith the Lord GOD; I do not this for your sakes, O house of Israel, but for mine holy name's sake, which ye have profaned among the heathen, whither ye went. (23) And I will sanctify my great name, which was profaned among the heathen, which ye have profaned in the midst of them; and the heathen shall know that I am the LORD, saith the Lord GOD, when I shall be sanctified in you before their eyes. (24) For I will take you from among the heathen, and gather you out of all countries, and will bring you into your own land. (25) Then will I sprinkle clean water upon you, and ye shall be clean: from all your filthiness, and from all your idols, will I cleanse you. (26) A new heart also will I give you, and a new spirit will I put within you: and I will take away the stony heart out of your flesh, and I will give you an heart of flesh. (27) And I will put my spirit within you, and cause you to walk in my statutes, and ye shall keep my judgments, and do them. (28) And ye shall dwell in the land that I gave to your fathers; and ye shall be my people, and I will be your God.

ISAIAH 61:1-11—(1) The Spirit of the Lord GOD is upon me; because the LORD hath anointed me to preach good tidings unto the meek; he hath sent me to bind up the brokenhearted, to proclaim liberty to the captives, and the opening of the prison to them that are bound; (2) To proclaim the acceptable year of the LORD, and the day of vengeance of our God; to comfort all that mourn; (3) To appoint unto them that mourn in Zion, to give unto them beauty for ashes, the oil of joy for mourning, the garment of praise for the spirit of heaviness; that they might be called trees of righteousness, the planting of the LORD, that he might be glorified. (4) And they shall build the old wastes, they shall raise up the former desolations, and they shall repair the waste cities, the desolations of many generations. (5) And strangers shall stand and feed your flocks, and the sons of the alien shall be your plowmen and your vinedressers. (6) But ye shall be named the Priests of the LORD: men shall call you the Ministers of our God: ye shall eat the riches of the Gentiles, and in their glory shall ye boast yourselves. (7) For your shame ye shall have double; and for confusion they shall rejoice in their portion: therefore in their land they shall possess the double: everlasting joy shall be unto them. (8) For I the LORD love judgment, I hate robbery for burnt offering; and I will direct their work in truth, and I will make an everlasting covenant with them. (9) And their seed shall be known among the Gentiles, and their offspring among the people: all that see them shall acknowledge them that they are the seed, which the LORD hath blessed. (10) I will greatly rejoice in the LORD, my soul shall be joyful in my God; for he hath clothed me with the garments of salvation, he hath covered me with the robe of righteousness, as a bridegroom decketh himself with ornaments, and as a bride adorneth herself with her jewels. (11) For as the earth bringeth forth her bud, and as the garden causeth the things that are sown in it to spring forth; so the Lord GOD will cause righteousness and praise to spring forth before all the nations.

LUKE 1:67-79—(67) And his father Zacharias was filled with the Holy Ghost, and prophesied, saying, (68) Blessed be the Lord God of Israel; for he hath visited and redeemed his people, (69) And hath raised up an horn of salvation for us in the house of his servant David; (70) As he spake by the mouth of his holy prophets, which have been since the world began: (71) That we should be saved from our enemies, and from the hand of all that hate us; (72) To perform the mercy promised to our fathers, and to remember his holy covenant; (73) The oath which he sware to our father Abraham, (74) That he would grant unto us, that we being delivered out of the hand of our enemies might serve him without fear, (75) In holiness and righteousness before him, all the days of our life. (76) And thou, child, shalt be called the prophet of the Highest: for thou shalt go before the face of the Lord to prepare his ways; (77) To give knowledge of salvation unto his people by the remission of their sins, (78) Through the tender mercy of our God; whereby the dayspring from on high hath visited us, (79) To give light to them that sit in darkness and in the shadow of death, to guide our feet into the way of peace.

The Promised Messiah In The
Volume Of The Book

PSALMS 40:7-8—(7) Then said I, Lo, I come: in the volume of the book it is written of me, (8) I delight to do thy will, O my God: yea, thy law is within my heart.

JOHN 5:46—For had ye believed Moses, ye would have believed me: for he wrote of me.

GENESIS 22:8—And Abraham said, My son, God will provide himself a lamb for a burnt offering: so they went both of them together.

DEUTERONOMY 18:15-19—(15) The LORD thy God will raise up unto thee a Prophet from the midst of thee, of thy brethren, like unto me; unto him ye shall hearken; (16) According to all that thou desiredst of the LORD thy God in Horeb in the day of the assembly, saying, Let me not hear again the voice of the LORD my God, neither let me see this great fire any more, that I die not. (17) And the LORD said unto me, They have well spoken that which they have spoken. (18) I will raise them up a Prophet from among their brethren, like unto thee, and will put my words in his mouth; and he shall speak unto them all that I shall command him.

(19) And it shall come to pass, that whosoever will not hearken unto my words, which he shall speak in my name, I will require it of him.

ISAIAH 9:6-7—(6) For unto us a child is born, unto us a son is given: and the government shall be upon his shoulder: and his name shall be called Wonderful, Counselor, The mighty God, The everlasting Father, The Prince of Peace (7) Of the increase of His government and peace there will be no end. He will reign on the throne of David and over his kingdom, to establish and sustain it with justice and righteousness from that time and forevermore.

ISAIAH 53:4-12—(4) Surely he hath borne our griefs, and carried our sorrows: yet we did esteem him stricken, smitten of God, and afflicted. (5) But he was wounded for our transgressions, he was bruised for our iniquities: the chastisement of our peace was upon him; and with his stripes we are healed. (6) All we like sheep have gone astray; we have turned every one to his own way; and the LORD hath laid on him the iniquity of us all. (7) He was oppressed, and he was afflicted, yet he opened not his mouth: he is brought as a lamb to the slaughter, and as a sheep before her shearers is dumb, so he openeth not his mouth. (8) He was taken from prison and from judgment: and who shall declare his generation? for he was cut off out of the land of the living: for the transgression of my people was he stricken. (9) And he made his grave with the wicked, and with the rich in his death; because he had done no violence, neither was any deceit in his mouth. (10) Yet it pleased the LORD to bruise him; he hath put him to grief: when thou shalt make his soul an offering for sin, he shall see his seed, he shall prolong his days, and the pleasure of the LORD shall prosper in his hand. (11) He shall see of the travail of his soul, and shall be satisfied: by his knowledge shall my righteous servant justify many; for he shall bear their iniquities. (12) Therefore will I divide him a portion with the great, and he shall divide the spoil with the strong; because he hath poured out his soul unto death: and he was numbered with the transgressors; and he bare the sin of many, and made intercession for the transgressors.

LUKE 24:44-49—(44) And he said unto them, These are the words which I spake unto you, while I was yet with you, that all things must be fulfilled, which were written in the law of Moses, and in the prophets, and in the psalms, concerning me. (45) Then opened he their understanding, that they might understand the scriptures, (46) And said unto them, Thus it is written, and thus it behooved Christ to suffer, and to rise from the dead the third day: (47) And that repentance and remission of sins should be preached in his name among all nations, beginning at Jerusalem. (48) And ye are witnesses of these things. (49) And, behold, I send the promise of my Father upon you: but tarry ye in the city of Jerusalem, until ye be endued with power from on high.

ROMANS 1:2 [b]
(which he had promised afore <u>by his prophets</u> in the Holy Scriptures,)

TMH prophets were raised up from the seed of the children of Israel.

AMOS 2:11—And I raised up of your sons for prophets, and of your young men for Nazarites. Is it not even thus, O ye children of Israel? Saith the Lord.

AMOS 3:7—Surely the Lord GOD will do nothing, but he revealeth his secret unto his servants the prophets.

PSALMS 147:19-20—(19) He sheweth his word unto Jacob, his statutes and his judgments unto Israel. (20) He hath not dealt so with any nation: and as for his judgments, they have not known them. Praise ye the LORD.

JEREMIAH 7:25—From the day your fathers came out of the land of Egypt until this day, I have sent you all My servants the prophets time and time again.

ROMANS 9:4—Who are Israelites; to whom pertaineth the adoption, and the glory, and the covenants, and the giving of the law, and the service *of God*, and the promises...

(Acts 26:6; Genesis 3:15; Exodus 12; Numbers 24:17; Psalms 16:8-11; 22:1-31, 110:1-4, 118:22-24; Isaiah 7:14, 9:1-2, 35:5-6, 42:1-7, 52:13, 53:12; Daniel 9:24-27; Hosea 11:1; Zechariah 9:9; Luke 22:37, Hebrews 10:7)

ROMANS 1:3 [a]
Concerning his Son Jesus Christ our Lord, <u>which was made</u> of the seed of David according to the flesh;

JOHN 1:1-3, 14—(1) <u>**In the beginning was the Word**, and the Word was with God, **and the Word was God**. (2) The same was in the beginning with God. (3) ***All things* were made by him; and without him *was not any thing made that was made***...(14) And **the *Word was made flesh***</u>, and dwelt among us, (and we beheld his glory, the glory as of the only begotten of the Father,) full of grace and truth.

GENESIS 1:1—In the beginning <u>God created the heaven and the earth</u>.

HEBREWS 2:9—But we see Jesus, who was *made* a little lower than the angels for the suffering of death, crowned with glory and honour; that he by the grace of God should taste death for every man.

JOHN 8:56-59—(56) Your father Abraham rejoiced to see my day: and he saw it, and was glad. (57) Then said the Jews unto him, Thou art not yet fifty years old, and hast thou seen Abraham? (58) Jesus said unto them, Verily, verily, I say unto you, Before Abraham was, I am. (59) Then took they up stones to cast at him: but Jesus hid himself, and went out of the temple, going through the midst of them, and so passed by.

HEBREWS 2:9—But we see Jesus, who was made a little lower than the angels for the suffering of death, crowned with glory and honour; that he by the grace of God should taste death for every man.

REVELATION 22:13—I am Alpha and Omega, the beginning and the end, the first and the last.

(Psalms 132:11; Isaiah 11:1-10; Galatians 4:4)

ROMANS 1:3 [b]
Concerning his Son Jesus Christ our Lord, which was made of the seed of David according to the flesh

MATTHEW 22:41-46—(41) While the Pharisees were gathered together, Jesus asked them, (42) Saying, What think ye of Christ? Whose son is he? They say unto him, The Son of David. (43) He saith unto them, How then doth David in spirit call him Lord, saying, (44) The LORD said unto my Lord, Sit thou on my right hand, till I make thine enemies thy footstool? (45) If David then call him Lord, how is he his son? (46) And no man was able to answer him a word, neither durst any man from that day forth ask him any more questions.

LUKE 1:32—He will be great and will be called the Son of the Most High. The Lord God will give Him the throne of His father David.

ISAIAH 9:7—Of the increase of his government and peace there shall be no end, upon the throne of David, and upon his kingdom, to order it, and to establish it with judgment and with justice from henceforth even for ever. The zeal of the LORD of hosts will perform this.

ISAIAH 16:5—...in loving devotion a throne will be established in the tent of David. A judge seeking justice and prompt in righteousness will sit on it in faithfulness.

ISAIAH 11:1-10—(1) And there shall come forth a rod out of the stem of Jesse, and a Branch shall grow out of his roots: (2) And the spirit of the

LORD shall rest upon him, the spirit of wisdom and understanding, the spirit of counsel and might, the spirit of knowledge and of the fear of the LORD; (3) And shall make him of quick understanding in the fear of the LORD: and he shall not judge after the sight of his eyes, neither reprove after the hearing of his ears: (4) But with righteousness shall he judge the poor, and reprove with equity for the meek of the earth: and he shall smite the earth with the rod of his mouth, and with the breath of his lips shall he slay the wicked. (5) And righteousness shall be the girdle of his loins, and faithfulness the girdle of his reins. (6) The wolf also shall dwell with the lamb, and the leopard shall lie down with the kid; and the calf and the young lion and the fatling together; and a little child shall lead them. (7) And the cow and the bear shall feed; their young ones shall lie down together: and the lion shall eat straw like the ox. (8) And the sucking child shall play on the hole of the asp, and the weaned child shall put his hand on the cockatrice' den. (9) They shall not hurt nor destroy in all my holy mountain: for the earth shall be full of the knowledge of the LORD, as the waters cover the sea. (10) And in that day there shall be a root of Jesse, which shall stand for an ensign of the people; to it shall the Gentiles seek: and his rest shall be glorious.

GENESIS 3:15—And I will put enmity between thee and the woman, and between thy seed and her seed; it shall bruise thy head, and thou shalt bruise his heel.

MATTHEW 1:16—And Jacob begat Joseph the husband of Mary, of whom was born Jesus, who is called Christ.

(Psalms 89:3-4, 132:11; Isaiah 11:1-10; Galatians 4:4)

ROMANS 1:4 [a]
And declared to be the Son of God with power, according to the spirit of holiness, by the resurrection from the dead:

MATTHEW 3:17—And lo a voice from heaven, saying, This is my beloved Son, in whom I am well pleased.

MATTHEW 16:16-17—(16) And Simon Peter answered and said, Thou art the Christ, the Son of the living God. (17) And Jesus answered and said unto him, Blessed art thou, Simon Barjona: for flesh and blood hath not revealed it unto thee, but my Father, which is in heaven.

MARK 9:7—And there was a cloud that overshadowed them: and a voice came out of the cloud, saying, This is my beloved Son: hear him.

2 PETER 1:17—For he received from God the Father honour and glory, when there came such a voice to him from the excellent glory, This is my beloved Son, in whom I am well pleased.

PSALMS 2:7—I will declare the decree: the LORD hath said unto me, Thou art my Son; this day have I begotten thee.

MATTHEW 1:20—But while he thought on these things, behold the angel of the Lord appeared unto him in a dream, saying, Joseph, thou son of David, fear not to take unto thee Mary thy wife: for that which is conceived in her is of the Holy Ghost.

(Luke 3:22; John 12:28; Acts 9:20, 13:33)

ROMANS 1:4 [b]
And declared to be the Son of God <u>with power, according to the spirit of holiness</u>, by the resurrection from the dead:

ACTS 10:38—How God anointed Jesus of Nazareth with the Holy Ghost and with power: who went about doing good, and healing all that were oppressed of the devil; for God was with him.

LUKE 4:32—And they were astonished at his doctrine: for his word was with power.

LUKE 21:27—And then shall they see the Son of man coming in a cloud with power and great glory.

JOHN 10:18—No man taketh it from me, but I lay it down of myself. I have power to lay it down, and I have power to take it again. This commandment have I received of my Father.

LUKE 3:22—And the Holy Ghost descended in a bodily shape like a dove upon him, and a voice came from heaven, which said, Thou art my beloved Son; in thee I am well pleased.

(Hebrews 9:14)

ROMANS 1:4 [c]
And declared to be the Son of God with power, according to the spirit of holiness, by the <u>resurrection from the dead</u>:

JOHN 11:25—Jesus said unto her, I am the resurrection, and the life: he that believeth in me, though he were dead, yet shall he live.

JOHN 5:21—For as the Father raiseth up the dead, and quickeneth them; even so the Son quickeneth whom he will.

COLOSSIANS 1:18—And he is the head of the body, the church: who is the beginning, the firstborn from the dead; that in all things he might have the preeminence.

1 PETER 1:3—Blessed be the God and Father of our Lord Jesus Christ, which according to his abundant mercy hath begotten us again unto a lively hope by the resurrection of Jesus Christ from the dead.

ROMANS 8:11—But if the Spirit of him that raised up Jesus from the dead dwell in you, he that raised up Christ from the dead shall also quicken your mortal bodies by his Spirit that dwelleth in you.

REVELATION 1:13-18—(13) And in the midst of the seven candlesticks one like unto the Son of man, clothed with a garment down to the foot, and girt about the paps with a golden girdle. (14) His head and his hairs were white like wool, as white as snow; and his eyes were as a flame of fire; (15) And his feet like unto fine brass, as if they burned in a furnace; and his voice as the sound of many waters. (16) And he had in his right hand seven stars: and out of his mouth went a sharp two-edged sword: and his countenance was as the sun shineth in his strength. (17) And when I saw him, I fell at his feet as dead. And he laid his right hand upon me, saying unto me, Fear not; I am the first and the last: (18) I am he that liveth, and was dead; and, behold, I am alive for evermore, Amen; and have the keys of hell and of death.

(Psalms 16:10-11; Acts 13:33; Hebrews 9:14)

ROMANS 1:5 [a]
By whom we have received grace and apostleship for obedience to the faith among all nations for his name

STRONG'S #651: "Apostleship"—*apostolé* (ἀποστολή)
USAGE: commission, duty of apostle, apostleship

Non-Israelite nations were never given apostleship. Can they follow our Messiah? Yes. But the service of apostleship was only bestowed upon those called to apostleship among the children of Israel. Only Israel was called to preach. Only Israel was called to service. Only Israel received the oracles of TMH. *Only Israel was sent and commissioned*. Non-Israelite nations were *never* called to do this, which is why we have the error of contemporary Christianity. They were not given the light of the scriptures. *(See commentary on Romans 11:12, pgs. 303-311)*

ROMANS 9:4-5—(4) Who are Israelites; **to whom pertaineth** the **adoption**, and the **glory**, and the **covenants**, and the **giving of the law**, and the **service of God**, and the **promises**; (5) Whose are the fathers, and of **whom as concerning the flesh Christ came**, who is over all, God blessed for ever. Amen.

JEREMIAH 31:31-33—(31) Behold, the days come, saith the LORD, that I will make a new covenant with the house of Israel, and with the house of Judah: (32) Not according to the covenant that I made with their fathers in the day that I took them by the hand to bring them out of the land of Egypt; which my covenant they brake, although I was an husband unto them, saith the LORD: (33) But this shall be the covenant that I will make with the house of Israel; After those days, saith the LORD, I will put my law in their inward parts, and write it in their hearts; and will be their God, and they shall be my people.

HEBREWS 8:8-10—(8) For finding fault with them, he saith, Behold, the days come, saith the Lord, when I will make a new covenant with the house of Israel and with the house of Judah: (9) Not according to the covenant that I made with their fathers in the day when I took them by the hand to lead them out of the land of Egypt; because they continued not in my covenant, and I regarded them not, saith the Lord. (10) For this is the covenant that I will make with the house of Israel after those days, saith the Lord; I will put my laws into their mind, and write them in their hearts: and I will be to them a God, and they shall be to me a people

---

ROMANS 1:5 [b]
By whom we have received grace and apostleship for obedience to the faith among all nations [ethnesin (ἔθνεσιν)] for his name

STRONG'S #1484: "Nations"—*ethnesin* (ἔθνεσιν)
USAGE: a race, people, nation; the nations, heathen world, Gentiles
ROOT WORD: *ethnos*

❧

Romans 1:5 points to the diaspora of the twelve tribes/twelve nations within Israel *(John 11:51-52, James 1:1)*, which TMH scattered to the four corners/among all nations of the earth.

EZEKIEL 12:15—And they shall know that I am the LORD, when I shall scatter them among the nations, and disperse them in the countries.

ZECHARIAH 7:14—But I scattered them with a whirlwind among all the nations whom they knew not. Thus the land was desolate after them, that no man passed through nor returned: for they laid the pleasant land desolate.

AMOS 9:9—For, lo, I will command, and I will sift the house of Israel among all nations, like as corn is sifted in a sieve, yet shall not the least grain fall upon the earth.

DEUTERONOMY 32:26—I said, I would scatter them into corners, I would make the remembrance of them to cease from among men.

JOHN 11:51-52—(51) And this spake he not of himself: but being high priest that year, he prophesied that Jesus should die for that nation (52) And not for that nation only, but that also he should gather together in one the children of God that were scattered abroad.

JAMES 1:1—James, a servant of God and of the Lord Jesus Christ, to the twelve tribes, which are scattered abroad, greetings.

LUKE 21:24—And they shall fall by the edge of the sword, and shall be led away captive into all nations: and Jerusalem shall be trodden down of the Gentiles, until the times of the Gentiles be fulfilled.

(1 Corinthians 15:10; Galatians 1:15-16; Ephesians 3:8)

ROMANS 1:6
Among whom are ye also the called of Jesus Christ.

STRONG'S #2822: "Called"—*klétos* (κλητός)
USAGE: called, invited, summoned by God to an office or to salvation

We can be sure the previous verse *(Romans 1:5)* pertains to Israel because only Israel is referred to as 'the called.' Jacob's children were called and chosen over all people to be a kingdom of kings, priests, and ministers of TMH God. *(Exodus 19:6, Isaiah 61:6; 1 Peter 2:9; Revelation 1:6, 5:8-10, 7:3-8)*

ISAIAH 48:12—Hearken unto me, O Jacob and Israel, my called; I am he; I am the first, I also am the last.

HEBREWS 9:15—And for this cause he is the mediator of the new testament, that by means of death, for the redemption of the transgressions that were under the first testament, they which are called might receive the promise of eternal inheritance.

1 CORINTHIANS 1:2, 24—(2) Unto the church of God which is at Corinth, to them that are sanctified in Christ Jesus, called to be saints, with all that in every place call upon the name of Jesus Christ our Lord, both theirs and ours...(24) But unto them which are called, both Jews and Greeks, Christ the power of God, and the wisdom of God.

REVELATION 17:14—These shall make war with the Lamb, and the Lamb shall overcome them: for he is Lord of lords, and King of kings: and they that are with him are called, and chosen, and faithful.

ISAIAH 45:3-4—(3) And I will give thee the treasures of darkness, and hidden riches of secret places, that thou mayest know that I, the Lord, which call thee by thy name, am the God of Israel. (4) For Jacob my servant's sake, and Israel mine elect, I have even called thee by thy name: I have surnamed thee, though thou hast not known me.

HOSEA 11:1—When Israel was a child, then I loved him, and called my son out of Egypt.

HEBREWS 8:7-10—(7) For if that first covenant had been faultless, then should no place have been sought for the second. (8) For finding fault with them, he saith, Behold, the days come, saith the Lord, when I will make a new covenant with the house of Israel and with the house of Judah: (9) Not according to the covenant that I made with their fathers in the day when I took them by the hand to lead them out of the land of Egypt; because they continued not in my covenant, and I regarded them not, saith the Lord. (10) For this is the covenant that I will make with the house of Israel after those days, saith the Lord; I will put my laws into their mind, and write them in their hearts: and I will be to them a God, and they shall be to me a people

(Jude 1:1)

ROMANS 1:7 [a1]
To all that be in Rome, beloved of God, <u>called to be saints</u>: Grace to you and peace from God our Father, and the Lord Jesus Christ.

STRONG'S #40: "Saint"—*hagios* (ἅγιος)
USAGE: set apart by (or for) God, holy, sacred

QUESTION: Was the entire world called to be saints?

ANSWER: No. TMH only bestowed the title of 'saints' to His chosen people, the children of Israel.

PSALMS 148:14—He also exalteth the horn of his people, the praise of all his saints; even of the children of Israel, a people near unto him. Praise ye the LORD.

PSALMS 149:1-2—(1) Praise ye the LORD. Sing unto the LORD a new song, and his praise in the congregation of saints. (2) Let Israel rejoice in him that made him: let the children of Zion be joyful in their King.

1 CORINTHIANS 1:1-2—(1) Paul, called to be an apostle of Jesus Christ through the will of God, and Sosthenes our brother, (2) Unto the church of God which is at Corinth, to them that are sanctified in Christ Jesus, called to be saints, with all that in every place call upon the name of Jesus Christ our Lord, both theirs and ours.

PSALMS 50:5—Gather my saints together unto me; those that have made a covenant with me by sacrifice.

> **QUESTION: Who made a covenant by sacrifice with TMH God of Israel?**
>
> **ANSWER: See *Deuteronomy 29:14-20, Jeremiah 31:31* et al.**

DEUTERONOMY 29:14-20—(14) I make this covenant and this oath, not with you alone, (15) but with him who stands here with us today before the Lord our God, as well as with him who is not here with us today (16) (for you know that we dwelt in the land of Egypt and that we came through the nations which you passed by, (17) and you saw their abominations and their idols which were among them—wood and stone and silver and gold); (18) so that there may not be among you man or woman or family or tribe, whose heart turns away today from the Lord our God, to go and serve the gods of these nations, and that there may not be among you a root bearing bitterness or wormwood; (19) and so it may not happen, when he hears the words of this curse, that he blesses himself in his heart, saying, 'I shall have peace, even though I follow the dictates of my heart'—as though the drunkard could be included with the sober. (20) The Lord would not spare him; for then the anger of the Lord and His jealousy would burn against that man, and every curse that is written in this book would settle on him, and the Lord would blot out his name from under heaven.

JEREMIAH 31:31-33—(31) Behold, the days come, saith the LORD, that I will make a new covenant with the house of Israel, and with the house of Judah: (32) Not according to the covenant that I made with their fathers in the day that I took them by the hand to bring them out of the land of Egypt; which my covenant they brake, although I was an husband unto them, saith the LORD: (33) But this shall be the covenant that I will make with the house of Israel; After those days, saith the LORD, I will put my law in their inward parts, and write it in their hearts; and will be their God, and they shall be my people.

ISAIAH 59:20-21—(20) And the Redeemer shall come to Zion, and unto them that turn from transgression in Jacob, saith the LORD. (21) As for me, this is my covenant with them, saith the LORD; My spirit that is upon thee, and my words which I have put in thy mouth, shall not depart out of thy mouth, nor out of the mouth of thy seed, nor out of the mouth of thy seed's seed, saith the LORD, from henceforth and for ever.

JEREMIAH 50:4-5—(4) In those days, and in that time, saith the LORD, the children of Israel shall come, they and the children of Judah together, going and weeping: they shall go, and seek the LORD their God. (5) They shall ask the way to Zion with their faces thitherward, saying, Come, and let us join ourselves to the LORD in a perpetual covenant that shall not be forgotten.

ROMANS 1:7 [a2]
To all that be in Rome, beloved of God, <u>called to be saints</u>: Grace to you and peace from God our Father, and the Lord Jesus Christ.

STRONG'S #40: "Saint"— *hagios* (ἅγιος)
USAGE: <u>set apart</u> by (or for) God, holy, sacred

> **QUESTION:** Was the entire world <u>set apart</u> by TMH? Or did He only select one specific group of people?
>
> **ANSWER:** See Exodus 33:16, 11:7, et al.

EXODUS 33:16—For wherein shall it be known here that I and thy people have found grace in thy sight? Is it not in that thou goest with us? <u>So shall we be separated, I and thy people, from all the people that are upon the face of the earth.</u>

EXODUS 11:7—But against any of the children of Israel shall not a dog move his tongue, against man or beast: that ye may know how that <u>the LORD doth put a difference between the Egyptians and Israel.</u>

(Romans 8:28)

ROMANS 1:7 [b]
To all that be in Rome, beloved of God, called to be saints: Grace to you and peace from <u>God our Father</u>, and the Lord Jesus Christ.

QUESTION: What group of people can rightfully call TMH their father?

ANSWER: The same people who are called 'the children of God.'

JOHN 11:45-52—(45) Then many of the Jews which came to Mary, and had seen the things which Jesus did, believed on him. (46) But some of them went their ways to the Pharisees, and told them what things Jesus had done. (47) Then gathered the chief priests and the Pharisees a council, and said, What do we? For this man doeth many miracles. (48) If we let him thus alone, all men will believe on him: and the Romans shall come and take away both our place and nation. (49) And one of them, named Caiaphas, being the high priest that same year, said unto them, Ye know nothing at all, (50) Nor consider that it is expedient for us, that one man should die for the people, and that the whole nation perish not. (51) And this spake he not of himself: but being high priest that year, he prophesied that Jesus should die for that nation; (52) And not for that nation only, but that also he should gather together in one the children of God that were scattered abroad.

QUESTION: Who are the children of God?

ANSWER: See Deuteronomy 32:26, James 1:1, *Galatians 4:4-6* and *Romans 9:6-13*.

DEUTERONOMY 32:26—I said, I would scatter them into corners, I would make the remembrance of them to cease from among men...

JAMES 1:1—James, a servant of God and of the Lord Jesus Christ, to the twelve tribes, which are scattered abroad, greetings.

GALATIANS 4:4-6—(4) But when the fullness of the time was come, God sent forth his Son, made of a woman, made under the law, (5) To redeem them that were under the law, that we might receive the adoption of sons. (6) And because ye are sons, God hath sent forth the Spirit of his Son into your hearts, crying, Abba, Father.

PSALMS 50:5—Gather my saints together unto me; those that have made a covenant with me by sacrifice.

ROMANS 9:6-13—(6) For they are not all Israel, which are of Israel: (7) Neither, because they are the seed of Abraham, are they all children: but, In Isaac shall thy seed be called. (8) That is, they, which are the children of the flesh, these are not the children of God: but the children of the promise are counted for the seed. (9) For this is the word of promise, At this time will I come, and Sara shall have a son. (10) And not only this; but when Rebecca also had conceived by one, even by our father Isaac; (11) [For the children being not yet born, neither having done any good or evil, that the purpose of God according to election might stand, not of works, but of him that calleth;] (12) It was said unto her, The elder shall serve the younger. (13) As it is written, Jacob have I loved, but Esau have I hated.

Romans 9:6-13, when read in context, makes it quite clear that the children of God come specifically from the *physical seed* of Abraham, through Isaac, and finally, through Jacob. Only Jacob's seed are considered God's children. And even within Jacob's seed, there's still a 'spiritual' sifting, since, as verse 6 says, 'they are not all Israel, which are Israel.' True Israel (AKA the Israel of God, *Galatians 6:16*) is born of the seed of Jacob *and* of the spirit of TMH. *(John 3:3-8)*

God's children are born-again/heart-circumcised Israelites.

1 JOHN 3:6-10—(6) Whosoever abideth in him sinneth not: whosoever sinneth hath not seen him, neither known him. (7) Little children, let no man deceive you: he that doeth righteousness is righteous, even as he is righteous. (8) He that committeth sin is of the devil; for the devil sinneth from the beginning. For this purpose the Son of God was manifested, that he might destroy the works of the devil. (9) Whosoever is born of God doth not commit sin; for his seed remaineth in him: and he cannot sin, because he is born of God. (10) In this the children of God are manifest, and the children of the devil: whosoever doeth not righteousness is not of God, neither he that loveth not his brother.

(Exodus 4:22; Deuteronomy 14:1; Hosea 1:10; Romans 8:15, 9:4; 1 Corinthians 1:3; 2 Corinthians 1:2)

ROMANS 1:8
First, I thank my God through Jesus Christ for you all, that your faith is spoken of throughout the whole world.

STRONG'S # 2889: "World"—*kosmos* (κόσμος)
USAGE: Usage: the world, universe; worldly affairs; the inhabitants of the world; adornment
STRONG'S DEFINITION: orderly arrangement, i.e. decoration; by implication, the world (in a wide or narrow sense, including its inhabitants, literally or figuratively (morally)—adorning, world.

❦

At the time *Romans* was written, the gospel hadn't been preached throughout the entire known world. In this instance, Paul was speaking about the 'world' or family of Israel.

ISAIAH 45:17—But Israel shall be saved in the LORD with an everlasting salvation: ye shall not be ashamed nor confounded world without end.

Definitions of 'world' include: timeframe, or structure/organization, or whole world. However, in *Romans 1:8*, the Greek word for "world," *kosmō* (κόσμῳ) can mean the universe, specific inhabitants of the world AKA a structured group/organization, or worldly affairs. Contextually, here *kosmō* is speaking about specific inhabitants, namely the people of Israel who are scattered among the nations. Similar usages in this context include: 'the wide-world of sports,' 'the writing world,' 'the world of Warcraft,' 'Sea World,' etc. With these points in mind, the 8th definition for *kosmos* in *Thayer's Greek Lexicon* fits better for *Romans 1:8* since we're talking about a select/elect/chosen group of people:

THAYER'S: "any aggregate or general collection of particulars of any sort."

Other scriptures that use *kosmō* are: *John 3:16-17; John 12:19, John 17:9, John 14-15, John 18:9, James 3:6; 1 John 2:15; 1 John 4:5.*Compare this with 'world' in *Revelation 3:10*. The Greek word used there is *oikoumenēs (οἰκουμένης)*, which means 'the whole world/the inhabited world.'

ROMANS 1:9
For God is my witness, whom I serve with my spirit in the gospel of his Son, that without ceasing I make mention of you always in my prayers

STRONG'S #2098: "Gospel"—*euaggelion (εὐαγγέλιον)*
USAGE: the good news of the coming of the Messiah, the gospel; the gen. after it expresses sometimes the giver (God), sometimes the subject (the Messiah, etc.), sometimes the human transmitter (an apostle).

TIDING: (ti'ding), The announcement of an event or occurrence not previously known; a piece of news; hence, in the plural, News; information. *The Century Dictionary And Cyclopedia, Vol. VIII, pg. 6331*

MATTHEW 9:35—And Jesus went about all the cities and villages, teaching in their synagogues, and preaching the gospel of the kingdom, and healing every sickness and every disease among the people.

> **QUESTION: What is the gospel/good tiding of the kingdom?**
> **ANSWER: Isaiah 61, et al.**

ISAIAH 61:1-11—(1) The Spirit of the Lord GOD is upon me; because the LORD hath anointed me to preach good tidings unto the meek; he hath sent me to bind up the brokenhearted, to proclaim liberty to the captives, and the opening of the prison to them that are bound; (2) To proclaim the acceptable year of the LORD, and the day of vengeance of our God; to comfort all that mourn; (3) To appoint unto them that mourn in Zion, to give unto them beauty for ashes, the oil of joy for mourning, the garment of praise for the spirit of heaviness; that they might be called trees of righteousness, the planting of the LORD, that he might be glorified. (4) And they shall build the old wastes, they shall raise up the former desolations, and they shall repair the waste cities, the desolations of many generations. (5) And strangers shall stand and feed your flocks, and the sons of the alien shall be your plowmen and your vinedressers. (6) But ye shall be named the Priests of the LORD: men shall call you the Ministers of our God: ye shall eat the riches of the Gentiles, and in their glory shall ye boast yourselves. (7) For your shame ye shall have double; and for confusion they shall rejoice in their portion: therefore in their land they shall possess the double: everlasting joy shall be unto them. (8) For I the LORD love judgment, I hate robbery for burnt offering; and I will direct their work in truth, and I will make an everlasting covenant with them. (9) And their seed shall be known among the Gentiles, and their offspring among the people: all that see them shall acknowledge them that they are the seed, which the LORD hath blessed. (10) I will greatly rejoice in the LORD, my soul shall be joyful in my God; for he hath clothed me with the garments of salvation, he hath covered me with the robe of righteousness, as a bridegroom decketh himself with ornaments, and as a bride adorneth herself with her jewels. (11) For as the earth bringeth forth her bud, and as the garden causeth the things that are sown in it to spring forth; so the Lord GOD will cause righteousness and praise to spring forth before all the nations.

ACTS 5:30-31—(30) The God of our fathers raised up Jesus, whom ye slew and hanged on a tree. (31) Him hath God exalted with his right hand to be a Prince and a Saviour, for to give repentance to Israel, and forgiveness of sins.

ACTS 1:6-8—(6) When they therefore were come together, they asked of him, saying, Lord, wilt thou at this time restore again the kingdom to Israel? (7) And he said unto them, It is not for you to know the times or the seasons, which the Father hath put in his own power. (8) But ye shall receive power, after that the Holy Ghost is come upon you: and ye shall be witnesses unto me both in Jerusalem, and in all Judaea, and in Samaria, and unto the uttermost part of the earth.

DANIEL 2:44—And in the days of these kings shall the God of heaven set up a kingdom, which shall never be destroyed: and the kingdom shall not be left to other people, but it shall break in pieces and consume all these kingdoms, and it shall stand forever.

DANIEL 7:18—But the saints of the most High shall take the kingdom, and possess the kingdom forever, even forever and ever.

LUKE 1:68-79—(68) Blessed be the Lord God of Israel; for he hath visited and redeemed his people, (69) And hath raised up an horn of salvation for us in the house of his servant David; (70) As he spake by the mouth of his holy prophets, which have been since the world began: (71) That we should be saved from our enemies, and from the hand of all that hate us; (72) To perform the mercy promised to our fathers, and to remember his holy covenant; (73) The oath which he sware to our father Abraham, (74) That he would grant unto us, that we being delivered out of the hand of our enemies might serve him without fear, (75) In holiness and righteousness before him, all the days of our life. (76) And thou, child, shalt be called the prophet of the Highest: for thou shalt go before the face of the Lord to prepare his ways; (77) To give knowledge of salvation unto his people by the remission of their sins, (78) Through the tender mercy of our God; whereby the dayspring from on high hath visited us, (79) To give light to them that sit in darkness and in the shadow of death, to guide our feet into the way of peace.

JOHN 11:49-52—(49) But one of them, named Caiaphas, who was high priest that year, said to them, "You know nothing at all! (50) You do not realize that it is better for you that one man die for the people than that the whole nation perish. (51) Caiaphas did not say this on his own. Instead, as high priest that year, he was prophesying that Jesus would die for the nation, (52) and not only for the nation, but also for the *scattered children of God*,* to gather them together into one.

---

* *Scattered children of God: (Psalms 44:11; Jeremiah 30:11, 50:17; Ezekiel 6:8, 11:16-17, 28:25; Zechariah 7:14; Romans 9:3-5; James 1:1)*

1 CORINTHIANS 15:1-4—(1) Moreover, brethren, I declare unto you the gospel which I preached unto you, which also ye have received, and wherein ye stand; (2) By which also ye are saved, if ye keep in memory what I preached unto you, unless ye have believed in vain. (3) For I delivered unto you first of all that which I also received, how that Christ died for our sins according to the scriptures; (4) And that he was buried, and that he rose again the third day according to the scriptures.

GALATIANS 4:4-6—(4) But when the fullness of the time was come, God sent forth his Son, made of a woman, made under the law, (5) To redeem them that were under the law, that we might receive the adoption of sons. (6) And because ye are sons, God hath sent forth the Spirit of his Son into your hearts, crying, Abba, Father.

"Gospel of His Son" = "Gospel of the Kingdom": (Matthew 4:23, 9:35, 24:14; Mark 1:14)

ROMANS 1:10-12

(10) Making request, if by any means now at length I might have a prosperous journey by the will of God to come unto you. (11) For I long to see you, that I may impart unto you some spiritual gift, to the end ye may be established; (12) That is, that I may be comforted together with you by the mutual faith both of you and me.

ACTS 11:23—Who, when he came, and had seen the grace of God, was glad, and exhorted them all, that with purpose of heart they would cleave unto the Lord.

ACTS 19:6—And when Paul had laid his hands upon them, the Holy Ghost came on them; and they spake with tongues, and prophesied.

ACTS 19:11-12—(11) And God wrought special miracles by the hands of Paul: (12) So that from his body were brought unto the sick handkerchiefs or aprons, and the diseases departed from them, and the evil spirits went out of them.

MARK 16:17-18—(17) And these signs shall follow them that believe; In my name shall they cast out devils; they shall speak with new tongues; (18) They shall take up serpents; and if they drink any deadly thing, it shall not hurt them; they shall lay hands on the sick, and they shall recover.

2 CORINTHIANS 4:13-14—(13) We having the same spirit of faith, according as it is written, I believed, and therefore have I spoken; we also believe, and therefore speak; (14) Knowing that he which raised up the Lord Jesus shall raise up us also by Jesus, and shall present us with you.

EPHESIANS 4:4-6—(4) There is one body, and one Spirit, even as ye are called in one hope of your calling; (5) One Lord, one faith, one baptism, (6) One God and Father of all, who is above all, and through all, and in you

---

ROMANS 1:13
Now I would not have you ignorant, brethren, that oftentimes I purposed to come unto you, (but was let hitherto,) that I might have some fruit <u>among you also, even as among other Gentiles</u>. *[ethnesin (ἔθνεσιν)]*

STRONG'S #1484: Gentiles—*Ethnesin* (ἔθνεσιν)
ROOT WORD: ethnos
USAGE: a race, people, nation; the nations, heathen world, Gentiles
DEFINITION: a race, a nation, the nations (as distinct from Israel)

※

As you can see, they added "as distinct from Israel" in the definition for Gentiles (*Ethnesin*). This is completely false. *(See Gentiles & Greeks, pg. 27 and The People Of Romans, pg. 53)*

When your theology teaches that Israelites are never referred to as Gentiles, you will always misinterpret scripture and build doctrines based on error. This is how Paul's writings are twisted because the twisters ignore history, context, and prophecy. **In order to uncover the truth, we *must* condition ourselves to look beyond these sleights of hand.**

In *Romans 1:13* where it says "among **you** also," and "among **other** gentiles," this implies that the first group ("you") is the same as the second ("other gentiles"). So the only question now is, which type of "gentiles" is he referring to? Non-Israelite Gentiles or Israelite Gentiles? *Romans 1:7* already gave the answer. Who did Paul write this epistle to?

ROMANS 1:7—To all that be in Rome, beloved of God, **called to be saints**: Grace to you and peace from God our Father and the Lord Jesus Christ.

Who are called to be saints? Again, Israel only: *Psalms 50:5; Psalms 148:14; Psalms 149:1-5; Isaiah 45:3-4; Isaiah 48:12; Hosea 11:1*

For another instance where 'Ethnos/Ethnesin/ethnōn is used to refer to Israelite Gentiles, see 'the fullness of the Gentiles' commentary on Romans 11:25 [c], pgs. 337-340

ROMANS 1:14
I am debtor both to the Greeks, [Hellēsin ("Ελλησίν")] and to the Barbarians; both to the wise, and to the unwise.

STRONG'S #1672: Greeks—*Hellēsin ("Ελληνσίν")*
ROOT WORD: *"Ελλην Héllēn, hel'-lane*; from G1671; a Hellen
USAGE: a Hellene, the native word for a Greek; it is, however, a term wide enough to include all Greek-speaking (i.e. educated) non-Jews.

STRONG'S #915: Barbarians — *barbaros (βάρβαρος)*
DEFINITION: of uncertain derivation; a foreigner (i.e. non-Greek)—barbarian(-rous).

❧

Notice the 'non-Jews" notation in the usage definition above for 'Greeks.' Once again we have intentional misdirection and misapplication. Here 'Greeks,' *Hellēsin ("Ελληνσίν")* refers to Greek-speaking people, and in this case, specifically, **Israelite Gentiles**. *(See 'The People Of Romans,' pg. 53)*

The term Barbarian has several definitions. It's used to describe those living outside the Greco/Roman Empire and/or the religion of Christianity. It's also applied to savage, uncivilized, or rude people. Lastly, it's used to describe those who speak a language unfamiliar to the hearer. In this context (and time-period) we're talking about anyone who didn't speak Greek, which is a pretty broad group of people.

TMH scattered Israelites everywhere, including the Barbary Coast, AKA North African coastal regions whose modern-day equivalent include Libya, Morocco, Tunisia, and Algeria. We see how vast the diaspora was by just the sampling of nations mentioned in *Acts 2*:

ACTS 2:5-11—(5) And there were dwelling at Jerusalem Jews, devout men, out of every nation under heaven. (6) Now when this was noised abroad, the multitude came together, and were confounded, because that every man heard them speak in his own language. (7) And they were all amazed and marveled, saying one to another, Behold, are not all these which speak Galileans? (8) And how hear we every man in our own tongue, wherein we were born? (9) Parthians, and Medes, and Elamites, and the dwellers in Mesopotamia, and in Judaea, and Cappadocia, in Pontus, and Asia, (10) Phrygia, and Pamphylia, in Egypt, <u>and in the parts</u>

of Libya about Cyrene, and strangers of Rome, Jews and proselytes, (11) Cretes and Arabians, we do hear them speak in our tongues the wonderful works of God.

Therefore, the Barbarians Paul is speaking of here (and the Scythians of *Colossians 3:11*) were diaspora Israelites. Paul (like Peter and the other apostles) was a spiritual fisherman, so if he went to the Barbarians, we can be sure the lost sheep of the house of Israel were among them.

COLOSSIANS 3:11—Where there is neither Greek nor Jew, circumcision nor uncircumcision, Barbarian, Scythian, bond nor free: but Christ is all, and in all.

ACTS 28:2—And the barbarous people shewed us no little kindness: for they kindled a fire, and received us every one, because of the present rain, and because of the cold.

1 CORINTHIANS 14:11—Therefore if I know not the meaning of the voice, I shall be unto him that speaketh a barbarian, and he that speaketh shall be a barbarian unto me.

DEUTERONOMY 32:26—I said, I would scatter them into corners, I would make the remembrance of them to cease from among men.

ZEPHANIAH 3:10—From beyond the rivers of Ethiopia my suppliants, even the daughter of my dispersed, shall bring mine offering.

ROMANS 1:15
So, as much as in me is, I am ready to preach the gospel to you that are at Rome also.

As seen previously in *Romans 1:5 [b]*, (pg. 83) Israelites were scattered everywhere, including Rome. In fact, Paul was a Roman citizen *(Acts 16:37-38)* who referred to himself as both a "Jew," *(Acts 21:39) and* an Israelite from the tribe of Benjamin. *(Romans 11:1)* Benjamites self-identified as Jews since most remained with the tribe of Judah after the Northern and Southern kingdoms split *(2 Chronicles 11, 1 Kings 12)*. They were therefore considered part of the House of Judah. *(Ezekiel 37:16)*

So just as Paul, an Israelite and a "Jew" from the tribe of Benjamin, was considered Roman, so too were the lost sheep of the house of Israel who were scattered in Rome, Greece, and elsewhere, considered Greeks/Gentiles.

ACTS 22:25-27—(25) And as they bound him with thongs, Paul said unto the centurion that stood by, Is it lawful for you to scourge a man that is a Roman, and uncondemned? (26) When the centurion heard that, he went and told the chief captain, saying, Take heed what thou doest: for this man is a Roman. (27) Then the chief captain came, and said unto him, Tell me, art thou a Roman? He said, Yea.

ACTS 23:25-27—(25) And he wrote a letter after this manner: (26) Claudius Lysias unto the most excellent governor Felix sendeth greeting. (27) This man was taken of the Jews, and should have been killed of them: then came I with an army, and rescued him, having understood that he was a Roman.

ACTS 28:16-28—(16) And when we came to Rome, the centurion delivered the prisoners to the captain of the guard: but Paul was suffered to dwell by himself with a soldier that kept him. (17) And it came to pass, that after three days Paul called the chief of the Jews together: and when they were come together, he said unto them, Men and brethren, though I have committed nothing against the people, or customs of our fathers, yet was I delivered prisoner from Jerusalem into the hands of the Romans. (18) Who, when they had examined me, would have let me go, because there was no cause of death in me. (19) But when the Jews spake against it, I was constrained to appeal unto Caesar; not that I had ought to accuse my nation of. (20) For this cause therefore have I called for you, to see you, and to speak with you: because that for the hope of Israel I am bound with this chain. (21) And they said unto him, We neither received letters out of Judaea concerning thee, neither any of the brethren that came shewed or spake any harm of thee. (22) But we desire to hear of thee what thou thinkest: for as concerning this sect, we know that everywhere it is spoken against. (23) And when they had appointed him a day, there came many to him into his lodging; to whom he expounded and testified the kingdom of God, persuading them concerning Jesus, both out of the law of Moses, and out of the prophets, from morning till evening. (24) And some believed the things, which were spoken, and some believed not. (25) And when they agreed not among themselves, they departed, after that Paul had spoken one word, Well spake the Holy Ghost by Esaias the prophet unto our fathers, (26) Saying, Go unto this people, and say, Hearing ye shall hear, and shall not understand; and seeing ye shall see, and not perceive: (27) For the heart of this people is waxed gross, and their ears are dull of hearing, and their eyes have they closed; lest they should see with their eyes, and hear with their ears, and understand with their heart, and should be converted, and I should heal them. (28) Be it known therefore unto you, that the salvation of God is sent unto the Gentiles, and that they will hear it.

ROMANS 1:16 [a]
For I am not ashamed of the gospel of Christ:
for it is the power of God unto salvation to every one that believeth; to the Jew first, and also to the Greek.

LUKE 9:26—For whosoever shall be ashamed of me and of my words, of him shall the Son of man be ashamed, when he shall come in his own glory, and in his Father's, and of the holy angels.

JOHN 13:37-38—(37) Peter said unto him, Lord, why cannot I follow thee now? I will lay down my life for thy sake. (38) Jesus answered him, Wilt thou lay down thy life for my sake? Verily, verily, I say unto thee, The cock shall not crow, till thou hast denied me thrice.

MARK 14:66-72—(66) And as Peter was beneath in the palace, there cometh one of the maids of the high priest: (67) And when she saw Peter warming himself, she looked upon him, and said, And thou also wast with Jesus of Nazareth. (68) But he denied, saying, I know not, neither understand I what thou sayest. And he went out into the porch; and the cock crew. (69) And a maid saw him again, and began to say to them that stood by, This is one of them. (70) And he denied it again. And a little after, they that stood by said again to Peter, Surely thou art [one] of them: for thou art a Galilaean, and thy speech agreeth thereto. (71) But he began to curse and to swear, saying, I know not this man of whom ye speak. (72) And the second time the cock crew. And Peter called to mind the word that Jesus said unto him, Before the cock crow twice, thou shalt deny me thrice. And when he thought thereon, he wept.

2 TIMOTHY 1:8—Be not thou therefore ashamed of the testimony of our Lord, nor of me his prisoner: but be thou partaker of the afflictions of the gospel according to the power of God.

JOHN 19:38-39—(38) And after this Joseph of Arimathaea, being a disciple of Jesus, but secretly for fear of the Jews, besought Pilate that he might take away the body of Jesus: and Pilate gave him leave. He came therefore, and took the body of Jesus. (39) And there came also Nicodemus, which at the first came to Jesus by night, and brought a mixture of myrrh and aloes, about an hundred pound weight.

(Luke 22:56-62, John 18:15-18)

ROMANS 1:16 [b]
For I am not ashamed of the gospel of Christ:
for it is the power of God unto <u>salvation to every one that believeth</u>; to the Jew first, and also to the Greek.

STRONG'S #4991: "Salvation"—*sótéria* (σωτηρία)
USAGE: welfare, prosperity, deliverance, preservation, salvation, safety

QUESTION: According to scripture, what is salvation, and who is it for?
ANSWER: See *Isaiah 46:13, Matthew 1:21, Luke 1:67-79* et al.

ISAIAH 46:13—I bring near my righteousness; it shall not be far off, and my salvation shall not tarry: and I will place salvation in Zion for Israel my glory.

MATTHEW 1:21—And she shall bring forth a son, and thou shalt call his name JESUS: for he shall save his people from their sins.

LUKE 1:67-79—(67) And his father Zacharias was filled with the Holy Ghost, and prophesied, saying, (68) Blessed [be] the Lord God of Israel; for he hath visited and redeemed his people, (69) And hath raised up an horn of salvation for us in the house of his servant David; (70) As he spake by the mouth of his holy prophets, which have been since the world began: (71) That we should be saved from our enemies, and from the hand of all that hate us; (72) To perform the mercy [promised] to our fathers, and to remember his holy covenant; (73) The oath which he sware to our father Abraham, (74) That he would grant unto us, that we being delivered out of the hand of our enemies might serve him without fear, (75) In holiness and righteousness before him, all the days of our life. (76) And thou, child, shalt be called the prophet of the Highest: for thou shalt go before the face of the Lord to prepare his ways; (77) To give knowledge of salvation unto his people by the remission of their sins, (78) Through the tender mercy of our God; whereby the dayspring from on high hath visited us, (79) To give light to them that sit in darkness and in the shadow of death, to guide our feet into the way of peace.

JOHN 11:49-52—(49) And one of them, named Caiaphas, being the high priest that same year, said unto them, Ye know nothing at all, (50) Nor consider that it is expedient for us, that one man should die for the people, and that the whole nation perish not. (51) And this spake he not of himself: but being high priest that year, he prophesied that Jesus should die for that nation; (52) And not for that nation only, but that also he should gather together in one the children of God that were scattered abroad.

ACTS 13:14, 22-24, 26—(14) But when they departed from Perga, they came to Antioch in Pisidia, and went into the synagogue on the Sabbath day, and sat down...(22) And when he had removed him, he raised up unto them David to be their king; to whom also he gave testimony, and said, I have found David the son of Jesse, a man after mine own heart, which shall fulfill all my will. (23) <u>Of this man's seed hath God according to his promise raised unto Israel a Saviour, Jesus</u>: (24) When John had first preached before his coming the baptism of <u>repentance to all the people of Israel</u>...(26) <u>Men and brethren, children of the stock of Abraham, and whosoever among you feareth God, to you is the word of this salvation sent.</u>

THE PSALMS OF SOLOMON 10:8—For good and merciful is God forever, and the assemblies of Israel shall glorify the name of the Lord. <u>The salvation of the Lord be upon the house of Israel unto everlasting gladness!</u>

JOHN 4:22—Ye worship ye know not what: we know what we worship: for salvation is of the Jews.

MATTHEW 15:24—But He answered and said, <u>'I was not sent except to the lost sheep of the house of Israel.'</u>

Although Messiah said He was only sent for Israel in *Matthew 15:24*, he *did* heal the Canaanite woman. (Verse 28) He helped her because of her righteous faith in Him. This is a prime example of a non-Israelite receiving mercy from our Messiah, and it is Gentiles like this faith-filled Canaanite woman who will follow our Messiah and cleave to Israel in the Kingdom of God. *(Zechariah 8:23)* *(For more information on non-Israelites in the kingdom, see The Strangers Among Us, pg. 426)*

However, the subject matter in this verse (salvation) is referring to Israel: Jews (Judah & their companions) and Greek Israelites. See "*Romans 1:16 [b]*" for the breakdown on Greek/Gentile Israelites.

Being saved and delivered from our enemies is salvation.

ROMANS 1:16 [c]
For I am not ashamed of the gospel of Christ: for it is the power of God unto salvation to every one that believeth; <u>to the Jew first</u>, and also to the Greek.

QUESTION: Why was <u>salvation</u> 'to the Jew first'?

ANSWER: (#1) "Jew" or 'Judah," means, "praised, celebrated."

GENESIS 29:35—And [Leah] conceived again and bore a son, and said, "Now I will praise the LORD." Therefore she called his name Judah. Then she stopped bearing.

The tribe of Judah's praiseworthiness and prominence is reiterated by Jacob. Ultimately, this is a prophecy about the coming Messiah, however, it is also relevant for the tribe of Judah:

> **GENESIS 49:8-9**—(8) Judah, your brothers shall praise you; your hand shall be on the neck of your enemies; your father's sons shall bow down to you. (9) Judah is a lion's whelp; from the prey, my son, you have gone up. He couches; he lies down as a lion, and as a lion, who dares rouse him up?

ANSWER: (#2) **Jacob/Israel also foretells Judah's leadership role in Genesis 49:10.**

> **GENESIS 49:10**—The scepter shall not depart from Judah, nor the ruler's staff from between his feet, until Shiloh comes, and to him shall be the obedience of the peoples.

ANSWER: (#3) **And last, but not least, Zechariah 12:7.**

> **ZECHARIAH 12:7**—The LORD also shall **save** the tents of **Judah first**, that the glory of the house of David and the glory of the inhabitants of Jerusalem do not magnify themselves against Judah.

Other bible versions render this same verse as: "the LORD will give salvation to the tents of Judah first..." Salvation means to save. Not only that, Messiah literally delivered the good news, or gospel to Judah first. Also notice the reason *Zechariah 12:7* gives for Judah to be first:

> "...that...the glory of the inhabitants of Jerusalem do not magnify themselves against Judah."

Paul, an expert in the Law, *always* pulled references from the OT, and other books. Therefore, his letters *must* be viewed and interpreted through these historical and prophetic documents.

ROMANS 1:16 [d]
For I am not ashamed of the gospel of Christ: for it is the power of God unto salvation to every one that believeth; to the Jew first, <u>and also to the Greek</u>. [*Hellēni* ('Ελληνι)]

QUESTION: How did Israelites become 'Greeks'?
ANSWER: See *1 Maccabees 1:41-50, 60-64, 4:1-5*.

1 MACCABEES 1:41-50—(41) Moreover king Antiochus wrote to his whole kingdom, that all should be one people, (42) and every one should leave his laws: so all the heathen agreed according to the commandment of the king. (43) Yea, many also of the Israelites consented to his religion, and sacrificed unto idols, and profaned the Sabbath. (44) For the king had sent letters by messengers unto Jerusalem and the cities of Judah that they should follow the strange laws of the land, (45) And forbid burnt offerings, and sacrifice, and drink offerings, in the temple; and that they should profane the sabbaths and festival days: (46) And pollute the sanctuary and holy people: (47) Set up altars, and groves, and chapels of idols, and sacrifice swine's flesh, and unclean beasts: (48) That they should also leave their children uncircumcised, and make their souls abominable with all manner of uncleanness and profanation: (49) To the end they might forget the law, and change all the ordinances. (50) And whosoever would not do according to the commandment of the king, he said, he should die.

1 MACCABEES 1:60-64—(60) At which time according to the commandment they put to death certain women, that had caused their children to be circumcised. (61) And they hanged the infants about their necks, and rifled their houses, and slew them that had circumcised them. (62) Howbeit many in Israel were fully resolved and confirmed in themselves not to eat any unclean thing. (63) Wherefore the rather to die, that they might not be defiled with meats, and that they might not profane the holy covenant: so then they died. (64) And there was very great wrath upon Israel.

1 MACCABEES 4:1-5—(1) Then took Gorgias five thousand footmen, and a thousand of the best horsemen, and removed out of the camp by night; (2) To the end he might rush in upon the camp of the Jews, and smite them suddenly. And the men of the fortress were his guides. (3) Now when Judas heard thereof he himself removed, and the valiant men with him, that he might smite the king's army, which was at Emmaus, (4) while as yet the forces were dispersed from the camp. (5) In the mean season came Gorgias by night into the camp of Judas: and when he found no man there, he sought them in the mountains: for said he, these fellows flee from us.

Just as a reminder, the subject is 'salvation' in *Romans 1:16*, which is for Israel. This includes "Jews" (the tribe of Judah and their companions Benjamin and Levi) as well as the Greek/Gentile Israelites (northern kingdom tribes and the scattered of the House of Judah living as Gentiles/Greeks).

1 CORINTHIANS 1:24—But unto them which are called, both Jews and Greeks, Christ the power of God, and the wisdom of God.

Who are 'the called'? Israel: both the House of Judah (Judah, Benjamin, and Levi) & the House of Israel (Ephraim). Again, we must remember to whom this epistle was written. Per *Romans 1:7*, to those who are called to be saints, and are, according to *Jeremiah*, loved by The Most High, with an everlasting love.

JEREMIAH 31:2-4—(2) Thus saith the LORD, The people which were left of the sword found grace in the wilderness; even Israel, when I went to cause him to rest. (3) The LORD hath appeared of old unto me, saying, Yea, I have loved thee with an everlasting love: therefore with lovingkindness have I drawn thee. (4) Again I will build thee, and thou shalt be built, O virgin of Israel: thou shalt again be adorned with thy tabrets, and shalt go forth in the dances of them that make merry.

(For a more extensive breakdown on Greek/Gentile Israelites, see Gentiles & Greeks, pg. 27 and The People Of Romans, pg. 53)

(Malachi 1:2; Ezekiel 20:31-32; Romans 9:4-5)

ROMANS 1:17
For therein is the righteousness of God revealed from faith to faith: as it is written, The just [Dikaios (δίκαιος)] shall live by faith.

STRONG'S #G1342: "Just"— *dikaios* (δίκαιος)
USAGE: just; especially, just in the eyes of God; righteous; the elect

THAYER'S: righteous, observing divine laws (n) a wide sense, upright, righteous, virtuous, keeping the commands of God of those who seem to themselves to be righteous, who pride themselves to be righteous, who pride themselves in their virtues, whether real or imagined

ఈ*ఈ

When we have faith, TMH considers us 'just,' but what justifies faith? Good works.

GENESIS 15:3-6—(3) And Abram said, Behold, to me thou hast given no seed: and, lo, one born in my house is mine heir. (4) And, behold, the word of the LORD came unto him, saying, This shall not be thine heir; but he that shall come forth out of thine own bowels shall be thine heir. (5) And he brought him forth abroad, and said, Look now toward heaven, and tell the stars, if thou be able to number them: and he said unto him, So shall thy seed be. (6) And he believed in the LORD; and he counted it to him for righteousness.

JAMES 2:21-25—(21) Was not Abraham our father justified by works, when he had offered Isaac his son upon the altar? (22) Seest thou how faith wrought with his works, and by works was faith made perfect? (23) And the scripture was fulfilled which saith, Abraham believed God, and it was imputed unto him for righteousness: and he was called the Friend of God. (24) Ye see then how that by works a man is justified, and not by faith only. (25) Likewise also was not Rahab the harlot justified by works, when she had received the messengers, and had sent them out another way?

These good works are not the 'works of the Law.' The works of the Law were the repeated sacrifices for sins as required by the sacrificial law of the Old Covenant. *Hebrews 10:1-23* outlines this. Good works are daily deeds and acknowledgements that demonstrate our faith. These show we believe what TMH said in His word, and as a result, we live in obedience to His commandments:

LUKE 6:46-49—(46) And why call ye me, Lord, Lord, and do not the things which I say? (47) Whosoever cometh to me, and heareth my sayings, and doeth them, I will shew you to whom he is like: (48) He is like a man which built an house, and digged deep, and laid the foundation on a rock: and when the flood arose, the stream beat vehemently upon that house, and could not shake it: for it was founded upon a rock. (49) But he that heareth, and doeth not, is like a man that without a foundation built an house upon the earth; against which the stream did beat vehemently, and immediately it fell; and the ruin of that house was great.

Without faith it's impossible to please TMH. *(Hebrews 11:6)* Yet without works our faith isn't faith. *It's dead.* Good works are a guarantor that our faith is true.

JAMES 2:14-20, 26—(14) What doth it profit, my brethren, though a man say he hath faith, and have not works? Can faith save him? (15) If a brother or sister be naked, and destitute of daily food, (16) and one of you say unto them, Depart in peace, be ye warmed and filled; notwithstanding ye give them not those things which are needful to the body; what doth it profit? (17) Even so faith, if it hath not works, is dead, being alone. (18) Yea, a man may say, Thou hast faith, and I have works: shew me thy faith without thy works, and I will shew thee my faith *by* my works. (19) Thou believest that there is one God; thou doest well: the devils also believe, and tremble. (20) But wilt thou know, O vain man, that faith without works is dead?...(26) For as the body without the spirit is dead, so faith without works is dead also.

Therefore, in order to be just/righteous, we must believe TMH. If we truly believe TMH, we do what He says by obeying His commandments. And if we obey His commandments, we'll produce fruit, i.e. good works. This is what it means to live by faith. *This* is what makes us 'just' in the eyes of TMH.

HABAKKUK 2:4—Behold, his soul, which is lifted up, is not upright in him: but the just shall live by his faith.

HEBREWS 10:38—Now the just shall live by faith: but if any man draw back, my soul shall have no pleasure in him.

ROMANS 1:18
For the wrath of God is revealed from heaven against <u>all ungodliness and unrighteousness of men who hold the truth in unrighteousness</u>

JOHN 14:6—Jesus said to him, I am the way, the truth, and the life. No one comes to the Father except through Me.

PSALMS 119:142—Thy righteousness is an everlasting righteousness, and thy law is the truth.

1 JOHN 3:4—Whosoever committeth sin transgresseth also the law: for sin is the transgression of the law.

2 THESSALONIANS 2:10-12—(10) And with all deceivableness of unrighteousness in them that perish; because they received not the love of the truth, that they might be saved. (11) And for this cause God shall send them strong delusion, that they should believe a lie: (12) That they all might be damned who believed not the truth, but had pleasure in unrighteousness.

(Acts 17:30; Ephesians 5:6)

ROMANS 1:19-20
(19) Because that which may be known of God is manifest in them; for God hath shewed it unto them. (20) For since the creation of the world His invisible attributes are clearly seen, being understood by the things that are made, even His eternal power and Godhead, so that they are without excuse

PSALMS 19:1—The heavens declare the glory of God; the skies proclaim the work of His hands.

PSALMS 97:6—The heavens proclaim His righteousness; all the peoples see His glory.

ISAIAH 45:7—I form the light, and create darkness: I make peace, and create evil: I the LORD do all these things.

JEREMIAH 31:35—Thus saith the LORD, which giveth the sun for a light by day, and the ordinances of the moon and of the stars for a light by night, which divideth the sea when the waves thereof roar; The LORD of hosts is his name.

(Acts 14:17)

ROMANS 1:21 [a]
Because that, <u>when they knew God</u>, they glorified him not as God , neither were thankful; but became vain in their imaginations, and their foolish heart was darkened.

Who are the "they" who *"knew God"* in verse 21? Remember to whom this letter was addressed. Remember the audience. Also remember scripture says only one nation has ever <u>known</u> TMH, and vice versa.

2 ESDRAS 3:18—Or is there any other people that knoweth thee beside Israel? Or what generation hath so believed thy covenants as Jacob?

AMOS 3:1-2—(1) Hear this word that the LORD hath spoken against you, O children of Israel, against the whole family which I brought up from the land of Egypt, saying, (2) You only have I known of all the families of the earth: therefore I will punish you for all your iniquities.

PSALMS 147:19-20—(19) He sheweth his word unto Jacob, his statutes and his judgments unto Israel. (20) He hath not dealt so with any nation: and as for his judgments, they have not known them. Praise ye the LORD.

2 ESDRAS 2:16—And those that be dead will I raise up again from their places, and bring them out of the graves: for I have known my name in Israel.

ADDITIONS TO ESTHER 10:9—And my nation is this Israel, which cried to God, and were saved: for the Lord hath saved his people, and the Lord hath delivered us from all those evils, and God hath wrought signs and great wonders, which have not been done among the Gentiles.

ROMANS 1:21 [b]
Because that, when they knew God, they glorified him not as God , <u>neither were thankful</u>; but became vain in their imaginations, and their foolish heart was darkened.

Remember again whom Paul is talking to and about. He was a former Pharisee, so everything he wrote came from an expertise in the Law and other prophetic books, all of which were about one people:
The children of Israel.

PSALMS 106:21—They forgat God their saviour, which had done great things in Egypt...

JEREMIAH 3:7-11, 20—(7) And I said after she had done all these *things*, Turn thou unto me. But she returned not. And her treacherous sister Judah saw *it*. (8) And I saw, when for all the causes whereby backsliding Israel committed adultery I had put her away, and given her a bill of divorce; yet her treacherous sister Judah feared not, but went and played the harlot also. (9) And it came to pass through the lightness of her whoredom, that she defiled the land, and committed adultery with stones and with stocks. (10) And yet for all this her treacherous sister Judah hath not turned unto me with her whole heart, but feignedly, saith the LORD. (11) And the LORD said unto me, The backsliding Israel hath justified herself more than treacherous Judah...(20) Surely as a wife treacherously departeth from her husband, so have ye dealt treacherously with me, O house of Israel, saith the LORD.

NEHEMIAH 9:16-17—(16) But they and our fathers dealt proudly, and hardened their necks, and hearkened not to thy commandments, (17) And refused to obey, neither were mindful of thy wonders that thou didst among them; but hardened their necks, and in their rebellion appointed a captain to return to their bondage: but thou art a God ready to pardon, gracious and merciful, slow to anger, and of great kindness, and forsookest them not.

2 KINGS 17:7-9—(7) For so it was, that the children of Israel had sinned against the Lord their God, which had brought them up out of the land of Egypt, from under the hand of Pharaoh king of Egypt, and had feared other gods, (8) And walked in the statutes of the heathen, whom the Lord cast out from before the children of Israel, and of the kings of Israel, which they had made. (9) And the children of Israel did secretly those things that were not right against the Lord their God, and they built them high places in all their cities, from the tower of the watchmen to the fenced city...

2 KINGS 17:15—And they rejected his statutes, and his covenant that he made with their fathers, and his testimonies which he testified against them; and they followed vanity, and became vain, and went after the heathen that were round about them, concerning whom the LORD had charged them, that they should not do like them.

(Deuteronomy 28:20; 29:26-29; Isaiah 1:4; Jeremiah 2:5; 2 Esdras 7:22-24;Acts 7:38-44)

ROMANS 1:21 [c]
Because that, when they knew God, they glorified him not as God , neither were thankful; but <u>became vain in their imaginations, and their foolish heart was darkened.</u>

The scripture says, *"their foolish heart was darkened."* If their hearts were darkened, that must mean they once held light. This again points to the people of Israel, namely the Northern Kingdom and some within the Southern Kingdom. They once walked in the light of The Most High's laws, statutes and commandments, but they fell into idolatry and wickedness, becoming like the heathen, and living in complete darkness.

ISAIAH 9:1-2—(1) Nevertheless the dimness shall not be such as was in her vexation, when at the first he lightly afflicted the land of <u>Zebulun</u> and the land of <u>Naphtali</u>, and afterward did more grievously afflict her by the way of the sea, beyond Jordan, in <u>Galilee of the nations</u>. (2) <u>The people that walked in darkness</u> have seen a great light: they that dwell in the land of the shadow of death, upon them hath the light shined.

MATTHEW 4:12-16—(12) Now when Jesus had heard that John was cast into prison, <u>he departed into Galilee</u>; (13) And leaving Nazareth, he came and dwelt in Capernaum, which is upon the sea coast, in the borders of Zabulon and Nephthalim: (14) <u>That it might be fulfilled which was spoken by Esaias the prophet, saying, (15) The land of Zabulon, and the land of Nephthalim, by the way of the sea, beyond Jordan, Galilee of the Gentiles; (16) The people which sat in darkness</u> saw great light; and to them which sat in the region and shadow of death light is sprung up.

PSALMS 107:10-12—(10) <u>Such as sit in darkness</u> and in the shadow of death, being bound in affliction and iron; (11) <u>Because they rebelled</u> against the words of God, and contemned the counsel of the most High: (12) Therefore he brought down their heart with labor; they fell down, and there was none to help.

EPHESIANS 4:17-19—(17) This I say therefore, and testify in the Lord, that ye henceforth walk not as other <u>Gentiles</u> walk, in the vanity of their mind, (18) Having the understanding darkened, being alienated from the life of God through the ignorance that is in them, because of the blindness of their heart: (19) Who being past feeling have given themselves over unto lasciviousness, to work all uncleanness with greediness.

ISAIAH 29:10-11—(10) For the LORD hath poured out upon you the spirit of deep sleep, and hath closed your eyes: the prophets and your rulers, the seers hath he covered. (11) And the vision of all is become unto you as the words of a book that is sealed, which men deliver to one that is learned, saying, Read this, I pray thee: and he saith, I cannot; for it is sealed.

MATTHEW 6:23—But if thine eye be evil, thy whole body shall be full of darkness. If therefore the light that is in thee be darkness, how great is that darkness

(Jeremiah 2:5)

ROMANS 1:22-23
(22) Professing themselves to be wise, they became fools, (23) and changed the glory of the uncorruptible God into an image made like to corruptible man, and to birds, and four-footed beasts, and creeping things.

JEREMIAH 2:11-13—(11) Hath a nation changed their gods, which are yet no gods? But my people have changed their glory for that which doth not profit. (12) Be astonished, O ye heavens, at this, and be horribly afraid, be ye very desolate, saith the LORD. (13) For my people have committed two evils; they have forsaken me the fountain of living waters, and hewed them out cisterns, broken cisterns, that can hold no water.

PSALMS 106:19-21—(19) They made a calf in Horeb, and worshipped the molten image. (20) Thus they changed their glory into the similitude of an ox that eateth grass. (21) They forgat God their saviour, which had done great things in Egypt.

WISDOM OF SOLOMON 12:24-25—(24) For they went far astray on the paths of error, accepting as gods those animals which even their enemies despised; they were deceived like foolish babes. (25) Therefore, as thoughtless children, thou didst send thy judgment to mock them.

EXODUS 32:4—And he received them at their hand, and fashioned it with a graving tool, after he had made it a molten calf: and they said,

These be thy gods, O Israel, which brought thee up out of the land of Egypt.

1 KINGS 12:28—Whereupon the king took counsel, and made two <u>calves of gold</u>, and said unto them, It is too much for you to go up to Jerusalem: behold thy gods, O Israel, which brought thee up out of the land of Egypt.

2 KINGS 17:16—And they left all the commandments of the LORD their God, and made them <u>molten images</u>, even two calves, and made a grove, and worshipped all the host of heaven, and served Baal.

JEREMIAH 44:16-18—(16) As for the word that thou hast spoken unto us in the name of the LORD, we will not hearken unto thee. (17) But we will certainly do whatsoever thing goeth forth out of our own mouth, to burn incense unto the queen of heaven, and to pour out drink offerings unto her, as we have done, we, and our fathers, our kings, and our princes, in the cities of Judah, and in the streets of Jerusalem: for then had we plenty of victuals, and were well, and saw no evil. (18<u>) But since we left off to burn incense to the queen of heaven, and to pour out drink offerings unto her</u>, we have wanted all things, and have been consumed by the sword and by the famine.

EZEKIEL 14:4-5—(4) Therefore speak to them, and say to them, 'Thus says the Lord God: "Everyone of the house of <u>Israel who sets up his idols in his heart</u>, and puts before him what causes him to stumble into iniquity, and then comes to the prophet, I the Lord will answer him who comes, according to the multitude of his idols, (5) that I may seize the house of Israel by their heart, because <u>they are all estranged from Me by their idols</u>.'

HOSEA 4:17—<u>Ephraim is joined to idols:</u> let him alone.

(Deuteronomy 4:15-19; Jeremiah 10:14, 11:10)

ROMANS 1:24
Wherefore <u>God also gave them up to uncleanness through the lusts of their own hearts, to dishonor their own bodies</u> between themselves

PSALMS 81:11-12—(11) <u>But my people would not hearken to my voice;</u> and Israel would none of me. (12) <u>So I gave them up unto their own hearts' lust:</u> and they walked in their own counsels.

ACTS 7:42—Then <u>God turned, and gave them up</u> to worship the host of heaven; as it is written in the book of the prophets, O ye house of Israel, have ye offered to me slain beasts and sacrifices by the space of forty years in the wilderness?

PSALMS 106:35-39—(35) But they mingled with the nations and adopted their customs. (36) They worshiped their idols, which became a snare to them. (37) They sacrificed their sons and their daughters to demons. (38) They shed innocent blood—the blood of their sons and daughters, whom they sacrificed to the idols of Canaan, and the land was polluted with blood. (39) They defiled themselves by their actions and prostituted themselves by their deeds.

WISDOM OF SOLOMON 12:3-7—(3) For it was thy will to destroy by the hands of our fathers both those old inhabitants of thy holy land, (4) Whom thou hatedst for doing most odious works of witchcrafts, and wicked sacrifices; (5) And also those merciless murderers of children, and devourers of man's flesh, and the feasts of blood, (6) With their priests out of the midst of their idolatrous crew, and the parents, that killed with their own hands souls destitute of help: (7) That the land, which thou esteemedst above all other, might receive a worthy colony of God's children.

EZRA 9:1-2—(1) Now when these things were done, the princes came to me, saying, The people of Israel, and the priests, and the Levites, have not separated themselves from the people of the lands, doing according to their abominations, even of the Canaanites, the Hittites, the Perizzites, the Jebusites, the Ammonites, the Moabites, the Egyptians, and the Amorites. (2) For they have taken of their daughters for themselves, and for their sons: so that the holy seed have mingled themselves with the people of those lands: yea, the hand of the princes and rulers hath been chief in this trespass.

JEREMIAH 3:20-21—(20) Surely as a wife treacherously departeth from her husband, so have ye dealt treacherously with me, O house of Israel, saith the LORD. (21) A voice was heard upon the high places, weeping and supplications of the children of Israel: for they have perverted their way, and they have forgotten the LORD their God.

EZEKIEL 22:10-11—(10) In thee have they discovered their fathers' nakedness: in thee have they humbled her that was set apart for pollution. (11) And one hath committed abomination with his neighbor's wife; and another hath lewdly defiled his daughter in law; and another in thee hath humbled his sister, his father's daughter.

HOSEA 4:17—Ephraim is joined to idols: let him alone.

1 PETER 4:1-3—(1) Forasmuch then as Christ hath suffered for us in the flesh, arm yourselves likewise with the same mind: for he that hath suffered in the flesh hath ceased from sin; (2) That he no longer should live the rest of his time in the flesh to the lusts of men, but to the will of God. (3) For the time past of our life may suffice us to have wrought the will of the Gentiles, when we walked in lasciviousness, lusts, excess of wine, revellings, banquetings, and abominable idolatries...

1 MACCABEES 1:13-15—(13) Then certain of the people were so forward herein, that they went to the king, who gave them license to do after the ordinances of the heathen: (14) Whereupon they built a place of exercise at Jerusalem according to the customs of the heathen: (15) And made themselves uncircumcised, and forsook the holy covenant, and joined themselves to the heathen, and were sold to do mischief.

(Judges 19:22-30; 2 Samuel 13:7-14; Proverbs 7:10-20; 1 Corinthians 6:18; Galatians 5:19; Ephesians 4:19, 5:3; Colossians 3:5)

ROMANS 1:25 [a]
Who changed the truth of God into a lie and worshipped and served the creature more than the Creator, who is blessed forever. Amen.

The WEB renders this verse as: *"who exchanged the truth of God for a lie."* Here Paul reiterates how TMH's rebellious children once had the truth, but threw it away. So what is the truth?

PSALMS 119:142—Thy righteousness *is* an everlasting righteousness, and thy law *is* the truth.

PSALMS 19:9—The fear of the LORD is clean, enduring forever: the judgments of the LORD are true and righteous altogether

PSALMS 119:160—Thy word *is* true *from* the beginning: and every one of thy righteous judgments *endureth* forever.

TMH's law is the truth, and only Israel was given the law.

ROMANS 9:4-5—(4) Who are Israelites; to whom *pertaineth* the adoption, and the glory, and the covenants, and the giving of the law, and the service *of God, and the promises;* (5) Whose *are* the fathers, and of whom as concerning the flesh Christ *came,* who is over all, God blessed for ever. Amen.

2 ESDRAS 5:27—And among all the multitudes of people thou hast gotten thee one people: and unto this people, whom thou lovedst, thou gavest a law that is approved of all.

PSALMS 147:19-20—(19) He sheweth his word unto Jacob, his statutes and his judgments unto Israel. (20) He hath not dealt so with any nation: and as for his judgments, they have not known them. Praise ye the LORD

ROMANS 3:1-2—(1) What advantage then hath the Jew? Or what profit is there of circumcision? (2) Much every way: chiefly, because that unto them were committed the oracles of God.

ROMANS 1:25 [b]
Who changed the truth of God into a lie and worshipped and served the creature more than the Creator, who is blessed forever. Amen.

EZEKIEL 20:39—As for you, O house of Israel, thus saith the Lord GOD; Go ye, serve ye every one his idols, and hereafter also, if ye will not hearken unto me: but pollute ye my holy name no more with your gifts, and with your idols.

HOSEA 11:2—As they called them, so they went from them: they sacrificed unto Baalim, and burned incense to graven images.

JEREMIAH 15:13—Because my people hath forgotten me, they have burned incense to vanity, and they have caused them to stumble in their ways from the ancient paths, to walk in paths, in a way not cast up;

HABAKKUK 2:18—What profiteth the graven image that the maker thereof hath graven it; the molten image, and a teacher of lies, that the maker of his work trusteth therein, to make dumb idols?

ACTS 14:11-16—(11) And when the people saw what Paul had done, they lifted up their voices, saying in the speech of Lycaonia, The gods are come down to us in the likeness of men. (12) And they called Barnabas, Jupiter; and Paul, Mercurius, because he was the chief speaker. (13) Then the priest of Jupiter, which was before their city, brought oxen and garlands unto the gates, and would have done sacrifice with the people. (14) Which when the apostles, Barnabas and Paul, heard of, they rent their clothes, and ran in among the people, crying out, (15) And saying, Sirs, why do ye these things? We also are men of like passions with you, and preach unto you that ye should turn from these vanities unto the living God, which made heaven, and earth, and the sea, and all things that are therein: (16) Who in times past suffered all nations to walk in their own ways.

(Isaiah 28:15, 44:20, Jeremiah 10:14; Amos 2:4; 1 Thessalonians 1:9; 2 Thessalonians 2:11-12)

ROMANS 1:26-27

(26) **For this cause God gave them up unto vile affections: for even their women did change the natural use into that which is against nature:** (27) **And likewise also the men, leaving the natural use of the woman, burned in their lust one toward another; men with men working that which is unseemly, and receiving in themselves that recompence of their error which was meet.**

1 KINGS 14:23-24—(23) For they also built them high places, and images, and groves, on every high hill, and under every green tree. (24) And there were also sodomites in the land: and they did according to all the abominations of the nations, which the LORD cast out before the children of Israel.

1 KINGS 15:12—And he banished the perverted persons from the land, and removed all the idols that his fathers had made.

1 KINGS 22:46—And the remnant of the sodomites, which remained in the days of his father Asa, he took out of the land.

(Leviticus 18:22-23; Psalms 81:12; Ephesians 5:3-12)

ROMANS 1:28 [a]
And even as they did not like <u>to retain God in their knowledge</u>, God gave them over to a reprobate mind, to do those things which are not convenient;

Retain: to keep in possession or use, to keep, not to lay aside, to keep, not to dismiss

❧

Per the above definition, to retain is to keep what one already has. However, the children of Israel were:

1. the only people who knew TMH *(2 Esdras 3:18, Psalms 147:19-20)*
2. the only people TMH knew. *(Amos 3:1-3)*

This means the people in *Romans 1:28* were those of the children of Israel who forsook their God. They alone had knowledge of TMH, knowledge no other nation of people enjoyed, but as *Romans 1:27-28* says, those who fell away forgot TMH.

JEREMIAH 2:32—Can a maid forget her ornaments, *or* a bride her attire? Yet my people have forgotten Me days without number.

HOSEA 4:6—My people are destroyed for lack of knowledge: because thou hast rejected knowledge, I will also reject thee, that thou shalt be no priest to me: seeing thou hast forgotten the law of thy God, I will also forget thy children.

ISAIAH 5:13—Therefore my people are gone into captivity, because they have no knowledge: and their honorable men are famished, and their multitude dried up with thirst.

ISAIAH 1:3—The ox knoweth his owner, and the ass his master's crib: *but* Israel doth not know, my people doth not consider.

JEREMIAH 17:4—And thou, even thyself, shalt discontinue from thine heritage that I gave thee; and I will cause thee to serve thine enemies in the land, which thou knowest not: for ye have kindled a fire in mine anger, *which* shall burn forever.

THE BOOK OF JUBILEES 1:8—And they will eat and be satisfied, and they will turn to strange gods, to (gods) which cannot deliver them from aught of their tribulation: and this witness shall be heard for a witness against them. For they will forget all My commandments, (even) all that I command them, and they will walk after the Gentiles, and after their uncleanness, and after their shame, and will serve their gods, and these will prove unto them an offence and a tribulation and an affliction and a snare.

2 MACCABEES 4:14-15—(14) That the priests had no courage to serve any more at the altar, but despising the temple, and neglecting the sacrifices, hastened to be partakers of the unlawful allowance in the place of exercise, after the game of Discus called them forth; (15) Not setting by the honors of their fathers, but liking the glory of the Grecians best of all.

2 ESDRAS 2:7—Let them be scattered abroad among the heathen, let their names be put out of the earth: for they have despised my covenant.

ROMANS 1:28 [b]
And even as they did not like to retain God in their knowledge, God gave them over to a <u>reprobate mind</u>, to do those things which are not convenient

ISAIAH 1:4-6—(4) Ah sinful nation, a people laden with iniquity, a seed of evildoers, children that are corrupters: they have forsaken the LORD, they have provoked the Holy One of Israel unto anger, they are gone away backward. (5) Why should ye be stricken any more? Ye will revolt more and more: <u>the whole head is sick, and the whole heart faint. (6) From the sole of the foot even unto the head there is no soundness in it</u>; but wounds, and bruises, and putrefying sores: they have not been closed, neither bound up, neither mollified with ointment.

DEUTERONOMY 28:28—The LORD shall smite thee with madness, and blindness, and astonishment of heart...

DEUTERONOMY 28:34—So that thou shalt be mad for the sight of thine eyes, which thou shalt see.

ISAIAH 30:12-13—(12) Wherefore thus saith the Holy One of Israel, Because ye despise this word, and trust in oppression and perverseness, and stay thereon: (13) Therefore this iniquity shall be to you as a breach ready to fall, swelling out in a high wall, whose breaking cometh suddenly at an instant.

ISAIAH 30:1—Woe to the rebellious children, saith the LORD, that take counsel, but not of me; and that cover with a covering, but not of my spirit, that they may add sin to sin.

(Psalms 81:12; Ephesians 5:3-5)

ROMANS 1:29-31

(29) Being filled with all unrighteousness, fornication, wickedness, covetousness, maliciousness; full of envy, murder, debate, deceit, malignity; whisperers, (30) backbiters, haters of God, despiteful, proud, boasters, inventors of evil things, disobedient to parents, (31) without understanding, covenant-breakers, without natural affection, implacable, unmerciful:

ISAIAH 30:9-13—(9) That this is a rebellious people, lying children, children that will not hear the law of the LORD: (10) Which say to the seers, See not; and to the prophets, Prophesy not unto us right things, speak unto us smooth things, prophesy deceits: (11) Get you out of the way, turn aside out of the path, cause the Holy One of Israel to cease from before us. (12) Wherefore thus saith the Holy One of Israel, because ye despise this word, and trust in oppression and perverseness, and stay thereon: (13) Therefore this iniquity shall be to you as a breach ready to fall, swelling out in a high wall, whose breaking cometh suddenly at an instant.

JEREMIAH 3:6-10—(6) The Lord said also to me in the days of Josiah the king: "Have you seen what backsliding Israel has done? She has gone up on every high mountain and under every green tree, and there played the harlot. (7) And I said, after she had done all these things, 'Return to Me.' But she did not return. And her treacherous sister Judah saw it. (8) Then I saw that for all the causes for which backsliding Israel had committed adultery, I had put her away and given her a certificate of divorce; yet her treacherous sister Judah did not fear, but went and played the harlot also. (9) So it came to pass, through her casual harlotry, that she defiled the land and committed adultery with stones and trees. (10) And yet for all this her treacherous sister Judah has not turned to Me with her whole heart, but in pretense," says the Lord.

JEREMIAH 11:8—Yet they obeyed not, nor inclined their ear, but walked every one in the imagination of their evil heart: therefore I will bring upon them all the words of this covenant, which I commanded them to do; but they did them not.

JEREMIAH 31:32—Not according to the covenant that I made with their fathers in the day that I took them by the hand to bring them out of the land of Egypt; which my covenant they brake, although I was an husband unto them, saith the LORD.

HOSEA 7:1-2, 8-16—(1) When I would have healed Israel, then the iniquity of Ephraim was discovered, and the wickedness of Samaria: for they commit falsehood; and the thief cometh in, and the troop of robbers spoileth without. (2) And they consider not in their hearts that I remember all their wickedness: now their own doings have beset them about; they are before my face...(8) Ephraim, he hath mixed himself among the people; Ephraim is a cake not turned. (9) Strangers have devoured his strength, and he knoweth it not: yea, gray hairs are here and there upon him, yet he knoweth not. (10) And the pride of Israel testifieth to his face: and they do not return to the LORD their God, nor seek him for all this. (11) Ephraim also is like a silly dove without heart: they call to Egypt, they go to Assyria. (12) When they shall go, I will spread my net upon them; I will bring them down as the fowls of the heaven; I will chastise them, as their congregation hath heard. (13) Woe unto them! for they have fled from me: destruction unto them! because they have transgressed against me: though I have redeemed them, yet they have spoken lies against me. (14) And they have not cried unto me with their heart, when they howled upon their beds: they assemble themselves for corn and wine, and they rebel against me. (15) Though I have bound and strengthened their arms, yet do they imagine mischief against me. (16) They return, but not to the most High: they are like a deceitful bow: their princes shall fall by the sword for the rage of their tongue: this shall be their derision in the land of Egypt.

2 PETER 2:14-15—(14) Having eyes full of adultery, and that cannot cease from sin; beguiling unstable souls: an heart they have exercised with covetous practices; cursed children: (15) Which have forsaken the right way, and are gone astray, following the way of Balaam the son of Bosor, who loved the wages of unrighteousness.

ROMANS 1:32
Who knowing the judgment of God, that they which commit such things are worthy of death, not only do the same, but have pleasure in them that do them.

Non-Israelites weren't given the law. *(Psalms 147:19-20; Amos 3:7; Romans 3:1-2, 9:4-5, 2 Esdras 5:27)* Only Israel knew the judgments of TMH. Non-Israelites weren't familiar with the strict penalties for specific sins, which per *Romans 1:32* were worthy of death under the Mosaic covenant. These laws, statutes, commandments, and punishments were only revealed to the children of Israel. Precepts for this verse, and the preceding ones, show us that both houses (Ephraim and Judah) were guilty of disobedience.

JEREMIAH 3:6-10—(6) The Lord said also to me in the days of Josiah the king: "Have you seen what backsliding Israel has done? She has gone up on every high mountain and under every green tree, and there played the harlot. (7) And I said, after she had done all these things, 'Return to Me.' But she did not return. And her treacherous sister Judah saw it. (8) Then I saw that for all the causes for which backsliding Israel had committed adultery, I had put her away and given her a certificate of divorce; yet her treacherous sister Judah did not fear, but went and played the harlot also. (9) So it came to pass, through her casual harlotry, that she defiled the land and committed adultery with stones and trees. (10) And yet for all this her treacherous sister Judah has not turned to Me with her whole heart, but in pretense," says the Lord.

HOSEA 7:1-6—(1) When I would have healed Israel, then the iniquity of Ephraim was discovered, and the wickedness of Samaria: for they commit falsehood; and the thief cometh in, and the troop of robbers spoileth without. (2) And they consider not in their hearts that I remember all their wickedness: now their own doings have beset them about; they are before my face. (3) They make the king glad with their wickedness, and the princes with their lies. (4) They are all adulterers, as an oven heated by the baker, who ceaseth from raising after he hath kneaded the dough, until it be leavened. (5) In the day of our king the princes have made him sick with bottles of wine; he stretched out his hand with scorners. (6) For they have made ready their heart like an oven, whiles they lie in wait: their baker sleepeth all the night; in the morning it burneth as a flaming fire.

PROVERBS 7:4-27—(4) Say unto wisdom, Thou art my sister; and call understanding thy kinswoman: (5) That they may keep thee from the strange woman, from the stranger which flattereth with her words. (6) For at the window of my house I looked through my casement, (7) And beheld among the simple ones, I discerned among the youths, a young man void of understanding, (8) Passing through the street near her corner; and he went the way to her house, (9) In the twilight, in the evening, in the black and dark night: (10) And, behold, there met him a woman with the attire of an harlot, and subtle of heart. (11) (She is loud and stubborn; her feet abide not in her house: (12) Now is she without, now in the streets, and lieth in wait at every corner.) (13) So she caught him, and kissed him, and with an impudent face said unto him, (14) I have peace offerings with me; this day have I payed my vows. (15) Therefore came I forth to meet thee, diligently to seek thy face, and I have found thee. (16) I have decked my bed with coverings of tapestry, with carved [works], with fine linen of Egypt. (17) I have perfumed my bed with myrrh, aloes, and cinnamon. (18) Come, let us take our fill of love until the morning: let us solace ourselves with loves. (19) For the good man is not at home, he is gone a long journey: (20) He hath taken a bag of money with him, [and] will come home at the day appointed. (21) With her much fair speech she caused him to yield, with the flattering of her lips she forced him. (22) He goeth after her straightway, as an ox goeth to the slaughter, or as a fool to the correction of the stocks; (23) Till a dart strike through his liver; as a bird hasteth to the snare, and knoweth not that it [is] for his life. (24) Hearken unto me now therefore, O ye children, and attend to the words of my mouth. (25) Let not thine heart decline to her ways, go not astray in her paths. (26) For she hath cast down many wounded: yea, many strong [men] have been slain by her. (27) Her house is the way to hell, going down to the chambers of death.

1 CORINTHIANS 5:1-2—(1) It is actually reported that there is sexual immorality among you, and of a kind that is intolerable even among pagans: A man has his father's wife. (2) And you are proud! Shouldn't you rather have been stricken with grief and removed from your fellowship the man who did this?

2 PETER 2:13—And shall receive the reward of unrighteousness, as they that count it pleasure to riot in the daytime. Spots they are and blemishes, sporting themselves with their own deceivings while they feast with you.

ROMANS 2

ROMANS 2:1
Therefore thou art inexcusable, O man, whosoever thou art that judgest: for wherein thou judgest another, thou condemnest thyself; for thou that judgest doest the same things.

MATTHEW 7:1-5—(1) Judge not, that ye be not judged. (2) For with what judgment ye judge, ye shall be judged: and with what measure ye mete, it shall be measured to you again. (3) And why beholdest thou the mote that is in thy brother's eye, but considerest not the beam that is in thine own eye? (4) Or how wilt thou say to thy brother, Let me pull out the mote out of thine eye; and, behold, a beam is in thine own eye? (5) Thou hypocrite, first cast out the beam out of thine own eye; and then shalt thou see clearly to cast out the mote out of thy brother's eye. * *(Luke 6:37-41)*

JOHN 8:7-9—(7) So when they continued asking him, he lifted up himself, and said unto them, He that is without sin among you, let him first cast a stone at her. (8) And again he stooped down, and wrote on the ground. (9) And they which heard it, being convicted by their own conscience, went out one by one, beginning at the eldest, even unto the last: and Jesus was left alone, and the woman standing in the midst.

ROMANS 14:10-13—(10) But why dost thou judge thy brother? Or why dost thou set at nought thy brother? For we shall all stand before the judgment seat of Christ. (11) For it is written, As I live, saith the Lord, every knee shall bow to me, and every tongue shall confess to God. (12) So then every one of us shall give account of himself to God. (13) Let us not therefore judge one another any more: but judge this rather, that no man put a stumbling block or an occasion to fall in his brother's way.

JAMES 4:11-12—(11) Speak not evil one of another, brethren. He that speaketh evil of his brother, and judgeth his brother, speaketh evil of the

---

* The saints (Israel) will judge the entire world (1 Corinthians 6:2). However, in the interim, we are to guide, counsel *and* judge each other, but by the spirit, not the flesh (1 Corinthians 2:15). How else are we to keep each other on the righteous path? (Deuteronomy 16:18; 1 Corinthians 5:1-5) The key is, we are to judge wisely (1 Kings 3:7-28); faithfully (Romans 3:21-23) righteously (Sirach 45:26, John 7:24), and without prejudice or bias. (Exodus 23:3; Leviticus 19:15, Deuteronomy 1:17; Zechariah 2:9; James 2:3-5) law, and judgeth the law: but if thou judge the law, thou art not a doer of the law, but a judge. (12) There is one lawgiver, who is able to save and to destroy: who art thou that judgest another?

ROMANS 2:2-4
(2) But we are sure that the judgment of God is according to truth against them, which commit such things. (3) And thinkest thou this, O man, that judgest them which do such things, and doest the same, that thou shalt escape the judgment of God? (4) Or despisest thou the riches of his goodness and forbearance and longsuffering; not knowing that the goodness of God leadeth thee to repentance?

JOHN 8:16—And yet if I judge, my judgment is true: for I am not alone, but I and the Father that sent me.

JOB 4:8—Even as I have seen, they that plow iniquity, and sow wickedness, reap the same.

GALATIANS 6:7—Be not deceived; God is not mocked: for whatsoever a man soweth, that shall he also reap.

ROMANS 9:22-23—(22) What if God, willing to shew his wrath, and to make his power known, endured with much longsuffering the vessels of wrath fitted to destruction: (23) and that he might make known the riches of his glory on the vessels of mercy, which he had afore prepared unto glory...

ISAIAH 30:18—And therefore will the LORD wait, that he may be gracious unto you, and therefore will he be exalted, that he may have mercy upon you: for the LORD is a God of judgment: blessed are all they that wait for him.

EPHESIANS 1:18—The eyes of your understanding being enlightened; that ye may know what is the hope of his calling, and what the riches of the glory of his inheritance in the saints...

2 PETER 3:9—The Lord is not slack concerning his promise, as some men count slackness; but is longsuffering to us-ward, not willing that any should perish, but that all should come to repentance.

(Exodus 34:4-7; Romans 3:25; Ephesians 1:7, 2:7)

ROMANS 2:5-6
(5) But after thy hardness and impenitent heart treasurest up unto thyself wrath against the day of wrath and revelation of the righteous judgment of God; (6) who will render to every man according to his deeds:

PSALMS 28:4—Give them according to their deeds, and according to the wickedness of their endeavors: give them after the work of their hands; render to them their desert.

PROVERBS 24:12—If thou sayest, Behold, we knew it not; doth not he that pondereth the heart consider it? And he that keepeth thy soul, doth not he know it? And shall not he render to every man according to his works?

2 ESDRAS 9:7-9—(7) And every one that shall be saved, and shall be able to escape by his works, and by faith, whereby ye have believed, (8) Shall be preserved from the said perils, and shall see my salvation in my land, and within my borders: for I have sanctified them for me from the beginning. (9) Then shall they be in pitiful case, which now have abused my ways: and they that have cast them away despitefully shall dwell in torments.

2 CORINTHIANS 5:10—For we must all appear before the judgment seat of Christ; that every one may receive the things done in his body, according to that he hath done, whether it be good or bad.

REVELATION 20:12-13—(12) And I saw the dead, small and great, stand before God; and the books were opened: and another book was opened, which is [the book] of life: and the dead were judged out of those things which were written in the books, according to their works. (13) And the sea gave up the dead, which were in it; and death and hell delivered up the dead, which were in them: and they were judged every man according to their works.

REVELATION 22:12—And, behold, I come quickly; and my reward is with me, to give every man according as his work shall be.

(Job 34:11; Matthew 16:27)

ROMANS 2:7-8
(7) To them who by patient continuance in well doing seek for glory and honor and immortality, eternal life: (8) But unto them that are contentious, and do not obey the truth, but obey unrighteousness, indignation and wrath

ROMANS 6:23—For the wages of sin is death; but the gift of God is eternal life through Jesus Christ our Lord.

DEUTERONOMY 30:19—I call heaven and earth to record this day against you, that I have set before you life and death, blessing and cursing: therefore choose life, that both thou and thy seed may live.

DEUTERONOMY 28:15—But it shall come to pass, if thou wilt not hearken unto the voice of the LORD thy God, to observe to do all his commandments and his statutes which I command thee this day; that all these curses shall come upon thee, and overtake thee...

ROMANS 1:18—For the wrath of God is revealed from heaven against all ungodliness and unrighteousness of men, who hold the truth in unrighteousness

ROMANS 5:21—That as sin hath reigned unto death, even so might grace reign through righteousness unto eternal life by Jesus Christ our Lord.

2 THESSALONIANS 2:10-12—(10) And with all deceivableness of unrighteousness in them that perish; because they received not the love of the truth, that they might be saved. (11) And for this cause God shall send them strong delusion, that they should believe a lie: (12) That they all might be damned who believed not the truth, but had pleasure in unrighteousness.

(Isaiah 66:16-18; 2 Thessalonians 1:8)

ROMANS 2:9-11

(9) **Tribulation and anguish, upon every soul of man that doeth evil, of the Jew first, and also of the Gentile** [Hellēnos (Ἕλληνος·)]; (10) **But glory, honor, and peace, to every man that worketh good, to the Jew first, and also to the Gentile** [Hellēni (Ἕλληνι)]: (11) **For there is no respect of persons with God.**

These verses should read, (verse 9) "and also of the <u>Greek</u>," and (verse 10) "and also to the <u>Greek</u>." The ESV, BSB, BLB, NASB, NKJV, CSB, CEV, and many other bibles translate these words as "Greek."

Contextually speaking, Paul is building a case—that the Circumcision (Judah) are in the same boat, spiritually speaking, as the Greek/Gentile Israelites (the Uncircumcision). Both have sinned. However, in a broader sense, it's also true that judgment begins with TMH's chosen people *(1 Peter 4:17, Amos 3:2)* therefore, both Israelite and non-Israelite will be judged because He is righteous and hates iniquity no matter the source.

DEUTERONOMY 10:17—For the LORD your God is God of gods, and Lord of lords, a great God, a mighty, and a terrible, which regardeth not persons, nor taketh reward.

DEUTERONOMY 1:17—Ye shall not respect persons in judgment; but ye shall hear the small as well as the great; ye shall not be afraid of the face of man; for the judgment is God's: and the cause that is too hard for you, bring it unto me, and I will hear it.

2 CHRONICLES 19:7—Wherefore now let the fear of the LORD be upon you; take heed and do it: for there is no iniquity with the LORD our God, nor respect of persons, nor taking of gifts.

EPHESIANS 6:9—And, ye masters, do the same things unto them, forbearing threatening: knowing that your Master also is in heaven; neither is there respect of persons with him.

COLOSSIANS 3:25—But he that doeth wrong shall receive for the wrong which he hath done: and there is no respect of persons.

1 PETER 1:17—And if ye call on the Father, who without respect of persons judgeth according to every man's work, pass the time of your sojourning here in fear

1 PETER 4:17—For the time is come that judgment must begin at the house of God: and if it first begin at us, what shall the end be of them that obey not the gospel of God?

AMOS 3:2—You only have I chosen among all the families of the earth; Therefore I will punish you for all your iniquities.

(Genesis 4:4-5; Exodus 2:25; Deuteronomy 16:19, Job 34:19, Matthew 20:16)

ROMANS 2:12-13

(12) For as many as have <u>sinned without law shall also perish without law</u>: and as many as have <u>sinned in the law shall be judged by the law</u>; (13) For not the hearers of the law are just before God, but the <u>doers of the law shall be justified</u>.

STRONG'S #1344: "Justified"—*dikaioó (δικαιόω)*
USAGE: make righteous, defend the cause of, plead for the righteousness (innocence) of, acquit, justify; hence: I regard as righteous.

From these two verses it's clear to see that the Law isn't done away with. Notice what Paul says above. Sinners without the Law will ***perish without*** the Law. Sinners under the Law are ***judged by*** the Law, however

those who obey the Law, whether under the Law or not, **will be justified**. Case in point, Rahab, the non-Israelite. *(James 2:25; Hebrews 11:31; Joshua 6:17)*

DEUTERONOMY 8:20—As the nations which the LORD destroyeth before your face, so shall ye perish; because ye would not be obedient unto the voice of the LORD your God.

PSALMS 73:27—For, lo, they that are far from thee shall perish: thou hast destroyed all them that go a whoring from thee.

2 ESDRAS 9:7-8—(7) And every one that shall be saved, and shall be able to escape by his works, and by faith, whereby ye have believed, (8) shall be preserved from the said perils, and shall see my salvation in my land, and within my borders: for I have sanctified them for me from the beginning.

MATTHEW 7:21—Not every one that saith unto me, Lord, Lord, shall enter into the kingdom of heaven; but he that doeth the will of my Father which is in heaven.

JAMES 1:22-25—(22) Be doers of the word, and not hearers only. Otherwise, you are deceiving yourselves. (23) For if any be a hearer of the word, and not a doer, he is like unto a man beholding his natural face in a glass: (24) For he beholdeth himself, and goeth his way, and straightway forgetteth what manner of man he was. (25) But whoso looketh into the perfect law of liberty, and continueth therein, he being not a forgetful hearer, but a doer of the work, this man shall be blessed in his deed.

JAMES 2:14-18—(14) What doth it profit, my brethren, though a man say he hath faith, and have not works? Can faith save him? (15) If a brother or sister be naked, and destitute of daily food, (16) and one of you say unto them, Depart in peace, be ye warmed and filled; notwithstanding ye give them not those things which are needful to the body; what doth it profit? (17) Even so faith, if it hath not works, is dead, being alone. (18) Yea, a man may say, Thou hast faith, and I have works: shew me thy faith without thy works, and I will shew thee my faith by my works.

After reading the above scriptures, one might ask, "Are we saved by faith or by works?" Here's the answer:

EPHESIANS 2:8-9—(8) For by grace are ye saved through faith; and that not of yourselves: it is the gift of God: (9) Not of works, lest any man should boast.

Salvation is a gift from TMH and works are the fruits of the circumcised heart. These fruits are a physical manifestation, or evidence that He is indeed dealing with us. Without this evidence, as *James 1:22* says, we deceive ourselves. This deception is the backdrop of *Matthew 7:23* where Messiah says, "I never knew you." Why? Because those who practice lawlessness are strangers to Him.

STRONG'S #458: "lawlessness"— *anomia* (ἄνομος);
DEFINITION: (1) properly, the condition of one without law — either because one is ignorant of it, or because of violating it. (2) contempt and violation of law, iniquity, wickedness

In *John 15:5* Messiah said good works are impossible to do without Him. Paul expounds on this point in Philippians:

PHILIPPIANS 2:12-13—(12) Wherefore, my beloved, as ye have always obeyed, not as in my presence only, but now much more in my absence, work out your own salvation with fear and trembling. (13) **For it is God which worketh in you both to will and to do of his good pleasure.**

Without a circumcised heart, one cannot produce good works or see the kingdom. *(John 3:3)* Therefore, salvation is a gift, whereas faith and good works are fruits of the Spirit. *(Galatians 5:22-23, 1 Corinthians 12:7-11)*

1 JOHN 3:6-9—(6) Whosoever abideth in him sinneth not: whosoever sinneth hath not seen him, neither known him. (7) Little children, let no man deceive you: he that doeth righteousness is righteous, even as he is righteous. (8) He that committeth sin is of the devil; for the devil sinneth from the beginning. For this purpose the Son of God was manifested, that he might destroy the works of the devil. (9) Whosoever is born of God doth not commit sin; **for his seed remaineth in him**: and he cannot sin, because he is born of God.

ROMANS 2:14-15
(14) **For when the Gentiles** [ethnē (ἔθνη)]**, which have not the law, do by nature the things contained in the law, these, having not the law, are a law unto themselves:** (15) **Which shew the work of the law written in their hearts, their conscience also bearing witness, and their thoughts the mean while accusing or else excusing one another**

JEREMIAH 31:31-34—(31) Behold, the days come, saith the LORD, that I will make a new covenant with the house of Israel, and with the house of Judah: (32) Not according to the covenant that I made with their fathers in the day that I took them by the hand to bring them out of the land of Egypt; which my covenant they brake, although I was an husband unto them, saith the LORD: (33) But this shall be the covenant that I will make with the house of Israel; After those days, saith the LORD, I will put my law in their inward parts, and write it in their hearts; and will be their God, and they shall be my people. (34) And they shall teach no more every man his neighbour, and every man his brother, saying, Know the LORD: for they shall all know me, from the least of them unto the greatest of them, saith the LORD: for I will forgive their iniquity, and I will remember their sin no more.

2 BARUCH 32:1—But as for you, if you prepare your hearts, so as to sow in them the fruits of the law, it shall protect you in that time in which the Mighty One is to shake the whole creation.

JOHN 14:26—But the Comforter, which is the Holy Ghost, whom the Father will send in my name, he shall teach you all things, and bring all things to your remembrance, whatsoever I have said unto you.

ROMANS 2:16
In the day when God shall judge the secrets of men by Jesus Christ according to my gospel.

ECCLESIASTES 12:14—For God shall bring every work into judgment, with every secret thing, whether it be good, or whether it be evil.

JOHN 5:22—For the Father judgeth no man, but hath committed all judgment unto the Son.

ACTS 10:42—And he commanded us to preach unto the people, and to testify that it is he which was ordained of God to be the Judge of quick and dead.

ACTS 17:31—Because he hath appointed a day, in the which he will judge the world in righteousness by that man whom he hath ordained; whereof he hath given assurance unto all men, in that he hath raised him from the dead.

1 CORINTHIANS 4:5—Therefore judge nothing before the time, until the Lord come, who both will bring to light the hidden things of darkness, and will make manifest the counsels of the hearts: and then shall every man have praise of God.

1 TIMOTHY 1:11—Because he hath appointed a day, in the which he will judge the world in righteousness by that man whom he hath ordained;

whereof he hath given assurance unto all men, in that he hath raised him from the dead.

REVELATION 20:12—And I saw the dead, small and great, stand before God; and the books were opened: and another book was opened, which is the book of life: and the dead were judged out of those things which were written in the books, according to their works.

ROMANS 2:17-18
(17) Behold, thou art called a Jew, and restest in the law, and makest thy boast of God (18) and knowest his will, and approvest the things that are more excellent, being instructed out of the law

ROMANS 3:1-2—(1) What advantage then hath the Jew? Or what profit is there of circumcision? (2) Much every way: chiefly, because that unto them were committed the oracles of God.

ROMANS 9:4—Who are Israelites; to whom pertaineth the adoption, and the glory, and the covenants, and the giving of the law, and the service of God, and the promises.

DEUTERONOMY 4:1-9—(1) Now therefore hearken, O Israel, unto the statutes and unto the judgments, which I teach you, for to do them, that ye may live, and go in and possess the land which the LORD God of your fathers giveth you. (2) Ye shall not add unto the word which I command you, neither shall ye diminish ought from it, that ye may keep the commandments of the LORD your God which I command you. (3) Your eyes have seen what the LORD did because of Baalpeor: for all the men that followed Baalpeor, the LORD thy God hath destroyed them from among you. (4) But ye that did cleave unto the LORD your God are alive every one of you this day. (5) Behold, I have taught you statutes and judgments, even as the LORD my God commanded me, that ye should do so in the land whither ye go to possess it. (6) Keep therefore and do them; for this is your wisdom and your understanding in the sight of the nations, which shall hear all these statutes, and say, Surely this great nation is a wise and understanding people. (7) For what nation is there so great, who hath God so nigh unto them, as the LORD our God is in all things that we call upon him for? (8) And what nation is there so great, that hath statutes and judgments so righteous as all this law, which I set before you this day? (9) Only take heed to thyself, and keep thy soul diligently, lest thou forget the things which thine eyes have seen, and lest they depart from thy heart all the days of thy life: but teach them thy sons, and thy sons' sons.

ROMANS 2:19-23

(19) And art confident that thou thyself art a guide of the blind, a light of them which are in darkness, (20) an instructor of the foolish, a teacher of babes, which hast the form of knowledge and of the truth in the law. (21) Thou therefore which teachest another, teachest thou not thyself? Thou that preachest a man should not steal, dost thou steal? (22) Thou that sayest a man should not commit adultery, dost thou commit adultery? Thou that abhorrest idols, dost thou commit sacrilege? (23) Thou that makest thy boast of the law, through breaking the law dishonourest thou God?

In the above verses, Paul is speaking directly to the Circumcision, AKA The House of Judah.

ISAIAH 48:1-4—(1) Hear ye this, O house of Jacob, which are called by the name of Israel, and are come forth out of the waters of Judah, which swear by the name of the LORD, and make mention of the God of Israel, but not in truth, nor in righteousness. (2) For they call themselves of the holy city, and stay themselves upon the God of Israel; The LORD of hosts is his name. (3) I have declared the former things from the beginning; and they went forth out of my mouth, and I shewed them; I did them suddenly, and they came to pass. (4) Because I knew that thou art obstinate, and thy neck is an iron sinew, and thy brow brass;

MICAH 3:11—The heads thereof judge for reward, and the priests thereof teach for hire, and the prophets thereof divine for money: yet will they lean upon the LORD, and say, Is not the LORD among us? None evil can come upon us.

MATTHEW 23:2-28—(2) The scribes and the Pharisees sit in Moses' seat: (3) All therefore whatsoever they bid you observe, that observe and do; but do not ye after their works: for they say, and do not. (4) For they bind heavy burdens and grievous to be borne, and lay them on men's shoulders; but they themselves will not move them with one of their fingers. (5) But all their works they do for to be seen of men: they make broad their phylacteries, and enlarge the borders of their garments, (6) And love the uppermost rooms at feasts, and the chief seats in the synagogues, (7) And greetings in the markets, and to be called of men, Rabbi, Rabbi. (8) But be not ye called Rabbi: for one is your Master, even Christ; and all ye are brethren. (9) And call no man your father upon the earth: for one is your Father, which is in heaven. (10) Neither be ye called masters: for one is your Master, even Christ. (11) But he that is greatest among you shall be your servant. (12) And whosoever shall exalt himself shall be abased; and he that shall humble himself shall be exalted. (13) But woe unto you, scribes and Pharisees, hypocrites! for ye shut up the kingdom of heaven against men: for ye neither go in yourselves, neither suffer ye them that are entering to go in. (14) Woe unto you, scribes and Pharisees, hypocrites! For ye devour widows' houses, and for a pretense make long prayer: therefore ye shall receive the greater damnation. (15) Woe unto you, scribes and Pharisees, hypocrites! For ye compass sea and land to make one proselyte, and when he is made, ye make him twofold more the child of hell than yourselves. (16) Woe unto you, ye blind guides, which say, Whosoever shall swear by the temple, it is nothing; but whosoever shall swear by the gold of the temple, he is a debtor! (17) Ye fools and blind: for whether is greater, the gold, or the temple that sanctifieth the gold? (18) And, Whosoever shall swear by the altar, it is nothing; but whosoever sweareth by the gift that is upon it, he is guilty. (19) Ye fools and blind: for whether is greater, the gift, or the altar that sanctifieth the gift? (20) Whoso therefore shall swear by the altar, sweareth by it, and by all things thereon. (21) And whoso shall swear by the temple, sweareth by it, and by him that dwelleth therein. (22) And he that shall swear by heaven, sweareth by the throne of God, and by him that sitteth thereon. (23) Woe unto you, scribes and Pharisees, hypocrites! for ye pay tithe of mint and anise and cumin, and have omitted the weightier matters of the law, judgment, mercy, and faith: these ought ye to have done, and not to leave the other undone. (24) Ye blind guides, which strain at a gnat, and swallow a camel. (25) Woe unto you, scribes and Pharisees, hypocrites! for ye make clean the outside of the cup and of the platter, but within they are full of extortion and excess. (26) Thou blind Pharisee, cleanse first that which is within the cup and platter, that the outside of them may be clean also. (27) Woe unto you, scribes and Pharisees, hypocrites! For ye are like unto whited sepulchers, which indeed appear beautiful outward, but are within full of dead men's bones, and of all uncleanness. (28) Even so ye also outwardly appear righteous unto men, but within ye are full of hypocrisy and iniquity.

MATTHEW 15:14—Let them alone: they be blind leaders of the blind. And if the blind lead the blind, both shall fall into the ditch.

2 TIMOTHY 3:5-8—(5) Having a form of godliness, but denying the power thereof: from such turn away. (6) For of this sort are they which creep into houses, and lead captive silly women laden with sins, led away with divers lusts, (7) Ever learning, and never able to come to the knowledge of the truth. (8) Now as Jannes and Jambres withstood Moses, so do these also resist the truth: men of corrupt minds, reprobate concerning the faith.

MALACHI 1:7-8—(7) Ye offer polluted bread upon mine altar; and ye say, Wherein have we polluted thee? In that ye say, The table of the LORD is contemptible. (8) And if ye offer the blind for sacrifice, is it not evil? And if ye offer the lame and sick, is it not evil? Offer it now unto thy governor; will he be pleased with thee, or accept thy person? saith the LORD of hosts.

MATTHEW 5:27-30—(27) Ye have heard that it was said by them of old time, Thou shalt not commit adultery: (28) But I say unto you, That whosoever looketh on a woman to lust after her hath committed adultery with her already in his heart. (29) And if thy right eye offend thee, pluck it out, and cast it from thee: for it is profitable for thee that one of thy members should perish, and not that thy whole body should be cast into hell. (30) And if thy right hand offend thee, cut it off, and cast it from thee: for it is profitable for thee that one of thy members should perish, and not that thy whole body should be cast into hell.

ROMANS 2:24-26

(24) **For the name of God is blasphemed among the Gentiles** [Ethnesin (ἔθνεσιν)]**, through you, as it is written.** (25) **For circumcision verily profiteth, if thou keep the law: but if thou be a breaker of the law, thy circumcision is made uncircumcision.** (26) **Therefore if the uncircumcision keep the righteousness of the law, shall not his uncircumcision be counted for circumcision?**

Because of the unrighteousness and hypocrisy among the Circumcision, TMH's name was blasphemed. How? They took TMH's name in vain *(Exodus 20:7)* by claiming to be His representatives (i.e. being in covenant with Him), while at the same time, practicing lawlessness. This is what it means to take His name in vain. That is why physical circumcision means nothing if the inward man is wicked.

So the Israelite Gentile, being uncircumcised in the flesh, yet circumcised in the heart, is counted as righteous. Thus, his uncircumcision becomes circumcision. An example of this is Abraham. Before he received the covenant of circumcision, TMH deemed him righteous because of his faith and obedience.

GENESIS 15:2-6—(2) And Abram said, Lord GOD, what wilt thou give me, seeing I go childless, and the steward of my house is this Eliezer of Damascus? (3) And Abram said, Behold, to me thou hast given no seed: and, lo, one born in my house is mine heir. (4) And, behold, the word of the LORD came unto him, saying, This shall not be thine heir; but he that shall come forth out of thine own bowels shall be thine heir. (5) And he brought him forth abroad, and said, Look now toward heaven, and tell the stars, if thou be able to number them: and he said unto him, So shall thy seed be. (6) And he believed in the LORD; and he counted it to him for righteousness.

ROMANS 4:9-12—(9) Cometh this blessedness then upon the circumcision only, or upon the uncircumcision also? for we say that faith was reckoned to Abraham for righteousness. (10) How was it then reckoned? when he was in circumcision, or in uncircumcision? Not in circumcision, but in uncircumcision. (11) And he received the sign of circumcision, a seal of the righteousness of the faith which he had yet being uncircumcised: that he might be the father of all them that believe, though they be not circumcised; that righteousness might be imputed unto them also: (12) And the father of circumcision to them who are not of the circumcision only, but who also walk in the steps of that faith of our father Abraham, which he had being yet uncircumcised.

JAMES 2:23—And the scripture was fulfilled which saith, Abraham believed God, and it was imputed unto him for righteousness: and he was called the Friend of God

ROMANS 2:27-29

(27) And shall not uncircumcision which is by nature, if it fulfill the law, judge thee, who by the letter and circumcision dost transgress the law? (28) For he is not a Jew, which is one outwardly; neither is that circumcision, which is outward in the flesh: (29) But he is a Jew, which is one inwardly; and circumcision is that of the heart, in the spirit, and not in the letter; whose praise is not of men, but of God.

Paul is once again addressing the Circumcision who believe their birthright and fleshly circumcision justifies them. He rightly concludes that their fleshly circumcision is made uncircumcision when they break the law, for no man is justified on his own. All have sinned and fall short of the grace of TMH. *(Romans 3:23; 1 John 1:10)*

Being born an Israelite doesn't justify. Circumcision of the flesh doesn't justify. Faith, and circumcision of the heart, which is the renewal of the mind by the indwelling of the Spirit, justifies.

JEREMIAH 4:3-4—(3) For thus saith the Lord to the men of Judah and Jerusalem, Break up your fallow ground, and sow not among thorns. (4) Circumcise yourselves to the Lord, and take away the foreskins of your heart, ye men of Judah and inhabitants of Jerusalem: lest my fury come forth like fire, and burn that none can quench it, because of the evil of your doings.

DEUTERONOMY 10:16—Circumcise therefore the foreskin of your heart, and be no more stiff-necked.

DEUTERONOMY 30:6—And the LORD thy God will circumcise thine heart, and the heart of thy seed, to love the LORD thy God with all thine heart, and with all thy soul, that thou mayest live.

TITUS 3:3-7—(3) For we ourselves also were sometimes foolish, disobedient, deceived, serving divers lusts and pleasures, living in malice and envy, hateful, and hating one another. (4) But after that the kindness and love of God our Saviour toward man appeared, (5) Not by works of righteousness which we have done, but according to his mercy he saved us, by the washing of regeneration, and renewing of the Holy Ghost; (6) Which he shed on us abundantly through Jesus Christ our Saviour; (7) That being justified by his grace, we should be made heirs according to the hope of eternal life.

GALATIANS 6:15—For in Christ Jesus neither circumcision availeth any thing, nor uncircumcision, but a new creature.

PHILIPPIANS 3:3—For we are the circumcision, which worship God in the spirit, and rejoice in Christ Jesus, and have no confidence in the flesh.

COLOSSIANS 2:11—In whom also ye are circumcised with the circumcision made without hands, in putting off the body of the sins of the flesh by the circumcision of Christ

GALATIANS 5:1-6—(1) Stand fast therefore in the liberty wherewith Christ hath made us free, and be not entangled again with the yoke of bondage. (2) Behold, I Paul say unto you, that if ye be circumcised, Christ shall profit you nothing. (3) For I testify again to every man that is circumcised, that he is a debtor to do the whole law. (4) Christ is become of no effect unto you, whosoever of you are justified by the law; ye are fallen from grace. (5) For we through the Spirit wait for the hope of righteousness by faith. (6) For in Jesus Christ neither circumcision availeth any thing, nor uncircumcision; but faith which worketh by love.

ROMANS 3

ROMANS 3:1-2
(1) What advantage then hath the Jew? Or what profit is there of circumcision? (2) Much every way: chiefly, because that unto them were committed the oracles of God.

In the beginning, the oracles of TMH were committed to the children of Israel via the Mosaic covenant.

DEUTERONOMY 4:5-8—(5) Behold, I have taught you statutes and judgments, even as the LORD my God commanded me, that ye should do so in the land whither ye go to possess it. (6) Keep therefore and do them; for this is your wisdom and your understanding in the sight of the nations, which shall hear all these statutes, and say, Surely this great nation is a wise and understanding people. (7) For what nation is there so great, who hath God so nigh unto them, as the LORD our God is in all things that we call upon him for? (8) And what nation is there so great, that hath statutes and judgments so righteous as all this law, which I set before you this day?

DEUTERONOMY 29:29—The secret things belong unto the LORD our God: but those things, which are revealed, belong unto us and to our children forever, that we may do all the words of this law.

PSALMS 147:19-20—(19) He sheweth his word unto Jacob, his statutes and his judgments unto Israel. (20) He hath not dealt so with any nation: and as for his judgments, they have not known them. Praise ye the LORD.

AMOS 3:1-2—(1) Hear this word that the LORD hath spoken against you, O children of Israel, against the whole family which I brought up from the land of Egypt, saying, (2) You only have I known of all the families of the earth: therefore I will punish you for all your iniquities.

2 ESDRAS 5:27—And among all the multitudes of people thou hast gotten thee one people: and unto this people, whom thou lovedst, thou gavest a law that is approved of all.

ROMANS 9:4-5—(4) Who are Israelites; to whom pertaineth the adoption, and the glory, and the covenants, and the giving of the law, and the service of God, and the promises (5) Whose are the fathers, and of whom as concerning the flesh Christ came, who is over all, God blessed for ever. Amen.

Later, the oracles of TMH were placed in Judah's care after TMH disowned Ephraim. The House of Judah was disobedient as well, but TMH didn't disown them.

HOSEA 1:6-9—(6) And she conceived again, and bare a daughter. And God said unto him, Call her name Loruhamah: <u>for I will no more have mercy upon the house of Israel; but I will utterly take them away</u>. (7) But I <u>will have mercy upon the house of Judah, and will save them by the LORD their God</u>, and will not save them by bow, nor by sword, nor by battle, by horses, nor by horsemen. (8) Now when she had weaned Loruhamah, she conceived, and bare a son. (9) <u>Then said God, Call his name Loammi: for ye are not my people, and I will not be your God</u>.

HOSEA 4:17—<u>Ephraim is joined to idols: let him alone</u>.

ISAIAH 7:8—For the head of Syria is Damascus, and the head of Damascus is Rezin; and within threescore and five years shall <u>Ephraim be broken, that it be not a people</u>.

2 KINGS 17:13-18—(13) Yet the LORD testified against Israel, and against Judah, by all the prophets, and by all the seers, saying, Turn ye from your evil ways, and keep my commandments and my statutes, according to all the law which I commanded your fathers, and which I sent to you by my servants the prophets. (14) Notwithstanding they would not hear, but hardened their necks, like to the neck of their fathers, that did not believe in the LORD their God. (15) And they rejected his statutes, and his covenant that he made with their fathers, and his testimonies which he testified against them; and they followed vanity, and became vain, and went after the heathen that were round about them, concerning whom the LORD had charged them, that they should not do like them. (16) And they left all the commandments of the LORD their God, and made them molten images, even two calves, and made a grove, and worshipped all the host of heaven, and served Baal. (17) And they caused their sons and their daughters to pass through the fire, and used divination and enchantments, and sold themselves to do evil in the sight of the LORD, to provoke him to anger. (18) <u>Therefore the LORD was very angry with Israel, and removed them out of his sight: there was none left but the tribe of Judah only</u>.

ROMANS 3:3-4

(3) For what if some did not believe? Shall their unbelief make the faith of God without effect? **(4)** **God forbid: yea, let God be true, but every man a liar; as it is written, that thou mightest be justified in thy sayings, and mightest overcome when thou art judged.**

NUMBERS 23:19—God is not a man, that he should lie; neither the son of man, that he should repent: hath he said, and shall he not do it? Or hath he spoken, and shall he not make it good?

PSALMS 51:4—Against thee, thee only, have I sinned, and done this evil in thy sight: that thou mightest be justified when thou speakest, and be clear when thou judgest.

DEUTERONOMY 32:4—He is the Rock, his work is perfect: for all his ways are judgment: a God of truth and without iniquity, just and right is he.

JOB 8:3-7—(3) Doth God pervert judgment? Or doth the Almighty pervert justice? (4) If thy children have sinned against him, and he have cast them away for their transgression; (5) if thou wouldest seek unto God betimes, and make thy supplication to the Almighty; (6) If thou wert pure and upright; surely now he would awake for thee, and make the habitation of thy righteousness prosperous. (7) Though thy beginning was small, yet thy latter end should greatly increase.

PSALMS 116:11—I said in my haste, All men are liars.

(Psalms 50:6; John 3:33)

ROMANS 3:5-8

(5) But if our unrighteousness commend the righteousness of God, what shall we say? Is God unrighteous who taketh vengeance? (I speak as a man) (6) God forbid: for then how shall God judge the world? (7) For if the truth of God hath more abounded through my lie unto his glory; why yet am I also judged as a sinner? (8) And not rather, (as we be slanderously reported, and as some affirm that we say,) Let us do evil that good may come? Whose damnation is just.

GENESIS 18:25—That be far from thee to do after this manner, to slay the righteous with the wicked: and that the righteous should be as the wicked, that be far from thee: Shall not the Judge of all the earth do right?

DEUTERONOMY 32:4—He is the Rock, his work is perfect: for all his ways are judgment: a God of truth and without iniquity, just and right is he.

2 CHRONICLES 19:7—Wherefore now let the fear of the LORD be upon you; take heed and do it: for there is no iniquity with the LORD our God, nor respect of persons, nor taking of gifts

PSALMS 18:30—As for God, his way is perfect: the word of the LORD is tried: he is a buckler to all those that trust in him.

ZEPHANIAH 3:5—The just LORD is in the midst thereof; he will not do iniquity: every morning doth he bring his judgment to light, he faileth not; but the unjust knoweth no shame.

ROMANS 3:9
What then? Are we better than they? No, in no wise: for we have before proved both Jews and Gentiles, [Hellēnas (Ἕλληνας)] that they are all under sin;

JEREMIAH 5:7-11—(7) How shall I pardon thee for this? Thy children have forsaken me, and sworn by them that are no gods: when I had fed them to the full, they then committed adultery, and assembled themselves by troops in the harlots' houses. (8) They were as fed horses in the morning: every one neighed after his neighbor's wife. (9) Shall I not visit for these things? saith the LORD: and shall not my soul be avenged on such a nation as this? (10) Go ye up upon her walls, and destroy; but make not a full end: take away her battlements; for they are not the LORD'S. (11) For the house of Israel and the house of Judah have dealt very treacherously against me, saith the LORD.

GALATIANS 3:22—But the scripture hath concluded all under sin, that the promise by faith of Jesus Christ might be given to them that believe.

PSALMS 106:6—We have sinned with our fathers, we have committed iniquity, we have done wickedly.

ECCLESIASTES 7:20—For there is not a just man upon earth, that doeth good, and sinneth not.

ROMANS 3:23—For all have sinned, and come short of the glory of God

1 JOHN 1:8—If we say that we have no sin, we deceive ourselves, and the truth is not in us.

(1 Kings 8:46-50; Proverbs 20:9; Jeremiah 33:8; Romans 2:12)

ROMANS 3:10-12
(10) As it is written, there is none righteous, no, not one: (11) There is none that understandeth, there is none that seeketh after God. (12) They are all gone out of the way, they are together become unprofitable; there is none that doeth good, no, not one.

ISAIAH 64:6—But we are all as an unclean thing, and all our righteousnesses are as filthy rags; and we all do fade as a leaf; and our iniquities, like the wind, have taken us away.

ECCLESIASTES 7:20—For there is not a just man upon earth, that doeth good, and sinneth not.

PSALMS 53:1-3—(1) The fool hath said in his heart, There is no God. Corrupt are they, and have done abominable iniquity: [there is] none that doeth good. (2) God looked down from heaven upon the children of men, to see if there were [any] that did understand, that did seek God. (3) Every one of them is gone back: they are altogether become filthy; there is none that doeth good, no, not one.

ISAIAH 41:26-29—(26) Who hath declared from the beginning, that we may know? And beforetime, that we may say, He is righteous? Yea, there is none that sheweth, yea, there is none that declareth, yea, there is none that heareth your words. (27) The first shall say to Zion, Behold, behold them: and I will give to Jerusalem one that bringeth good tidings. (28) For I beheld, and there was no man; even among them, and there was no counselor, that, when I asked of them, could answer a word. (29) Behold, they are all vanity; their works are nothing: their molten images are wind and confusion.

(Psalms 14:1-3; Psalms 36:1, Mark 10:18)

ROMANS 3:13-18
(13) Their throat is an open sepulcher; with their tongues they have used deceit; the poison of asps is under their lips: (14) Whose mouth is full of cursing and bitterness: (15) Their feet are swift to shed blood: (16) Destruction and misery are in their ways: (17) And the way of peace have they not known: (18) There is no fear of God before their eyes.

PSALMS 5:9—For there is no faithfulness in their mouth; their inward part is very wickedness; their throat is an open sepulcher; they flatter with their tongue.

ISAIAH 59:3-8—(3) For your hands are defiled with blood, and your fingers with iniquity; your lips have spoken lies, your tongue hath muttered perverseness. (4) None calleth for justice, nor any pleadeth for truth: they trust in vanity, and speak lies; they conceive mischief, and bring forth iniquity. (5) They hatch cockatrice' eggs, and weave the spider's web: he that eateth of their eggs dieth, and that which is crushed breaketh out into a viper. (6) Their webs shall not become garments, neither shall they cover themselves with their works: their works are works of iniquity, and the act of violence is in their hands. (7) Their feet run to evil, and they make haste to shed innocent blood: their thoughts are thoughts of iniquity; wasting and destruction are in their paths. (8) The way of peace they know not; and there is no judgment in their goings: they have made them crooked paths: whosoever goeth therein shall not know peace.

PSALMS 140:3—(1) Deliver me, O LORD, from the evil man: preserve me from the violent man; (2) Which imagine mischiefs in their heart; continually are they gathered together for war. (3) They have sharpened their tongues like a serpent; adders' poison is under their lips. Selah.

PROVERBS 1:15-16—(15) My son, walk not thou in the way with them; refrain thy foot from their path: (16) for their feet run to evil, and make haste to shed blood.

(Psalms 10:5-7; Psalms 36:1; James 3:8)

ROMANS 3:19-20

(19) Now we know that what things soever the law saith, it saith to them who are under the law: that every mouth may be stopped, and all the world may become guilty before God. (20) Therefore by the deeds of the law there shall no flesh be justified in his sight: for by the law is the knowledge of sin.

PSALMS 143:1-2—(1) Hear my prayer, O Lord give ear to my supplications: in thy faithfulness answer me, and in thy righteousness (2) and enter not into judgment with thy servant: for in thy sight shall no man living be justified.

ROMANS 2:12—For as many as have sinned without law shall also perish without law: and as many as have sinned in the law shall be judged by the law.

ROMANS 7:7-10—(7) What shall we say then? Is the law sin? God forbid. Nay, I had not known sin, but by the law: for I had not known lust, except the law had said, Thou shalt not covet. (8) But sin, taking occasion by the commandment, wrought in me all manner of concupiscence. For without the law sin was dead. (9) For I was alive without the law once: but when the commandment came, sin revived, and I died. (10) And the commandment, which was ordained to life, I found to be unto death.

ROMANS 3:21-22
(21) **But now the righteousness of God without the law is manifested, being witnessed by the law and the prophets;** (22) **Even the righteousness of God which is by faith of Jesus Christ unto all and upon all them that believe: for there is no difference:**

1 PETER 1:10—Of which salvation the prophets have enquired and searched diligently, who prophesied of the grace that should come unto you.

ACTS 13:39—And by him all that believe are justified from all things, from which ye could not be justified by the law of Moses.

ACTS 10:43—To him give all the prophets witness, that through his name whosoever believeth in him shall receive remission of sins.

ROMANS 1:17—For therein is the righteousness of God revealed from faith to faith: as it is written, the just shall live by faith.

ROMANS 8:3—For what the law could not do, in that it was weak through the flesh, God sending his own Son in the likeness of sinful flesh, and for sin, condemned sin in the flesh:

GALATIANS 2:16—Knowing that a man is not justified by the works of the law, but by the faith of Jesus Christ, even we have believed in Jesus Christ, that we might be justified by the faith of Christ, and not by the works of the law: for by the works of the law shall no flesh be justified.

GALATIANS 3:11—But that no man is justified by the law in the sight of God, it is evident: for, the just shall live by faith.

GALATIANS 3:28—There is neither Jew nor Greek, there is neither bond nor free, there is neither male nor female: for ye are all one in Christ Jesus.

COLOSSIANS 3:11—Where there is neither Greek nor Jew, circumcision nor uncircumcision, Barbarian, Scythian, bond nor free: but Christ is all, and in all.

JOHN 5:45-47—(45) Do not think that I will accuse you to the Father: there is one that accuseth you, even Moses, in whom ye trust. (46) For had ye believed Moses, ye would have believed me: for he wrote of me. (47) But if ye believe not his writings, how shall ye believe my words?

DANIEL 9:24—Seventy weeks are determined upon thy people and upon thy holy city, to finish the transgression, and to make an end of sins, and to make reconciliation for iniquity, and to bring in everlasting righteousness, and to seal up the vision and prophecy, and to anoint the most Holy.

ROMANS 3:23
For all have sinned, and come short of the glory of God;

ROMANS 3:9—What then? Are we better than they? No, in no wise: for we have before proved both Jews and Gentiles, that they are all under sin.

GALATIANS 3:22—But the scripture hath concluded all under sin, that the promise by faith of Jesus Christ might be given to them that believe.

ROMANS 3:24
Being justified freely by his grace through the redemption that is in Christ Jesus:

HEBREWS 9:12-15—(12) Neither by the blood of goats and calves, but by his own blood he entered in once into the holy place, having obtained eternal redemption for us. (13) For if the blood of bulls and of goats, and the ashes of an heifer sprinkling the unclean, sanctifieth to the purifying of the flesh: (14) How much more shall the blood of Christ, who through the eternal Spirit offered himself without spot to God, purge your conscience from dead works to serve the living God? (15) And for this cause he is the mediator of the new testament, that by means of death, for the redemption of the transgressions that were under the first testament, they which are called might receive the promise of eternal inheritance.

EPHESIANS 1:7—In whom we have redemption through his blood, the forgiveness of sins, according to the riches of his grace.

MATTHEW 20:28—Even as the Son of man came not to be ministered unto, but to minister, and to give his life a ransom for many.

EPHESIANS 2:8—For by grace are ye saved through faith; and that not of yourselves: it is the gift of God

1 TIMOTHY 2:6—Who gave himself a ransom for all, to be testified in due time.

TITUS 3:5, 7—(5) Not by works of righteousness which we have done, but according to his mercy he saved us, by the washing of regeneration, and renewing of the Holy Ghost...(7) That being justified by his grace, we should be made heirs according to the hope of eternal life.

(Colossians 1:14; 1 Peter 1:18)

ROMANS 3:25
Whom God hath set forth to be a propitiation through faith in his blood, to declare his righteousness for the remission of sins that are past, through the forbearance of God;

HEBREWS 9:15—And for this cause he is the mediator of the new testament, that by means of death, for the redemption of the transgressions that were under the first testament, they which are called might receive the promise of eternal inheritance.

COLOSSIANS 1:20—And, having made peace through the blood of his cross, by him to reconcile all things unto himself; by him, I say, whether they be things in earth, or things in heaven.

EPHESIANS 2:13—But now in Christ Jesus ye who sometimes were far off are made nigh by the blood of Christ.

(Exodus 12:13, Leviticus 16:16)

ROMANS 3:26-27
(26) To declare, I say, at this time his righteousness: that he might be just, and the justifier of him which believeth in Jesus. (27) Where is boasting then? It is excluded. By what law? Of works? Nay: but by the law of faith.

ROMANS 5:1—Therefore being justified by faith, we have peace with God through our Lord Jesus Christ.

GALATIANS 3:23-25—(23) But before faith came, we were kept under the law, shut up unto the faith which should afterwards be revealed. (24) Wherefore the law was our schoolmaster to bring us unto Christ, that we might be justified by faith. (25) But after that faith is come, we are no longer under a schoolmaster.

PHILIPPIANS 3:9—And be found in him, not having mine own righteousness, which is of the law, but that which is through the faith of Christ, the righteousness which is of God by faith

(Romans 2:17, 23)

ROMANS 3:28
Therefore we conclude that a man is justified by faith without the deeds of the law.

EPHESIANS 2:8-9—(8) For by grace are ye saved through faith; and that not of yourselves: it is the gift of God: (9) Not of works, lest any man should boast.

GALATIANS 2:16—Knowing that a man is not justified by the works of the law, but by the faith of Jesus Christ, even we have believed in Jesus Christ, that we might be justified by the faith of Christ, and not by the works of the law: for by the works of the law shall no flesh be justified.

ROMANS 3:21—But now the righteousness of God without the law is manifested, being witnessed by the law and the prophets

ROMANS 4:6—Even as David also describeth the blessedness of the man, unto whom God imputeth righteousness without works.

ROMANS 3:29-30
(29) Is he the God of the Jews only? Is he not also of the Gentiles? [ethnōn (ἐθνῶν)]; Yes, of the Gentiles [ethnōn (ἐθνῶν)] also: (30) seeing it is one God, which shall justify the circumcision by faith, and uncircumcision through faith.

This is a summation of the argument he opened with in *Romans 3:9*—that the Circumcision and the Uncircumcision of Israel were in the same boat. He didn't suddenly decide to start talking about non-Israelites in this verse. He's speaking about the *same* people he's been speaking about from the beginning—Israel.

Here, the Greek word ethnōn (ἐθνῶν) once again refers to Israelite Gentiles—the Uncircumcision. We know this because (1) this letter was addressed to the saints *(Romans 1:7)* (2) only Israelites are called to be saints *(Psalms 50:5; Psalms 148:14; Psalms 149:5-9; Wisdom of Solomon 4:15)*; (3) Israel is the only nation TMH' has ever known and the only nation that's ever known Him, *(Jeremiah 3:14, Amos 3:1-2, 2 Esdras 2:16, and 2 Esdras 3:32)* and (4) TMH is only called **the God of Israel** in the Bible. *(2 Samuel 23:3; 2 Chronicles 13:5; Judges 11:21; 21:3; Psalms 68:8, 35; Ezra 4:1-2)*

ROMANS 9:23-27—(23) And that he might make known the riches of his glory on the vessels of mercy, which he had afore prepared unto glory, (24) Even us, whom he hath called, not of the Jews only, but also of the Gentiles? (25) As he saith also in Osee, I will call them my people, which were not my people; and her beloved, which was not beloved. (26) And it shall come to pass, that in the place where it was said unto them, Ye are not my people; there shall they be called the children of the living God. (27) Esaias also crieth concerning Israel, Though the number of the children (of Israel be as the sand of the sea, a remnant shall be saved.

ROMANS 10:12—For there is no difference between the Jew and the Greek: for the same Lord over all is rich unto all that call upon him.

COLOSSIANS 3:11—Where there is neither Greek nor Jew, circumcision nor uncircumcision, Barbarian, Scythian, bond nor free: but Christ is all, and in all.

THE BOOK OF JUBILEES 15:30-32—(30) For Ishmael and his sons and his brothers and Esau, the Lord did not cause to approach Him, and he chose them not because they are the children of Abraham, because He knew them, but He chose Israel to be His people. (31) And He sanctified it, and gathered it from amongst all the children of men; for there are many nations and many peoples, and all are His, and over all hath He placed spirits in authority to lead them astray from Him. (32) But over Israel He did not appoint any angel or spirit, for He alone is their ruler, and He will preserve them and require them at the hand of His angels and his spirits, and at the hand of all His powers in order that He may preserve them and bless them, and that they may be His and He may be theirs from henceforth forever.

ROMANS 3:31
Do we then make void the law through faith?
God forbid: yea, we establish the law.

ROMANS 2:13—For not the hearers of the law are just before God, but the doers of the law shall be justified.

ROMANS 8:4—That the righteousness of the law might be fulfilled in us, who walk not after the flesh, but after the Spirit.

JAMES 1:22—But be ye doers of the word, and not hearers only, deceiving your own selves.

MATTHEW 7:21—Not every one that saith unto me, Lord, Lord, shall enter into the kingdom of heaven; but he that doeth the will of my Father which is in heaven.

LUKE 6:46-49—(46) And why call ye me, Lord, Lord, and do not the things which I say? (47) Whosoever cometh to me, and heareth my sayings, and doeth them, I will shew you to whom he is like: (48) He is like a man which built an house, and digged deep, and laid the foundation on a rock: and when the flood arose, the stream beat vehemently upon that house, and could not shake it: for it was founded upon a rock. (49) But he that heareth, and doeth not, is like a man that without a foundation built an house upon the earth; against which the stream did beat vehemently, and immediately it fell; and the ruin of that house was great.

JAMES 2:18-22—(18) Yea, a man may say, Thou hast faith, and I have works: shew me thy faith without thy works, and I will shew thee my faith by my works. (19) Thou believest that there is one God; thou doest well: the devils also believe, and tremble. (20) But wilt thou know, O vain man, that faith without works is dead? (21) Was not Abraham our father justified by works, when he had offered Isaac his son upon the altar? (22) Seest thou how faith wrought with his works, and by works was faith made perfect?

(John 1:17; James 2:8; Romans 13:8)

ROMANS 4

ROMANS 4:1-3
(1) **What shall we say then that Abraham our father, as pertaining to the flesh, hath found?** (2) **For if Abraham were justified by works, he hath whereof to glory; but not before God.** (3) **For what saith the scripture? Abraham believed God, and it was counted unto him for righteousness.**

Abraham's belief in TMH's divine promises made him righteous. As an aside, notice Paul didn't say, "Abraham my father." He said, "**_our_** father." Only the children of Israel can call Abraham their father. *(See Romans 9:7-9, pg. 244)* This is more evidence that the Gentiles Paul is speaking to are Israelites.

GENESIS 15:3-6—(3) And Abram said, Behold, to me thou hast given no seed: and, lo, one born in my house is mine heir. (4) And, behold, the word of the LORD came unto him, saying, This shall not be thine heir; but **he that shall come forth out of thine own bowels shall be thine heir**. (5) And he brought him forth abroad, and said, Look now toward heaven, and tell the stars, if thou be able to number them: and he said unto him, So shall thy seed be. (6) And he believed in the LORD; and he counted it to him for righteousness.

GALATIANS 3:6—Even as Abraham believed God, and it was accounted to him for righteousness.

1 MACCABEES 2:52—Was not Abraham found faithful in temptation, and it was imputed unto him for righteousness?

JAMES 2:21, 23—(21) Was not Abraham our father justified by works, when he had offered Isaac his son upon the altar? *...(23) And the scripture was fulfilled which saith, Abraham believed God, and it was imputed unto him for righteousness: and he was called the Friend of God.

*Re: *James 2:21,23* above: On the surface, this appears to be a contradiction of *Romans 4:2*, but it's not. Contextually speaking, James' argument was that faith without works is dead—i.e., a lie—illegitimate. Therefore, our works become justifiers only in the sense that they demonstrate or prove the legitimacy of our faith. Hence James' statement in *James 2:19*: *"Thou believest that there is one God; thou doest well: the devils also believe, and tremble."* Simply believing that there's a God isn't enough. Saying you love TMH isn't enough.

As the saying goes, 'Talk is cheap' *(Isaiah 29:13).*

Along with believing TMH, Abraham showed his faith by doing what he was told. In other words, he demonstrated his faith with obedience:

1. By leaving the idols of his father and his home behind [Ur (Mesopotamia)] for the land of Canaan (this was before TMH's covenant of circumcision) when TMH told him to leave. *(Genesis 12:1-9)*
2. Being willing to sacrifice his son Isaac when TMH tested him. *(Genesis 22:1-19)*

This is how faith and works go hand-in-hand. We're to believe and follow every word that comes out of the mouth of TMH. *(Deuteronomy 8:3)* We practice lawlessness *(Matthew 7:21-27)* when we don't obey His commandments. *(Luke 6:46)*
Righteousness equals lawfulness.

LAW

STRONG'S #3551: "law"—*nomos* (νόμος)
USAGE: usage, custom, law; in NT: of law in general, plur: of divine laws; of a force or influence impelling to action; of the Mosaic law; meton: of the books which contain the law, the Pentateuch, the Old Testament scriptures in general.

THAYER'S: *νόμος, νόμου, ὁ* (*νέμω* to divide, distribute, apportion), in secular authors from Hesiod down, anything established, anything received by usage, a custom, usage, law; in the Sept. very often for תּוֹרָה, also for חֹק, דָּת, etc. In the N. T. a command, law; and 1. of any law whatsoever: *διά ποίου νόμου*; *Romans 3:27*; *νόμος δικαιοσύνης*, a law or rule producing a state approved of God, i. e. by the observance of which we are approved of God, *Romans 9:31*, cf. Meyer (see Weiss edition), Fritzsche, Philippi at the passage; a precept or injunction: *κατά νόμον ἐντολῆς σαρκίνης*, *Hebrews 7:16*; plural of the things prescribed by the divine will, *Hebrews 8:10*

RIGHTEOUS

STRONG'S #G1342: "righteous"—*dikaios* (δίκαιος)
USAGE: just; especially, just in the eyes of God; righteous; the elect
THAYER'S DEFINITION: in a wide sense, upright, righteous, virtuous, keeping the commands of God.

(Isaiah 51:2; Hebrews 11:8; Revelation 22:12)

ROMANS 4:4-5
(4) Now to him that worketh is the reward not reckoned of grace, but of debt. (5) But to him that worketh not, but believeth on him that justifieth the ungodly, his faith is counted for righteousness.

Paul isn't saying good works don't count. He's saying faith is what justifies us, and works, which are demonstrations of faith, move in tangent with this faith. Ours isn't a works-based salvation. Salvation is a free gift, yet obedience to TMH's commandments is the *evidence* that we are walking with Him. Therefore, how do we show TMH that we truly want and appreciate His free gift? By loving Him.

2 JOHN 1:6—And this is love: that we walk after his commandments. This is the commandment that, as ye have heard from the beginning, ye should walk in it.

So it is TMH's grace that saves us via our *true* faith in the Messiah's sacrifice, a faith which was once and for all delivered to the saints. *(Jude 1:3)* **Works of the Law** can't save us. Messiah's blood does.

ACTS 15:11—But we believe that through the grace of the Lord Jesus Christ we shall be saved, even as they.

ROMANS 3:22—Even the righteousness of God, which is by faith of Jesus Christ unto all and upon all them that believe: for there is no difference.

ROMANS 11:6—And if by grace, then is it no more of works: otherwise grace is no more grace. But if it be of works, then is it no more grace: otherwise work is no more work.

EPHESIANS 2:8-9—(8) For by grace are ye saved through faith; and that not of yourselves: it is the gift of God: (9) Not of works, lest any man should boast.

However, we mar our good works when we get puffed up because pride nullifies faith.

LUKE 18:9-14—(9) And he spake this parable unto certain which trusted in themselves that they were righteous, and despised others: (10) Two men went up into the temple to pray; the one a Pharisee, and the other a publican. (11) The Pharisee stood and prayed thus with himself, God, I thank thee, that I am not as other men are, extortioners, unjust, adulterers, or even as this publican. (12) I fast twice in the week, I give tithes of all that I possess. (13) And the publican, standing afar off, would not lift up so much as his eyes unto heaven, but smote upon his breast, saying, God be merciful to me a sinner. (14) I tell you, this man went down to his house justified rather than the other: for every one that exalteth himself shall be abased; and he that humbleth himself shall be exalted.

This is why we should never forget this scripture:

PHILIPPIANS 2:12-13—(12) Wherefore, my beloved, as ye have always obeyed, not as in my presence only, but now much more in my absence, work out your own salvation with fear and trembling. (13) **For it is God which worketh in you** both to will and to do of his good pleasure.

ROMANS 4:6-8
(6) Even as David also describeth the blessedness of the man, unto whom God imputeth righteousness without works, (7) Saying, Blessed are they whose iniquities are forgiven, and whose sins are covered, (8) Blessed is the man to whom the Lord will not impute sin.

We are saved by grace because *"all have sinned, and come short of the glory of God."* (Romans 3:23) For Messiah is the author and finisher of our faith, (Hebrews 12:2) while our righteous Father corrects and forgives us when we *'come short'* (i.e. stumble) *and* repent:

PSALMS 32:1-2, 5—(1) Blessed is he whose transgression is forgiven, whose sin is covered. (2) Blessed is the man unto whom the LORD imputeth not iniquity, and in whose spirit there is no guile...(5) I acknowledged my sin unto thee, and mine iniquity have I not hid. I said, I will confess my transgressions unto the LORD; and thou forgavest the iniquity of my sin. Selah.

PHILIPPIANS 2:12-13—(12)...work out your own salvation with fear and trembling. (13) For it is God which worketh in you both to will and to do of his good pleasure.

PSALMS 31:1—In thee, O LORD, do I put my trust; let me never be ashamed: deliver me in thy righteousness.

(Psalms 103:3; 78:38; 85:2; Jeremiah 31:34; Luke 13:5; Acts 2:38; Revelation 2:4-5; Revelation 2:21; Revelation 3:2-3; Revelation 3:19)

ROMANS 4:9-10
(9) **Cometh this blessedness then upon the circumcision only, or upon the uncircumcision also? For we say that faith was reckoned to Abraham for righteousness:** (10) **how was it then reckoned? When he was in circumcision, or in uncircumcision? Not in circumcision, but in uncircumcision;**

Here Paul makes the point that the TMH's promise to Abraham, and Abraham's subsequent show of faith in believing the promise, came *before* the covenant commandment of circumcision.

GENESIS 15:5-6—(5) And he brought him forth abroad, and said, Look now toward heaven, and tell the stars, if thou be able to number them: and he said unto him, So shall thy seed be. (6) And he believed in the LORD; and he counted it to him for righteousness.

GENESIS 17: 1, 9-11—(1) And when Abram was ninety years old and nine, the LORD appeared to Abram, and said unto him, I am the Almighty God; walk before me, and be thou perfect...(9) And God said unto Abraham, Thou shalt keep my covenant therefore, thou, and thy seed after thee in their generations. (10) This is my covenant, which ye shall keep, between me and you and thy seed after thee; every man child among you shall be circumcised. (11) And ye shall circumcise the flesh of your foreskin; and it shall be a token of the covenant betwixt me and you.

ROMANS 4:11
And he received the sign of circumcision, a seal of the righteousness of the faith, which he had yet being, uncircumcised: that he might be the father of all them that believe, though they be not circumcised; that righteousness might be imputed unto them also:

Abraham was deemed righteous even before the commandment of circumcision. His faith justified him. This is why he is the father of both the Circumcision (Jew) and the Uncircumcision (Israelite Greeks and Northern Kingdom Israelites of the diaspora who were living as Gentiles) because he exercised righteousness by believing TMH before and after circumcision.

GENESIS 15:5-6—(5) And he brought him forth abroad, and said, Look now toward heaven, and tell the stars, if thou be able to number them: and he said unto him, So shall thy seed be. (6) And he believed in the LORD; and he counted it to him for righteousness.

GENESIS 17:10-11—(10) This is my covenant, which ye shall keep, between me and you and thy seed after thee; Every man child among you shall be circumcised. (11) And ye shall circumcise the flesh of your foreskin; and it shall be a token of the covenant betwixt me and you.

GALATIANS 3:7—Know ye therefore that they which are of faith, the same are the children of Abraham.

(Romans 9:6-13)

ROMANS 4:12-13

(12) And the father of circumcision to them who are not of the circumcision only, but who also walk in the steps of that faith of our father Abraham, which he had being yet uncircumcised. (13) For the promise, that he should be the heir of the world, was not to Abraham, or to his seed, through the law, but through the righteousness of faith.

ROMANS 9:6-13—(6) It is not as though God's word has failed. For not all who are descended from Israel are Israel. (7) Nor because they are Abraham's descendants are they all his children. On the contrary, "Through Isaac your offspring will be reckoned." (8) So it is not the children of the flesh who are God's children, but it is the children of the promise who are regarded as offspring. (9) For this is what the promise stated: "At the appointed time I will return, and Sarah will have a son." (10) Not only that, but Rebecca's children were conceived by one man, our father Isaac. (11) Yet before the twins were born or had done anything good or bad, in order that God's plan of election might stand, (12) not by works but by Him who calls, she was told, "The older will serve the younger." (13) So it is written: "Jacob I loved, but Esau I hated."

HEBREWS 11:9—By faith he sojourned in the land of promise, as in a strange country, dwelling in tabernacles with Isaac and Jacob, the heirs with him of the same promise.

GENESIS 17:4-6—(4) As for me, behold, my covenant is with thee, and thou shalt be a father of many nations. (5) Neither shall thy name any more be called Abram, but thy name shall be Abraham; for a father of many nations have I made thee. (6) And I will make thee exceeding fruitful, and I will make nations of thee, and kings shall come out of thee.

GENESIS 22:17—That in blessing I will bless thee, and in multiplying I will multiply thy seed as the stars of the heaven, and as the sand which is upon the sea shore; and thy seed shall possess the gate of his enemies

GENESIS 45:3-5—(3) ...and I will perform the oath which I sware unto Abraham thy father; (4) and I will make thy seed to multiply as the stars of heaven, and will give unto thy seed all these countries; and in thy seed shall all the nations of the earth be blessed; (5) because that Abraham obeyed my voice, and kept my charge, my commandments, my statutes, and my laws.

ROMANS 4:18-22—(18) Who against hope believed in hope, that he might become the father of many nations, according to that which was spoken, So shall thy seed be. (19) And being not weak in faith, he considered not his own body now dead, when he was about an hundred years old, neither yet the deadness of Sara's womb: (20) He staggered not at the promise of God through unbelief; but was strong in faith, giving glory to God; (21) And being fully persuaded that, what he had promised, he was able also to perform. (22) And therefore it was imputed to him for righteousness.

GALATIANS 3:18—For if the inheritance be of the law, it is no more of promise: but God gave it to Abraham by promise.

ROMANS 4:14-15

(14) For if they which are of the law be heirs, faith is made void, and the promise made of none effect: (15) because the law worketh wrath: for where no law is, there is no transgression.

ROMANS 3:20—Therefore by the deeds of the law there shall no flesh be justified in his sight: for by the law is the knowledge of sin.

ROMANS 5:13-20—(13) For until the law sin was in the world: but sin is not imputed when there is no law. (14) Nevertheless death reigned from Adam to Moses, even over them that had not sinned after the similitude of Adam's transgression, who is the figure of him that was to come. (15) But not as the offence, so also is the free gift. For if through the offence of one many be dead, much more the grace of God, and the gift by grace, which is by one man, Jesus Christ, hath abounded unto many. (16) And not as it was by one that sinned, [so is] the gift: for the judgment [was] by one to condemnation, but the free gift is of many offences unto justification. (17) For if by one man's offence death reigned by one; much more they which receive abundance of grace and of the gift of righteousness shall reign in life by one, Jesus Christ. (18) Therefore as by the offence of one judgment came upon all men to condemnation; even so by the righteousness of one the free gift came upon all men unto justification of life. (19) For as by one man's disobedience many were made sinners, so by the obedience of one shall many be made righteous. (20) Moreover the law entered, that the offence might abound. But where sin abounded, grace did much more abound:

ROMANS 7:5-13—(5) For when we were in the flesh, the motions of sins, which were by the law, did work in our members to bring forth fruit unto death. (6) But now we are delivered from the law, that being dead wherein we were held; that we should serve in newness of spirit, and not in the oldness of the letter. (7) What shall we say then? Is the law sin? God forbid. Nay, I had not known sin, but by the law: for I had not known lust, except the law had said, Thou shalt not covet. (8) But sin, taking occasion by the commandment, wrought in me all manner of concupiscence. For without the law sin was dead. (9) For I was alive without the law once: but when the commandment came, sin revived, and I died. (10) And the commandment, which was ordained to life, I found to be unto death. (11) For sin, taking occasion by the commandment, deceived me, and by it slew [me]. (12) Wherefore the law is holy, and the commandment holy, and just, and good. (13) Was then that which is good made death unto me? God forbid. But sin, that it might appear sin, working death in me by that which is good; that sin by the commandment might become exceeding sinful.

GALATIANS 3:10, 18—(10) For as many as are of the works of the law are under the curse: for it is written, Cursed is every one that continueth not in all things which are written in the book of the law to do them...(18) For if the inheritance be of the law, it is no more of promise: but God gave it to Abraham by promise.

2 CORINTHIANS 3:7-9—(7) But if the ministration of death, written and engraven in stones, was glorious, so that the children of Israel could not steadfastly behold the face of Moses for the glory of his countenance; which glory was to be done away: (8) How shall not the ministration of the spirit be rather glorious? (9) For if the ministration of condemnation be glory, much more doth the ministration of righteousness exceed in glory.

2 CORINTHIANS 3:13-16—(13) And not as Moses, which put a veil over his face, that the children of Israel could not steadfastly look to the end of that which is abolished: (14) But their minds were blinded: for until this day remaineth the same veil untaken away in the reading of the old testament; which veil is done away in Christ. (15) But even unto this day, when Moses is read, the veil is upon their heart. (16) Nevertheless when it shall turn to the Lord, the veil shall be taken away. *(Exodus 34:29-35)*

ROMANS 4:16-18

(16) Therefore it is of faith that it might be by grace; to the end the promise might be sure to all the seed; not to that only which is of the law, but to that also which is of the faith of Abraham; who is the father of us all, (17) As it is written, I have made thee a father of many nations,) before him whom he believed, even God, who quickeneth the dead, and calleth those things which be not as though they were. (18) Who against hope believed in hope, that he might become the father of many nations, according to that which was spoken, So shall thy seed be...

STRONG'S #G4690: "seed"—*sperma (σπέρμα)*
DEFINITION: something sown, i.e. seed (including the male "sperm"); by implication, offspring; specially, a remnant (figuratively, as if kept over for planting):—issue, seed.
USAGE: (a) seed, commonly of cereals, (b) offspring, descendants

THAYER'S: the semen virile; α. properly: Leviticus 15:16-18; Leviticus 18:20f, etc.; (probably also Hebrews 11:11, cf. καταβολή 1, and see below); often in secular writings. By metonymy the product of this semen, seed, children, offspring, progeny; family, race, posterity

(For a breakdown on Abraham's seed, see the commentary throughout Romans 9, which begins on pg. 224.)

GENESIS 15:5—And he brought him forth abroad, and said, 'Look now toward heaven, and tell the stars, if thou be able to number them: and he said unto him, So shall thy seed be.'

GENESIS 17:4-5—(4) As for me, behold, my covenant is with thee, and thou shalt be a father of many nations. (5) Neither shall thy name any more be called Abram, but thy name shall be Abraham; for a father of many nations have I made thee.

GENESIS 21:10—Wherefore she said unto Abraham, Cast out this bondwoman and her son: for the son of this bondwoman shall not be heir with my son, even with Isaac.

ISAIAH 51:2—Look unto Abraham your father, and unto Sarah that bare you: for I called him alone, and blessed him, and increased him.

ISAIAH 59:20-21—(20) And the Redeemer shall come to Zion, **and unto them** that turn from transgression *in Jacob*, saith the LORD. (21) As for me, this is my covenant with them, saith the LORD; My spirit that is upon thee, and my words which I have put in thy mouth, shall not depart out of thy mouth, nor out of the mouth of thy seed, nor out of the mouth of thy seed's seed, saith the LORD, from henceforth and for ever.

EZEKIEL 37:15-23—(15) The word of the LORD came again unto me, saying, (16) Moreover, thou son of man, take thee one stick, and write upon it, For Judah, and for the children of Israel his companions: then take another stick, and write upon it, For Joseph, the stick of Ephraim, and for all the house of Israel his companions: (17) And join them one to another into one stick; and they shall become one in thine hand. (18) And when the children of thy people shall speak unto thee, saying, Wilt thou not shew us what thou meanest by these? (19) Say unto them, Thus saith the Lord GOD; Behold, I will take the stick of Joseph, which is in the hand of Ephraim, and the tribes of Israel his fellows, and will put them with him, even with the stick of Judah, and make them one stick, and they shall be one in mine hand. (20) And the sticks whereon thou writest shall be in thine hand before their eyes. (21) And say unto them, Thus saith the Lord GOD; Behold, I will take the children of Israel from among the heathen, whither they be gone, and will gather them on every side, and bring them into their own land: (22) And I will make them one nation in the land upon the mountains of Israel; and one king shall be king to them all: and they shall be no more two nations, neither shall they be divided into two kingdoms any more at all: (23) Neither shall they defile themselves any more with their idols, nor with their detestable things, nor with any of their transgressions: but I will save them out of all their dwelling places, wherein they have sinned, and will cleanse them: so shall they be my people, and I will be their God.

HEBREWS 8:10—For this is the covenant that I will make with the house of Israel after those days, saith the Lord; I will put my laws into their mind, and write them in their hearts: and I will be to them a God, and they shall be to me a people:

HEBREWS 10:15-18—(15) Whereof the Holy Ghost also is a witness to us: for after that he had said before, (16) This is the covenant that I will make with them after those days, saith the Lord, I will put my laws into their hearts, and in their minds will I write them; (17) And their sins and iniquities will I remember no more. (18) Now where remission of these is, there is no more offering for sin.

(Romans 3:24; Galatians 3:22)

ROMANS 4:19-20

(19) And being not weak in faith, he considered not his own body now dead, when he was about an hundred years old, neither yet the deadness of Sara's womb: (20) He staggered not at the promise of God through unbelief; but was strong in faith, giving glory to God

This scripture solidifies the fact that Paul is referring to an actual seed line here and in previous verses.

GENESIS 17:17-23—(17) Then Abraham fell upon his face, and laughed, and said in his heart, Shall a child be born unto him that is an hundred years old? And shall Sarah, that is ninety years old, bear? (18) And Abraham said unto God, O that Ishmael might live before thee! (19) And God said, Sarah thy wife shall bear thee a son indeed; and thou shalt call his name Isaac: and I will establish my covenant with him for an everlasting covenant, and with his seed after him. (20) And as for Ishmael, I have heard thee: Behold, I have blessed him, and will make him fruitful, and will multiply him exceedingly; twelve princes shall he beget, and I will make him a great nation. (21) But my covenant will I establish with Isaac, which Sarah shall bear unto thee at this set time in the next year. (22) And he left off talking with him, and God went up from Abraham. (23) And Abraham took Ishmael his son, and all that were born in his house, and all that were bought with his money, every male among the men of Abraham's house; and circumcised the flesh of their foreskin in the selfsame day, as God had said unto him.

HEBREWS 11:11—Through faith also Sara herself received strength to conceive seed, and was delivered of a child when she was past age, because she judged him faithful who had promised.

(Genesis 18:9-15; Genesis 21:6-7)

ROMANS 4:21-22

(21) And being fully persuaded that, what he had promised, he was able also to perform. (22) And therefore it was imputed to him for righteousness.

GENESIS 15:6—And he believed in the LORD; and he counted it to him for righteousness.

GENESIS 18:14—Is any thing too hard for the LORD? At the time appointed I will return unto thee, according to the time of life, and Sarah shall have a son.

JEREMIAH 32:27—Behold, I am the LORD, the God of all flesh: is there anything too hard for me?

PSALMS 115:3—But our God is in the heavens: he hath done whatsoever he hath pleased.

LUKE 1:37—For with God nothing shall be impossible.

HEBREWS 11:19—Accounting that God was able to raise him up, even from the dead; from whence also he received him in a figure.

ROMANS 4:23-24
(23) Now it was not written for his sake alone, that it was imputed to him; (24) but for us also, to whom it shall be imputed, if we believe on him that raised up Jesus our Lord from the dead

ROMANS 15:4—For whatsoever things were written aforetime were written for our learning, that we through patience and comfort of the scriptures might have hope.

PSALMS 102:18—This shall be written for the generation to come: and the people which shall be created shall praise the LORD.

2 TIMOTHY 3:16-17—(16) All scripture is given by inspiration of God, and is profitable for doctrine, for reproof, for correction, for instruction in righteousness: (17) That the man of God may be perfect, thoroughly furnished unto all good works.

ROMANS 8:32-34—(32) He that spared not his own Son, but delivered him up for us all, how shall he not with him also freely give us all things? (33) Who shall lay any thing to the charge of God's elect? It is God that justifieth. (34) Who is he that condemneth? It is Christ that died, yea rather, that is risen again, who is even at the right hand of God, who also maketh intercession for us.

1 PETER 1:21—Who by him do believe in God, that raised him up from the dead, and gave him glory; that your faith and hope might be in God.

ROMANS 4:25
Who was delivered for our offences, and was raised again for our justification.

ACTS 5:30-31—(30) The God of our fathers raised up Jesus, whom ye slew and hanged on a tree. (31) Him hath God exalted with his right hand to be a Prince and a Saviour, for to give repentance to Israel, and forgiveness of sins.

ISAIAH 53:4-10—(4) Surely he hath borne our griefs, and carried our sorrows: yet we did esteem him stricken, smitten of God, and afflicted. (5) But he was wounded for our transgressions, he was bruised for our iniquities: the chastisement of our peace was upon him; and with his stripes we are healed. (6) All we like sheep have gone astray; we have turned every one to his own way; and the LORD hath laid on him the iniquity of us all. (7) He was oppressed, and he was afflicted, yet he opened not his mouth: he is brought as a lamb to the slaughter, and as a sheep before her shearers is dumb, so he openeth not his mouth. (8) He was taken from prison and from judgment: and who shall declare his generation? For he was cut off out of the land of the living: for the transgression of my people was he stricken. (9) And he made his grave with the wicked, and with the rich in his death; because he had done no violence, neither was any deceit in his mouth. (10) Yet it pleased the LORD to bruise him; he hath put him to grief: when thou shalt make his soul an offering for sin, he shall see his seed, he shall prolong his days, and the pleasure of the LORD shall prosper in his hand.

MATTHEW 1:21—And she shall bring forth a son, and thou shalt call his name JESUS: for he shall save his people from their sins.

LUKE 1:76-77—(76) And thou, child, shalt be called the prophet of the Highest: for thou shalt go before the face of the Lord to prepare his ways; (77) To give knowledge of salvation unto his people by the remission of their sins.

MATTHEW 15:24—But he answered and said, I am not sent but unto the lost sheep of the house of Israel.

JOHN 11:49-52—(49) And one of them, named Caiaphas, being the high priest that same year, said unto them, Ye know nothing at all, (50) Nor consider that it is expedient for us, that one man should die for the people, and that the whole nation perish not. (51) And this spake he not of himself: but being high priest that year, he prophesied that Jesus should die for that nation; (52) And not for that nation only, but that also he should gather together in one the children of God that were scattered abroad.

2 CORINTHIANS 5:21—For he hath made him to be sin for us, who knew no sin; that we might be made the righteousness of God in him.

GALATIANS 1:4—Who gave himself for our sins, that he might deliver us from this present evil world, according to the will of God and our Father.

HEBREWS 9:28—So Christ was once offered to bear the sins of many; and unto them that look for him shall he appear the second time without sin unto salvation.

1 PETER 2:24—Who his own self bare our sins in his own body on the tree that we, being dead to sins, should live unto righteousness: by whose stripes ye were healed.

1 PETER 3:18—For Christ also hath once suffered for sins, the just for the unjust, that he might bring us to God, being put to death in the flesh, but quickened by the Spirit.

ROMANS 5

ROMANS 5:1-2
(1) Therefore being justified by faith, we have peace with God through our Lord Jesus Christ: (2) by whom also we have access by faith into this grace wherein we stand, and rejoice in hope of the glory of God.

ROMANS 3:28-30—(28) Therefore we conclude that a man is justified by faith without the deeds of the law. (29) Is he the God of the Jews only? Is he not also of the Gentiles? Yes, of the Gentiles also: (30) seeing it is one God, which shall justify the circumcision by faith, and uncircumcision through faith.

EPHESIANS 2:14, 18—(14) For he is our peace, who hath made both one, and hath broken down the middle wall of partition between us...(18) For through him we both have access by one Spirit unto the Father.

EPHESIANS 3:12—In whom we have boldness and access with confidence by the faith of him.

HEBREWS 3:6—But Christ as a son over his own house; whose house are we, if we hold fast the confidence and the rejoicing of the hope firm unto the end.

2 JOHN 1:9—Whosoever transgresseth, and abideth not in the doctrine of Christ, hath not God. He that abideth in the doctrine of Christ, he hath both the Father and the Son.

ROMANS 5:3-4
(3) And not only so, but we glory in tribulations also: knowing that tribulation worketh patience; (4) and patience, experience; and experience, hope

JAMES 1:2-3, 12—(2) My brethren, count it all joy when ye fall into divers temptations; (3) Knowing this, that the trying of your faith worketh patience...(12) Blessed is the man that endureth temptation: for when he is tried, he shall receive the crown of life, which the Lord hath promised to them that love him.

1 PETER 4:12-14—(12) Beloved, think it not strange concerning the fiery trial which is to try you, as though some strange thing happened unto you: (13) But rejoice, inasmuch as ye are partakers of Christ's sufferings; that, when his glory shall be revealed, ye may be glad also with exceeding joy. (14) If ye be reproached for the name of Christ, happy are ye; for the spirit of glory and of God resteth upon you: on their part he is evil spoken of, but on your part he is glorified.

2 CORINTHIANS 8:2—How that in a great trial of affliction the abundance of their joy and their deep poverty abounded unto the riches of their liberality.

2 CORINTHIANS 12:10—Therefore I take pleasure in infirmities, in reproaches, in necessities, in persecutions, in distresses for Christ's sake: for when I am weak, then am I strong.

ACTS 5:41—And they departed from the presence of the council, rejoicing that they were counted worthy to suffer shame for his name.

MATTHEW 5:11-12—(11) Blessed are ye, when men shall revile you, and persecute you, and shall say all manner of evil against you falsely, for my sake. (12) Rejoice, and be exceeding glad: for great is your reward in heaven: for so persecuted they the prophets which were before you.

ROMANS 5:5
And hope maketh not ashamed; because the love of God is shed abroad in our hearts by the Holy Ghost, which is given unto us.

JOHN 14:16-17—(16) And I will pray the Father, and he shall give you another Comforter, that he may abide with you for ever; (17) Even the Spirit of truth; whom the world cannot receive, because it seeth him not, neither knoweth him: but ye know him; for he dwelleth with you, and shall be in you.

JOHN 14:26—But the Comforter, which is the Holy Ghost, whom the Father will send in my name, he shall teach you all things, and bring all things to your remembrance, whatsoever I have said unto you.

JOHN 16:13—Howbeit when he, the Spirit of truth, is come, he will guide you into all truth: for he shall not speak of himself; but whatsoever he shall hear, that shall he speak: and he will shew you things to come.

GALATIANS 4:6—And because ye are sons, God hath sent forth the Spirit of his Son into your hearts, crying, Abba, Father.

2 CORINTHIANS 1:22—Who hath also sealed us, and given the earnest of the Spirit in our hearts.

ACTS 2:33—Therefore being by the right hand of God exalted, and having received of the Father the promise of the Holy Ghost, he hath shed forth this, which ye now see and hear

(Ephesians 1:13)

ROMANS 5:6-8

(6) For when we were yet without strength, in due time Christ died for the ungodly. (7) For scarcely for a righteous man will one die: yet peradventure for a good man some would even dare to die. (8) But God commendeth his love toward us, in that, while we were yet sinners, Christ died for us.

Though The House of Judah continued to practice the Law and its customs, *both* houses of Israel were in sin when Messiah laid down his life. Neither the Circumcision nor the Uncircumcision were justified before TMH. If either were, the law of sacrifice would still be in effect.

This is why both were still considered law transgressors: the Circumcision for its hypocrisy and blind obedience to the commandments of men, and the Uncircumcision for its fall into lawlessness and idolatry.

Even so, Messiah died for all of Israel, regardless. His blood covers His repentant brethren's transgressions.

MATTHEW 1:21—And she shall bring forth a son, and thou shalt call his name JESUS: for he shall save his people from their sins.

LUKE 1:76-77—(76) And thou, child, shalt be called the prophet of the Highest: for thou shalt go before the face of the Lord to prepare his ways; (77) To give knowledge of salvation unto his people by the remission of their sins.

JOHN 11:49-52—(49) And one of them, named Caiaphas, being the high priest that same year, said unto them, Ye know nothing at all, (50) Nor consider that it is expedient for us, that one man should die for the people, and that the whole nation perish not. (51) And this spake he not of himself: but being high priest that year, he prophesied that Jesus should die for that nation; (52) And not for that nation only, but that also he should gather together in one the children of God that were scattered abroad.

THE PSALMS OF SOLOMON 10:8—For good and merciful is God forever, and the assemblies of Israel shall glorify the name of the Lord. The salvation of the Lord be upon the house of Israel unto everlasting gladness!

ROMANS 3:25—Whom God hath set forth to be a propitiation through faith in his blood, to declare his righteousness for the remission of sins that are past, through the forbearance of God.

MATTHEW 15:24—But he answered and said, I am not sent but unto the lost sheep of the house of Israel.

JOHN 3:16— For God so loved the world, that he gave his only begotten Son, that whosoever believeth in him should not perish, but have everlasting life.

ISAIAH 53:5—But he was wounded for our transgressions, he was bruised for our iniquities: the chastisement of our peace was upon him; and with his stripes we are healed.

JOHN 15:13—Greater love hath no man than this, that a man lay down his life for his friends.

ROMANS 4:25—Who was delivered for our offences, and was raised again for our justification.

ROMANS 8:32—He that spared not his own Son, but delivered him up for us all, how shall he not with him also freely give us all things?

HEBREWS 9:14—How much more shall the blood of Christ, who through the eternal Spirit offered himself without spot to God, purge your conscience from dead works to serve the living God?

1 PETER 3:18—For Christ also hath once suffered for sins, the just for the unjust, that he might bring us to God, being put to death in the flesh, but quickened by the Spirit.

ROMANS 5:9
Much more then, being now justified by his blood, we shall be saved from wrath through him.

1 THESSALONIANS 1:10—And to wait for his Son from heaven, whom he raised from the dead, even Jesus, which delivered us from the wrath to come.

1 THESSALONIANS 5:9-11—(9) For God hath not appointed us to wrath, but to obtain salvation by our Lord Jesus Christ, (10) Who died for us, that, whether we wake or sleep, we should live together with him. (11)

Wherefore comfort yourselves together, and edify one another, even as also ye do.

JEREMIAH 32:34—Behold, I will gather them out of all countries, whither I have driven them in mine anger, and in my fury, and in great wrath; and I will bring them again unto this place, and I will cause them to dwell safely.

JOHN 3:36—He that believeth on the Son hath everlasting life: and he that believeth not the Son shall not see life; but the wrath of God abideth on him.

SIRACH 5:6-7—(6) And say not His mercy is great; he will be pacified for the multitude of my sins: for mercy and wrath come from him, and his indignation resteth upon sinners. (7) Make no tarrying to turn to the Lord, and put not off from day to day: for suddenly shall the wrath of the Lord come forth, and in thy security thou shalt be destroyed, and perish in the day of vengeance.

2 ESDRAS 15:37—And there shall be great fearfulness and trembling upon earth: and they that see the wrath shall be afraid, and trembling shall come upon them.

BARUCH 2:13—Let thy wrath turn from us: for we are but a few left among the heathen, where thou hast scattered us.

HEBREWS 4:1-3—(1) Let us therefore fear, lest, a promise being left us of entering into his rest, any of you should seem to come short of it. (2) For unto us was the gospel preached, as well as unto them: but the word preached did not profit them, not being mixed with faith in them that heard it. (3) For we which have believed do enter into rest, as he said, As I have sworn in my wrath, if they shall enter into my rest: although the works were finished from the foundation of the world.

(Jeremiah 51:6, 44-45; Isaiah 48:20; 52:11-12; Sirach 1:21; 2 Maccabees 8:5; Matthew 3:7; 2 Corinthians 6:17)

ROMANS 5:10
For if, when we were enemies, we were reconciled to God by the death of his Son, much more, being reconciled, we shall be saved by his life.

2 CORINTHIANS 5:18-20—(18) And all things are of God, who hath reconciled us to himself by Jesus Christ, and hath given to us the ministry of reconciliation; (19) To wit, that God was in Christ, reconciling the world unto himself, not imputing their trespasses unto them; and hath committed unto us the word of reconciliation. (20) Now then we are ambassadors for Christ, as though God did beseech you by us: we pray you in Christ's stead, be ye reconciled to God.

COLOSSIANS 1:20-21—(20) And, having made peace through the blood of his cross, by him to reconcile all things unto himself; by him, I say, whether they be things in earth, or things in heaven. (21) And you, that were sometime alienated and enemies in your mind by wicked works, yet now hath he reconciled.

EPHESIANS 2:13, 16—(13) But now in Christ Jesus ye who sometimes were far off are made nigh by the blood of Christ...(16) And that he might reconcile both unto God in one body by the cross, having slain the enmity thereby

MARK 2:17—When Jesus heard it, he saith unto them, They that are whole have no need of the physician, but they that are sick: I came not to call the righteous, but sinners to repentance.

ROMANS 3:25—Whom God hath set forth to be a propitiation through faith in his blood, to declare his righteousness for the remission of sins that are past, through the forbearance of God

ROMANS 8:32—He that spared not his own Son, but delivered him up for us all, how shall he not with him also freely give us all things?

1 TIMOTHY 1:15—This is a faithful saying, and worthy of all acceptation, that Christ Jesus came into the world to save sinners; of whom I am chief

1 JOHN 1:7—But if we walk in the light, as he is in the light, we have fellowship one with another, and the blood of Jesus Christ his Son cleanseth us from all sin.

ROMANS 5:11-13

(11) And not only so, but we also joy in God through our Lord Jesus Christ, by whom we have now received the atonement. (12) Wherefore, as by one man sin entered into the world, and death by sin; and so death passed upon all men, for that all have sinned: (13) for until the law, sin was in the world: but sin is not imputed when there is no law.

Just to be clear, there was never a time when TMH's Law didn't exist, nor a time when it was or will ever be nullified. In fact, the first blood sacrifice may have happened in the Garden after the first sin since TMH clothed Adam and Eve with animal skins. *(Genesis 3:21)* However, Abel's blood sacrifice *(Genesis 4:4)*, and Cain's less than satisfactory offering *(Genesis 4:6)* are recorded, the end resulting in Abel's murder. This 'oral law' followed Noah on the ark when the clean and unclean animals were separated and counted. *(Genesis 7:1-3; The Book Of Jasher 6:1-10)*

TMH's Law was still in play after the flood, when Noah cursed Canaan for his father Ham's disgraceful behavior. *(Genesis 9:21-22, 24-25, Exodus 20:12)* Shem and Japheth's honorable response to the same situation and Noah's subsequent blessing showed the Law in full force as well. *(Genesis 9:23, 26-27)*

We also saw it with Abraham when he paid tithes to Melchizedek, king of Salem, *(Genesis 14:17-20; Hebrews 7:1-10)* as well as with Job who is said to have lived before, or during the time of Abraham. He purified his children via burnt offerings to TMH just in case they sinned against Him. *(Job 1:4-5)* So if the Law always existed, but sin didn't, what is Paul referring to here? Simple. There was never a time when the Law didn't exist, so Paul must be referring to <u>Moses' written deliverance of the Law via the Old Covenant</u>, because, as we've seen above, TMH's Law has existed in oral form *(Genesis 26:5)* from the beginning.

> **GENESIS 2:17**—But of the tree of the knowledge of good and evil, thou shalt not eat of it: for in the day that thou eatest thereof thou shalt surely die.
>
> **GENESIS 3:6**—And when the woman saw that the tree was good for food, and that it was pleasant to the eyes, and a tree to be desired to make one wise, she took of the fruit thereof, and did eat, and gave also unto her husband with her; and he did eat.
>
> **GENESIS 3:19**—In the sweat of thy face shalt thou eat bread, till thou return unto the ground; for out of it wast thou taken: for dust thou art, and unto dust shalt thou return.
>
> **1 CORINTHIANS 15:21-22**—(21) For since by man came death, by man came also the resurrection of the dead. (22) For as in Adam all die, even so in Christ shall all be made alive.
>
> **1 JOHN 3:4**—Whosoever committeth sin transgresseth also the law: for sin is the transgression of the law.
>
> **ROMANS 4:15**—Because the law worketh wrath: for where no law is, there is no transgression.

ROMANS 5:14
Nevertheless death reigned from Adam to Moses, even over them that had not sinned after the similitude of Adam's transgression, who is the figure of him that was to come.

1 CORINTHIANS 15:21-22—(21) For since by man came death, by man came also the resurrection of the dead. (22) For as in Adam all die, even so in Christ shall all be made alive.

1 CORINTHIANS 15:45—And so it is written, The first man Adam was made a living soul; the last Adam was made a quickening spirit.

ROMANS 8:20-21—(20) For the creature was made subject to vanity, not willingly, but by reason of him who hath subjected the same in hope, (21) Because the creature itself also shall be delivered from the bondage of corruption into the glorious liberty of the children of God.

MATTHEW 1:21—And she shall bring forth a son, and thou shalt call his name JESUS: for he shall save his people from their sins.

ROMANS 5:15-16
(15) But not as the offence, so also is the free gift. For if through the offence of one many be dead, much more the grace of God, and the gift by grace, which is by one man, Jesus Christ, hath abounded unto many. (16) And not as it was by one that sinned, so is the gift: for the judgment was by one to condemnation, but the free gift is of many offences unto justification.

ISAIAH 53:11—He shall see of the travail of his soul, and shall be satisfied: by his knowledge shall my righteous servant justify many; for he shall bear their iniquities.

1 CORINTHIANS 15:20—(20) But now is Christ risen from the dead, and become the firstfruits of them that slept. (21) For since by man came death, by man came also the resurrection of the dead. (22) For as in Adam all die, even so in Christ shall all be made alive. (23) But every man in his own order: Christ the firstfruits; afterward they that are Christ's at his coming.

MATTHEW 1:21—And she shall bring forth a son, and thou shalt call his name JESUS: for he shall save his people from their sins.

2 CORINTHIANS 5:14—For the love of Christ constraineth us; because we thus judge, that if one died for all, then were all dead.

ROMANS 5:17
For if by one man's offence death reigned by one; much more they which receive abundance of grace and of the gift of righteousness shall reign in life by one, Jesus Christ.

1 CORINTHIANS 15:20-23—(20) But now is Christ risen from the dead, and become the firstfruits of them that slept. (21) For since by man came death, by man came also the resurrection of the dead. (22) For as in Adam all die, even so in Christ shall all be made alive. (23) But every man in his own order: Christ the firstfruits; afterward they that are Christ's at his coming.

1 CORINTHIANS 15:45-49—(45) And so it is written, The first man Adam was made a living soul; the last Adam was made a quickening spirit. (46) Howbeit that was not first which is spiritual, but that which is natural; and afterward that which is spiritual. (47) The first man is of the earth, earthy: the second man is the Lord from heaven. (48) As is the earthy, such are they also that are earthy: and as is the heavenly, such are they also that are heavenly. (49) And as we have borne the image of the earthy, we shall also bear the image of the heavenly.

GENESIS 2:15-16-17—(15) And the LORD God took the man, and put him into the garden of Eden to dress it and to keep it. (16) And the LORD God commanded the man, saying, Of every tree of the garden thou mayest freely eat: (17) But of the tree of the knowledge of good and evil, thou shalt not eat of it: for in the day that thou eatest thereof thou shalt surely die.

GENESIS 3:6-7—(6) And when the woman saw that the tree was good for food, and that it was pleasant to the eyes, and a tree to be desired to make one wise, she took of the fruit thereof, and did eat, and gave also unto her husband with her; and he did eat. (7) And the eyes of them both were opened, and they knew that they were naked; and they sewed fig leaves together, and made themselves aprons.

GENESIS 3:14-19—(14) And the LORD God said unto the serpent, Because thou hast done this, thou art cursed above all cattle, and above every beast of the field; upon thy belly shalt thou go, and dust shalt thou eat all the days of thy life: (15) And I will put enmity between thee and the woman, and between thy seed and her seed; it shall bruise thy head, and thou shalt bruise his heel. (16) Unto the woman he said, I will greatly multiply thy sorrow and thy conception; in sorrow thou shalt bring forth children; and thy desire shall be to thy husband, and he shall rule over thee. (17) And unto Adam he said, Because thou hast hearkened unto the voice of thy wife, and hast eaten of the tree, of which I commanded thee, saying, Thou shalt not eat of it: cursed is the ground for thy sake; in sorrow shalt thou eat of it all the days of thy life; (18) Thorns also and thistles shall it bring forth to thee; and thou shalt eat the herb of the field; (19) In the sweat of thy face shalt thou eat bread, till thou return unto the ground; for out of it wast thou taken: for dust thou art, and unto dust shalt thou return.

ROMANS 5:18-19

(18) Therefore as by the offence of one judgment came upon all men to condemnation; even so by the righteousness of one the free gift came upon all men unto justification of life. (19) For as by one man's disobedience many were made sinners, so by the obedience of one shall many be made righteous.

ISAIAH 53:11-12—(11) He shall see of the travail of his soul, and shall be satisfied: by his knowledge shall my righteous servant justify many; for he shall bear their iniquities. (12) Therefore will I divide him a portion with the great, and he shall divide the spoil with the strong; because he hath poured out his soul unto death: and he was numbered with the transgressors; and he bare the sin of many, and made intercession for the transgressors.

ROMANS 4:21-25—(21) And being fully persuaded that, what he had promised, he was able also to perform. (22) And therefore it was imputed to him for righteousness. (23) Now it was not written for his sake alone, that it was imputed to him; (24) But for us also, to whom it shall be imputed, if we believe on him that raised up Jesus our Lord from the dead; (25) Who was delivered for our offences, and was raised again for our justification.

JOHN 12:32—And I, if I be lifted up from the earth, will draw all men unto me.

1 CORINTHIANS 15:21—For since by man came death, by man came also the resurrection of the dead.

1 CORINTHIANS 15:45—And so it is written, The first man Adam was made a living soul; the last Adam was made a quickening spirit.

HEBREWS 2:9—But we see Jesus, who was made a little lower than the angels for the suffering of death, crowned with glory and honour; that he by the grace of God should taste death for every man.

PHILIPPIANS 2:8-9—(8) And being found in fashion as a man, he humbled himself, and became obedient unto death, even the death of the cross. (9) Wherefore God also hath highly exalted him, and given him a name, which is above every name.

ROMANS 5:20-21

(20) Moreover the law entered, that the offence might abound. But where sin abounded, grace did much more abound: (21) that as sin hath reigned unto death, even so might grace reign through righteousness unto eternal life by Jesus Christ our Lord.

JOHN 1:17—For the law was given by Moses, but grace and truth came by Jesus Christ.

JOHN 15:22—If I had not come and spoken unto them, they had not had sin: but now they have no cloak for their sin.

ROMANS 4:15—Because the law worketh wrath: for where no law is, there is no transgression.

1 TIMOTHY 1:14—And the grace of our Lord was exceeding abundant with faith and love which is in Christ Jesus.

ROMANS 2:7—To them who by patient continuance in well doing seek for glory and honour and immortality, eternal life

LUKE 7:47—Wherefore I say unto thee, her sins, which are many, are forgiven; for she loved much: but to whom little is forgiven, the same loveth little.

ROMANS 6

ROMANS 6:1-3
(1) **What shall we say then? Shall we continue in sin, that grace may abound?** (2) **God forbid. How shall we that are dead to sin, live any longer therein?** (3) **Know ye not, that so many of us as were baptized into Jesus Christ were baptized into his death?**

1 JOHN 3:4-10—(4) Whosoever committeth sin transgresseth also the law: for sin is the transgression of the law. (5) And ye know that he was manifested to take away our sins; and in him is no sin. (6) Whosoever abideth in him sinneth not: whosoever sinneth hath not seen him, neither known him. (7) Little children, let no man deceive you: he that doeth righteousness is righteous, even as he is righteous. (8) He that committeth sin is of the devil; for the devil sinneth from the beginning. For this purpose the Son of God was manifested, that he might destroy the works of the devil. (9) Whosoever is born of God doth not commit sin; for his seed remaineth in him: and he cannot sin, because he is born of God. (10) In this the children of God are manifest, and the children of the devil: whosoever doeth not righteousness is not of God, neither he that loveth not his brother.

ROMANS 5:21—That as sin hath reigned unto death, even so might grace reign through righteousness unto eternal life by Jesus Christ our Lord.

GALATIANS 2:19-21—(19) For I through the law am dead to the law, that I might live unto God. (20) I am crucified with Christ: nevertheless I live; yet not I, but Christ liveth in me: and the life which I now live in the flesh I live by the faith of the Son of God, who loved me, and gave himself for me (21) I do not frustrate the grace of God: for if righteousness come by the law, then Christ is dead in vain.

GALATIANS 3:27—For as many of you as have been baptized into Christ have put on Christ.

COLOSSIANS 3:3-11—(3) For ye are dead, and your life is hid with Christ in God. (4) When Christ, who is our life, shall appear, then shall ye also appear with him in glory. (5) Mortify therefore your members which are upon the earth; fornication, uncleanness, inordinate affection, evil concupiscence, and covetousness, which is idolatry: (6) For which things' sake the wrath of God cometh on the children of disobedience: (7) In the which ye also walked some time, when ye lived in them. (8) But now ye also put off all these; anger, wrath, malice, blasphemy, filthy communication out of your mouth. (9) Lie not one to another, seeing that ye have put off the old man with his deeds; (10) And have put on the new man, which is renewed in knowledge after the image of him that created him: (11) Where there is neither Greek nor Jew, circumcision nor uncircumcision, Barbarian, Scythian, bond nor free: but Christ is all, and in all.

ROMANS 6:4-5

(4) Therefore we are buried with him by baptism into death: that like as Christ was raised up from the dead by the glory of the Father, even so we also should walk in newness of life. (5) For if we have been planted together in the likeness of his death, we shall be also in the likeness of his resurrection:

2 CORINTHIANS 5:17—Therefore if any man be in Christ, he is a new creature: old things are passed away; behold, all things are become new.

COLOSSIANS 3:10—And have put on the new man, which is renewed in knowledge after the image of him that created him.

ROMANS 8:11—But if the Spirit of him that raised up Jesus from the dead dwell in you, he that raised up Christ from the dead shall also quicken your mortal bodies by his Spirit that dwelleth in you.

1 CORINTHIANS 6:14—And God hath both raised up the Lord, and will also raise up us by his own power.

JOHN 11:40—Jesus saith unto her, Said I not unto thee, that, if thou wouldest believe, thou shouldest see the glory of God?

GALATIANS 3:27—For as many of you as have been baptized into Christ have put on Christ.

GALATIANS 6:15—For in Christ Jesus neither circumcision availeth any thing, nor uncircumcision, but a new creature.

EPHESIANS 2:5—Even when we were dead in sins, hath quickened us together with Christ, (by grace ye are saved;)

EPHESIANS 4:23-24—(23) And be renewed in the spirit of your mind; (24) And that ye put on the new man, which after God is created in righteousness and true holiness.

PHILIPPIANS 3:10-11—(10) That I may know him, and the power of his resurrection, and the fellowship of his sufferings, being made conformable unto his death; (11) If by any means I might attain unto the resurrection of the dead.

COLOSSIANS 2:12—Buried with him in baptism, wherein also ye are risen with him through the faith of the operation of God, who hath raised him from the dead.

ROMANS 6:6-7
(6) Knowing this, that our old man is crucified with him, that the body of sin might be destroyed, that henceforth we should not serve sin. (7) For he that is dead is freed from sin.

EPHESIANS 4:22—That ye put off concerning the former conversation the old man, which is corrupt according to the deceitful lusts

GALATIANS 5:24—And they that are Christ's have crucified the flesh with the affections and lusts.

GALATIANS 2:20—I am crucified with Christ: nevertheless I live; yet not I, but Christ liveth in me: and the life which I now live in the flesh I live by the faith of the Son of God, who loved me, and gave himself for me.

GALATIANS 6:14—But God forbid that I should glory, save in the cross of our Lord Jesus Christ, by whom the world is crucified unto me, and I unto the world.

COLOSSIANS 2:11—In whom also ye are circumcised with the circumcision made without hands, in putting off the body of the sins of the flesh by the circumcision of Christ

1 PETER 4:1—Forasmuch then as Christ hath suffered for us in the flesh, arm yourselves likewise with the same mind: for he that hath suffered in the flesh hath ceased from sin.

LUKE 9:24—For whosoever will save his life shall lose it: but whosoever will lose his life for my sake, the same shall save it

ROMANS 6:8-10
(8) Now if we be dead with Christ, we believe that we shall also live with him: (9) knowing that Christ being raised from the dead dieth no more; death hath no more dominion over him. (10) For in that he died, he died unto sin once: but in that he liveth, he liveth unto God.

2 TIMOTHY 2:11—It is a faithful saying: For if we be dead with him, we shall also live with him.

LUKE 20:38—For he is not a God of the dead, but of the living: for all live unto him.

HEBREWS 9:27-28—(27) And as it is appointed unto men once to die, but after this the judgment: (28) So Christ was once offered to bear the sins of many; and unto them that look for him shall he appear the second time without sin unto salvation.

HEBREWS 10:10—By the which will we are sanctified through the offering of the body of Jesus Christ once for all.

REVELATION 1:18—I am he that liveth, and was dead; and, behold, I am alive for evermore, Amen; and have the keys of hell and of death.

ROMANS 6:11-12

(11) **Likewise reckon ye also yourselves to be dead indeed unto sin, but alive unto God through Jesus Christ our Lord.** (12) **Let not sin therefore reign in your mortal body, that ye should obey it in the lusts thereof.**

PSALMS 19:13—Keep back thy servant also from presumptuous sins; let them not have dominion over me: then shall I be upright, and I shall be innocent from the great transgression.

PSALMS 119:133—Order my steps in thy word: and let not any iniquity have dominion over me.

PSALMS 51:9-12—(9) Hide thy face from my sins, and blot out all mine iniquities. (10) Create in me a clean heart, O God; and renew a right spirit within me. (11) Cast me not away from thy presence; and take not thy holy spirit from me. (12) Restore unto me the joy of thy salvation; and uphold me with thy free spirit.

ROMANS 7:4, 6—(4) Wherefore, my brethren, ye also are become dead to the law by the body of Christ; that ye should be married to another, even to him who is raised from the dead, that we should bring forth fruit unto God...(6) But now we are delivered from the law, that being dead wherein we were held; that we should serve in newness of spirit, and not in the oldness of the letter.

GALATIANS 2:19—For I through the law am dead to the law, that I might live unto God.

ROMANS 6:13-14

(13) Neither yield ye your members as instruments of unrighteousness unto sin: but yield yourselves unto God, as those that are alive from the dead, and your members as instruments of righteousness unto God. (14) For sin shall not have dominion over you: for ye are not under the law, but under grace.

ROMANS 12:1—I beseech you therefore, brethren, by the mercies of God, that ye present your bodies a living sacrifice, holy, acceptable unto God, which is your reasonable service.

ROMANS 7:4-6—(4) Wherefore, my brethren, ye also are become dead to the law by the body of Christ; that ye should be married to another, even to him who is raised from the dead, that we should bring forth fruit unto God. (5) For when we were in the flesh, the motions of sins, which were by the law, did work in our members to bring forth fruit unto death. (6) But now we are delivered from the law, that being dead wherein we were held; that we should serve in newness of spirit, and not in the oldness of the letter.

ROMANS 8:2—For the law of the Spirit of life in Christ Jesus hath made me free from the law of sin and death.

GALATIANS 5:18—But if ye be led of the Spirit, ye are not under the law.

COLOSSIANS 3:5—Mortify therefore your members which are upon the earth; fornication, uncleanness, inordinate affection, evil concupiscence, and covetousness, which is idolatry

1 PETER 4:2—That he no longer should live the rest of his time in the flesh to the lusts of men, but to the will of God.

JAMES 4:1—From whence come wars and fightings among you? Come they not hence, even of your lusts that war in your members?

1 PETER 2:24—Who his own self bare our sins in his own body on the tree, that we, being dead to sins, should live unto righteousness: by whose stripes ye were healed.

JOHN 1:17—For the law was given by Moses, but grace and truth came by Jesus Christ.

ROMANS 6:15-16

(15) What then? Shall we sin, because we are not under the law, but under grace? God forbid. (16) Know ye not, that to whom ye yield yourselves servants to obey, his servants ye are to whom ye obey; whether of sin unto death, or of obedience unto righteousness?

MATTHEW 6:24—No man can serve two masters: for either he will hate the one, and love the other; or else he will hold to the one, and despise the other. Ye cannot serve God and mammon.

JOHN 8:34—Jesus answered them, Verily, verily, I say unto you, Whosoever committeth sin is the servant of sin.

ROMANS 6:10—For in that he died, he died unto sin once: but in that he liveth, he liveth unto God.

2 PETER 2:19—While they promise them liberty, they themselves are the servants of corruption: for of whom a man is overcome, of the same is he brought in bondage.

JOSHUA 24:15—And if it seem evil unto you to serve the LORD, choose you this day whom ye will serve; whether the gods which your fathers served that were on the other side of the flood, or the gods of the Amorites, in whose land ye dwell: but as for me and my house, we will serve the LORD.

ROMANS 6:17-18

(17) But God be thanked, that ye were the servants of sin, but ye have obeyed from the heart that form of doctrine, which was delivered you. (18) Being then made free from sin, ye became the servants of righteousness.

1 CORINTHIANS 7:22—For he that is called in the Lord, being a servant, is the Lord's freeman: likewise also he that is called, being free, is Christ's servant.

1 PETER 2:16—As free, and not using your liberty for a cloak of maliciousness, but as the servants of God.

GALATIANS 5:1—Stand fast therefore in the liberty wherewith Christ hath made us free, and be not entangled again with the yoke of bondage.

JOHN 8:32—And ye shall know the truth, and the truth shall make you free.

(2 Timothy 1:13; Matthew 25:19-21; John 3:7; Revelation 1:1, 19:10, Amos 3:7)

ROMANS 6:19
I speak after the manner of men because of the infirmity of your flesh: for as ye have yielded your members servants to uncleanness and to iniquity unto iniquity; even so now yield your members servants to righteousness unto holiness.

1 CORINTHIANS 6:15—Know ye not that your bodies are the members of Christ? Shall I then take the members of Christ, and make them the members of an harlot? God forbid.

1 CORINTHIANS 6:19—What? Know ye not that your body is the temple of the Holy Ghost which is in you, which ye have of God, and ye are not your own.

ROMANS 6:13—Neither yield ye your members as instruments of unrighteousness unto sin: but yield yourselves unto God, as those that are alive from the dead, and your members as instruments of righteousness unto God.

ROMANS 6:20-21
(20) For when ye were the servants of sin, ye were free from righteousness. (21) What fruit had ye then in those things whereof ye are now ashamed? For the end of those things is death.

JOHN 8:34—Jesus answered them, Verily, verily, I say unto you, Whosoever committeth sin is the servant of sin.

1 TIMOTHY 5:6—But she that liveth in pleasure is dead while she liveth.

2 PETER 2:10-13—(10) But chiefly them that walk after the flesh in the lust of uncleanness, and despise government. Presumptuous are they, selfwilled, they are not afraid to speak evil of dignities. (11) Whereas angels, which are greater in power and might, bring not railing accusation against them before the Lord. (12) But these, as natural brute beasts, made to be taken and destroyed, speak evil of the things that they understand not; and shall utterly perish in their own corruption; (13) And shall receive the reward of unrighteousness, as they that count it pleasure to riot in the day time.

ROMANS 1:32—Who knowing the judgment of God, that they which commit such things are worthy of death, not only do the same, but have pleasure in them that do them.

ROMANS 7:5—For when we were in the flesh, the motions of sins, which were by the law, did work in our members to bring forth fruit unto death.

ROMANS 8:6, 13—(6) For to be carnally minded is death; but to be spiritually minded is life and peace...(13) For if ye live after the flesh, ye shall die: but if ye through the Spirit do mortify the deeds of the body, ye shall live.

ROMANS 6:22-23

(22) But now being made free from sin, and become servants to God, ye have your fruit unto holiness, and the end everlasting life. (23) For the wages of sin is death; but the gift of God is eternal life through Jesus Christ our Lord.

ROMANS 2:7—To them who by patient continuance in well doing seek for glory and honour and immortality, eternal life.

ROMANS 5:12-17—(12) Wherefore, as by one man sin entered into the world, and death by sin; and so death passed upon all men, for that all have sinned. (13) (For until the law sin was in the world: but sin is not imputed when there is no law. (14) Nevertheless death reigned from Adam to Moses, even over them that had not sinned after the similitude of Adam's transgression, who is the figure of him that was to come. (15) But not as the offence, so also is the free gift. For if through the offence of one many be dead, much more the grace of God, and the gift by grace, which is by one man, Jesus Christ, hath abounded unto many. (16) And not as it was by one that sinned, so is the gift: for the judgment was by one to condemnation, but the free gift is of many offences unto justification. (17) For if by one man's offence death reigned by one; much more they which receive abundance of grace and of the gift of righteousness shall reign in life by one, Jesus Christ.)

ROMANS 6:18—Being then made free from sin, ye became the servants of righteousness.

1 PETER 1:3-4—(3) Blessed be the God and Father of our Lord Jesus Christ, which according to his abundant mercy hath begotten us again unto a lively hope by the resurrection of Jesus Christ from the dead, (4) To an inheritance incorruptible, and undefiled, and that fadeth not away, reserved in heaven for you.

GENESIS 2:17—But of the tree of the knowledge of good and evil, thou shalt not eat of it: for in the day that thou eatest thereof thou shalt surely die.

ROMANS 7

ROMANS 7:1-3

(1) Know ye not, brethren, (for I speak to them that know the law,) how that the law hath dominion over a man as long as he liveth? (2) For the woman which hath an husband is bound by the law to her husband so long as he liveth; but if the husband be dead, she is loosed from the law of her husband. (3) So then if, while her husband liveth, she be married to another man, she shall be called an adulteress: but if her husband be dead, she is free from that law; so that she is no adulteress, though she be married to another man.

A woman who weds a man has made a covenant with him. If he dies, she is no longer bound by this covenant, and therefore would not be considered an adulteress if she marries another man (entering into a second—or new—covenant) because the first covenant would have been dissolved. *However*, notice the overall covenant law of marriage *still stands*—that a woman isn't free to marry again unless she's a widow. So in essence, the covenant law of marriage is a law within THE LAW, the latter of which is still very much in effect.

In other words, TMH's law is eternal.

DEUTERONOMY 24:1-4—(1) When a man hath taken a wife, and married her, and it come to pass that she find no favor in his eyes, because he hath found some uncleanness in her: then let him write her a bill of divorcement, and give it in her hand, and send her out of his house. (2) And when she is departed out of his house, she may go and be another man's wife. (3) And if the latter husband hate her, and write her a bill of divorcement, and giveth it in her hand, and sendeth her out of his house; or if the latter husband die, which took her to be his wife; (4) Her former husband, which sent her away, may not take her again to be his wife, after that she is defiled; for that is abomination before the LORD: and thou shalt not cause the land to sin, which the LORD thy God giveth thee for an inheritance.

JEREMIAH 3:1—They say, If a man put away his wife, and she go from him, and become another man's, shall he return unto her again? Shall not that land be greatly polluted? But thou hast played the harlot with many lovers; yet return again to me, saith the LORD.

MATTHEW 5:32—But I say unto you, That whosoever shall put away his wife, saving for the cause of fornication, causeth her to commit adultery: and whosoever shall marry her that is divorced committeth adultery.

1 CORINTHIANS 7:39—The wife is bound by the law as long as her husband liveth; but if her husband be dead, she is at liberty to be married to whom she will; only in the Lord.

ROMANS 7:4
Wherefore, my brethren, ye also are become dead to the law by the body of Christ; that ye should be married to another, even to him who is raised from the dead, that we should bring forth fruit unto God.

Once we consider the point made in *Romans 7:1-3*, that the first husband is dead, yet the eternal Law still stands, we see how Messiah's death freed us from the law of sin and death. *(Romans 8:2)*

2 CORINTHIANS 5:21—For he hath made him to be sin for us, who knew no sin; that we might be made the righteousness of God in him.

The death sentence provision within the Law was fulfilled by Messiah's sacrifice, once and for all. Death was the penalty (the law of sin and death), but He paid the price for us, making the need for perpetual animal sacrifices obsolete. This was not an alteration or an abolishment of the law. It was the fulfillment of that *law within the Law*.

Likewise, we die to the law of sin within our flesh, *(Romans 7:23)* and are reborn. *(John 3:3)* We are therefore new creatures, *(2 Corinthians 5:17, Galatians 6:15)* for the old man/woman has passed away. This frees us to marry another—we who were once defiled, have been made clean. *(John 15:3; Acts 10:15)* Our husband is the risen Messiah, who personifies the New Covenant, and the law of the spirit. *(Romans 8:2)* This same Messiah was TMH's complete Word—the Law (torah) & the prophets—before He died, and He was the complete Word after His resurrection. Through this sacred marriage, we 'know' Him and He 'knows' us. By this He then comes into us (His wife) and plants the seed of His word within our hearts.

1 JOHN 3:9—Whosoever is born of God doth not commit sin; for his seed remaineth in him: and he cannot sin, because he is born of God.

JEREMIAH 31-31-34—(31) Behold, the days come, saith the LORD, that I will make a new covenant with the house of Israel, and with the house of Judah: (32) Not according to the covenant that I made with their fathers in the day that I took them by the hand to bring them out of the land of Egypt; which my covenant they brake, although I was an husband unto them, saith the LORD: (33) But this shall be the covenant that I will make with the house of Israel; After those days, saith the LORD, I will put my law in their inward parts, and write it in their hearts; and will be their God, and they shall be my people. (34) And they shall teach no more every man his neighbour, and every man his brother, saying, Know the LORD: for they shall all know me, from the least of them unto the greatest of them, saith the LORD: for I will forgive their iniquity, and I will remember their sin no more.

ROMANS 8:2—For the law of the Spirit of life in Christ Jesus hath made me free from the law of sin and death.

GALATIANS 2:19—For I through the law am dead to the law, that I might live unto God.

GALATIANS 5:18-22—(18) But if ye be led of the Spirit, ye are not under the law. (19) Now the works of the flesh are manifest, which are these; Adultery, fornication, uncleanness, lasciviousness, (20) Idolatry, witchcraft, hatred, variance, emulations, wrath, strife, seditions, heresies, (21) Envyings, murders, drunkenness, revelings, and such like: of the which I tell you before, as I have also told you in time past, that they which do such things shall not inherit the kingdom of God. (22) But the fruit of the Spirit is love, joy, peace, longsuffering, gentleness, goodness, faith...

EPHESIANS 2:15-16—(15) Having abolished in his flesh the enmity, even the law of commandments contained in ordinances; for to make in himself of twain one new man, so making peace; (16) And that he might reconcile both unto God in one body by the cross, having slain the enmity thereby:

COLOSSIANS 1:22—In the body of his flesh through death, to present you holy and unblameable and unreproveable in his sight

COLOSSIANS 2:14—Blotting out the handwriting of ordinances that was against us, which was contrary to us, and took it out of the way, nailing it to his cross.

(Psalms 40:7; John 1:1, 14; Hebrews 10:7)

ROMANS 7:5
For when we were in the flesh, the motions of sins, which were by the law, did work in our members to bring forth fruit unto death.

We transgressed our old covenant continuously because we followed it in the flesh. These transgressions (sins) resulted in the penalty (curse) of death. This was the ultimate consequence (curse) of breaking the old covenant, for the wages of sin is death *(Romans 6:23)*.

ROMANS 6:13—Neither yield ye your members as instruments of unrighteousness unto sin: but yield yourselves unto God, as those that are alive from the dead, and your members as instruments of righteousness unto God.

ROMANS 6:21—What fruit had ye then in those things whereof ye are now ashamed? For the end of those things is death.

1 CORINTHIANS 6:15—Know ye not that your bodies are the members of Christ? shall I then take the members of Christ, and make them the members of an harlot? God forbid.

GALATIANS 5:19—Now the works of the flesh are manifest, which are these; Adultery, fornication, uncleanness, lasciviousness

JAMES 1:15—Then when lust hath conceived, it bringeth forth sin: and sin, when it is finished, bringeth forth death.

ROMANS 7:6
But now we are delivered from the law, that being dead wherein we were held; that we should serve in newness of spirit, and not in the oldness of the letter.

Here Paul isn't saying we're being delivered or made free from TMH's Law (Torah) overall since it's still a sin to kill, covet, dishonor the Sabbath, eat shellfish, and all the other commandments we're always held accountable for. So he must be talking about something else, and that something else is the **penalty** (curse of the law) Messiah endured via His sacrifice for our sins.

That penalty was death.

While death is the ultimate curse, (Galatians 3:13) the curses, as outlined in *Deuteronomy 28:15-68* are included in the 'curse of the law' as well.

We must remember, TMH's Law is *not* a curse. Again and again throughout scripture, we read that TMH's law is perfect (Psalms 19:7), holy (Romans 7:12, 2 Peter 2:21), good (1 Timothy 1:8; Romans 7:16), and the truth. (Psalms 119:142)

There *are* curses within the Law, *(Deuteronomy 28:15-68, 30:7)* but the Law in itself is not a curse. It's a perfect standard that could never make us perfect in our imperfect, sinful flesh. That is, *not* without a renewal of the mind and spirit. (Matthew 5:48, Ephesians 4:23, Colossians 3:10, 2 Corinthians 4:16)

This is why the Law must be written on our hearts and minds forever. *(Jeremiah 31:31-34)*

So for those who think TMH's Law is a curse, why would He write a curse *into* our hearts and minds forever? He wouldn't.

Woe to them who call good evil and evil good! *(Isaiah 5:20)*

Again, the *curse of the Law* is the penalty imbedded within the Law. That penalty is triggered because of sin, and sin is transgression of the Law. We must obey TMH's commandments, however now, thanks to TMH's love and grace, we do so by His Spirit. This is the circumcision of the heart, AKA: being born again. This circumcision process helps our spirit overpower and subdue our sinful flesh.

COLOSSIANS 2:11—In whom also ye are circumcised with the circumcision made without hands, in putting off the body of the sins of the flesh by the circumcision of Christ

HEBREWS 10:16—For this is the covenant that I will make with the house of Israel after those days, saith the Lord; I will put my laws into their mind, and write them in their hearts: and I will be to them a God, and they shall be to me a people.

JEREMIAH 31:31-33—(31) Behold, the days come, saith the LORD, that I will make a new covenant with the house of Israel, and with the house of Judah: (32) Not according to the covenant that I made with their fathers in the day that I took them by the hand to bring them out of the land of Egypt; which my covenant they brake, although I was an husband unto them, saith the LORD: (33) But this shall be the covenant that I will make with the house of Israel; After those days, saith the LORD, I will put my law in their inward parts, and write it in their hearts; and will be their God, and they shall be my people.

JOHN 3:3—Jesus answered and said unto him, Verily, verily, I say unto thee, except a man be born again, he cannot see the kingdom of God.

ROMANS 2:29—But he is a Jew, which is one inwardly; and circumcision is that of the heart, in the spirit, and not in the letter; whose praise is not of men, but of God.

1 PETER 1:18-25—(18) Forasmuch as ye know that ye were not redeemed with corruptible things, as silver and gold, from your vain conversation received by tradition from your fathers; (19) But with the precious blood of Christ, as of a lamb without blemish and without spot: (20) Who verily was foreordained before the foundation of the world, but was manifest in these last times for you, (21) Who by him do believe in God, that raised him up from the dead, and gave him glory; that your faith and hope might be in God. (22) Seeing ye have purified your souls in obeying the truth through the Spirit unto unfeigned love of the brethren, see that ye love one another with a pure heart fervently: (23) Being born again, not of corruptible seed, but of incorruptible, by the word of God, which liveth and abideth for ever. (24) For all flesh is as grass, and all the glory of man as the flower of grass. The grass withereth, and the flower thereof falleth away: (25) But the word of the Lord endureth for ever. And this is the word, which by the gospel is preached unto you.

(2 Corinthians 3:6; Jeremiah 4:4; Deuteronomy 30:6)

ROMANS 7:7-8

(7) What shall we say then? Is the law sin? God forbid. Nay, I had not known sin, but by the law: for I had not known lust, except the law had said, Thou shalt not covet. (8) But sin, taking occasion by the commandment, wrought in me all manner of concupiscence. For without the law sin was dead.

Paul makes it clear that the Law isn't sin or a curse. The curse of the Law comes from *breaking* the Law *via* sin. And sin (i.e. lawlessness/iniquity) is the flesh's natural reaction to the Law, a reaction that manifests in rebellion against TMH's righteous commandments. We overcome this fleshly rebellion by meditating on TMH word and walking in the newness of the spirit through faith. *(Joshua 1:8; Psalms 119:9-16; James 1:22-25)*

ROMANS 3:20, 28—Therefore by the deeds of the law there shall no flesh be justified in his sight: for by the law is the knowledge of sin...(28) Therefore we conclude that a man is justified by faith without the deeds of the law.

ROMANS 4:15—Because the law worketh wrath: for where no law is, there is no transgression.

ROMANS 8:9—But ye are not in the flesh, but in the Spirit, if so be that the Spirit of God dwell in you. Now if any man have not the Spirit of Christ, he is none of his.

1 CORINTHIANS 15:56—The sting of death is sin; and the strength of sin is the law.

GALATIANS 5:13—For, brethren, ye have been called unto liberty; only use not liberty for an occasion to the flesh, but by love serve one another.

1 JOHN 3:9—Whosoever is born of God doth not commit sin; for his seed remaineth in him: and he cannot sin, because he is born of God.

ROMANS 7:9-10

(9) For I was alive without the law once: but when the commandment came, sin revived, and I died. (10) And the commandment, which was ordained to life, I found to be unto death.

TMH's commandments are good. They were meant to keep us safe, healthy, and in right standing with Him. But the sin within takes every occasion to entice us to rebel, which results in wrath. In essence, our flesh is in a constant war with the good, righteous laws of our Creator, Father, and God.

As it is written, sin is the transgression of the Law, *(1 John 3:4)* and the wages of sin is death. *(Romans 6:23)* It is only by TMH's Spirit that we can obey Him and produce good works. *(Philippians 2:12-13)* Without His Spirit, our flesh remains at constant war with TMH, a war we cannot win.

LEVITICUS 18:5—Ye shall therefore keep my statutes, and my judgments: which if a man do, he shall live in them: I am the LORD.

DEUTERONOMY 4:1—Now therefore hearken, O Israel, unto the statutes and unto the judgments, which I teach you, for to do them, that ye may live, and go in and possess the land, which the LORD God of your fathers giveth you.

DEUTERONOMY 30:17-19—(17) But if thine heart turn away, so that thou wilt not hear, but shalt be drawn away, and worship other gods, and serve them; (18) I denounce unto you this day, that ye shall surely perish, and that ye shall not prolong your days upon the land, whither thou passest over Jordan to go to possess it. (19) I call heaven and earth to record this day against you, that I have set before you life and death, blessing and cursing: therefore choose life, that both thou and thy seed may live.

EZEKIEL 20:11-13, 21—(11) And I gave them my statutes, and shewed them my judgments, which if a man do, he shall even live in them. (12) Moreover also I gave them my Sabbaths, to be a sign between me and them, that they might know that I am the LORD that sanctify them. (13) But the house of Israel rebelled against me in the wilderness: they walked not in my statutes, and they despised my judgments, which if a man do, he shall even live in them; and my sabbaths they greatly polluted: then I said, I would pour out my fury upon them in the wilderness, to consume them...(21) Notwithstanding the children rebelled against me: they walked not in my statutes, neither kept my judgments to do them, which if a man do, he shall even live in them; they polluted my sabbaths: then I said, I would pour out my fury upon them, to accomplish my anger against them in the wilderness.

In the gospels, Messiah basically repeated what Moses wrote in the Torah—that following TMH's commands are the ways to life. However, as *Matthew 19:16-22* demonstrates, and the scriptures that follow it below show, our flesh is at war with His perfect laws:

MATTHEW 19:16-22—(16) And, behold, one came and said unto him, Good Master, what good thing shall I do, that I may have eternal life? (17) And he said unto him, Why callest thou me good? There is none good but one, that is, God: <u>but if thou wilt enter into life, keep the commandments.</u> (18) He saith unto him, Which? Jesus said, Thou shalt do no murder, Thou shalt not commit adultery, Thou shalt not steal, Thou shalt not bear false witness, (19) Honour thy father and thy mother: and, Thou shalt love thy neighbour as thyself. (20) The young man saith unto him, All these things have I kept from my youth up: what lack I yet? (21) Jesus said unto him, <u>If thou wilt be perfect, go and sell that thou hast, and give to the poor, and thou shalt have treasure in heaven: and come and follow me.</u> (22) But when the young man heard that saying, <u>he went away sorrowful: for he had great possessions.</u>

LUKE 10:25-28—(25) And, behold, a certain lawyer stood up, and tempted him, saying, <u>Master, what shall I do to inherit eternal life?</u> (26) He said unto him, What is written in the law? How readest thou? (27) And he answering said, <u>Thou shalt love the Lord thy God with all thy heart, and with all thy soul, and with all thy strength, and with all thy mind; and thy neighbour as thyself.</u> (28) And he said unto him, Thou hast answered right: this do and thou shalt live.

MATTHEW 26:41—Watch and pray, that ye enter not into temptation: the spirit indeed is willing, but the flesh is weak.

ROMANS 10:4-11—(4) <u>For Christ is the end of the law for righteousness to every one that believeth.</u> (5) For Moses describeth the righteousness which is of the law, That the man which doeth those things shall live by them. (6) But the <u>righteousness, which is of faith,</u> speaketh on this wise, Say not in thine heart, Who shall ascend into heaven? (that is, to bring Christ down from above:) (7) Or, Who shall descend into the deep? (that is, to bring up Christ again from the dead.) (8) But what saith it? The word is nigh thee, even in thy mouth, and in thy heart: that is, the word of faith, which we preach; (9) That if thou shalt confess with thy mouth the Lord Jesus, and shalt believe in thine heart that God hath raised him from the dead, thou shalt be saved. (10) <u>For with the heart man believeth unto righteousness; and with the mouth confession is made unto salvation.</u> (11) For the scripture saith, Whosoever believeth on him shall not be ashamed.

ROMANS 7:11
For sin, taking occasion by the commandment deceived me, and by it slew me.

Just as the serpent beguiled Eve, our sinful flesh beguiles us. It's a never-ending battle.

GENESIS 3:2-4, 13—(2) And the woman said unto the serpent, We may eat of the fruit of the trees of the garden: (3) But of the fruit of the tree which is in the midst of the garden, God hath said, Ye shall not eat of it, neither shall ye touch it, lest ye die. (4) And the serpent said unto the woman, Ye shall not surely die...(13) And the LORD God said unto the woman, What is this that thou hast done? And the woman said, The serpent beguiled me, and I did eat.

JAMES 1:13-15—(13) Let no man say when he is tempted, I am tempted of God: for God cannot be tempted with evil, neither tempteth he any man: (14) But every man is tempted, when he is drawn away of his own lust, and enticed. (15) Then when lust hath conceived, it bringeth forth sin: and sin, when it is finished, bringeth forth death.

JEREMIAH 17:9—The heart is deceitful above all things, and desperately wicked: who can know it.

EPHESIANS 4:20-27—(20) But ye have not so learned Christ; (21) If so be that ye have heard him, and have been taught by him, as the truth is in Jesus: (22) That ye put off concerning the former conversation the old man, which is corrupt according to the deceitful lusts; (23) And be renewed in the spirit of your mind; (24) And that ye put on the new man, which after God is created in righteousness and true holiness. (25) Wherefore putting away lying, speak every man truth with his neighbour: for we are members one of another. (26) Be ye angry, and sin not: let not the sun go down upon your wrath: (27) Neither give place to the devil.

HEBREWS 2:16-18—(16) For verily he took not on him the nature of angels; but he took on him the seed of Abraham. (17) Wherefore in all things it behoved him to be made like unto his brethren, that he might be a merciful and faithful high priest in things pertaining to God, to make reconciliation for the sins of the people. (18) For in that he himself hath suffered being tempted, he is able to succor them that are tempted.

HEBREWS 4:15—For we have not an high priest which cannot be touched with the feeling of our infirmities; but was in all points tempted like as we are, yet without sin.

ROMANS 7:12
Wherefore the law is holy, and the commandment holy, and just, and good.

PSALMS 19:7-14—(7) The law of the LORD is perfect, converting the soul: the testimony of the LORD is sure, making wise the simple. (8) The statutes of the LORD are right, rejoicing the heart: the commandment of the LORD is pure, enlightening the eyes. (9) The fear of the LORD is clean, enduring forever: the judgments of the LORD are true and righteous altogether. (10) More to be desired are they than gold, yea, than much fine gold: sweeter also than honey and the honeycomb. (11) Moreover by them is thy servant warned: and in keeping of them there is great reward. (12) Who can understand his errors? cleanse thou me from secret faults. (13) Keep back thy servant also from presumptuous sins; let them not have dominion over me: then shall I be upright, and I shall be innocent from the great transgression. (14) Let the words of my mouth, and the meditation of my heart, be acceptable in thy sight, O LORD, my

1 TIMOTHY 1:8—But we know that the law is good, if a man use it lawfully.

ROMANS 7:13
Was then that which is good made death unto me? God forbid. But sin, that it might appear sin, working death in me by that which is good; that sin by the commandment might become exceeding sinful.

ROMANS 3:20—Therefore by the deeds of the law there shall no flesh be justified in his sight: for by the law is the knowledge of sin.

ROMANS 5:20-21—(20) Moreover the law entered, that the offence might abound. But where sin abounded, grace did much more abound: (21) That as sin hath reigned unto death, even so might grace reign through righteousness unto eternal life by Jesus Christ our Lord.

1 CORINTHIANS 15:56—The sting of death is sin; and the strength of sin is the law.

ROMANS 7:14-15
(14) For we know that the law is spiritual: but I am carnal, sold under sin. (15) For that which I do I allow not: for what I would, that do I not; but what I hate, that do I.

GALATIANS 5:17—For the flesh lusteth against the Spirit, and the Spirit against the flesh: and these are contrary the one to the other: so that ye cannot do the things that ye would.

PSALMS 40:12—For innumerable evils have compassed me about: mine iniquities have taken hold upon me, so that I am not able to look up; they are more than the hairs of mine head: therefore my heart faileth me.

JEREMIAH 17:9—The heart is deceitful above all things, and desperately wicked: who can know it?

PRAYER OF MANASSEH—My transgressions, O Lord, are multiplied: my transgressions are multiplied, and I am not worthy to behold and see the height of heaven for the multitude of mine iniquities. I am bowed down with many iron bands, that I cannot lift up mine head, neither have any release: for I have provoked thy wrath, and done evil before thee: I did not thy will, neither kept I thy commandments: I have set up abominations, and have multiplied offences. Now therefore I bow the knee of mine heart, beseeching thee of grace. I have sinned, O Lord, I have sinned, and I acknowledge mine iniquities.

PSALMS 19:11-13—(11) Moreover by them is thy servant warned: and in keeping of them there is great reward. (12) Who can understand his errors? Cleanse thou me from secret faults. (13) Keep back thy servant also from presumptuous sins; let them not have dominion over me: then shall I be upright, and I shall be innocent from the great transgression.

1 CORINTHIANS 3:1—And I, brethren, could not speak unto you as unto spiritual, but as unto carnal, even as unto babes in Christ.

(1 Kings 21:20; 2 Kings 17:17, Matthew 26:41; Mark 14:38)

ROMANS 7:16-20

(16) **If then I do that which I would not, I consent unto the law that it is good.** (17) **Now then it is no more I that do it, but sin that dwelleth in me.** (18) **For I know that in me (that is, in my flesh,) dwelleth no good thing: for to will is present with me; but how to perform that which is good I find not.** (19) **For the good that I would I do not: but the evil, which I would not, that I do.** (20) **Now if I do that I would not, it is no more I that do it, but sin that dwelleth in me.**

JEREMIAH 17:9—The heart is deceitful above all things, and desperately wicked: who can know it?

GENESIS 6:5—And GOD saw that the wickedness of man was great in the earth, and that every imagination of the thoughts of his heart was only evil continually.

GENESIS 8:21—And the LORD smelled a sweet savor; and the LORD said in his heart, I will not again curse the ground any more for man's sake; for the imagination of man's heart is evil from his youth; neither will I again smite any more every thing living, as I have done.

MATTHEW 15:18-19—(18) But those things which proceed out of the mouth come forth from the heart; and they defile the man. (19) For out of the heart proceed evil thoughts, murders, adulteries, fornications, thefts, false witness, blasphemies.

JOB 15:14—What is man, that he should be clean? And he which is born of a woman, that he should be righteous?

PSALMS 51:5—Behold, I was shapen in iniquity; and in sin did my mother conceive me.

(Isaiah 56:3; Mark 7:21, Ephesians 2:3)

ROMANS 7:21-23

(21) **I find then a law, that, when I would do good, evil is present with me.** (22) **For I delight in the law of God after the inward man:** (23) **But I see another law in my members, warring against the law of my mind, and bringing me into captivity to the law of sin which is in my members.**

Contextually speaking, the law we are to die to is the law of sin and death, that is, the law of our sinful flesh. This is the law that wars with our spirit, because our spirits delight in the Law of TMH.

GALATIANS 5:17—For the flesh lusteth against the Spirit, and the Spirit against the flesh: and these are contrary the one to the other: so that ye cannot do the things that ye would.

MATTHEW 26:41—Watch and pray, that ye enter not into temptation: the spirit indeed is willing, but the flesh is weak.

ROMANS 6:13, 19—(13) Neither yield ye your members as instruments of unrighteousness unto sin: but yield yourselves unto God, as those that are alive from the dead, and your members as instruments of righteousness unto God...(19) I speak after the manner of men because of the infirmity of your flesh: for as ye have yielded your members servants to uncleanness and to iniquity unto iniquity; even so now yield your members servants to righteousness unto holiness.

PSALMS 1:2—But his delight is in the law of the LORD; and in his law doth he meditate day and night.

PSALMS 40:8—I delight to do thy will, O my God: yea, thy law is within my heart.

PSALMS 119:35—Make me to go in the path of thy commandments; for therein do I delight.

(Deuteronomy 30:6; Psalms 37:31, 40:8; Jeremiah 31:33; Hebrews 8:10; Hebrews 10:16)

ROMANS 7:24-25

(24) O wretched man that I am! Who shall deliver me from the body of this death? (25) I thank God through Jesus Christ our Lord. So then with the mind I myself serve the law of God; but with the flesh the law of sin.

Paul isn't surrendering to his flesh here. On the contrary, he's making a distinction to describe the ever-present war all believers engage in. Our job is to master our flesh and subdue it by the Spirit of TMH.

PHILIPPIANS 2:12-13—(12) Therefore, my beloved, as you have always obeyed, not as in my presence only, but now much more in my absence, work out your own salvation with fear and trembling; (13) for it is God who works in you both to will and to do for His good pleasure.

EPHESIANS 3:16—That he would grant you, according to the riches of his glory, to be strengthened with might by his Spirit in the inner man.

PHILIPPIANS 4:13—I can do all things through Christ which strengthened me.

LUKE 18:27—And he said, The things which are impossible with men are possible with God.

ROMANS 8:2—For the law of the Spirit of life in Christ Jesus hath made me free from the law of sin and death

ROMANS 6:6—Knowing this, that our old man is crucified with him, that the body of sin might be destroyed, that henceforth we should not serve sin.

ROMANS 8:23—And not only they, but ourselves also, which have the firstfruits of the Spirit, even we ourselves groan within ourselves, waiting for the adoption, to wit, the redemption of our body.

2 CORINTHIANS 4:16—For which cause we faint not; but though our outward man perish, yet the inward man is renewed day by day.

GALATIANS 5:24—And they that are Christ's have crucified the flesh with the affections and lusts.

1 CORINTHIANS 10:13—There hath no temptation taken you but such as is common to man: but God is faithful, who will not suffer you to be tempted above that ye are able; but will with the temptation also make a way to escape, that ye may be able to bear it.

1 CORINTHIANS 15:57—But thanks be to God, which giveth us the victory through our Lord Jesus Christ.

1 PETER 4:1—Forasmuch then as Christ hath suffered for us in the flesh, arm yourselves likewise with the same mind: for he that hath suffered in the flesh hath ceased from sin

(Matthew 10:38)

ROMANS 8

ROMANS 8:1
There is therefore now no condemnation to them, which are in Christ Jesus, who walk not after the flesh, but after the Spirit.

GALATIANS 5:16—This I say then, Walk in the Spirit, and ye shall not fulfill the lust of the flesh.

GALATIANS 5:25—If we live in the Spirit, let us also walk in the Spirit.

1 CORINTHIANS 1:30—But of him are ye in Christ Jesus, who of God is made unto us wisdom, and righteousness, and sanctification, and redemption.

1 CORINTHIANS 6:9-11—(9) Know ye not that the unrighteous shall not inherit the kingdom of God? Be not deceived: neither fornicators, nor idolaters, nor adulterers, nor effeminate, nor abusers of themselves with mankind, (10) Nor thieves, nor covetous, nor drunkards, nor revilers, nor extortioners, shall inherit the kingdom of God. (11) And such were some of you: but ye are washed, but ye are sanctified, but ye are justified in the name of the Lord Jesus, and by the Spirit of our God.

ROMANS 8:2-3
(2) For the law of the Spirit of life in Christ Jesus hath made me free from <u>the law of sin and death</u>. (3) For what the law could not do, in that it was weak through the flesh, God sending his own Son in the likeness of sinful flesh, and for sin, condemned sin in the flesh:

Excerpt from the commentary for *Romans 7:21-23*, pg. 190:

"Therefore, contextually speaking, the law we are to die to is the law of sin and death, that is, the law of our sinful flesh. This is the law that wars with our spirit, because our spirits delight in the Law of TMH."

ACTS 13:38-39—(38) Be it known unto you therefore, men and brethren, that through this man is preached unto you the forgiveness of sins: (39) And by him all that believe are justified from all things, from which ye could not be justified by the law of Moses.

Because of the law of sin and death that reigns within our sinful bodies, the Law of Moses with its perpetual sacrifices and ordinances can never justify us. However, the indwelling Spirit that enables us to be obedient to TMH's eternal laws, which have not and will never change, justifies us.

HEBREWS 10:1-2—(1) For the law having a shadow of good things to come, and not the very image of the things, can never with those sacrifices which they offered year by year continually make the comers thereunto perfect. (2) For then would they not have ceased to be offered? because that the worshippers once purged should have had no more conscience of sins.

HEBREWS 7:19—For the law made nothing perfect, but the bringing in of a better hope did; by the which we draw nigh unto God.

2 CORINTHIANS 5:21—For he hath made him to be sin for us, who knew no sin; that we might be made the righteousness of God in him.

1 CORINTHIANS 15:45—And so it is written, The first man Adam was made a living soul; the last Adam was made a quickening spirit.

HEBREWS 10:10, 14—(10) By the which will we are sanctified through the offering of the body of Jesus Christ once for all...(14) For by one offering he hath perfected for ever them that are sanctified.

GALATIANS 3:13—Christ hath redeemed us from the **curse of the law**, being made a curse for us: for it is written, Cursed is every one that hangeth on a tree.

HEBREWS 9:15—And for this cause he is the mediator of the new testament, that by means of death, for the redemption of the transgressions that were under the first testament, they which are called might receive the promise of eternal inheritance.

ROMANS 6:18, 22—(18) Being then made free from sin, ye became the servants of righteousness...(22) But now being made free from sin, and become servants to God, ye have your fruit unto holiness, and the end everlasting life.

GALATIANS 5:1—Stand fast therefore in the liberty wherewith Christ hath made us free, and be not entangled again with the yoke of bondage.

ROMANS 8:4
That the righteousness of the law might be fulfilled in us, who walk not after the flesh, but after the Spirit.

GALATIANS 2:20—I am crucified with Christ: nevertheless I live; yet not I, but Christ liveth in me: and the life which I now live in the flesh I live by the faith of the Son of God, who loved me, and gave himself for me.

ROMANS 6:4—Therefore we are buried with him by baptism into death: that like as Christ was raised up from the dead by the glory of the Father, even so we also should walk in newness of life.

EPHESIANS 4:22-24—(22) That ye put off concerning the former conversation the old man, which is corrupt according to the deceitful lusts; (23) And be renewed in the spirit of your mind; (24) And that ye put on the new man, which after God is created in righteousness and true holiness.

PSALMS 51:6-12—(6) Behold, thou desirest truth in the inward parts: and in the hidden part thou shalt make me to know wisdom. (7) Purge me with hyssop, and I shall be clean: wash me, and I shall be whiter than snow. (8) Make me to hear joy and gladness; that the bones which thou hast broken may rejoice. (9) Hide thy face from my sins, and blot out all mine iniquities. (10) Create in me a clean heart, O God; and renew a right spirit within me. (11) Cast me not away from thy presence; and take not thy holy spirit from me. (12) Restore unto me the joy of thy salvation; and uphold me with thy free spirit.

GALATIANS 5:16—This I say then, walk in the Spirit, and ye shall not fulfill the lust of the flesh.

ROMANS 13:14—But put ye on the Lord Jesus Christ, and make not provision for the flesh, to fulfill the lusts thereof.

ROMANS 8:5-8
(5) **For they that are after the flesh do mind the things of the flesh; but they that are after the Spirit the things of the Spirit.** (6) **For to be carnally minded is death; but to be spiritually minded is life and peace.** (7) **Because the carnal mind is enmity against God: for it is not subject to the law of God, neither indeed can be.** (8) **So then they that are in the flesh cannot please God.**

JOHN 3:6—That which is born of the flesh is flesh; and that which is born of the Spirit is spirit.

1 CORINTHIANS 2:14—But the natural man receiveth not the things of the Spirit of God: for they are foolishness unto him: neither can he know them, because they are spiritually discerned.

ROMANS 6:21—What fruit had ye then in those things whereof ye are now ashamed? For the end of those things is death.

GALATIANS 5:17-25—(17) For the flesh lusteth against the Spirit, and the Spirit against the flesh: and these are contrary the one to the other: so that ye cannot do the things that ye would. (18) But if ye be led of the Spirit, ye are not under the law. (19) Now the works of the flesh are manifest, which are [these]; Adultery, fornication, uncleanness, lasciviousness, (20) Idolatry, witchcraft, hatred, variance, emulations, wrath, strife, seditions, heresies, (21) Envyings, murders, drunkenness, revellings, and such like: of the which I tell you before, as I have also told [you] in time past, that they which do such things shall not inherit the kingdom of God. (22) But the fruit of the Spirit is love, joy, peace, longsuffering, gentleness, goodness, faith, (23) Meekness, temperance: against such there is no law. (24) And they that are Christ's have crucified the flesh with the affections and lusts. (25) If we live in the Spirit, let us also walk in the Spirit.

ROMANS 7:12-18—(12) Wherefore the law is holy, and the commandment holy, and just, and good. (13) Was then that which is good made death unto me? God forbid. But sin, that it might appear sin, working death in me by that which is good; that sin by the commandment might become exceeding sinful. (14) For we know that the law is spiritual: but I am carnal, sold under sin. (15) For that which I do I allow not: for what I would, that do I not; but what I hate, that do I. (16) If then I do that which I would not, I consent unto the law that it is good. 17Now then it is no more I that do it, but sin that dwelleth in me. (18) For I know that in me (that is, in my flesh,) dwelleth no good thing: for to will is present with me; but how to perform that which is good I find not.

JAMES 4:4—Ye adulterers and adulteresses, know ye not that the friendship of the world is enmity with God? Whosoever therefore will be a friend of the world is the enemy of God.

GALATIANS 6:8—For he that soweth to his flesh shall of the flesh reap corruption; but he that soweth to the Spirit shall of the Spirit reap life everlasting.

REVELATION 22:14-15—(14) Blessed are they that do his commandments, that they may have right to the tree of life, and may enter in through the gates into the city. (15) For without are dogs, and sorcerers, and whoremongers, and murderers, and idolaters, and whosoever loveth and maketh a lie.

ROMANS 8:9
But ye are not in the flesh, but in the Spirit, if so be that the Spirit of God dwell in you. Now if any man have not the Spirit of Christ, he is none of his.

2 CORINTHIANS 13:5—Examine yourselves, whether ye be in the faith; prove your own selves. Know ye not your own selves, how that Jesus Christ is in you, except ye be reprobates?

JOHN 14:17—Even the Spirit of truth; whom the world cannot receive, because it seeth him not, neither knoweth him: but ye know him; for he dwelleth with you, and shall be in you.

1 CORINTHIANS 6:19—What? Know ye not that your body is the temple of the Holy Ghost which is in you, which ye have of God, and ye are not your own? For ye are bought with a price: therefore glorify God in your body, and in your spirit, which are God's.

JOHN 3:34—For he whom God hath sent speaketh the words of God: for God giveth not the Spirit by measure unto him.

1 CORINTHIANS 3:16—Know ye not that ye are the temple of God, and that the Spirit of God dwelleth in you?

1 JOHN 3:9—Whosoever is born of God doth not commit sin; for his seed remaineth in him: and he cannot sin, because he is born of God.

1 JOHN 3:24—And he that keepeth his commandments dwelleth in him, and he in him. And hereby we know that he abideth in us, by the Spirit which he hath given us.

ROMANS 8:10-11
(10) And if Christ be in you, the body is dead because of sin; but the Spirit is life because of righteousness. (11) But if the Spirit of him that raised up Jesus from the dead dwell in you, he that raised up Christ from the dead shall also quicken your mortal bodies by his Spirit that dwelleth in you.

PSALMS 16:10—For thou wilt not leave my soul in hell; neither wilt thou suffer thine Holy One to see corruption.

PSALMS 49:15—But God will redeem my soul from the power of the grave: for he shall receive me. Selah

JOB 19:25-27—(25) For I know that my redeemer liveth, and that he shall stand at the latter day upon the earth: (26) and though after my skin worms destroy this body, yet in my flesh shall I see God: (27) Whom I shall see for myself, and mine eyes shall behold, and not another; though my reins be consumed within me.

1 CORINTHIANS 6:14—And God hath both raised up the Lord, and will also raise up us by his own power.

JOHN 5:24-29—(24) Verily, verily, I say unto you, He that heareth my word, and believeth on him that sent me, hath everlasting life, and shall not come into condemnation; but is passed from death unto life. (25) Verily, verily, I say unto you, The hour is coming, and now is, when the dead shall hear the voice of the Son of God: and they that hear shall live. (26) For as the Father hath life in himself; so hath he given to the Son to have life in himself; (27) and hath given him authority to execute judgment also, because he is the Son of man. (28) Marvel not at this: for the hour is coming, in the which all that are in the graves shall hear his voice, (29) and shall come forth; they that have done good, unto the resurrection of life; and they that have done evil, unto the resurrection of damnation.

JOHN 6:39—And this is the Father's will which hath sent me, that of all which he hath given me I should lose nothing, but should raise it up again at the last day

1 CORINTHIANS 15:20-28—(20) But now is Christ risen from the dead, and become the firstfruits of them that slept. (21) For since by man came death, by man came also the resurrection of the dead. (22) For as in Adam all die, even so in Christ shall all be made alive. (23) But every man in his own order: Christ the firstfruits; afterward they that are Christ's at his coming. (24) Then cometh the end, when he shall have delivered up the kingdom to God, even the Father; when he shall have put down all rule and all authority and power. (25) For he must reign, till he hath put all enemies under his feet. (26) The last enemy that shall be destroyed is death. (27) For he hath put all things under his feet. But when he saith, all things are put under him, it is manifest that he is excepted, which did put all things under him. (28) And when all things shall be subdued unto him, then shall the Son also himself be subject unto him that put all things under him, that God may be all in all.

1 CORINTHIANS 15:42-57—(42) So also is the resurrection of the dead. It is sown in corruption; it is raised in incorruption: (43) It is sown in dishonor; it is raised in glory: it is sown in weakness; it is raised in power: (44) It is sown a natural body; it is raised a spiritual body. There is a natural body, and there is a spiritual body. (45) And so it is written, The first man Adam was made a living soul; the last Adam was made a quickening spirit. (46) Howbeit that was not first which is spiritual, but that which is natural; and afterward that which is spiritual. (47) The first man is of the earth, earthy: the second man is the Lord from heaven. (48) As is the earthy, such are they also that are earthy: and as is the heavenly, such are they also that are heavenly. (49) And as we have borne the image of the earthy, we shall also bear the image of the heavenly. (50) Now this I say, brethren, that flesh and blood cannot inherit the kingdom of God; neither doth corruption inherit incorruption. (51) Behold, I shew you a mystery; We shall not all sleep, but we shall all be changed, (52) In a moment, in the twinkling of an eye, at the last trump: for the trumpet shall sound, and the dead shall be raised incorruptible, and we shall be changed. (53) For this corruptible must put on incorruption, and this mortal must put on immortality. (54) So when this corruptible shall have put on incorruption, and this mortal shall have put on immortality, then shall be brought to pass the saying that is written, Death is swallowed up in victory. (55) O death, where is thy sting? O grave, where is thy victory? (56) The sting of death is sin; and the strength of sin is the law. (57) But thanks be to God, which giveth us the victory through our Lord Jesus Christ.

PHILIPPIANS 3:7-11—(7) But what things were gain to me, those I counted loss for Christ. (8) Yea doubtless, and I count all things but loss for the excellency of the knowledge of Christ Jesus my Lord: for whom I have suffered the loss of all things, and do count them but dung, that I may win Christ, (9) And be found in him, not having mine own righteousness, which is of the law, but that which is through the faith of Christ, the righteousness which is of God by faith: (10) That I may know him, and the power of his resurrection, and the fellowship of his sufferings, being made conformable unto his death; (11) If by any means I might attain unto the resurrection of the dead.

1 THESSALONIANS 4:13-18—(13) But I would not have you to be ignorant, brethren, concerning them which are asleep, that ye sorrow not, even as others which have no hope. (14) For if we believe that Jesus died and rose again, even so them also which sleep in Jesus will God bring with him. (15) For this we say unto you by the word of the Lord, that we, which are alive and remain unto the coming of the Lord shall not prevent them which are asleep. (16) For the Lord himself shall descend from heaven with a shout, with the voice of the archangel, and with the trump of God: and the dead in Christ shall rise first: (17) Then we which are alive and remain shall be caught up together with them in the clouds, to meet the Lord in the air: and so shall we ever be with the Lord. (18) Wherefore comfort one another with these words.

REVELATION 20:4-6—(4) And I saw thrones, and they sat upon them, and judgment was given unto them: and I saw the souls of them that were beheaded for the witness of Jesus, and for the word of God, and which had not worshipped the beast, neither his image, neither had received his mark upon their foreheads, or in their hands; and they lived and reigned with Christ a thousand years. (5) But the rest of the dead lived not again until the thousand years were finished. This is the first resurrection. (6) Blessed and holy is he that hath part in the first resurrection: on such the second death hath no power, but they shall be priests of God and of Christ, and shall reign with him a thousand years.

(Ezekiel 37; Luke 14:14, 20:35-36; John 5:21, 11:24)

ROMANS 8:12-13
(12) Therefore, brethren, we are debtors, not to the flesh, to live after the flesh. (13) For if ye live after the flesh, ye shall die: but if ye through the Spirit do mortify the deeds of the body, ye shall live.

ROMANS 6:14—For sin shall not have dominion over you: for ye are not under the law, but under grace.

GALATIANS 5:16-25—(16) This I say then, Walk in the Spirit, and ye shall not fulfill the lust of the flesh. (17) For the flesh lusteth against the Spirit, and the Spirit against the flesh: and these are contrary the one to the other: so that ye cannot do the things that ye would. (18) But if ye be led of the Spirit, ye are not under the law. (19) Now the works of the flesh are manifest, which are these; Adultery, fornication, uncleanness, lasciviousness, (20) Idolatry, witchcraft, hatred, variance, emulations, wrath, strife, seditions, heresies, (21) envyings, murders, drunkenness, revelings, and such like: of the which I tell you before, as I have also told you in time past, that they which do such things shall not inherit the kingdom of God. (22) But the fruit of the Spirit is love, joy, peace, longsuffering, gentleness, goodness, faith, (23) meekness, temperance: against such there is no law. (24) And they that are Christ's have crucified the flesh with the affections and lusts. (25) If we live in the Spirit, let us also walk in the Spirit.

GALATIANS 6:8—For he that soweth to his flesh shall of the flesh reap corruption; but he that soweth to the Spirit shall of the Spirit reap life everlasting.

EPHESIANS 4:22—That ye put off concerning the former conversation the old man, which is corrupt according to the deceitful lusts.

COLOSSIANS 3:5—Mortify therefore your members which are upon the earth; fornication, uncleanness, inordinate affection, evil concupiscence, and covetousness, which is idolatry.

ROMANS 8:14 [a]
For as many as are led by the Spirit of God, they are the sons of God.

JOHN 14:26—But the Helper, the Holy Spirit, whom the Father will send in My name, He will teach you all things, and bring to your remembrance all things that I said to you.

JOHN 16:13—Howbeit when he, the Spirit of truth, is come, he will guide you into all truth: for he shall not speak of himself; but whatsoever he shall hear, that shall he speak: and he will shew you things to come.

1 CORINTHIANS 2:9—(9) But as it is written, Eye hath not seen, nor ear heard, neither have entered into the heart of man, the things which God hath prepared for them that love him. (10) But God hath revealed them unto us by his Spirit: for the Spirit searcheth all things, yea, the deep things of God. (11) For what man knoweth the things of a man, save the spirit of man, which is in him? Even so the things of God knoweth no man, but the Spirit of God. (12) Now we have received, not the spirit of the world, but the spirit, which is of God; that we might know the things that are freely given to us of God. (13) Which things also we speak, not in the words which man's wisdom teacheth, but which the Holy Ghost teacheth; comparing spiritual things with spiritual. (14) But the natural man receiveth not the things of the Spirit of God: for they are foolishness unto him: neither can he know them, because they are spiritually discerned. (15) But he that is spiritual judgeth all things, yet he himself is judged of no man. (16) For who hath known the mind of the Lord, that he may instruct him? But we have the mind of Christ.

GALATIANS 5:16—This I say then, walk in the Spirit, and ye shall not fulfill the lust of the flesh.

GALATIANS 5:18—But if ye be led of the Spirit, ye are not under the law.

ROMANS 8:14 [b]
For as many as are led by the Spirit of God, they are the sons of God.

GALATIANS 4:4-7—(4) But when the fullness of the time was come, God sent forth his Son, made of a woman, made under the law, (5) To redeem them that were under the law, that we might receive the adoption of sons. (6) And because ye are sons, God hath sent forth the Spirit of his Son into your hearts, crying, Abba, Father. (7) Wherefore thou art no more a servant, but a son; and if a son, then an heir of God through Christ.

ROMANS 9:3-11—(3) For I could wish that myself were accursed from Christ for my brethren, my kinsmen according to the flesh: (4) <u>Who are Israelites; to whom pertaineth the adoption</u>, and the glory, and the covenants, and the giving of the law, and the service of God, and the promises; (5) Whose are the fathers, and of whom as concerning the flesh Christ came, who is over all, God blessed for ever. Amen. (6) Not as though the word of God hath taken none effect. <u>For they are not all Israel, which are of Israel: (7) Neither, because they are the seed of Abraham, are they all children: but, In Isaac shall thy seed be called. (8) That is, They which are the children of the flesh, these are not the children of God: but the children of the promise are counted for the seed.</u> (9) For this is the word of promise, At this time will I come, and Sara shall have a son. (10) And not only this; but when Rebecca also had conceived by one, even by our father Isaac; (11) (For the children being not yet born, neither having done any good or evil, that the purpose of God according to election might stand, not of works, but of him that calleth;)

JOHN 1:12-13—(12) But as many as received him, to them gave he power to become the sons of God, even to them that believe on his name: (13) Which were born, not of blood, nor of the will of the flesh, nor of the will of man, but of God

JOHN 11:48-52—(48) If we let him thus alone, all men will believe on him: and the Romans shall come and take away both our place and nation. (49) And one of them, named Caiaphas, being the high priest that same year, said unto them, Ye know nothing at all, (50) Nor consider that it is expedient for us, that one man should die for the people, and that the whole nation perish not. (51) And this spake he not of himself: but being high priest that year, he prophesied that Jesus should die for that nation; <u>(52) And not for that nation only, but that also he should gather together in one the children of God that were scattered abroad.</u>

JAMES 1:1—James, a servant of God and of the Lord Jesus Christ, to the twelve tribes, which are scattered abroad, greeting.

ROMANS 8:15 [a]
For ye have not received the <u>spirit of bondage again to fear; but ye have received the Spirit of adoption, whereby we cry, Abba, Father.</u>

Until we're born again (circumcision of the heart), we're in bondage to sin. Without the Spirit, we bow to the whims of our flesh.

JOHN 8:34—Jesus answered them, Verily, verily, I say unto you, Whosoever committeth sin is the servant of sin.

ROMANS 6:16—Know ye not, that to whom ye yield yourselves servants to obey, his servants ye are to whom ye obey; whether of sin unto death, or of obedience unto righteousness?

ROMANS 6:20—For when ye were the servants of sin, ye were free from righteousness.

1 CORINTHIANS 2:12—Now we have received, not the spirit of the world, but the spirit which is of God; that we might know the things that are freely given to us of God.

2 TIMOTHY 1:7—For God hath not given us the spirit of fear; but of power, and of love, and of a sound mind.

2 PETER 2:19—While they promise them liberty, they themselves are the servants of corruption: for of whom a man is overcome, of the same is he brought in bondage.

(Matthew 6:24)

ROMANS 8:15 [b]
For ye have not received the spirit of bondage again to fear; but ye have received the Spirit of adoption, whereby we cry, Abba, Father.

ROMANS 9:3-5—(3) For I could wish that myself were accursed from Christ for my brethren, my kinsmen according to the flesh: (4) Who are Israelites; to whom pertaineth the adoption, and the glory, and the covenants, and the giving of the law, and the service of God, and the promises; (5) Whose are the fathers, and of whom as concerning the flesh Christ came, who is over all, God blessed for ever. Amen.

GALATIANS 4:4-7—(4) But when the fullness of the time was come, God sent forth his Son, made of a woman, made under the law, (5) To redeem them that were under the law, that we might receive the adoption of sons. (6) And because ye are sons, God hath sent forth the Spirit of his Son into your hearts, crying, Abba, Father. (7) Wherefore thou art no more a servant, but a son; and if a son, then an heir of God through Christ.

EPHESIANS 1:5—Having predestinated us unto the adoption of children by Jesus Christ to himself, according to the good pleasure of his will

ROMANS 8:16-17

(16) **The Spirit itself beareth witness with our spirit, that we are the children of God:** **(17)** **And if children, then heirs; heirs of God, and joint-heirs with Christ; if so be that we suffer with him, that we may be also glorified together.**

ACTS 14:22—Confirming the souls of the disciples, and exhorting them to continue in the faith, and that we must through much tribulation enter into the kingdom of God.

ACTS 26:18—To open their eyes, and to turn them from darkness to light, and from the power of Satan unto God, that they may receive forgiveness of sins, and inheritance among them, which are sanctified by faith that is in me.

ROMANS 9:3-5—(3) For I could wish that myself were accursed from Christ for my brethren, my kinsmen according to the flesh: (4) Who are Israelites; to whom pertaineth the adoption, and the glory, and the covenants, and the giving of the law, and the service of God, and the promises; (5) Whose are the fathers, and of whom as concerning the flesh Christ came, who is over all, God blessed for ever. Amen.

2 CORINTHIANS 1:7—And our hope of you is steadfast, knowing, that as ye are partakers of the sufferings, so shall ye be also of the consolation.

GALATIANS 4:5-7—(5) To redeem them that were under the law, that we might receive the adoption of sons. (6) And because ye are sons, God hath sent forth the Spirit of his Son into your hearts, crying, Abba, Father. (7) Wherefore thou art no more a servant, but a son; and if a son, then an heir of God through Christ.

PHILIPPIANS 1:29—For unto you it is given in the behalf of Christ, not only to believe on him, but also to suffer for his sake

ROMANS 8:18

For I reckon that the sufferings of this present time are not worthy to be compared with the glory, which shall be revealed in us.

JOHN 14:12—Verily, verily, I say unto you, He that believeth on me, the works that I do shall he do also; and greater works than these shall he do; because I go unto my Father.

ROMANS 6:5—For if we have been planted together in the likeness of his death, we shall be also in the likeness of his resurrection.

1 CORINTHIANS 2:9—But as it is written: "Eye has not seen, nor ear heard, Nor have entered into the heart of man The things which God has prepared for those who love Him."

1 CORINTHIANS 15:42-49—(42) So also is the resurrection of the dead. It is sown in corruption; it is raised in incorruption: (43) It is sown in dishonor; it is raised in glory: it is sown in weakness; it is raised in power: (44) It is sown a natural body; it is raised a spiritual body. There is a natural body, and there is a spiritual body. (45) And so it is written, The first man Adam was made a living soul; the last Adam was made a quickening spirit. (46) Howbeit that was not first which is spiritual, but that which is natural; and afterward that which is spiritual. (47) The first man is of the earth, earthy: the second man is the Lord from heaven. (48) As is the earthy, such are they also that are earthy: and as is the heavenly, such are they also that are heavenly. (49) And as we have borne the image of the earthy, we shall also bear the image of the heavenly.

1 CORINTHIANS 15:52-53—(52) In a moment, in the twinkling of an eye, at the last trump: for the trumpet shall sound, and the dead shall be raised incorruptible, and we shall be changed. (53) For this corruptible must put on incorruption, and this mortal must put on immortality.

2 CORINTHIANS 4:17—For our light affliction, which is but for a moment, worketh for us a far more exceeding and eternal weight of glory

1 PETER 1:6-7—(6) Wherein ye greatly rejoice, though now for a season, if need be, ye are in heaviness through manifold temptations: (7) That the trial of your faith, being much more precious than of gold that perisheth, though it be tried with fire, might be found unto praise and honour and glory at the appearing of Jesus Christ:

1 PETER 4:13—But rejoice, inasmuch as ye are partakers of Christ's sufferings; that, when his glory shall be revealed, ye may be glad also with exceeding joy.

1 JOHN 3:2—Beloved, now are we the sons of God, and it doth not yet appear what we shall be: but we know that, when he shall appear, we shall be like him; for we shall see him as he is.

LUKE 17:20-21—(20) And when he was demanded of the Pharisees, when the kingdom of God should come, he answered them and said, The kingdom of God cometh not with observation: (21) Neither shall they say, Lo here! or, lo there! for, behold, the kingdom of God is within you.

ROMANS 8:19
For the earnest expectation of the creature waiteth for the manifestation of the sons of God.

ISAIAH 11:6-9—(6) The wolf also shall dwell with the lamb, and the leopard shall lie down with the kid; and the calf and the young lion and the fatling together; and a little child shall lead them. (7) And the cow and the bear shall feed; their young ones shall lie down together: and the lion shall eat straw like the ox. (8) And the sucking child shall play on the hole of the asp, and the weaned child shall put his hand on the cockatrice' den. (9) They shall not hurt nor destroy in all my holy mountain: for the earth shall be full of the knowledge of the LORD, as the waters cover the sea.

ISAIAH 14:4-10—(4) That thou shalt take up this proverb against the king of Babylon, and say, How hath the oppressor ceased! The golden city ceased! (5) The LORD hath broken the staff of the wicked, and the scepter of the rulers. (6) He who smote the people in wrath with a continual stroke, he that ruled the nations in anger, is persecuted, and none hindereth. (7) The whole earth is at rest, and is quiet: they break forth into singing. (8) Yea, the fir trees rejoice at thee, and the cedars of Lebanon, saying, Since thou art laid down, no feller is come up against us. (9) Hell from beneath is moved for thee to meet thee at thy coming: it stirreth up the dead for thee, even all the chief ones of the earth; it hath raised up from their thrones all the kings of the nations. (10) All they shall speak and say unto thee, Art thou also become weak as we? Art thou become like unto us?

ISAIAH 55:12-13—(12) For ye shall go out with joy, and be led forth with peace: the mountains and the hills shall break forth before you into singing, and all the trees of the field shall clap their hands. (13) Instead of the thorn shall come up the fir tree, and instead of the brier shall come up the myrtle tree: and it shall be to the LORD for a name, for an everlasting sign that shall not be cut off.

ISAIAH 65:24-25—(24) And it shall come to pass, that before they call, I will answer; and while they are yet speaking, I will hear. (25) The wolf and the lamb shall feed together, and the lion shall eat straw like the bullock: and dust shall be the serpent's meat. They shall not hurt nor destroy in all my holy mountain, saith the LORD.

2 ESDRAS 11:40-46—(40) And the fourth came, and overcame all the beasts that were past, and had power over the world with great fearfulness, and over the whole compass of the earth with much wicked oppression; and so long time dwelt he upon the earth with deceit. (41) For the earth hast thou not judged with truth. (42) For thou hast afflicted the

PRECEPTS FOR ROMANS

meek, thou hast hurt the peaceable, thou hast loved liars, and destroyed the dwellings of them that brought forth fruit, and hast cast down the walls of such as did thee no harm. (43) Therefore is thy wrongful dealing come up unto the Highest, and thy pride unto the Mighty. (44) The Highest also hath looked upon the proud times, and, behold, they are ended, and his abominations are fulfilled. (45) And therefore appear no more, thou eagle, nor thy horrible wings, nor thy wicked feathers nor thy malicious heads, nor thy hurtful claws, nor all thy vain body: (46) That all the earth may be refreshed, and may return, being delivered from thy violence, and that she may hope for the judgment and mercy of him that made her.

2 PETER 3:12-13—(12) Looking for and hasting unto the coming of the day of God, wherein the heavens being on fire shall be dissolved, and the elements shall melt with fervent heat? (13) Nevertheless we, according to his promise, look for new heavens and a new earth, wherein dwelleth righteousness.

ROMANS 9:4—Who are Israelites; to whom pertaineth the adoption, and the glory, and the covenants, and the giving of the law, and the service of God, and the promises.

PROVERBS 29:2—When the righteous are in authority, the people rejoice: but when the wicked beareth rule, the people mourn.

REVELATION 11:18—And the nations were angry, and thy wrath is come, and the time of the dead, that they should be judged, and that thou shouldest give reward unto thy servants the prophets, and to the saints, and them that fear thy name, small and great; and shouldest destroy them which destroy the earth.

VISION OF EZRA 1:48-49—(48) And he saw visions of a furnace against the setting sun, burning with great fire into which were sent many kings and princes of this world; (49) and many thousands of poor people were accusing them and saying 'They through their power, wounded us and dragged free men into servitude.'

APOCALYPSE OF ELIJAH 4:7-12—(7) Then when Elijah and Enoch hear that the shameless one has revealed himself in the holy place, they will come down and fight with him, saying (8) 'Are you indeed not ashamed? When you attach yourself to the saints, because you are always estranged. (9) You have been hostile to those who belong to heaven. You have acted against those belonging to the earth. (10) You have been hostile to the thrones. You have acted against the angels. You are always a stranger. (11) You have fallen from heaven like the morning stars. You were changed, and your tribe became dark for you. (12) But you are not ashamed. You are the Devil.

ROMANS 8:20-22

(20) For the creature was made subject to vanity, not willingly, but by reason of him who hath subjected the same in hope, (21) Because the creature itself also shall be delivered from the bondage of corruption into the glorious liberty of the children of God. (22) For we know that the whole creation groaneth and travaileth in pain together until now.

GENESIS 3:17-19—(17) And unto Adam he said, Because thou hast hearkened unto the voice of thy wife, and hast eaten of the tree, of which I commanded thee, saying, Thou shalt not eat of it: cursed is the ground for thy sake; in sorrow shalt thou eat of it all the days of thy life; (18) Thorns also and thistles shall it bring forth to thee; and thou shalt eat the herb of the field; (19) In the sweat of thy face shalt thou eat bread, till thou return unto the ground; for out of it wast thou taken: for dust thou art, and unto dust shalt thou return.

JEREMIAH 12:4, 11—(4) How long shall the land mourn, and the herbs of every field wither, for the wickedness of them that dwell therein? The beasts are consumed, and the birds; because they said, He shall not see our last end...(11) They have made it desolate, and being desolate it mourneth unto me; the whole land is made desolate, because no man layeth it to heart.

1 CORINTHIANS 15:42, 50—(42) So also is the resurrection of the dead. It is sown in corruption; it is raised in incorruption...(50) Now this I say, brethren, that flesh and blood cannot inherit the kingdom of God; neither doth corruption inherit incorruption.

ROMANS 8:23

And not only they, but ourselves also, which have the firstfruits of the Spirit, even we ourselves groan within ourselves, waiting for the adoption, to wit, the redemption of our body.

2 CORINTHIANS 5:2-5—(2) For in this we groan, earnestly desiring to be clothed upon with our house which is from heaven: (3) If so be that being clothed we shall not be found naked. (4) For we that are in this tabernacle do groan, being burdened: not for that we would be unclothed, but clothed upon, that mortality might be swallowed up of life. (5) Now he that hath wrought us for the selfsame thing is God, who also hath given unto us the earnest of the Spirit.

EPHESIANS 1:10-14—(10) That in the dispensation of the fullness of times he might gather together in one all things in Christ, both which are in heaven, and which are on earth; even in him: (11) In whom also we have obtained an inheritance, being predestinated according to the purpose of him who worketh all things after the counsel of his own will: (12) That we should be to the praise of his glory, who first trusted in Christ. (13) In whom ye also trusted, after that ye heard the word of truth, the gospel of your salvation: in whom also after that ye believed, ye were sealed with that holy Spirit of promise, (14) Which is the earnest of our inheritance until the redemption of the purchased possession, unto the praise of his glory.

LUKE 20:36—Neither can they die any more: for they are equal unto the angels; and are the children of God, being the children of the resurrection.

LUKE 21:28—And when these things begin to come to pass, then look up, and lift up your heads; for your redemption draweth nigh.

JOHN 20:22—And when he had said this, he breathed on them, and saith unto them, Receive ye the Holy Ghost.

ROMANS 8:15—For ye have not received the spirit of bondage again to fear; but ye have received the Spirit of adoption, whereby we cry, Abba, Father.

ACTS 10:45—And they of the circumcision, which believed, were astonished, as many as came with Peter, because that on the Gentiles also was poured out the gift of the Holy Ghost.

EPHESIANS 4:30—And grieve not the holy Spirit of God, whereby ye are sealed unto the day of redemption.

JAMES 1:18—(17) Every good gift and every perfect gift is from above, and cometh down from the Father of lights, with whom is no variableness, neither shadow of turning. (18) Of his own will begat he us with the word of truth, that we should be a kind of firstfruits of his creatures.

(Acts 2)

ROMANS 8:24-25

(24) For we are saved by hope: but hope that is seen is not hope: for what a man seeth, why doth he yet hope for? (25) But if we hope for that we see not, then do we with patience wait for it.

2 CORINTHIANS 5:7—For we walk by faith, not by sight.

2 CORINTHIANS 4:18—While we look not at the things, which are seen, but at the things, which are not seen: for the things, which are, seen are temporal; but the things, which are not seen, are eternal.

PSALMS 37:7-11—(7) Rest in the LORD, and wait patiently for him: fret not thyself because of him who prospereth in his way, because of the man who bringeth wicked devices to pass. (8) Cease from anger, and forsake wrath: fret not thyself in any wise to do evil. (9) For evildoers shall be cut off: but those that wait upon the LORD, they shall inherit the earth. (10) For yet a little while, and the wicked shall not be: yea, thou shalt diligently consider his place, and it shall not be. (11) But the meek shall inherit the earth; and shall delight themselves in the abundance of peace.

SIRACH 2:6-18—(6) Believe in him, and he will help thee; order thy way aright, and trust in him. (7) Ye that fear the Lord, wait for his mercy; and go not aside, lest ye fall. (8) Ye that fear the Lord, believe him; and your reward shall not fail. (9) Ye that fear the Lord, hope for good, and for everlasting joy and mercy. (10) Look at the generations of old, and see; did ever any trust in the Lord, and was confounded? or did any abide in his fear, and was forsaken? Or whom did he ever despise, that called upon him? (11) For the Lord is full of compassion and mercy, longsuffering, and very pitiful, and forgiveth sins, and saveth in time of affliction. (12) Woe be to fearful hearts, and faint hands, and the sinner that goeth two ways! (13) Woe unto him that is fainthearted! for he believeth not; therefore shall he not be defended. (14) Woe unto you that have lost patience! and what will ye do when the Lord shall visit you? (15) They that fear the Lord will not disobey his Word; and they that love him will keep his ways. (16) They that fear the Lord will seek that which is well, pleasing unto him; and they that love him shall be filled with the law. (17) They that fear the Lord will prepare their hearts, and humble their souls in his sight, (18) Saying, We will fall into the hands of the Lord, and not into the hands of men: for as his majesty is, so is his mercy.

PSALMS 147:11-12—(11) The LORD taketh pleasure in them that fear him, in those that hope in his mercy. (12) Praise the LORD, O Jerusalem; praise thy God, O Zion.

ISAIAH 40:31—But they that wait upon the LORD shall renew their strength; they shall mount up with wings as eagles; they shall run, and not be weary; and they shall walk, and not faint

HEBREWS 3;6—But Christ as a son over his own house; whose house are we, if we hold fast the confidence and the rejoicing of the hope firm unto the end

HEBREWS 11:1—Now faith is the substance of things hoped for, the evidence of things not seen.

ROMANS 8:26-27

(26) **Likewise the Spirit also helpeth our infirmities: for we know not what we should pray for as we ought: but the Spirit itself maketh intercession for us with groanings which cannot be uttered.** (27) **And he that searcheth the hearts knoweth what is the mind of the Spirit, because he maketh intercession for the saints according to the will of God.**

JOHN 14:16—And I will pray the Father, and he shall give you another Comforter, that he may abide with you forever

ROMANS 8:34—Who is he that condemneth? It is Christ that died, yea rather, that is risen again, who is even at the right hand of God, who also maketh intercession for us.

HEBREWS 7:23-28—(23) And they truly were many priests, because they were not suffered to continue by reason of death: (24) But this man, because he continueth ever, hath an unchangeable priesthood. (25) Wherefore he is able also to save them to the uttermost that come unto God by him, seeing he ever liveth to make intercession for them. (26) For such an high priest became us, who is holy, harmless, undefiled, separate from sinners, and made higher than the heavens; (27) Who needeth not daily, as those high priests, to offer up sacrifice, first for his own sins, and then for the people's: for this he did once, when he offered up himself. (28) For the law maketh men high priests which have infirmity; but the word of the oath, which was since the law, maketh the Son, who is consecrated forevermore.

ISAIAH 53:11-12—(11) He shall see of the travail of his soul, and shall be satisfied: by his knowledge shall my righteous servant justify many; for he shall bear their iniquities. (12) Therefore will I divide him a portion with the great, and he shall divide the spoil with the strong; because he hath poured out his soul unto death: and he was numbered with the transgressors; and he bare the sin of many, and made intercession for the transgressors.

(1 Chronicles 28:9; 1 Samuel 16:7; Jeremiah 17:10; 1 John 5:14)

ROMANS 8:28
And we know that all things work together for good to them that love God, to them who are the called according to his purpose.

JEREMIAH 32:27—Behold, I am the LORD, the God of all flesh: is there any thing too hard for me?

MATTHEW 19:26—But Jesus beheld them, and said unto them, With men this is impossible; but with God all things are possible.

LUKE 1:37—For with God nothing shall be impossible.

ISAIAH 45:7—I form the light, and create darkness: I make peace, and create evil: I the LORD do all these things.

EPHESIANS 1:9-12—(9) Having made known unto us the mystery of his will, according to his good pleasure which he hath purposed in himself (10) That in the dispensation of the fullness of times he might gather together in one all things in Christ, both which are in heaven, and which are on earth; even in him: (11) In whom also we have obtained an inheritance, being predestinated according to the purpose of him who worketh all things after the counsel of his own will: (12) That we should be to the praise of his glory, who first trusted in Christ.

ISAIAH 25:1—O LORD, thou art my God; I will exalt thee, I will praise thy name; for thou hast done wonderful things; thy counsels of old are faithfulness and truth.

ROMANS 9:11—For the children being not yet born, neither having done any good or evil, that the purpose of God according to election might stand, not of works, but of him that calleth.

2 TIMOTHY 1:9—Who hath saved us, and called us with an holy calling, not according to our works, but according to his own purpose and grace, which was given us in Christ Jesus before the world began.

ROMANS 8:29
For whom he did foreknow, he also did predestinate to be <u>conformed to the image of his Son</u>, that he might be the firstborn among many brethren.

EPHESIANS 1:5—Having predestinated us unto the adoption of children by Jesus Christ to himself, according to the good pleasure of his will.

EPHESIANS 1:11—In whom also we have obtained an inheritance, being predestinated according to the purpose of him who worketh all things after the counsel of his own will.

1 PETER 1:2—Elect according to the foreknowledge of God the Father, through sanctification of the Spirit, unto obedience and sprinkling of the blood of Jesus Christ: Grace unto you, and peace, be multiplied.

PSALMS 147:19-20—(19) He sheweth his word unto Jacob, his statutes and his judgments unto Israel. (20) He hath not dealt so with any nation:

and as for his judgments, they have not known them. Praise ye the LORD.

ISAIAH 41:8-10—(8) But thou, Israel, art my servant, Jacob whom I have chosen, the seed of Abraham my friend. (9) Thou whom I have taken from the ends of the earth, and called thee from the chief men thereof, and said unto thee, Thou art my servant; I have chosen thee, and not cast thee away. (10) Fear thou not; for I am with thee: be not dismayed; for I am thy God: I will strengthen thee; yea, I will help thee; yea, I will uphold thee with the right hand of my righteousness.

ISAIAH 45:3-4—(3) And I will give thee the treasures of darkness, and hidden riches of secret places, that thou mayest know that I, the LORD, which call thee by thy name, am the God of Israel. (4) For Jacob my servant's sake, and Israel mine elect, I have even called thee by thy name: I have surnamed thee, though thou hast not known me.

AMOS 3:2—You only have I known of all the families of the earth: therefore I will punish you for all your iniquities.

ROMANS 11:2—God hath not cast away his people which he foreknew.

(Isaiah 43:1)

ROMANS 8:30 [a]
Moreover whom he did predestinate, them he also <u>called</u>: and whom he called, them he also justified: and whom he justified, them he also glorified.

ISAIAH 48:12—Hearken unto me, O Jacob and Israel, my called; I am he; I am the first, I also am the last.

1 CORINTHIANS 1:9—God is faithful, by whom ye were called unto the fellowship of his Son Jesus Christ our Lord.

EPHESIANS 4:4—There is one body, and one Spirit, even as ye are called in one hope of your calling.

1 PETER 2:21—For even hereunto were ye called: because Christ also suffered for us, leaving us an example, that ye should follow his steps.

1 PETER 3:9—Not rendering evil for evil, or railing for railing: but contrariwise blessing; knowing that ye are thereunto called, that ye should inherit a blessing.

ISAIAH 45:3-4—(3) And I will give thee the treasures of darkness, and hidden riches of secret places, that thou mayest know that I, the Lord, which call thee by thy name, am the God of Israel. (4) For Jacob my servant's sake, and Israel mine elect, I have even called thee by thy name: I have surnamed thee, though thou hast not known me.

HOSEA 11:1—When Israel was a child, then I loved him, and called my son out of Egypt.

ROMANS 8:30 [b]
Moreover whom he did predestinate, them he also called: and whom he called, them he also justified: and whom he justified, them he also glorified.

STRONG'S # 1344: "justified"—*dikaioó (δικαιόω)*
USAGE: make righteous, defend the cause of, plead for the righteousness (innocence) of, acquit, justify; hence: I regard as righteous.

STRONG'S # 1392: "glorified"—*doxazó (δοξάζω)*
USAGE: glorify, honor, bestow glory on.

---

1 CORINTHIANS 6:11—And such were some of you: but ye are washed, but ye are sanctified, but ye are justified in the name of the Lord Jesus, and by the Spirit of our God.

ROMANS 9:4-5—(4) Who are **Israelites; to whom pertaineth** the adoption, and **the glory**...

2 CORINTHIANS 3:18—But we all, with open face beholding as in a glass the glory of the Lord, are changed into the same image from glory to glory, even as by the Spirit of the Lord.

1 PETER 1:2—Elect according to the foreknowledge of God the Father, through sanctification of the Spirit, unto obedience and sprinkling of the blood of Jesus Christ: Grace unto you, and peace, be multiplied.

1 PETER 2:9—But ye are a chosen generation, a royal priesthood, an holy nation, a peculiar people; that ye should shew forth the praises of him who hath called you out of darkness into his marvelous light.

ISAIAH 61:2-9—(2) To proclaim the acceptable year of the LORD, and the day of vengeance of our God; to comfort all that mourn; (3) To appoint unto them that mourn in Zion, to give unto them beauty for ashes, the oil of joy for mourning, the garment of praise for the spirit of heaviness; that they might be called trees of righteousness, the planting of the LORD, that he might be glorified...(9) And their seed shall be known among the Gentiles, and their offspring among the people: all that see them shall acknowledge them, that they *are* the seed, which the LORD hath blessed.

1 JOHN 3:2—Beloved, now are we the sons of God, and it doth not yet appear what we shall be: but we know that, when he shall appear, we shall be like him; for we shall see him as he is.

ZEPHANIAH 3:19-20—(19) Behold, at that time I will undo all that afflict thee: and I will save her that halteth, and gather her that was driven out; and I will get them praise and fame in every land where they have been put to shame. (20) At that time will I bring you again, even in the time that I gather you: for I will make you a name and a praise among all people of the earth, when I turn back your captivity before your eyes, saith the LORD.

ZECHARIAH 8:13—And it shall come to pass, that as ye were a curse among the heathen, O house of Judah, and house of Israel; so will I save you, and ye shall be a blessing: fear not, but let your hands be strong.

ROMANS 8:31
What shall we then say to these things? If God be for us, who can be against us?

TMH is for His children when we love Him. We demonstrate this love by keeping His commandments. *(John 14:15, 2 John 1:6)* As we yield to the Holy Spirit's leading, we produce righteous fruit, for it is TMH who does a good work in us. *(Philippians 2:12-13)* Therefore, if we follow His instructions, no weapon formed against us will prosper. *(Isaiah 54)* Obedience fuels *all* TMH's blessings.

ISAIAH 54:13-17—(13) ...all thy children shall be taught of the LORD; and great shall be the peace of thy children. (14) In righteousness shalt thou be established: thou shalt be far from oppression; for thou shalt not fear: and from terror; for it shall not come near thee. (15) Behold, they shall surely gather together, but not by me: whosoever shall gather together against thee shall fall for thy sake. (16) Behold, I have created the smith that bloweth the coals in the fire, and that bringeth forth an instrument for his work; and I have created the waster to destroy. (17) No weapon that is formed against thee shall prosper; and every tongue that shall rise against thee in judgment thou shalt condemn. This is the heritage of the servants of the LORD, and their righteousness is of me, saith the LORD.

EXODUS 23:20-22—(20) Behold, I send an Angel before thee, to keep thee in the way, and to bring thee into the place which I have prepared. (21) Beware of him, and obey his voice, provoke him not; for he will not pardon your transgressions: for my name is in him. (22) But if thou shalt indeed obey his voice, and do all that I speak; then I will be an enemy unto thine enemies, and an adversary unto thine adversaries.

DEUTERONOMY 28:1-2—(1) And it shall come to pass, if thou shalt hearken diligently unto the voice of the LORD thy God, to observe and to do all his commandments which I command thee this day, that the LORD thy God will set thee on high above all nations of the earth: (2) And all these blessings shall come on thee, and overtake thee, if thou shalt hearken unto the voice of the LORD thy God.

PSALMS 91—(1) He that dwelleth in the secret place of the most High shall abide under the shadow of the Almighty. (2) I will say of the LORD, He is my refuge and my fortress: my God; in him will I trust. (3) Surely he shall deliver thee from the snare of the fowler, and from the noisome pestilence. (4) He shall cover thee with his feathers, and under his wings shalt thou trust: his truth shall be thy shield and buckler. (5) Thou shalt not be afraid for the terror by night; nor for the arrow that flieth by day; (6) Nor for the pestilence that walketh in darkness; nor for the destruction that wasteth at noonday. (7) A thousand shall fall at thy side, and ten thousand at thy right hand; but it shall not come nigh thee. (8) Only with thine eyes shalt thou behold and see the reward of the wicked. (9) Because thou hast made the LORD, which is my refuge, even the most High, thy habitation; (10) There shall no evil befall thee, neither shall any plague come nigh thy dwelling. (11) For he shall give his angels charge over thee, to keep thee in all thy ways. (12) They shall bear thee up in their hands, lest thou dash thy foot against a stone. (13) Thou shalt tread upon the lion and adder: the young lion and the dragon shalt thou trample under feet. (14) Because he hath set his love upon me, therefore will I deliver him: I will set him on high, because he hath known my name. (15) He shall call upon me, and I will answer him: I will be with him in trouble; I will deliver him, and honour him. (16) With long life will I satisfy him, and shew him my salvation.

PSALMS 41:11—By this I know that thou favorest me, because mine enemy doth not triumph over me.

PSALMS 56:9—When I cry unto thee, then shall mine enemies turn back: this I know; for God is for me.

PSALMS 118:5-6—(5) I called upon the LORD in distress: the LORD answered me, and set me in a large place. (6) The LORD is on my side; I will not fear: what can man do unto me?

PSALMS 147:11—The LORD taketh pleasure in them that fear him, in those that hope in his mercy.

ISAIAH 44:1-8—(1) Yet now hear, O Jacob my servant; and Israel, whom I have chosen: (2) Thus saith the LORD that made thee, and formed thee from the womb, which will help thee; Fear not, O Jacob, my servant; and thou, Jesurun, whom I have chosen. (3) For I will pour water upon him that is thirsty, and floods upon the dry ground: I will pour my spirit upon thy seed, and my blessing upon thine offspring. (4) Thou art my King, O God: command deliverances for Jacob. (5) Through thee will we push down our enemies: through thy name will we tread them under that rise up against us. (6) For I will not trust in my bow, neither shall my sword save me. (7) But thou hast saved us from our enemies, and hast put them to shame that hated us. (8) In God we boast all the day long, and praise thy name forever. Selah.

1 JOHN 4:4—Ye are of God, little children, and have overcome them: because greater is he that is in you, than he that is in the world.

THE BOOK OF JUBILEES 18:15-16—(15)...And thy seed shall inherit the cities of its enemies, (16) and in thy seed shall all nations of the earth be blessed; because thou hast obeyed My voice, and I have shown to all that thou art faithful unto Me in all that I have said unto thee: Go in peace.

THE BOOK OF JUBILEES 19:27-30—(27) Jacob, my beloved son, whom my soul loveth, may God bless thee from above the firmament, and may He give thee all the blessings wherewith He blessed Adam, and Enoch, and Noah, and Shem; and all the things of which He told me, and all the things which He promised to give me, may he cause to cleave to thee and to thy seed forever, according to the days of heaven above the earth. (28) And the Spirits of Mastêmâ shall not rule over thee or over thy seed to turn thee from the Lord, who is thy God from henceforth forever. (29) And may the Lord God be a father to thee and thou the first-born son, and to the people always. (30) Go in peace, my son.' And they both went forth together from Abraham.

The Book of Jubilees 31:20—Blessed be he that blesseth thee, and all that hate thee and afflict thee and curse thee shall be rooted out and destroyed from the earth and be accursed.

(Numbers 14:9, 24:8-9; 1 Kings 8:57; Psalms 18:19, Psalms 91; Jeremiah 20:11; 1 Thessalonians 1:4-12)

ROMANS 8:32
He that spared not his own Son, but delivered him up for us all, how shall he not with him also freely give us all things?

LUKE 11:13—If ye then, being evil, know how to give good gifts unto your children: how much more shall your heavenly Father give the Holy Spirit to them that ask him?

2 ESDRAS 9:13—And therefore be thou not curious how the ungodly shall be punished, and when: but enquire how the righteous shall be saved, whose the world is, and for whom the world is created.

1 CORINTHIANS 2:9—But as it is written: "Eye has not seen, nor ear heard, Nor have entered into the heart of man The things which God has prepared for those who love Him."

JAMES 1:12—Blessed is the man that endureth temptation: for when he is tried, he shall receive the crown of life, which the Lord hath promised to them that love him.

JOHN 16:23-24—(23) And in that day ye shall ask me nothing. Verily, verily, I say unto you, Whatsoever ye shall ask the Father in my name, he will give it you. (24) Hitherto have ye asked nothing in my name: ask, and ye shall receive, that your joy may be full.

ROMANS 5:6, 10—(6) For when we were yet without strength, in due time Christ died for the ungodly...(10) For if, when we were enemies, we were reconciled to God by the death of his Son, much more, being reconciled, we shall be saved by his life.

(Genesis 22:12; Romans 8:1)

ROMANS 8:33 [a]
Who shall lay any thing to the charge of God's elect? It is God that justifieth.

Who are TMH's elect? Israel.

ISAIAH 45:4—For Jacob my servant's sake, and Israel mine elect, I have even called thee by thy name: I have surnamed thee, though thou hast not known me.

ISAIAH 65:9—And I will bring forth a seed out of Jacob, and out of Judah an inheritor of my mountains: and mine elect shall inherit it, and my servants shall dwell there.

ISAIAH 65:22—They shall not build, and another inhabit; they shall not plant, and another eat: for as the days of a tree are the days of my people, and mine elect shall long enjoy the work of their hands.

MATTHEW 24:22, 24, 31—(22) And except those days should be shortened, there should no flesh be saved: but for the elect's sake those days shall be shortened...(24) For there shall arise false Christs, and false prophets, and shall shew great signs and wonders; insomuch that, if it were possible, they shall deceive the very elect...(31) And he shall send his angels with a great sound of a trumpet, and they shall gather together his elect from the four winds, from one end of heaven to the other.

LUKE 18:7—And shall not God avenge his own elect, which cry day and night unto him, though he bear long with them?

WISDOM OF SOLOMON 3:9—They that put their trust in him shall understand the truth: and such as be faithful in love shall abide with him: for grace and mercy is to his saints, and he hath care for his elect.

SIRACH 47:22—But the Lord will never leave off his mercy, neither shall any of his works perish, neither will he abolish the posterity of his elect, and the seed of him that loveth him he will not take away: wherefore he gave a remnant unto Jacob, and out of him a root unto David.

PSALMS 155:21—Deliver Israel, your elect one; and those of the house of Jacob, your chosen one.

ROMANS 8:33 [b]
Who shall lay any thing to the charge of God's elect? It is God that justifieth.

The accuser of the brethren *(Revelation 12:10)* charges TMH's elect night and day. Therefore, it is imperative that we walk uprightly.

ISAIAH 50:8-9—(8) He is near that justifieth me; who will contend with me? Let us stand together: who is mine adversary? Let him come near to me. (9) Behold, the Lord GOD will help me; who is he that shall condemn me? Lo, they all shall wax old as a garment; the moth shall eat them up.

PSALMS 91:1-8—(1) He that dwelleth in the secret place of the most High shall abide under the shadow of the Almighty. (2) I will say of the LORD, He is my refuge and my fortress: my God; in him will I trust. (3) Surely he shall deliver thee from the snare of the fowler, and from the noisome pestilence. (4) He shall cover thee with his feathers, and under his wings shalt thou trust: his truth shall be thy shield and buckler. (5) Thou shalt not be afraid for the terror by night; nor for the arrow that flieth by day; (6) Nor for the pestilence that walketh in darkness; nor for the destruction that wasteth at noonday. (7) A thousand shall fall at thy side, and ten thousand at thy right hand; but it shall not come nigh thee. (8) Only with thine eyes shalt thou behold and see the reward of the wicked.

1 PETER 2:11-15—(11) Dearly beloved, I beseech you as strangers and pilgrims, abstain from fleshly lusts, which war against the soul; (12) Having your conversation honest among the Gentiles: that, whereas they speak against you as evildoers, they may by your good works, which they shall behold, glorify God in the day of visitation. (13) Submit yourselves to every ordinance of man for the Lord's sake: whether it be to the king, as supreme; (14) Or unto governors, as unto them that are sent by him for the punishment of evildoers, and for the praise of them that do well. (15) For so is the will of God, that with well doing ye may put to silence the ignorance of foolish men.

ROMANS 8:34
Who is he that condemneth? It is Christ that died, yea rather, that is risen again, who is even at the right hand of God, who also maketh intercession for us.

MARK 16:19—So then after the Lord had spoken unto them, he was received up into heaven, and sat on the right hand of God.

JOHN 3:18—He that believeth on him is not condemned: but he that believeth not is condemned already, because he hath not believed in the name of the only begotten Son of God.

COLOSSIANS 3:1—If ye then be risen with Christ, seek those things which are above, where Christ sitteth on the right hand of God.

HEBREWS 1:3—Who being the brightness of his glory, and the express image of his person, and upholding all things by the word of his power, when he had by himself purged our sins, sat down on the right hand of the Majesty on high

HEBREWS 7:25—Wherefore he is able also to save them to the uttermost that come unto God by him, seeing he ever liveth to make intercession for them.

HEBREWS 9:24—For Christ is not entered into the holy places made with hands, which are the figures of the true; but into heaven itself, now to appear in the presence of God for us.

1 JOHN 2:1—My little children, these things write I unto you, that ye sin not. And if any man sin, we have an advocate with the Father, Jesus Christ the righteous.

REVELATION 12:10—And I heard a loud voice saying in heaven, Now is come salvation, and strength, and the kingdom of our God, and the power of his Christ: for the accuser of our brethren is cast down, which accused them before our God day and night.

ROMANS 8:35-36

(35) Who shall separate us from the love of Christ? Shall tribulation, or distress, or persecution, or famine, or nakedness, or peril, or sword? (36) As it is written, For thy sake we are killed all the day long; we are accounted as sheep for the slaughter.

PSALMS 44:11-14—(11) Thou hast given us like sheep appointed for meat; and hast scattered us among the heathen. (12) Thou sellest thy people for nought, and dost not increase thy wealth by their price. (13) Thou makest us a reproach to our neighbors, a scorn and a derision to them that are round about us. (14) Thou makest us a byword among the heathen, a shaking of the head among the people.

PSALMS 44:22—Yea, for thy sake are we killed all the day long; we are counted as sheep for the slaughter.

JEREMIAH 50:17—Israel is a scattered sheep; the lions have driven him away: first the king of Assyria hath devoured him; and last this Nebuchadnezzar king of Babylon hath broken his bones.

PSALMS 43:1-5—(1) Judge me, O God, and plead my cause against an ungodly nation: O deliver me from the deceitful and unjust man. (2) For thou art the God of my strength: why dost thou cast me off? Why go I mourning because of the oppression of the enemy? (3) O send out thy light and thy truth: let them lead me; let them bring me unto thy holy hill, and to thy tabernacles. (4) Then will I go unto the altar of God, unto God my exceeding joy: yea, upon the harp will I praise thee, O God my God. (5) Why art thou cast down, O my soul? And why art thou disquieted within me? Hope in God: for I shall yet praise him, who is the health of my countenance, and my God.

(Deuteronomy 28:15-69)

ROMANS 8:37-39

(37) Nay, in all these things we are more than conquerors through him that loved us. (38) For I am persuaded, that neither death, nor life, nor angels, nor principalities, nor powers, nor things present, nor things to come, (39) Nor height, nor depth, nor any other creature, shall be able to separate us from the love of God, which is in Christ Jesus our Lord.

JEREMIAH 31:3-4—(3) The LORD hath appeared of old unto me, saying, Yea, I have loved thee with an everlasting love: therefore with lovingkindness have I drawn thee. (4) Again I will build thee, and thou shalt be built, O virgin of Israel: thou shalt again be adorned with thy tabrets, and shalt go forth in the dances of them that make merry.

MALACHI 1:2—I have loved you, saith the LORD. Yet ye say, Wherein hast thou loved us? Was not Esau Jacob's brother?" saith the LORD: Yet I loved Jacob....

ROMANS 5:8—But God commendeth his love toward us, in that, while we were yet sinners, Christ died for us.

1 CORINTHIANS 15:57—But thanks be to God, which giveth us the victory through our Lord Jesus Christ.

2 CORINTHIANS 2:14—Now thanks be unto God, which always causeth us to triumph in Christ, and maketh manifest the savor of his knowledge by us in every place.

REVELATION 3:9—Behold, I will make them of the synagogue of Satan, which say they are Jews, and are not, but do lie; behold, I will make them to come and worship before thy feet, and to know that I have loved thee.

EPHESIANS 6:12—For we wrestle not against flesh and blood, but against principalities, against powers, against the rulers of the darkness of this world, against spiritual wickedness in high places.

COLOSSIANS 2:10, 15—(10) And ye are complete in him, which is the head of all principality and power...(15) And having spoiled principalities and powers, he made a shew of them openly, triumphing over them in it.

1 KINGS 10:9—Blessed be the LORD thy God, which delighted in thee, to set thee on the throne of Israel: because the LORD loved Israel forever, therefore made he thee king, to do judgment and justice.

DEUTERONOMY 7:7-8—(7) The LORD did not set his love upon you, nor choose you, because ye were more in number than any people; for ye were the fewest of all people: (8) But because the LORD loved you, and because he would keep the oath, which he had sworn unto your fathers, hath the LORD brought you out with a mighty hand, and redeemed you out of the house of bondmen, from the hand of Pharaoh king of Egypt.

ISAIAH 49:14-17, 22-26—(14) But Zion said, The LORD hath forsaken me, and my Lord hath forgotten me. (15) Can a woman forget her sucking child, that she should not have compassion on the son of her womb? yea, they may forget, yet will I not forget thee. (16) Behold, I have graven thee upon the palms of my hands; thy walls are continually before me. (17) Thy children shall make haste; thy destroyers and they that made thee waste shall go forth of thee...(22) Thus saith the Lord GOD, Behold, I will lift up mine hand to the Gentiles, and set up my standard to the people: and they shall bring thy sons in their arms, and thy daughters shall be carried upon their shoulders. (23) And kings shall be thy nursing fathers, and their queens thy nursing mothers: they shall bow down to thee with their face toward the earth, and lick up the dust of thy feet; and thou shalt know that I am the LORD: for they shall not be ashamed that wait for me. (24) Shall the prey be taken from the mighty, or the lawful captive delivered? (25) But thus saith the LORD, Even the captives of the mighty shall be taken away, and the prey of the terrible shall be delivered: for I will contend with him that contendeth with thee, and I will save thy children. (26) And I will feed them that oppress thee with their own flesh; and they shall be drunken with their own blood, as with sweet wine: and all flesh shall know that I the LORD am thy Saviour and thy Redeemer, the mighty One of Jacob.

ROMANS 9

ROMANS 9:1-2
(1) I say the truth in Christ, I lie not, my conscience also bearing me witness in the Holy Ghost, (2) That I have great heaviness and continual sorrow in my heart.

Paul carried a huge burden to preach the gospel of the kingdom, most likely due to how he persecuted believers before he came into the truth.

ACTS 7:55-59—(55) But [Stephen], being full of the Holy Ghost, looked up steadfastly into heaven, and saw the glory of God, and Jesus standing on the right hand of God, (56) And said, Behold, I see the heavens opened, and the Son of man standing on the right hand of God. (57) Then they cried out with a loud voice, and stopped their ears, and ran upon him with one accord, (58) And cast him out of the city, and stoned him: and the witnesses laid down their clothes at a young man's feet, whose name was Saul. (59) And they stoned Stephen, calling upon God, and saying, Lord Jesus, receive my spirit.

ACTS 22:19-20—(19) And I said, Lord, they know that I imprisoned and beat in every synagogue them that believed on thee: (20) And when the blood of thy martyr Stephen was shed, I also was standing by, and consenting unto his death, and kept the raiment of them that slew him.

ROMANS 10:1—Brethren, my heart's desire and prayer to God for Israel is, that they might be saved.

1 CORINTHIANS 15:9-11—(9) For I am the least of the apostles, that am not meet to be called an apostle, because I persecuted the church of God. (10) But by the grace of God I am what I am: and his grace which was bestowed upon me was not in vain; but I labored more abundantly than they all: yet not I, but the grace of God which was with me. (11) Therefore whether it were I or they, so we preach, and so ye believed.

ROMANS 9:3-4 [a]
(3) For I could wish that myself were accursed from Christ <u>for my brethren, my kinsmen according to the flesh</u> (4)[a] <u>who are Israelites; to whom pertaineth the adoption</u>, and the glory, and the covenants, and the giving of the law, and the service of God, and the promises...

GALATIANS 4:4-5—(4) But when the fullness of the time was come, God sent forth his Son, made of a woman, made under the law, (5) To redeem them that were under the law, that we might receive the adoption of sons.

EXODUS 4:22—And thou shalt say unto Pharaoh, Thus saith the LORD, Israel is my son, even my firstborn.

ROMANS 8:14-15—(14) For as many as are led by the Spirit of God, they are the sons of God. (15) For ye have not received the spirit of bondage again to fear; but ye have received the Spirit of adoption, whereby we cry, Abba, Father.

ROMANS 8:23—And not only they, but ourselves also, which have the firstfruits of the Spirit, even we ourselves groan within ourselves, waiting for the adoption, to wit, the redemption of our body.

EPHESIANS 1:5—Having predestinated us unto the adoption of children by Jesus Christ to himself, according to the good pleasure of his will

---

ROMANS 9:4 [b]
Who are Israelites; to whom pertaineth the adoption, and the glory, and the covenants, and the giving of the law, and the service of God, and the promises...

PSALMS 149—(1) Praise ye the LORD. Sing unto the LORD a new song, and his praise in the congregation of saints. (2) Let Israel rejoice in him that made him: let the children of Zion be joyful in their King. (3) Let them praise his name in the dance: let them sing praises unto him with the timbrel and harp. (4) For the LORD taketh pleasure in his people: he will beautify the meek with salvation. (5) **Let the saints be joyful in glory**: let them sing aloud upon their beds. (6) Let the high praises of God be in their mouth, and a two-edged sword in their hand; (7) to execute vengeance upon the heathen, and punishments upon the people; (8) To bind their kings with chains, and their nobles with fetters of iron; (9) To execute upon them the judgment written: **this honor have all his saints**. Praise ye the LORD.

ISAIAH 62:2-4—(2) **And the Gentiles shall see thy righteousness, and all kings thy glory:** and thou shalt be called by a new name, which the mouth of the LORD shall name. (3) **Thou shalt also be a crown of glory** in the hand of the LORD, and a royal diadem in the hand of thy God. (4) Thou shalt no more be termed Forsaken; neither shall thy land any more be termed Desolate: but thou shalt be called Hephzibah, and thy land Beulah: for the LORD delighteth in thee, and thy land shall be married.

ZECHARIAH 12:7—The LORD also shall save the tents of Judah first, **that the glory of the house of David and the glory of the inhabitants of Jerusalem do not magnify themselves against Judah.**

ROMANS 8:18-19—(18) For I reckon that the sufferings of this present time are not worthy to be compared with **the glory, which shall be revealed in us.** (19) For the earnest expectation of the creature waiteth for the manifestation of the sons of God.

ACTS 29:10-12 *[Lost Chapter]*—(10) And at even the Holy Ghost fell upon Paul, and he prophesied, saying, Behold in the last days the God of Peace shall dwell in the cities, and the inhabitants thereof shall be numbered; and in the seventh numbering of the people, their eyes shall be opened, **and the glory of their inheritance shine forth before them.** And nations shall come up to worship on the Mount that testifieth of the patience and long suffering of a servant of the Lord. (11) And in the latter days new tidings of the Gospel shall issue forth out of Jerusalem, and the hearts of the people shall rejoice, and behold, fountains shall be opened, and there shall be no more plague. (12) In those days there shall be wars and rumors of wars; and a king shall rise up, and his sword shall be for the healing of the nations, and his peacemaking shall abide, and the glory of his kingdom a wonder among princes.

BARUCH 4:24—Like as now the neighbors of Sion have seen your captivity: so shall they see shortly your salvation from our God, which shall come upon you with great glory, and brightness of the Everlasting.

BARUCH 5:5-6—(5) Arise, O Jerusalem, and stand on high, and look about toward the east, and behold thy children gathered from the west unto the east by the word of the Holy One, rejoicing in the remembrance of God. (6) For they departed from thee on foot, and were led away of their enemies: but God bringeth them unto thee exalted with glory, as children of the kingdom.

2 BARUCH 51:3-6—(3) Also (as for) the glory of those who have now been justified in My law, who have had understanding in their life, and who have planted in their heart the root of wisdom, then their splendor shall be glorified in changes, and the form of their face shall be turned into the light of their beauty, that they may be able to acquire and receive the world which does not die, which is then promised to them. (4) For over this above all shall those who come then lament, that they rejected My law, and stopped their ears that they might not hear wisdom or receive understanding. (5) When therefore they see those, over whom they are now exalted, (but) who shall then be exalted and glorified more than they, they shall respectively be transformed, the latter into the splendor of angels, and the former shall yet more waste away in wonder at the visions and in the beholding of the forms. (6) For they shall first behold and afterwards depart to be tormented.

DEUTERONOMY 28:1—And it shall come to pass, if thou shalt hearken diligently unto the voice of the LORD thy God, to observe and to do all his commandments which I command thee this day, that the LORD thy God will set thee on high above all nations of the earth.

(1 Samuel 4:21; Isaiah 60:1-4; 2 Baruch 32:1-6; 1 Maccabees 2:12-13)

ROMANS 9:4 [c]
Who are Israelites; to whom pertaineth the adoption, and the glory, and the covenants, and the giving of the law, and the service of God, and the promises...

GENESIS 17:2, 7—(2) And I will make my covenant between me and thee, and will multiply thee exceedingly...(7) And I will establish my covenant between me and thee and thy seed after thee in their generations for an everlasting covenant, to be a God unto thee, and to thy seed after thee.

DEUTERONOMY 29:1,10-15—(1) These are the words of the covenant, which the LORD commanded Moses to make with the children of Israel in the land of Moab, beside the covenant which he made with them in Horeb...(10) Ye stand this day all of you before the LORD your God; your captains of your tribes, your elders, and your officers, with all the men of Israel, (11) Your little ones, your wives, and thy stranger that is in thy camp, from the hewer of thy wood unto the drawer of thy water: (12) That thou shouldest enter into covenant with the LORD thy God, and into his oath, which the LORD thy God maketh with thee this day: (13) That he may establish thee to day for a people unto himself, and that he may be unto thee a God, as he hath said unto thee, and as he hath sworn unto thy fathers, to Abraham, to Isaac, and to Jacob. (14) Neither with you only do I make this covenant and this oath; (15) But with him that standeth here with us this day before the LORD our God, and also with him that is not here with us this day.

LEVITICUS 26:39-46—(39) And they that are left of you shall pine away in their iniquity in your enemies' lands; and also in the iniquities of their fathers shall they pine away with them. (40) If they shall confess their iniquity, and the iniquity of their fathers, with their trespass which they trespassed against me, and that also they have walked contrary unto me; (41) And that I also have walked contrary unto them, and have brought them into the land of their enemies; if then their uncircumcised hearts be humbled, and they then accept of the punishment of their iniquity: (42)

Then will I remember my covenant with Jacob, and also my covenant with Isaac, and also my covenant with Abraham will I remember; and I will remember the land. (43) The land also shall be left of them, and shall enjoy her sabbaths, while she lieth desolate without them: and they shall accept of the punishment of their iniquity: because, even because they despised my judgments, and because their soul abhorred my statutes. (44) And yet for all that, when they be in the land of their enemies, I will not cast them away, neither will I abhor them, to destroy them utterly, and to break my covenant with them: for I am the LORD their God. (45) But I will for their sakes remember the covenant of their ancestors, whom I brought forth out of the land of Egypt in the sight of the heathen, that I might be their God: I am the LORD. (46) These are the statutes and judgments and laws, which the LORD made between him and the children of Israel in mount Sinai by the hand of Moses.

PSALMS 50:5—Gather my saints together unto me; those that have made a covenant with me by sacrifice.

JEREMIAH 31:31-33—(31) Behold, the days come, saith the LORD, that I will make a new covenant with the house of Israel, and with the house of Judah: (32) Not according to the covenant that I made with their fathers in the day that I took them by the hand to bring them out of the land of Egypt; which my covenant they brake, although I was an husband unto them, saith the LORD: (33) But this shall be the covenant that I will make with the house of Israel; After those days, saith the LORD, I will put my law in their inward parts, and write it in their hearts; and will be their God, and they shall be my people.

LUKE 1:72—To perform the mercy promised to our fathers, and to remember his holy covenant.

LUKE 22:19-20—(19) And he took bread, and gave thanks, and brake [it], and gave unto them, saying, This is my body which is given for you: this do in remembrance of me. (20) Likewise also the cup after supper, saying, This cup is the new testament in my blood, which is shed for you.

ACTS 3:25—Ye are the children of the prophets, and of the covenant which God made with our fathers, saying unto Abraham, And in thy seed shall all the kindreds of the earth be blessed.

HEBREWS 8:7-13—(7) For if that first covenant had been faultless, then should no place have been sought for the second. (8) For finding fault with them, he saith, Behold, the days come, saith the Lord, when I will make a new covenant with the house of Israel and with the house of Judah: (9) Not according to the covenant that I made with their fathers in the day when I took them by the hand to lead them out of the land of

Egypt; because they continued not in my covenant, and I regarded them not, saith the Lord. (10) For this is the covenant that I will make with the house of Israel after those days, saith the Lord; I will put my laws into their mind, and write them in their hearts: and I will be to them a God, and they shall be to me a people: (11) And they shall not teach every man his neighbour, and every man his brother, saying, Know the Lord: for all shall know me, from the least to the greatest. (12) For I will be merciful to their unrighteousness, and their sins and their iniquities will I remember no more. (13) In that he saith, A new covenant, he hath made the first old. Now that which decayeth and waxeth old is ready to vanish away.

HEBREWS 9:15—And for this cause he is the mediator of the new testament, that by means of death, for the redemption of the transgressions that were under the first testament, they which are called might receive the promise of eternal inheritance.

(Deuteronomy 29:1; Jeremiah 34:18; Ezekiel 16:60)

ROMANS 9:4 [d]
Who are Israelites; to whom pertaineth the adoption, and The glory, and the covenants, and the giving of the law, and the service of God, and the promises;

LEVITICUS 26:46—These are the statutes and judgments and laws, which the LORD made between him and the children of Israel in mount Sinai by the hand of Moses.

DEUTERONOMY 4:8—And what nation is there so great, that hath statutes and judgments so righteous as all this law, which I set before you this day.

PSALMS 147:19-20—(19) He sheweth his word unto Jacob, his statutes and his judgments unto Israel. (20) He hath not dealt so with any nation: and as for his judgments, they have not known them. Praise ye the LORD.

AMOS 3:7—Surely the Lord GOD will do nothing, but he revealeth his secret unto his servants the prophets.

ROMANS 3:1-2—(1) What advantage then hath the Jew? Or what profit is there of circumcision? (2) Much every way: chiefly, because that unto them were committed the oracles of God.

GALATIANS 4:4-5—(4) But when the fullness of the time was come, God sent forth his Son, made of a woman, made under the law, (5) To redeem them that were under the law, that we might receive the adoption of sons.

2 ESDRAS 5:27—And among all the multitudes of people thou hast gotten thee one people: and unto this people, whom thou lovedst, thou gavest a law that is approved of all.

BOOK OF ENOCH 104:12-13—(12) Then, I know another mystery, that books will be given to the righteous and the wise to become a cause of joy and uprightness and much wisdom. (13) And to them shall the books be given, and they shall believe in them and rejoice over them, and then shall all the righteous who have learnt therefrom all the paths of uprightness be recompensed.

ROMANS 9:4 [e]
Who are Israelites; to whom pertaineth the adoption, and the glory, and the covenants, and the giving of the law, <u>and the service of God</u>, and the promises...

HEBREWS 9:1, 6—(1) <u>Then verily the first covenant</u> had also ordinances of <u>divine service</u>, and a worldly sanctuary...(6) Now when these things were thus ordained, the priests went always into the first tabernacle, accomplishing <u>the service of God</u>.

EXODUS 19:5—Now therefore, if ye will obey my voice indeed, and keep my covenant, then ye shall be <u>a peculiar treasure unto me above all people</u>: for all the earth is mine.

LEVITICUS 20:26—And ye <u>shall be holy unto me</u>: for I the LORD am holy, and have severed you from other people, that <u>ye should be mine</u>.

LEVITICUS 25:55—For unto me <u>the children of Israel are servants; they are my servants</u> whom I brought forth out of the land of Egypt: I am the LORD your God.

DEUTERONOMY 7:6—For thou art an holy people unto the LORD thy God: the LORD thy <u>God hath chosen thee to be a special people</u> unto himself, <u>above all people that are upon the face of the earth</u>.

DEUTERONOMY 14:2—For thou art an holy people unto the LORD thy God, and <u>the LORD hath chosen thee to be a peculiar people unto himself, above all the nations that are upon the earth</u>.

DEUTERONOMY 26:18-19—(18) And the LORD hath avouched thee this day to be <u>his peculiar people</u>, as he hath promised thee, and that thou shouldest keep all his commandments; (19) And to make thee high above all nations which he hath made, in praise, and in name, and in honour; and that thou mayest be an holy people unto the LORD thy God, as he hath spoken.

DEUTERONOMY 28:9—The LORD shall establish thee an holy people unto himself, as he hath sworn unto thee, if thou shalt keep the commandments of the LORD thy God, and walk in his ways.

ISAIAH 41:8-9—(8) But thou, Israel, art my servant, Jacob whom I have chosen, the seed of Abraham my friend. (9) Thou whom I have taken from the ends of the earth, and called thee from the chief men thereof, and said unto thee, Thou art my servant; I have chosen thee, and not cast thee away.

ISAIAH 61:6—But ye shall be named the Priests of the LORD: men shall call you the Ministers of our God: ye shall eat the riches of the Gentiles, and in their glory shall ye boast yourselves.

AMOS 3:7—Surely the Lord GOD will do nothing, but he revealeth his secret unto his servants the prophets.

ADDITIONS TO ESTHER 10:9-12—(9) And my nation is this Israel, which cried to God, and were saved: for the Lord hath saved his people, and the Lord hath delivered us from all those evils, and God hath wrought signs and great wonders, which have not been done among the Gentiles. (10) Therefore hath he made two lots, one for the people of God, and another for all the Gentiles. (11) And these two lots came at the hour, and time, and Day of Judgment, before God among all nations. (12) So God remembered his people, and justified his inheritance.

1 PETER 2:9—But ye are a chosen generation, a royal priesthood, an holy nation, a peculiar people; that ye should shew forth the praises of him who hath called you out of darkness into his marvelous light...

REVELATION 1:5-6—(5) And from Jesus Christ, who is the faithful witness, and the first begotten of the dead, and the prince of the kings of the earth. Unto him that loved us, and washed us from our sins in his own blood, (6) and hath made us kings and priests unto God and his Father; to him be glory and dominion forever and ever. Amen.

REVELATION 5:8-10—(8) And when he had taken the book, the four beasts and four and twenty elders fell down before the Lamb, having every one of them harps, and golden vials full of odors, which are the prayers of saints. (9) And they sung a new song, saying, Thou art worthy to take the book, and to open the seals thereof: for thou wast slain, and hast redeemed us to God by thy blood out of every kindred, and tongue, and people, and nation; (10) And hast made us unto our God kings and priests: and we shall reign on the earth.

REVELATION 7:3-8—(3) Saying, Hurt not the earth, neither the sea, nor the trees, till we have sealed the servants of our God in their foreheads. (4) And I heard the number of them, which were sealed: and there were sealed an hundred and forty and four thousand of all the tribes of the children of Israel. (5) Of the tribe of Judah were sealed twelve thousand. Of the tribe of Reuben were sealed twelve thousand. Of the tribe of Gad were sealed twelve thousand. (6) Of the tribe of Asher were sealed twelve thousand. Of the tribe of Naphtali were sealed twelve thousand. Of the tribe of Manassas were sealed twelve thousand. (7) Of the tribe of Simeon were sealed twelve thousand. Of the tribe of Levi were sealed twelve thousand. Of the tribe of Issachar were sealed twelve thousand. (8) Of the tribe of Zebulon were sealed twelve thousand. Of the tribe of Joseph were sealed twelve thousand. Of the tribe of Benjamin were sealed twelve thousand.

THE BOOK OF JUBILEES 16:18—For he should become the portion of the Most High, and all his seed had fallen into the possession of God, that it should be unto the Lord a people for (His) possession above all nations and that it should become a kingdom and priests and a holy nation.

ROMANS 9:4 [f]
Who are Israelites; to whom pertaineth the adoption, and the glory, and the covenants, and the giving of the law, and the service of God, and the promises...

GENESIS 15:18-21—(18) In the same day the LORD made a covenant with Abram, saying, Unto thy seed have I given this land, from the river of Egypt unto the great river, the river Euphrates: (19) The Kenites, and the Kenizzites, and the Kadmonites, (20) And the Hittites, and the Perizzites, and the Rephaims, (21) And the Amorites, and the Canaanites, and the Girgashites, and the Jebusites.

GENESIS 21:10—Wherefore she said unto Abraham, Cast out this bondwoman and her son: for the son of this bondwoman shall not be heir with my son, even with Isaac.

DEUTERONOMY 1:8—Behold, I have set the land before you: go in and possess the land which the LORD sware unto your fathers, Abraham, Isaac, and Jacob, to give unto them and to their seed after them.

PRECEPTS FOR ROMANS

DEUTERONOMY 6:3—Hear therefore, O Israel, and observe to do it; that it may be well with thee, and that ye may increase mightily, as the LORD God of thy fathers hath promised thee, in the land that floweth with milk and honey.

DEUTERONOMY 28:1-13—(1) And it shall come to pass, if thou shalt hearken diligently unto the voice of the LORD thy God, to observe and to do all his commandments which I command thee this day, that the LORD thy God will set thee on high above all nations of the earth: (2) And all these blessings shall come on thee, and overtake thee, if thou shalt hearken unto the voice of the LORD thy God. (3) Blessed shalt thou be in the city, and blessed shalt thou be in the field. (4) Blessed shall be the fruit of thy body, and the fruit of thy ground, and the fruit of thy cattle, the increase of thy kine, and the flocks of thy sheep. (5) Blessed shall be thy basket and thy store. (6) Blessed shalt thou be when thou comest in, and blessed shalt thou be when thou goest out. (7) The LORD shall cause thine enemies that rise up against thee to be smitten before thy face: they shall come out against thee one way, and flee before thee seven ways. (8) The LORD shall command the blessing upon thee in thy storehouses, and in all that thou settest thine hand unto; and he shall bless thee in the land which the LORD thy God giveth thee. (9) The LORD shall establish thee an holy people unto himself, as he hath sworn unto thee, if thou shalt keep the commandments of the LORD thy God, and walk in his ways. (10) And all people of the earth shall see that thou art called by the name of the LORD; and they shall be afraid of thee. (11) And the LORD shall make thee plenteous in goods, in the fruit of thy body, and in the fruit of thy cattle, and in the fruit of thy ground, in the land which the LORD sware unto thy fathers to give thee. (12) The LORD shall open unto thee his good treasure, the heaven to give the rain unto thy land in his season, and to bless all the work of thine hand: and thou shalt lend unto many nations, and thou shalt not borrow. (13) And the LORD shall make thee the head, and not the tail; and thou shalt be above only, and thou shalt not be beneath; if that thou hearken unto the commandments of the LORD thy God, which I command thee this day, to observe and to do them.

2 ESDRAS 6:9, 59—(9) For Esau is the end of the world, and Jacob is the beginning of it that followeth…(59) If the world now be made for our sakes, why do we not possess an inheritance with the world? How long shall this endure?

2 ESDRAS 2:8:1—And he answered me, saying, The most High hath made this world for many, but the world to come for few.

2 ESDRAS 7:11—Because for their sakes I made the world: and when Adam transgressed my statutes, then was decreed that now is done.

ACTS 2:39—For the promise is unto you, and to your children, and to all that are afar off, even as many as the Lord our God shall call.

ACTS 5:29-31—(29) Then Peter and the other apostles answered and said, We ought to obey God rather than men. (30) The God of our fathers raised up Jesus, whom ye slew and hanged on a tree. (31) Him hath God exalted with his right hand [to be] a Prince and a Saviour, for to give repentance to Israel, and forgiveness of sins.

ACTS 13:23-24, 32-35—(23) Of this man's seed hath God according to his promise raised unto Israel a Saviour, Jesus: (24) When John had first preached before his coming the baptism of repentance to all the people of Israel...(32) And we declare unto you glad tidings, how that the promise which was made unto the fathers (33) God hath fulfilled the same unto us their children, in that he hath raised up Jesus again; as it is also written in the second psalm, Thou art my Son, this day have I begotten thee. (34) And as concerning that he raised him up from the dead, now no more to return to corruption, he said on this wise, I will give you the sure mercies of David. (35) Wherefore he saith also in another psalm, Thou shalt not suffer thine Holy One to see corruption.

ROMANS 9:6-13—(6) Not as though the word of God hath taken none effect. For they are not all Israel, which are of Israel: (7) Neither, because they are the seed of Abraham, are they all children: but, In Isaac shall thy seed be called. (8) That is, They which are the children of the flesh, these are not the children of God: but the children of the promise are counted for the seed. (9) For this is the word of promise, At this time will I come, and Sara shall have a son. (10) And not only this; but when Rebekah also had conceived by one, even by our father Isaac; (11) (For the children being not yet born, neither having done any good or evil, that the purpose of God according to election might stand, not of works, but of him that calleth;) (12) It was said unto her, The elder shall serve the younger. (13) As it is written, Jacob have I loved, but Esau have I hated.

HEBREWS 6:17—Wherein God, willing more abundantly to shew unto the heirs of promise the immutability of his counsel, confirmed it by an oath.

HEBREWS 9:15—And for this cause he is the mediator of the new testament, that by means of death, for the redemption of the transgressions that were under the first testament, they which are called might receive the promise of eternal inheritance.

GALATIANS 3:16-17—(16) Now to Abraham and his seed were the promises made. He saith not, And to seeds, as of many; but as of one, And to thy seed, which is Christ. (17) And this I say, that the covenant, that was confirmed before of God in Christ, the law, which was four hundred and thirty years after, cannot disannul, that it should make the promise of none effect. **

Re: Galatians 3:16—The line *"He saith not, And to seeds, as of many, but as of one,"* is often misinterpreted to imply that the seed referred to here is not the children of Israel. It's assumed this seed only refers to Messiah. This is incorrect. Actually, the scripture applies to both the Messiah *and* the children of Israel. Sarah's son Isaac is the initial seed of promise because it was with him that the first selection/rejection began, i.e. Isaac vs. Ishmael. Notice the wording:

"...He saith not, and to seeds, as of many...." —These *"seeds, as of many,"* are Ishmael, Zimran, Jokshan, Medan, Midian, Ishbak, Shahs, and their descendants. These are the seeds Abraham had with Hagar, Keturah and his concubine.

"...but as of one..."—That *'one'* seed is Isaac and Isaac's seed thereafter, which includes Jacob, Jacob's children, and their descendants.

"*AND* to thy seed, which is Christ." The *"and"* in this sentence makes it clear that Messiah is included in this group, but is also ***distinct***.

Romans 4:16 agrees: "Therefore it is of faith, that it might be by grace; to the end **the promise** might be sure **to *all* the seed...**"

So *Galatians 3:16-17* and *Romans 4:16* line up perfectly with *Romans 9:4*. The keyword in all these scriptures is: **PROMISE(S)**.

This is the essence of Sarah's prophetic declaration in *Genesis*:

GENESIS 21:10—Wherefore she said unto Abraham, Cast out this bondwoman and her son: for the son of this bondwoman shall not be heir with my son, even with Isaac.

The Book of Jubilees drives the point home:

THE BOOK OF JUBILEES 15:30-32—(30) For Ishmael and his sons and his brothers and Esau, the Lord did not cause to approach Him, and he chose them not because they are the children of Abraham, because He knew them, but He chose Israel to be His people. (31) And He sanctified it, and gathered it from amongst all the children of men; for there are many nations and many peoples, and all are His, and over all hath He placed spirits in authority to lead them astray from Him. (32) But over Israel He did not appoint any angel or spirit, for He alone is their ruler, and He will preserve them and require them at the hand of His angels and his spirits, and at the hand of all His powers in order that He may preserve them and bless them, and that they may be His and He may be theirs from henceforth forever.

ROMANS 9:5 [a1]
Whose are the fathers, and of whom as concerning the flesh Christ came, who is over all, God blessed forever. Amen.

Abraham

GENESIS 12:1-3—(1) Now the LORD had said unto Abram, Get thee out of thy country, and from thy kindred, and from thy father's house, unto a land that I will shew thee: (2) And I will make of thee a great nation, and I will bless thee, and make thy name great; and thou shalt be a blessing: (3) And I will bless them that bless thee, and curse him that curseth thee: and in thee shall all families of the earth be blessed.

GENESIS 17:4-7—(4) As for me, behold, my covenant is with thee, and thou shalt be a father of many nations. (5) Neither shall thy name any more be called Abram, but thy name shall be Abraham; for a father of many nations have I made thee. (6) And I will make thee exceeding fruitful, and I will make nations of thee, and kings shall come out of thee. (7) And I will establish my covenant between me and thee and thy seed after thee in their generations for an everlasting covenant, to be a God unto thee, and to thy seed after thee.

GENESIS 17:9-11—(9) And God said unto Abraham, Thou shalt keep my covenant therefore, thou, and thy seed after thee in their generations. (10) This is my covenant, which ye shall keep, between me and you and thy seed after thee; Every man-child among you shall be circumcised. (11) And ye shall circumcise the flesh of your foreskin; and it shall be a token of the covenant betwixt me and you.

2 ESDRAS 3:12-15—(12) And it happened, that when they that dwelt upon the earth began to multiply, and had gotten them many children, and were a great people, they began again to be more ungodly than the first. (13) Now when they lived so wickedly before thee, thou didst choose thee a man from among them, whose name was Abraham. (14) Him thou lovedst, and unto him only thou shewedst thy will: (15) And madest an everlasting covenant with him, promising him that thou wouldest never forsake his seed.

GALATIANS 3:16—Now to Abraham and his seed were the promises made. He saith not, And to seeds, as of many; but as of one, and to thy seed, which is Christ.

THE BOOK OF JUBILEES 18:15-16—(15) And he said: 'By Myself have I sworn, saith the Lord, because thou hast done this thing, and hast not withheld thy son, thy beloved son, from Me, that in blessing I will bless thee, and in multiplying I will multiply thy seed as the stars of heaven, and as the sand which is on the seashore. And thy seed shall inherit the cities of its enemies, (16) and in thy seed shall all nations of the earth be blessed; because thou hast obeyed My voice, and I have shown to all that thou art faithful unto Me in all that I have said unto thee: Go in peace.

(Genesis 12:6-7, 13:14-15, 15:18-21, 18:17-19; 2 Esdras 3:12-13, Hebrews 11:8-19)

ROMANS 9:5 [a2]
Whose are the fathers, and of whom as concerning the flesh Christ came, who is over all, God blessed forever. Amen.

Isaac

GENESIS 17:19-21—(19) And God said, Sarah thy wife shall bear thee a son indeed; and thou shalt call his name Isaac: and I will establish my covenant with him for an everlasting covenant, and with his seed after him. (20) And as for Ishmael, I have heard thee: Behold, I have blessed him, and will make him fruitful, and will multiply him exceedingly; twelve princes shall he beget, and I will make him a great nation. (21) But my covenant will I establish with Isaac, which Sarah shall bear unto thee at this set time in the next year.

GENESIS 21:9-12—(9) And Sarah saw the son of Hagar the Egyptian, which she had born unto Abraham, mocking. (10) Wherefore she said unto Abraham, Cast out this bondwoman and her son: for the son of this bondwoman shall not be heir with my son, even with Isaac. (11) And the thing was very grievous in Abraham's sight because of his son. (12) And God said unto Abraham, Let it not be grievous in thy sight because of the lad, and because of thy bondwoman; in all that Sarah hath said unto thee, hearken unto her voice; for in Isaac shall thy seed be called.

4 MACCABEES 16:18—For whom also our father Abraham was ready to sacrifice his son Isaac, who was to be the father of our nation: and Isaac shrank not on seeing the paternal hand, armed with a knife, descending upon him.

GALATIANS 4:22-23, 28—(22) For it is written, that Abraham had two sons, the one by a bondmaid, the other by a freewoman. (23) But he who was of the bondwoman was born after the flesh; but he of the freewoman was by promise...(28) Now we, brethren, as Isaac was, are the children of promise.

SIRACH 44:22—With Isaac did he establish likewise for Abraham his father's sake the blessing of all men, and the covenant, And made it rest upon the head of Jacob. He acknowledged him in his blessing, and gave him an heritage, and divided his portions; among the twelve tribes did he part them.

(Genesis 25:11; Romans 9:7-10; Hebrews 11:17-19; Sirach 44:22)

ROMANS 9:5 [a3]
Whose are the fathers, and of whom as concerning the flesh Christ came, who is over all, God blessed forever. Amen.

Jacob/Israel

GENESIS 25:22-26—(22) And the children struggled together within her; and she said, If it be so, why am I thus? And she went to inquire of the LORD. (23) And the LORD said unto her, Two nations are in thy womb, and two manner of people shall be separated from thy bowels; and the one people shall be stronger than the other people; and the elder shall serve the younger. (24) And when her days to be delivered were fulfilled, behold, there were twins in her womb. (25) And the first came out red, all over like an hairy garment; and they called his name Esau. (26) And after that came his brother out, and his hand took hold on Esau's heel; and his name was called Jacob: and Isaac was threescore years old when she bare them.

GENESIS 27:26-29—(26) And his father Isaac said unto him, Come near now, and kiss me, my son. (27) And he came near, and kissed him: and he smelled the smell of his raiment, and blessed him, and said, See, the smell of my son is as the smell of a field which the LORD hath blessed: (28) Therefore God give thee of the dew of heaven, and the fatness of the earth, and plenty of corn and wine: (29) Let people serve thee, and nations bow down to thee: be lord over thy brethren, and let thy mother's sons bow down to thee: cursed be every one that curseth thee, and blessed be he that blesseth thee.

MALACHI 1:2-3—(2) I have loved you, saith the LORD. Yet ye say, Wherein hast thou loved us? Was not Esau Jacob's brother? saith the LORD: yet I loved Jacob, (3) And I hated Esau, and laid his mountains and his heritage waste for the dragons of the wilderness.

2 ESDRAS 6:9—For Esau is the end of the world, and Jacob is the beginning of it that followeth.

GENESIS 32:24-28—(24) And Jacob was left alone; and there wrestled a man with him until the breaking of the day. (25) And when he saw that he prevailed not against him, he touched the hollow of his thigh; and the hollow of Jacob's thigh was out of joint, as he wrestled with him. (26) And he said, Let me go, for the day breaketh. And he said, I will not let thee go, except thou bless me. (27) And he said unto him, What is thy name? And he said, Jacob. (28) And he said, Thy name shall be called no more Jacob, but Israel: for as a prince hast thou power with God and with men, and hast prevailed.

THE BOOK OF JUBILEES 19:27-30—(27) Jacob, my beloved son, whom my soul loveth, may God bless thee from above the firmament, and may He give thee all the blessings wherewith He blessed Adam, and Enoch, and Noah, and Shem; and all the things of which He told me, and all the things which He promised to give me, may he cause to cleave to thee and to thy seed forever, according to the days of heaven above the earth. (28) And the Spirits of Mastêmâ shall not rule over thee or over thy seed to turn thee from the Lord, who is thy God from henceforth forever. (29) And may the Lord God be a father to thee and thou the first-born son, and to the people always. (30) Go in peace, my son.' And they both went forth together from Abraham.

MALACHI 1:2—I have loved you, saith the LORD. Yet ye say, Wherein hast thou loved us? *Was* not Esau Jacob's brother? saith the LORD: yet I loved Jacob...

(2 Esdras 6:6-9; Sirach 44:21-22; 4 Ezra 5:7-10; Book of Jubilees 19:27-30; Romans 9:13)

ROMANS 9:5 [a4]
Whose are the fathers, and of whom as concerning the flesh Christ came, who is over all, God blessed forever. Amen.

The Twelve Patriarchs

GENESIS 49:28—All these are the twelve tribes of Israel: and this is it that their father spake unto them, and blessed them; every one according to his blessing he blessed them.

Reuben *(Genesis 49:3-4)*; **Simeon and Levi** *(Genesis 49:5-7)*; **Judah** *(Genesis 49:8-12)*; **Zebulun** *(Genesis 49:13)*; **Issachar** *(Genesis 49:14-15)*; **Dan** *(Genesis 49:16-18)*; **Gad** *(Genesis 49:19)*; **Asher** *(Genesis 49:20)*; **Naphtali** *(Genesis 49:21)*; **Joseph** *(Genesis 49:22-26)*; **Benjamin** *(Genesis 49:27)*; **Ephraim & Manasseh** *(Genesis 48:11-20, Hebrews 11:21)*

ROMANS 9:5 [b]
Whose are the fathers, <u>and of whom as concerning the flesh Christ came, who is over all, God blessed forever. Amen.</u>

MATTHEW 1:21—And she shall bring forth a son, and thou shalt call his name JESUS: <u>for he shall save his people from their sins.</u>

MATTHEW 15:24—But he answered and said, <u>I am not sent but unto the lost sheep of the house of Israel.</u>

ACTS 5:29-31—(29) Then Peter and the other apostles answered and said, We ought to obey God rather than men. (30) <u>The God of our fathers raised up Jesus,</u> whom ye slew and hanged on a tree. (31) Him hath God exalted with his right hand to be a Prince and a Saviour, for <u>to give repentance to Israel, and forgiveness of sins.</u>

LUKE 1:76-77—(76) And thou, child, shalt be called the prophet of the Highest: for thou shalt go before the face of the Lord to prepare his ways; (77) <u>To give knowledge of salvation unto his people by the remission of their sins.</u>

JOHN 11:48-52—(48) If we let him thus alone, all men will believe on him: and the Romans shall come and take away both our place and nation. (49) And one of them, named Caiaphas, being the high priest that same year, said unto them, Ye know nothing at all, (50) Nor consider that it is expedient for us, <u>that one man should die for the people, and that the whole nation perish not.</u> (51) And this spake he not of himself: but being high priest that year, he prophesied that Jesus should die for that nation; (52) <u>And not for that nation only, but that also he should gather together in one the children of God that were scattered abroad.</u>

DEUTERONOMY 10:15—Only the LORD had a delight in thy fathers to love them, <u>and he chose their seed after them, even you above all people, as it is this day.</u>

ISAIAH 53:3-6—(3) He is despised and rejected of men; a man of sorrows, and acquainted with grief: and we hid as it were our faces from him; he was despised, and we esteemed him not. (4) <u>Surely he hath borne our griefs, and carried our sorrows</u>: yet we did esteem him stricken, smitten of God, and afflicted. (5) <u>But he was wounded for our transgressions, he was bruised for our iniquities: the chastisement of our peace was upon him; and with his stripes we are healed. (6) All we like sheep have gone astray; we have turned every one to his own way; and the LORD hath laid on him the iniquity of us all.</u>

JEREMIAH 23:6—In his days Judah shall be saved, and Israel shall dwell safely: and this is his name whereby he shall be called, THE LORD OUR RIGHTEOUSNESS.

JAMES 1:1—James, a servant of God and of the Lord Jesus Christ, to the twelve tribes, which are scattered abroad, greeting.

ROMANS 9:6
Not as though the word of God hath taken none effect.
For they are not all Israel, which are of Israel:

As the saying goes, "Not all skin-folk are kinfolk."

JUDGES 9:1-6—(1) And Abimelech the son of Jerubbaal went to Shechem unto his mother's brethren, and communed with them, and with all the family of the house of his mother's father, saying, (2) Speak, I pray you, in the ears of all the men of Shechem, Whether is better for you, either that all the sons of Jerubbaal, which are threescore and ten persons, reign over you, or that one reign over you? Remember also that I am your bone and your flesh. (3) And his mother's brethren spake of him in the ears of all the men of Shechem all these words: and their hearts inclined to follow Abimelech; for they said, He is our brother. (4) And they gave him threescore and ten pieces of silver out of the house of Baalberith, wherewith Abimelech hired vain and light persons, which followed him. (5) And he went unto his father's house at Ophrah, and slew his brethren the sons of Jerubbaal, being threescore and ten persons, upon one stone: notwithstanding yet Jotham the youngest son of Jerubbaal was left; for he hid himself. (6) And all the men of Shechem gathered together, and all the house of Millo, and went, and made Abimelech king, by the plain of the pillar that was in Shechem

2 CHRONICLES 21:4—Now when Jehoram was established over the kingdom of his father, he strengthened himself and killed all his brothers with the sword, and also others of the princes of Israel.

JUDGES 19:16, 20-22—(16) And, behold, there came an old man from his work out of the field at even, which was also of mount Ephraim; and he sojourned in Gibeah: but the men of the place were Benjamites...(20) And the old man said, Peace be with thee; howsoever let all thy wants lie upon me; only lodge not in the street. (21) So he brought him into his house, and gave provender unto the asses: and they washed their feet, and did eat and drink. (22) Now as they were making their hearts merry, behold, the men of the city, certain sons of Belial, beset the house round about, and beat at the door, and spake to the master of the house, the old man, saying, Bring forth the man that came into thine house, that we may know him.

1 SAMUEL 18:6-12—(6) And it came to pass as they came, when David was returned from the slaughter of the Philistine, that the women came out of all cities of Israel, singing and dancing, to meet king Saul, with tabrets, with joy, and with instruments of music. (7) And the women answered one another as they played, and said, Saul hath slain his thousands, and David his ten thousands. (8) And Saul was very wroth, and the saying displeased him; and he said, They have ascribed unto David ten thousands, and to me they have ascribed but thousands: and what can he have more but the kingdom? (9) And Saul eyed David from that day and forward. (10) And it came to pass on the morrow, that the evil spirit from God came upon Saul, and he prophesied in the midst of the house: and David played with his hand, as at other times: and there was a javelin in Saul's hand. (11) And Saul cast the javelin; for he said, I will smite David even to the wall with it. And David avoided out of his presence twice. (12) And Saul was afraid of David, because the LORD was with him, and was departed from Saul.

1 KINGS 19:1-2—(1) And Ahab told Jezebel all that Elijah had done, and withal how he had slain all the prophets with the sword. (2) Then Jezebel sent a messenger unto Elijah, saying, So let the gods do to me, and more also, if I make not thy life as the life of one of them by to morrow about this time.

2 MACCABEES 4:12-15—(12) John the father of Eupolemus built gladly a place of exercise under the tower itself, and brought the chief young men under his subjection, and made them wear a hat. (13) Now such was the height of Greek fashions, and increase of heathenish manners, through the exceeding profaneness of Jason, that ungodly wretch, and no high priest; (14) That the priests had no courage to serve any more at the altar, but despising the temple, and neglecting the sacrifices, hastened to be partakers of the unlawful allowance in the place of exercise, after the game of Discus called them forth; (15) Not setting by the honors of their fathers, but liking the glory of the Grecians best of all.

MATTHEW 10:21-22, 35-36—(21) Now brother will deliver up brother to death, and a father his child; and children will rise up against parents and cause them to be put to death. (22) And you will be hated by all for My name's sake. But he who endures to the end will be saved...(35) For I am come to set a man at variance against his father, and the daughter against her mother, and the daughter in law against her mother in law. (36) And a man's foes shall be they of his own household.

MARK 8:31—And he began to teach them, that the Son of man must suffer many things, and be rejected of the elders, and of the chief priests, and scribes, and be killed, and after three days rise again.

MARK 14:10—And Judas Iscariot, one of the twelve, went unto the chief priests, to betray him unto them.

LUKE 8:19-20—(19) Then came to him his mother and his brethren, and could not come at him for the press. (20) And it was told him by certain which said, Thy mother and thy brethren stand without, desiring to see thee. (21) And he answered and said unto them, My mother and my brethren are these which hear the word of God, and do it.

LUKE 12:52-53—(52) For from henceforth there shall be five in one house divided, three against two, and two against three. (53) The father shall be divided against the son, and the son against the father; the mother against the daughter, and the daughter against the mother; the mother in law against her daughter in law, and the daughter in law against her mother in law.

JOHN 8:37-47—(37) I know that ye are Abraham's seed; but ye seek to kill me, because my word hath no place in you. (38) I speak that which I have seen with my Father: and ye do that which ye have seen with your father. (39) They answered and said unto him, Abraham is our father. Jesus saith unto them, If ye were Abraham's children, ye would do the works of Abraham. (40) But now ye seek to kill me, a man that hath told you the truth, which I have heard of God: this did not Abraham. (41) Ye do the deeds of your father. Then said they to him, We be not born of fornication; we have one Father, even God. (42) Jesus said unto them, If God were your Father, ye would love me: for I proceeded forth and came from God; neither came I of myself, but he sent me. (43) Why do ye not understand my speech? Even because ye cannot hear my word. (44) Ye are of your father the devil, and the lusts of your father ye will do. He was a murderer from the beginning, and abode not in the truth, because there is no truth in him. When he speaketh a lie, he speaketh of his own: for he is a liar, and the father of it. (45) And because I tell you the truth, ye believe me not. (46) Which of you convinceth me of sin? And if I say the truth, why do ye not believe me? (47) He that is of God heareth God's words: ye therefore hear them not, because ye are not of God.

ACTS 20:30—Also of your own selves shall men arise, speaking perverse things, to draw away disciples after them.

1 CORINTHIANS 11:19—For there must be also heresies among you, that they which are approved may be made manifest among you.

1 JOHN 2:19—They went out from us, but they were not of us; for if they had been of us, they would no doubt have continued with us: but they went out, that they might be made manifest that they were not all of us.

(Deuteronomy 13:6-10; Matthew 7:21; Romans 4:16; 2 John 1:7)

ROMANS 9:7-9
(7) Neither, because they are the seed of Abraham, are they all children: but, In Isaac shall thy seed be called. (8) That is, they which are the children of the flesh, these are not the children of God: but the children of the promise are counted for the seed. (9) For this is the word of promise, At this time will I come, and Sara shall have a son.

Abraham had many sons, but the seed of promise was Isaac. The children of the flesh are Abraham's other sons. The children of the promise come from an actual seed (not spiritual) of a man (Isaac), who fathered Jacob, who then fathered the twelve tribes of Israel. These are TMH's chosen, an actual bloodline of people. TMH rightfully told Abraham that rather than Eliezer, his loyal, but *unrelated* servant, the blessings and promises would be on a people Abraham would *physically* father.

The Christian doctrine of 'Spiritual Israel' is wicked. Any teaching that seeks to replace TMH's chosen people with others is blasphemous. *(Revelation 2:9)* There is no such thing as 'spiritual Israel' as defined by Christian doctrine. *Romans 9:6-11* shows who true Israel is.

GENESIS 15:3-4—(3) And Abram said, Behold, to me thou hast given no seed: and, lo, one born in my house is mine heir. (4) And, behold, the word of the LORD came unto him, saying, This shall not be thine heir; but **he that shall come forth out of thine own bowels shall be thine heir**.

GENESIS 18:10, 14—(10) And he said, I will certainly return unto thee according to the time of life; and, lo, Sarah thy wife shall have a son. And Sarah heard it in the tent door, which was behind him…(14) Is any thing too hard for the LORD? At the time appointed I will return unto thee, according to the time of life, and Sarah shall have a son.

GENESIS 21:9-12—(9) And Sarah saw the son of Hagar the Egyptian, which she had born unto Abraham, mocking. (10) Wherefore she said unto Abraham, Cast out this bondwoman and her son: for the son of this bondwoman shall not be heir with my son, even with Isaac. (11) And the thing was very grievous in Abraham's sight because of his son. (12) And God said unto Abraham, Let it not be grievous in thy sight because of the lad, and because of thy bondwoman; in all that Sarah hath said unto thee, hearken unto her voice; for **in Isaac shall thy seed be called**.

GALATIANS 4:22-23, 28—(22) For it is written, that Abraham had two sons, the one by a bondmaid, the other by a freewoman. (23) But he who was of the bondwoman was born after the flesh; but he of the freewoman was by promise...(28) Now we, brethren, as Isaac was, are the children of promise.

HEBREWS 11:17-19—(17) By faith Abraham, when he was tried, offered up Isaac: and he that had received the promises offered up his only begotten son, (18) Of whom it was said, That in Isaac shall thy seed be called: (19) Accounting that God was able to raise him up, even from the dead; from whence also he received him in a figure.

SIRACH 44:22—With Isaac did he establish likewise for Abraham his father's sake the blessing of all men, and the covenant, And made it rest upon the head of Jacob. He acknowledged him in his blessing, and gave him an heritage, and divided his portions; among the twelve tribes did he part them.

THE BOOK OF JUBILEES 15:30-32—(30) For Ishmael and his sons and his brothers and Esau, the Lord did not cause to approach Him, and he chose them not because they are the children of Abraham, because He knew them, but He chose Israel to be His people. (31) And He sanctified it, and gathered it from amongst all the children of men; for there are many nations and many peoples, and all are His, and over all hath He placed spirits in authority to lead them astray from Him. (32) But over Israel He did not appoint any angel or spirit, for He alone is their ruler, and He will preserve them and require them at the hand of His angels and his spirits, and at the hand of all His powers in order that He may preserve them and bless them, and that they may be His and He may be theirs from henceforth forever.

(Romans 4:16; Galatians 3:29, 6:16)

ROMANS 9:10-11

(10) **And not only this; but when Rebecca also had conceived by one, even by our father Isaac;** (11) **(For the children being not yet born, neither having done any good or evil, that the purpose of God according to <u>election</u> might stand, not of works, but of him that calleth)**

This is where the term "elect" comes from, wherein TMH narrows down His choice to one bloodline of people. Those of the election are the children of Israel.

GENESIS 25:21-27—(21) And Isaac entreated the LORD for his wife, because she was barren: and the LORD was entreated of him, and Rebekah his wife conceived. (22) And the children struggled together within her; and she said, If it be so, why am I thus? And she went to enquire of the LORD. (23) And the LORD said unto her, <u>Two nations are in thy womb, and two manner of people shall be separated from thy bowels;</u> and the <u>one people shall be stronger than the other people; and the elder shall serve the younger.</u> (24) And when her days to be delivered were fulfilled, behold, there were twins in her womb. (25) And the first came out red, all over like an hairy garment; and they called his name Esau. (26) And after that came his brother out, and his hand took hold on Esau's heel; and his name was called Jacob: and Isaac was threescore years old when she bare them. (27) And the boys grew: and Esau was a cunning hunter, a man of the field; and Jacob was a plain man, dwelling in tents.

GENESIS 27:27-29—(27) And he came near, and kissed him: and he smelled the smell of his raiment, and blessed him, and said, See, the smell of my son is as the smell of a field which the LORD hath blessed: (28) Therefore God give thee of the dew of heaven, and the fatness of the earth, and plenty of corn and wine: (29) Let people serve thee, and nations bow down to thee: be lord over thy brethren, and let thy mother's sons bow down to thee: <u>cursed be every one that curseth thee, and blessed be he that blesseth thee.</u>

ISAIAH 45:4—For Jacob my servant's sake, and <u>Israel mine elect</u>, I have even called thee by thy name: I have surnamed thee, though thou hast not known me.

SIRACH 46:1—Jesus the son a Nave was valiant in the wars, and was the successor of Moses in prophecies, who according to his name was made great for the saving of <u>the elect of God</u>, and taking vengeance of the enemies that rose up against them, that he might set Israel in their inheritance.

SIRACH 47:22—But the Lord will never leave off his mercy, neither shall any of his works perish, neither <u>will he abolish the posterity of his elect</u>, and the seed of him that loveth him he will not take away: wherefore he gave a remnant unto Jacob, and out of him a root unto David.

PSALMS 155:21—<u>Deliver Israel, your elect one; and those of the house of Jacob, your chosen one.</u> (This Psalm was removed from the bible)

ROMANS 9:12
It was said unto her, The elder shall serve the younger.

GENESIS 25:23—And the LORD said unto her, Two nations are in thy womb, and two manner of people shall be separated from thy bowels; and the one people shall be stronger than the other people; and the elder shall serve the younger.

GENESIS 25:29-34—(29) And Jacob sod pottage: and Esau came from the field, and he was faint: (30) And Esau said to Jacob, Feed me, I pray thee, with that same red pottage; for I am faint: therefore was his name called Edom. (31) And Jacob said, Sell me this day thy birthright. (32) And Esau said, Behold, I am at the point to die: and what profit shall this birthright do to me? (33) And Jacob said, Swear to me this day; and he sware unto him: and he sold his birthright unto Jacob. (34) Then Jacob gave Esau bread and pottage of lentils; and he did eat and drink, and rose up, and went his way: thus Esau despised his birthright.

OBADIAH 1:19-21—(19) And *they of* the south shall possess the mount of Esau; and *they of* the plain the Philistines: and they shall possess the fields of Ephraim, and the fields of Samaria: and Benjamin *shall possess* Gilead. (20) And the captivity of this host of the children of Israel *shall possess* that of the Canaanites, *even* unto Zarephath; and the captivity of Jerusalem, which *is* in Sepharad, shall possess the cities of the south. (21) And saviours shall come up on mount Zion to judge the mount of Esau; and the kingdom shall be the LORD'S.

MATTHEW 20:16—So the last shall be first, and the first last: for many be called, but few chosen.

ROMANS 9:13
As it is written, Jacob have I loved, but Esau have I hated.

Esau also goes by the names Edom, Daughter of Edom, Seir, Mount Seir, Idumea, the Wicked, and the Daughter of Babylon.

So why does TMH hate Esau? And why, according to *Zondervan's Compact Bible Dictionary,* (Pg. 142) are Esau and his descendants the only nation not promised mercy from TMH? The scriptures give a definitive answer:

GENESIS 27:41-42—(41) And Esau hated Jacob because of the blessing wherewith his father blessed him: and Esau said in his heart, The days of mourning for my father are at hand; then will I slay my brother Jacob. (42) And these words of Esau her elder son were told to Rebekah: and she sent and called Jacob her younger son, and said unto him, Behold, thy brother Esau, as touching thee, doth comfort himself, purposing to kill thee.

JEREMIAH 49:10—But I have made Esau bare, I have uncovered his secret places, and he shall not be able to hide himself: his seed is spoiled, and his brethren, and his neighbors, and he is not.

EZEKIEL 25:12-14—(12) Thus saith the Lord GOD; Because that Edom hath dealt against the house of Judah by taking vengeance, and hath greatly offended, and revenged himself upon them; (13) Therefore thus saith the Lord GOD; I will also stretch out mine hand upon Edom, and will cut off man and beast from it; and I will make it desolate from Teman; and they of Dedan shall fall by the sword. (14) And I will lay my vengeance upon Edom by the hand of my people Israel: and they shall do in Edom according to mine anger and according to my fury; and they shall know my vengeance, saith the Lord GOD.

EZEKIEL 35:2-3—(2) Son of man, set thy face against mount Seir, and prophesy against it, (3) And say unto it, Thus saith the Lord GOD; Behold, O mount Seir, I am against thee, and I will stretch out mine hand against thee, and I will make thee most desolate.

EZEKIEL 35:5-15—(5) Because thou hast had a perpetual hatred, and hast shed the blood of the children of Israel by the force of the sword in the time of their calamity, in the time that their iniquity had an end: (6) Therefore, as I live, saith the Lord GOD, I will prepare thee unto blood, and blood shall pursue thee: sith thou hast not hated blood, even blood shall pursue thee. (7) Thus will I make mount Seir most desolate, and cut off from it him that passeth out and him that returneth. (8) And I will fill his mountains with his slain men: in thy hills, and in thy valleys, and in all thy rivers, shall they fall that are slain with the sword. (9) I will make thee perpetual desolations, and thy cities shall not return: and ye shall know that I am the LORD. (10) Because thou hast said, These two nations and these two countries shall be mine, and we will possess it; whereas the LORD was there: (11) Therefore, as I live, saith the Lord GOD, I will even do according to thine anger, and according to thine envy which thou hast used out of thy hatred against them; and I will make myself known among them, when I have judged thee. (12) And thou shalt know that I am the LORD, and that I have heard all thy blasphemies which thou hast spoken against the mountains of Israel, saying, They are laid desolate, they are given us to consume. (13) Thus with your mouth ye have boasted against me, and have multiplied your words against me: I have heard them. (14) Thus saith the Lord GOD; When the whole earth rejoiceth, I will make thee desolate. (15) As thou didst rejoice at the inheritance of the house of Israel, because it was desolate, so will I do unto thee: thou shalt be desolate, O mount Seir, and all Idumea, even all of it: and they shall know that I am the LORD.

EZEKIEL 36:5—Therefore thus saith the Lord GOD; Surely in the fire of my jealousy have I spoken against the residue of the heathen, and against all Idumea, which have appointed my land into their possession with the joy of all their heart, with despiteful minds, to cast it out for a prey.

PSALMS 137:7-8—(7) Remember, O LORD, against the sons of Edom the day of Jerusalem, who said, "Raze it, raze it to its very foundation." (8) O daughter of Babylon, you devastated one, how blessed will be the one who repays you with the recompense with which you have repaid us.

JOEL 3:19—Egypt shall be a desolation, and Edom shall be a desolate wilderness, for the violence against the children of Judah, because they have shed innocent blood in their land.

AMOS 1:9, 11-12—(9) Thus saith the LORD; For three transgressions of Tyrus, and for four, I will not turn away the punishment thereof; because they delivered up the whole captivity to Edom, and remembered not the brotherly covenant...(11) Thus saith the LORD; For three transgressions of Edom, and for four, I will not turn away the punishment thereof; because he did pursue his brother with the sword, and did cast off all pity, and his anger did tear perpetually, and he kept his wrath forever: (12) But I will send a fire upon Teman, which shall devour the palaces of Bozrah.

OBADIAH 1:10-15—(10) For thy violence against thy brother Jacob shame shall cover thee, and thou shalt be cut off forever. (11) In the day that thou stoodest on the other side, in the day that the strangers carried away captive his forces, and foreigners entered into his gates, and cast lots upon Jerusalem, even thou wast as one of them. (12) But thou shouldest not have looked on the day of thy brother in the day that he became a stranger; neither shouldest thou have rejoiced over the children of Judah in the day of their destruction; neither shouldest thou have spoken proudly in the day of distress. (13) Thou shouldest not have entered into the gate of my people in the day of their calamity; yea, thou shouldest not have looked on their affliction in the day of their calamity, nor have laid hands on their substance in the day of their calamity; (14) Neither shouldest thou have stood in the crossway, to cut off those of his that did escape; neither shouldest thou have delivered up those of his that did remain in the day of distress. (15) For the day of the LORD is near upon all the heathen: as thou hast done, it shall be done unto thee: thy reward shall return upon thine own head.

ISAIAH 34:4-8—(4) And all the host of heaven shall be dissolved, and the heavens shall be rolled together as a scroll: and all their host shall fall down, as the leaf falleth off from the vine, and as a falling fig from the fig tree. (5) For my sword shall be bathed in heaven: behold, it shall come down upon Idumea, and upon the people of my curse, to judgment. (6) The sword of the LORD is filled with blood, it is made fat with fatness, and with the blood of lambs and goats, with the fat of the kidneys of rams: for the LORD hath a sacrifice in Bozrah, and a great slaughter in the land of Idumea. (7) And the unicorns shall come down with them, and the bullocks with the bulls; and their land shall be soaked with blood, and their dust made fat with fatness. (8) For it is the day of the LORD'S vengeance, and the year of recompenses for the controversy of Zion.

ISAIAH 63:1-6—(1) Who is this that cometh from Edom, with dyed garments from Bozrah? this that is glorious in his apparel, travelling in the greatness of his strength? I that speak in righteousness, mighty to save. (2) Wherefore art thou red in thine apparel, and thy garments like him that treadeth in the winefat? (3) I have trodden the winepress alone; and of the people there was none with me: for I will tread them in mine anger, and trample them in my fury; and their blood shall be sprinkled upon my garments, and I will stain all my raiment. (4) For the day of vengeance is in mine heart, and the year of my redeemed is come. (5) And I looked, and there was none to help; and I wondered that there was none to uphold: therefore mine own arm brought salvation unto me; and my fury, it upheld me. (6) And I will tread down the people in mine anger, and make them drunk in my fury, and I will bring down their strength to the earth.

JEREMIAH 49:16-18—(16) Thy terribleness hath deceived thee, and the pride of thine heart, O thou that dwellest in the clefts of the rock, that holdest the height of the hill: though thou shouldest make thy nest as high as the eagle, I will bring thee down from thence, saith the LORD. (17) Also Edom shall be a desolation: every one that goeth by it shall be astonished, and shall hiss at all the plagues thereof. (18) As in the overthrow of Sodom and Gomorrah and the neighbour cities thereof, saith the LORD, no man shall abide there, neither shall a son of man dwell in it.

JEREMIAH 49:20-22—(20) Therefore hear the counsel of the LORD, that he hath taken against Edom; and his purposes, that he hath purposed against the inhabitants of Teman: Surely the least of the flock shall draw them out: surely he shall make their habitations desolate with them. (21) The earth is moved at the noise of their fall, at the cry the noise thereof was heard in the Red Sea. (22) Behold, he shall come up and fly as the eagle, and spread his wings over Bozrah: and at that day shall the heart of the mighty men of Edom be as the heart of a woman in her pangs.

LAMENTATIONS 4:19-22—(19) Our persecutors are swifter than the eagles of the heaven: they pursued us upon the mountains, they laid wait for us in the wilderness. (20) The breath of our nostrils, the anointed of the LORD, was taken in their pits, of whom we said, Under his shadow we shall live among the heathen. (21) Rejoice and be glad, O daughter of Edom, that dwellest in the land of Uz; the cup also shall pass through unto thee: thou shalt be drunken, and shalt make thyself naked. (22) The punishment of thine iniquity is accomplished, O daughter of Zion; he will no more carry thee away into captivity: he will visit thine iniquity, O daughter of Edom; he will discover thy sins.

MALACHI 1:2-4—(2) I have loved you, saith the LORD. Yet ye say, Wherein hast thou loved us? Was not Esau Jacob's brother? saith the LORD: yet I loved Jacob, (3) And I hated Esau, and laid his mountains and his heritage waste for the dragons of the wilderness. (4) Whereas Edom saith, We are impoverished, but we will return and build the desolate places; thus saith the LORD of hosts, They shall build, but I will throw down; and they shall call them, The border of wickedness, and, The people against whom the LORD hath indignation forever.

2 ESDRAS 6:9—For Esau is the end of the world, and Jacob is the beginning of it that followeth.

THE BOOK OF JUBILEES 24:3-7—(3) And Jacob sod lentil pottage, and Esau came from the field hungry. And he said to Jacob his brother: 'Give me of this red pottage.' And Jacob said to him: 'Sell to me thy [primogeniture, this] birthright and I will give thee bread, and also some of this lentil pottage.' (4) And Esau said in his heart: 'I shall die; of what profit to me is this birthright? (5) 'And he said to Jacob: 'I give it to thee.' And Jacob said: 'Swear to me, this day,' and he sware unto him. (6) And Jacob gave his brother Esau bread and pottage, and he eat till he was satisfied, and Esau despised his birthright; for this reason was Esau's name called Edom, on account of the red pottage which Jacob gave him for his birthright. (7) And Jacob became the elder, and Esau was brought down from his dignity.

APOCALYPSE OF ELIJAH 4:7-12—(7) Then when Elijah and Enoch hear that the shameless one has revealed himself in the holy place, they will come down and fight with him, saying (8) 'Are you indeed not ashamed? When you attach yourself to the saints, because you are always estranged. (9) You have been hostile to those who belong to heaven. You have acted against those belonging to the earth. (10) You have been hostile to the thrones. You have acted against the angels. You are always a stranger. (11) You have fallen from heaven like the morning stars. You were changed, and your tribe became dark for you. (12) But you are not ashamed. You are the Devil.

ROMANS 9:21-22—(21) Hath not the potter power over the clay, of the same lump to make one vessel unto honour, and another unto dishonor? (22) What if God, willing to shew his wrath, and to make his power known, endured with much longsuffering the vessels of wrath fitted to destruction.

HEBREWS 12:16-17—(16) Lest there be any fornicator, or profane person, as Esau, who for one morsel of meat sold his birthright. (17) For ye know how that afterward, when he would have inherited the blessing, he was rejected: for he found no place of repentance, though he sought it carefully with tears.

(Genesis 25:29-34; 1 Esdras 8:69; Words of Gad the Seer 2:78, 80-83, 2:85-86)

ROMANS 9:14-16

(14) What shall we say then? Is there unrighteousness with God? God forbid. (15) For he saith to Moses, I will have mercy on whom I will have mercy, and I will have compassion on whom I will have compassion. (16) So then it is not of him that willeth, nor of him that runneth, but of God that sheweth mercy.

EXODUS 33:19—And he said, I will make all my goodness pass before thee, and I will proclaim the name of the LORD before thee; and will be gracious to whom I will be gracious, and will shew mercy on whom I will shew mercy.

DEUTERONOMY 32:4—He is the Rock, his work is perfect: for all his ways are judgment: a God of truth and without iniquity, just and right is he.

EXODUS 34:6—And the LORD passed by before him, and proclaimed, The LORD, The LORD God, merciful and gracious, longsuffering, and abundant in goodness and truth

PSALMS 118:1-4—(1) O give thanks unto the LORD; for he is good: because his mercy endureth forever. (2) Let Israel now say, that his mercy endureth forever. (3) Let the house of Aaron now say, that his mercy endureth forever. (4) Let them now that fear the LORD say, that his mercy endureth forever.

ROMANS 9:17-18

(17) For the scripture saith unto Pharaoh, Even for this same purpose have I raised thee up, that I might shew my power in thee, and that my name might be declared

throughout all the earth. **(18) Therefore hath he mercy on whom he will have mercy, and whom he will he hardeneth.**

EXODUS 4:21—And the LORD said unto Moses, When thou goest to return into Egypt, see that thou do all those wonders before Pharaoh, which I have put in thine hand: but I will harden his heart, that he shall not let the people go.

EXODUS 9:16—And in very deed for this cause have I raised thee up, for to shew in thee my power; and that my name may be declared throughout all the earth.

JEREMIAH 18:6—O house of Israel, cannot I do with you as this potter? saith the LORD. Behold, as the clay is in the potter's hand, so are ye in mine hand, O house of Israel.

ROMANS 9:19-21

(19) Thou wilt say then unto me, Why doth he yet find fault? For who hath resisted his will? (20) Nay but, O man, who art thou that repliest against God? Shall the thing formed say to him that formed it, Why hast thou made me thus? (21) Hath not the potter power over the clay, of the same lump to make one vessel unto honour and another unto dishonor?

ISAIAH 45:9—Woe unto him that striveth with his Maker! Let the potsherd strive with the potsherds of the earth. Shall the clay say to him that fashioneth it, What makest thou? Or thy work, He hath no hands?

JEREMIAH 18:6—O house of Israel, cannot I do with you as this potter? saith the LORD. Behold, as the clay is in the potter's hand, so are ye in mine hand, O house of Israel.

ISAIAH 29:16—Surely your turning of things upside down shall be esteemed as the potter's clay: for shall the work say of him that made it, He made me not? Or shall the thing framed say of him that framed it, He had no understanding?

WISDOM OF SOLOMON 15:7—For the potter, tempering soft earth, fashioneth every vessel with much labor for our service: yea, of the same clay he maketh both the vessels that serve for clean uses, and likewise also all such as serve to the contrary: but what is the use of either sort, the potter himself is the judge.

2 TIMOTHY 2:20—But in a great house there are not only vessels of gold and of silver, but also of wood and of earth; and some to honour, and some to dishonor.

2 CLEMENT 8:2—For we are clay in the hand of the artisan. As in the case of a potter: if he's making a vessel that becomes twisted or crushed in his hands, he then remolds it; but if he has already put it in the kiln, he can no longer fix it. So too with us. While we are still in the world, we should repent from our whole heart of the evil we have done in the flesh, so the Lord will save us—while there is still time for repentance.

2 CHRONICLES 20:6—And said, O LORD God of our fathers, art not thou God in heaven? And rulest not thou over all the kingdoms of the heathen? And in thine hand is there not power and might, so that none is able to withstand thee?

ROMANS 9:22
What if God, willing to shew his wrath, and to make his power known, endured with much longsuffering the vessels of wrath fitted to destruction:

Judgment begins with the house of TMH, *(1 Peter 4:17)* so His children are punished speedily *(Amos 3:2)* however, TMH allows non-Israelites time to store up wrath until an appointed time of judgment:

PROVERBS 16:4—The LORD hath made all things for himself: yea, even the wicked for the day of evil.

ECCLESIASTES 8:11—Because sentence against an evil work is not executed speedily, therefore the heart of the sons of men is fully set in them to do evil.

PSALMS 50:21—These things hast thou done, and I kept silence; thou thoughtest that I was altogether such an one as thyself: but I will reprove thee, and set them in order before thine eyes.

ISAIAH 42:13-15—(13) The LORD shall go forth as a mighty man, he shall stir up jealousy like a man of war: he shall cry, yea, roar; he shall prevail against his enemies. (14) I have long time holden my peace; I have been still, and refrained myself: now will I cry like a travailing woman; I will destroy and devour at once. (15) I will make waste mountains and hills, and dry up all their herbs; and I will make the rivers islands, and I will dry up the pools.

GENESIS 15:16—But in the fourth generation they shall come hither again: for the iniquity of the Amorites is not yet full.

ROMANS 9:23-24
(23) And that he might make known the <u>riches of his glory</u> on the vessels of mercy, which he had <u>afore prepared unto glory</u>, (24) Even us, <u>whom he hath called</u>, not of the Jews only, but also of the Gentiles? *[ethnōn (ἐθνῶν)]*

As stated previously, throughout the NT, *Ethnos (nations, people, heathen, gentiles...etc.)* is used to describe both Israelites and non-Israelites. *(See The People Of Romans, pg. 53)* So as with any verse, in order to determine which group Paul is speaking about here, we need to examine the context.

In verse 23 above, we read: "that he might <u>make known the riches of his glory **on the vessels of mercy, which he prepared unto glory.**</u>" From this, we can just go back to *Romans 9:4*, which states that the 'glory' has been given to the Israelites. So once again, Paul is speaking about Israelite Gentiles of the diaspora. For more proof, go to the next verse, *Romans 9:25-26*.

ROMANS 9:4—Who are Israelites; to whom pertaineth the adoption, <u>and the glory</u>, and the covenants, and the giving of the law, and the service of God, and the promises.

ISAIAH 48:12—Hearken unto me, O Jacob and <u>Israel, my called</u>; I am he; I am the first, I also am the last.

HOSEA 11:1—When Israel was a child, then I loved him, and called my son out of Egypt.

ISAIAH 45:3-4—(3) And I will give thee the treasures of darkness, and hidden riches of secret places, that thou mayest know that I, the Lord, which call thee by thy name, am the God of Israel. (4) For Jacob my servant's sake, and <u>Israel mine elect, I have even called thee by thy name: I have surnamed thee, though thou hast not known me</u>.

ROMANS 2:4—Or despisest thou the <u>riches of his goodness</u> and forbearance and longsuffering; not knowing that the goodness of God leadeth thee to repentance?

ROMANS 3:29—Is he the God of the Jews only? Is he not also of the Gentiles? Yes, of the Gentiles also

ROMANS 8:28-30—(28) And we know that all things work together for good to them that love God, to them who are the called according to his purpose. (29) For whom he did foreknow, he also did predestinate to be conformed to the image of his Son, that he might be the firstborn among many brethren. (30) Moreover whom he did predestinate, them he also called: and whom he called, <u>them he also justified: and whom he justified, them he also glorified</u>.

COLOSSIANS 1:27—To whom God would make known what is the <u>riches of the glory</u> of this mystery among the Gentiles; which is Christ in you, <u>the hope of glory</u>

ROMANS 9:25-26
(25) **As he saith also in Osee, I will call them my people, which were not my people; and her beloved, which was not beloved.** (26) **And it shall come to pass, that in the place where it was said unto them, Ye are not my people; there shall they be called the children of the living God.**

This verse quotes a prophecy in *Hosea* (Osee) concerning the Israelites, the same people (Northern & Southern kingdoms) Paul is speaking of in *Romans 9:23-24*.

HOSEA 1:10-11—(10) Yet the number of **the children of Israel** shall be as the sand of the sea, which cannot be measured nor numbered; and it shall come to pass, <u>that in the place where it was **said unto them**, Ye are not my people, **there it shall be said unto *them***, Ye are the sons of the living God.</u> <u>(11) Then shall the **children of Judah** and the **children of Israel** be gathered together</u>, and appoint themselves one head, and they shall come up out of the land: for great shall be the day of Jezreel.

HOSEA 2:23—And I will sow her unto me in the earth; and I will have mercy upon her that had not obtained mercy; and I will say to them which were not my people, Thou art my people; and they shall say, Thou art my God.

1 PETER 2:9-10—(9) But ye are a chosen generation, a royal priesthood, an holy nation, a peculiar people; that ye should shew forth the praises of him who hath called you out of darkness into his marvelous light: (10) Which in time past [were] not a people, but are now the people of God: which had not obtained mercy, but now have obtained mercy.

ROMANS 9:27
Esaias also crieth concerning Israel, though the number of the children of Israel be as the sand of the sea, a remnant shall be saved:

ISAIAH 10:20-23—(20) And it shall come to pass in that day, that the remnant of Israel, and such as are escaped of the house of Jacob, shall no more again stay upon him that smote them; but shall stay upon the LORD, the Holy One of Israel, in truth. (21) The remnant shall return, [even] the remnant of Jacob, unto the mighty God. (22) For though thy people Israel be as the sand of the sea, yet a remnant of them shall return: the consumption decreed shall overflow with righteousness. (23) For the Lord GOD of hosts shall make a consumption, even determined, in the midst of all the land.

ROMANS 9:6—Not as though the word of God hath taken none effect. For they are not all Israel, which are of Israel

ROMANS 11:5—Even so then at this present time also there is a remnant according to the election of grace.

ROMANS 9:28-29
(28) For he will finish the work, and cut it short in righteousness: because a short work will the Lord make upon the earth. (29) And as Esaias said before, Except the Lord of Sabaoth had left us a seed, we had been as Sodom, and been made like unto Gomorrah.

ISAIAH 1:9-10,12-17—(9) Except the LORD of hosts had left unto us a very small remnant, we should have been as Sodom, and we should have been like unto Gomorrah. (10) Hear the word of the LORD, ye rulers of Sodom; give ear unto the law of our God, ye people of Gomorrah. To what purpose is the multitude of your sacrifices unto me? saith the LORD: I am full of the burnt offerings of rams, and the fat of fed beasts; and I delight not in the blood of bullocks, or of lambs, or of he goats...(12) When ye come to appear before me, who hath required this at your hand, to tread my courts? (13) Bring no more vain oblations; incense is an abomination unto me; the new moons and sabbaths, the calling of assemblies, I cannot away with; it is iniquity, even the solemn meeting. (14) Your new moons and your appointed feasts my soul hateth: they are a trouble unto me; I am weary to bear them. (15) And when ye spread forth your hands, I will hide mine eyes from you: yea, when ye make many prayers, I will not hear: your hands are full of blood. (16) Wash you, make you clean; put away the evil of your doings from before mine eyes; cease to do evil; (17) Learn to do well; seek judgment, relieve the oppressed, judge the fatherless, plead for the widow.

ISAIAH 10:23—For the Lord GOD of hosts shall make a consumption, even determined, in the midst of all the land.

ISAIAH 13:19—And Babylon, the glory of kingdoms, the beauty of the Chaldees' excellency, shall be as when God overthrew Sodom and Gomorrah.

ISAIAH 28:22—Now therefore be ye not mockers, lest your bands be made strong: for I have heard from the Lord GOD of hosts a consumption, even determined upon the whole earth.

ROMANS 9:30
What shall we say then? That the Gentiles, which followed not after righteousness, have attained to righteousness, even the righteousness which is of faith.

ROMANS 1:17—For therein is the righteousness of God revealed from faith to faith: as it is written, The just shall live by faith.

ROMANS 3:21—But now the righteousness of God without the law is manifested, being witnessed by the law and the prophets.

ROMANS 4:11—And he received the sign of circumcision, a seal of the righteousness of the faith which he had yet being uncircumcised: that he might be the father of all them that believe, though they be not circumcised; that righteousness might be imputed unto them also

ROMANS 10:3, 6—(3) For they being ignorant of God's righteousness, and going about to establish their own righteousness, have not submitted themselves unto the righteousness of God...(6) But the righteousness which is of faith speaketh on this wise, Say not in thine heart, Who shall ascend into heaven? (that is, to bring Christ down from above:)

ROMANS 9:31
But Israel, which followed after the law of righteousness, hath not attained to the law of righteousness.

ISAIAH 8:14—And he shall be for a sanctuary; but for a stone of stumbling and for a rock of offence to both the houses of Israel, for a gin and for a snare to the inhabitants of Jerusalem.

ISAIAH 28:16—Therefore thus saith the Lord GOD, Behold, I lay in Zion for a foundation a stone, a tried stone, a precious corner stone, a sure foundation: he that believeth shall not make haste.

MATTHEW 15:1-6—(1) Then came to Jesus scribes and Pharisees, which were of Jerusalem, saying, (2) Why do thy disciples transgress the tradition of the elders? For they wash not their hands when they eat bread. (3) But he answered and said unto them, Why do ye also transgress the commandment of God by your tradition? (4) For God commanded, saying, Honour thy father and mother: and, He that curseth father or mother, let him die the death. (5) But ye say, Whosoever shall say to his father or his mother, It is a gift, by whatsoever thou mightest be profited by me; (6) And honour not his father or his mother, he shall be free. Thus have ye made the commandment of God of none effect by your tradition.

MARK 7:7-13—(7) Howbeit in vain do they worship me, teaching for doctrines the commandments of men. (8) For laying aside the commandment of God, ye hold the tradition of men, [as] the washing of pots and cups: and many other such like things ye do. (9) And he said unto them, Full well ye reject the commandment of God, that ye may keep your own tradition. (10) For Moses said, Honour thy father and thy mother; and, Whoso curseth father or mother, let him die the death: (11) But ye say, If a man shall say to his father or his mother, It is Corban, that is to say, a gift, by whatsoever thou mightest be profited by me; [he shall be free]. (12) And ye suffer him no more to do ought for his father or his mother; (13) Making the word of God of none effect through your tradition, which ye have delivered: and many such like things do ye.

LUKE 11:37-52—(37) And as he spake, a certain Pharisee besought him to dine with him: and he went in, and sat down to meat. (38) And when the Pharisee saw it, he marveled that he had not first washed before dinner. (39) And the Lord said unto him, Now do ye Pharisees make clean the outside of the cup and the platter; but your inward part is full of ravening and wickedness. (40) Ye fools, did not he that made that which is without make that which is within also? (41) But rather give alms of such things as ye have; and, behold, all things are clean unto you. (42) But woe unto you, Pharisees! for ye tithe mint and rue and all manner of herbs, and pass over judgment and the love of God: these ought ye to have done, and not to leave the other undone. (43) Woe unto you, Pharisees! For ye love the uppermost seats in the synagogues, and greetings in the markets. (44) Woe unto you, scribes and Pharisees, hypocrites! For ye are as graves which appear not, and the men that walk over them are not aware of them. (45) Then answered one of the lawyers, and said unto him, Master, thus saying thou reproachest us also. (46) And he said, Woe unto you also, ye lawyers! For ye lade men with burdens grievous to be borne, and ye yourselves touch not the burdens with one of your fingers. (47) Woe unto you! For ye build the sepulchers of the prophets, and your fathers killed them. (48) Truly ye bear witness that ye allow the deeds of your fathers: for they indeed killed them, and ye build their sepulchers. (49) Therefore also said the wisdom of God, I will send them prophets and apostles, and some of them they shall slay and persecute: (50) That the blood of all the prophets, which was shed from the foundation of the world, may be required of this generation; (51) From the blood of Abel unto the blood of Zacharias, which perished between the altar and the temple: verily I say unto you, It shall be required of this generation. (52) Woe unto you, lawyers! for ye have taken away the key of knowledge: ye entered not in yourselves, and them that were entering in ye hindered.

ROMANS 10:2-4—(2) For I bear them record that they have a zeal of God, but not according to knowledge. (3) For they being ignorant of God's righteousness, and going about to establish their own righteousness, have not submitted themselves unto the righteousness of God. (4) For Christ [is] the end of the law for righteousness to every one that believeth.

GALATIANS 5:4—Christ is become of no effect unto you, whosoever of you are justified by the law; ye are fallen from grace.

1 PETER 2:6—Wherefore also it is contained in the scripture, Behold, I lay in Sion a chief corner stone, elect, precious: and he that believeth on him shall not be confounded.

ROMANS 9:32-33

(32) Wherefore? Because they sought it not by faith, but as it were by the works of the law. For they stumbled at that stumblingstone; (33) As it is written, Behold, I lay in Sion a stumblingstone and rock of offence: and whosoever believeth on him shall not be ashamed.

PSALMS 118:22—The stone which the builders refused is become the head stone of the corner.

ISAIAH 8:14-22—(14) And he shall be for a sanctuary; but for a stone of stumbling and for a rock of offence to both the houses of Israel, for a gin and for a snare to the inhabitants of Jerusalem. (15) And many among them shall stumble, and fall, and be broken, and be snared, and be taken. (16) Bind up the testimony, seal the law among my disciples. (17) And I will wait upon the LORD, that hideth his face from the house of Jacob, and I will look for him. (18) Behold, I and the children whom the LORD hath given me are for signs and for wonders in Israel from the LORD of hosts, which dwelleth in mount Zion. (19) And when they shall say unto you, Seek unto them that have familiar spirits, and unto wizards that peep, and that mutter: should not a people seek unto their God? For the living to the dead? (20) To the law and to the testimony: if they speak not according to this word, it is because there is no light in them. (21) And they shall pass through it, hardly bestead and hungry: and it shall come to pass, that when they shall be hungry, they shall fret themselves, and curse their king and their God, and look upward. (22) And they shall look unto the earth; and behold trouble and darkness, dimness of anguish; and they shall be driven to darkness.

ISAIAH 8:14—And he shall be for a sanctuary; but for a stone of stumbling and for a rock of offence to both the houses of Israel, for a gin and for a snare to the inhabitants of Jerusalem.

ISAIAH 28:16—Therefore thus saith the Lord GOD, Behold, I lay in Zion for a foundation a stone, a tried stone, a precious corner stone, a sure foundation: he that believeth shall not make haste.

MATTHEW 21:42—Jesus saith unto them, Did ye never read in the scriptures, The stone which the builders rejected, the same is become the head of the corner: this is the Lord's doing, and it is marvelous in our eyes?

LUKE 2:34—And Simeon blessed them, and said unto Mary his mother, Behold, this child is set for the fall and rising again of many in Israel; and for a sign which shall be spoken against

LUKE 18:10-14—(10) Two men went up into the temple to pray; the one a Pharisee, and the other a publican. (11) The Pharisee stood and prayed thus with himself, God, I thank thee, that I am not as other men are, extortioners, unjust, adulterers, or even as this publican. (12) I fast twice in the week, I give tithes of all that I possess. (13) And the publican, standing afar off, would not lift up so much as his eyes unto heaven, but smote upon his breast, saying, God be merciful to me a sinner. (14) I tell you, this man went down to his house justified rather than the other: for every one that exalteth himself shall be abased; and he that humbleth himself shall be exalted.

ROMANS 10:11—For the scripture saith, Whosoever believeth on him shall not be ashamed.

1 CORINTHIANS 1:23—But we preach Christ crucified, unto the Jews a stumbling block, and unto the Greeks foolishness.

1 PETER 2:6-8—(6) Wherefore also it is contained in the scripture, Behold, I lay in Sion a chief corner stone, elect, precious: and he that believeth on him shall not be confounded. (7) Unto you therefore which believe [he is] precious: but unto them, which be disobedient, the stone which the builders disallowed, the same is made the head of the corner, (8) And a stone of stumbling, and a rock of offence, [even to them] which stumble at the word, being disobedient: whereunto also they were appointed.

ROMANS 10

ROMANS 10:1 [a]
Brethren, my heart's desire and prayer to God for Israel is, that they might be saved.

LEVITICUS 20:26—And ye shall be holy unto me: for I the LORD am holy, and have severed you from other people, that ye should be mine.

DEUTERONOMY 14:2—For thou art an holy people unto the LORD thy God, and the LORD hath chosen thee to be a peculiar people unto himself, above all the nations that are upon the earth.

2 SAMUEL 7:23-24—(23) And what one nation in the earth is like thy people, even like Israel, whom God went to redeem for a people to himself, and to make him a name, and to do for you great things and terrible, for thy land, before thy people, which thou redeemedst to thee from Egypt, from the nations and their gods? (24) For thou hast confirmed to thyself thy people Israel to be a people unto thee forever: and thou, LORD, art become their God.

1 CHRONICLES 17:21—And what one nation in the earth is like thy people Israel, whom God went to redeem to be his own people, to make thee a name of greatness and terribleness, by driving out nations from before thy people, whom thou hast redeemed out of Egypt?

2 BARUCH 48:20—For this is the nation, which you have chosen, and these are the people, to whom you find no equal.

ROMANS 9:2-5—(2) That I have great heaviness and continual sorrow in my heart. (3) For I could wish that myself were accursed from Christ for my brethren, my kinsmen according to the flesh: (4) Who are Israelites; to whom pertaineth the adoption, and the glory, and the covenants, and the giving of the law, and the service of God, and the promises; (5) Whose are the fathers, and of whom as concerning the flesh Christ came, who is over all, God blessed for ever. Amen.

ROMANS 10:1 [b]
Brethren, my heart's desire and prayer to God for Israel is, that they might be saved. *[sótéria (σωτηρία)]*

STRONG'S #G4991: "salvation"—*sótéria* (σωτηρία)
USAGE: welfare, prosperity, deliverance, preservation, salvation, safety

BIBLICAL CONTEXT: "Blessed be the Lord God of Israel; for he hath visited and redeemed his people, and hath raised up an horn of salvation for us in the house of his servant David; as he spake by the mouth of his holy prophets, which have been since the world began: That we should be saved from our enemies, and from the hand of all that hate us; to perform the mercy promised to our fathers, and to remember his holy covenant; the oath which he sware to our father Abraham, that he would grant unto us, that we being delivered out of the hand of our enemies might serve him without fear, in holiness and righteousness before him, all the days of our life. And thou, child, shalt be called the prophet of the Highest: for thou shalt go before the face of the Lord to prepare his ways; to give knowledge of salvation unto his people by the remission of their sins" *(Luke 1:68-77)*

From a Hebrew perspective, to be "saved" is to be safe, at home, in your own lands, *away* from your enemies. We were delivered **to** our enemies because of our sins (transgressing the law). Therefore we won't be saved *from* our enemies and all who hate us until we become righteous, justified, sanctified (set-apart), and born-again...i.e. the circumcision of the heart.

So salvation is a *physical act*. Justification, sanctification, and righteousness are *spiritual acts*, which come from 'circumcision of the heart.'

PHILIPPIANS 2:12-13—(12) Wherefore, my beloved, as ye have always obeyed, not as in my presence only, but now much more in my absence, work out your own salvation with fear and trembling. (13) For it is God which worketh in you both to will and to do of his good pleasure.

TMH is the great physician who works on our willing hearts. This is a joint effort between the believer and the Father. It involves our spiritual submission to His will. He prunes, cultivates, and shapes us into clean vessels. Salvation/redemption is the physical act of saving us via our Kinsmen/Redeemer/Messiah. Being saved from sin is being saved from the consequences of our transgressing the law, which are the curses. These include separation from TMH, enemies and oppressors ruling over us, and eventually death. There is no salvation without spiritual circumcision. You can't have one without the other. TMH won't let us step foot into the Kingdom until we're born again.

Therefore, the circumcised heart has a great deliverance coming.

2 CHRONICLES 6:24-25—(24) And if thy people Israel be put to the worse before the enemy, because they have sinned against thee; and shall return and confess thy name, and pray and make supplication before thee in this house; (25) Then hear thou from the heavens, and forgive the sin of thy people Israel, and bring them again unto the land which thou gavest to them and to their fathers.

PSALMS 136:22-24—(22) Even an heritage unto Israel his servant: for his mercy endureth for ever. (23) Who remembered us in our low estate: for his mercy endureth forever: (24) and hath redeemed us from our enemies: for his mercy endureth forever.

JEREMIAH 31:10-11—(10) Hear the word of the LORD, O ye nations, and declare it in the isles afar off, and say, He that scattered Israel will gather him, and keep him, as a shepherd doth his flock. (11) For the LORD hath redeemed Jacob, and ransomed him from the hand of him that was stronger than he.

ZECHARIAH 9:16—And the LORD their God shall save them in that day as the flock of his people: for they shall be as the stones of a crown, lifted up as an ensign upon his land.

JOEL 3:18, 27, 31-32—(18) Then will the LORD be jealous for his land, and pity his people...(27) And ye shall know that I am in the midst of Israel, and that I am the LORD your God, and none else: and my people shall never be ashamed...(31) The sun shall be turned into darkness, and the moon into blood, before the great and the terrible day of the LORD come. (32) And it shall come to pass, that whosoever shall call on the name of the LORD shall be delivered: for in mount Zion and in Jerusalem shall be deliverance, as the LORD hath said, and in the remnant whom the LORD shall call.

MATTHEW 1:21—And she shall bring forth a son, and thou shalt call his name JESUS: for he shall save his people from their sins.

MATTHEW 10:22—And ye shall be hated of all men for my name's sake: but he that endureth to the end shall be saved.

LUKE 1:68-79—(68) Blessed be the Lord God of Israel; for he hath visited and redeemed his people, (69) and hath raised up an horn of salvation for us in the house of his servant David; (70) as he spake by the mouth of his holy prophets, which have been since the world began: (71) that we should be saved from our enemies, and from the hand of all that hate us; (72) to perform the mercy promised to our fathers, and to remember his holy covenant; (73) the oath which he sware to our father Abraham, (74) that he would grant unto us, that we being delivered out of the hand of our enemies might serve him without fear, (75) in holiness and righteousness before him, all the days of our life. (76) And thou, child, shalt be called the prophet of the Highest: for thou shalt go before the face of the Lord to prepare his ways; (77) to give knowledge of salvation unto his people by the remission of their sins, (78) through the tender mercy of our God; whereby the dayspring from on high hath visited us, (79) to give light to them that sit in darkness and in the shadow of death, to guide our feet into the way of peace.

ACTS 5:31—Him hath God exalted with his right hand to be a Prince and a Saviour, for to give repentance to Israel, and forgiveness of sins.

(Psalms 85:9; Isaiah 43:1; 44:23, 46:13, 48:20; 51:11, 62:11; Jeremiah 23:3)

ROMANS 10:2
For I bear them record that they have a zeal of God, but not according to knowledge.

HOSEA 4:6—My people are destroyed for lack of knowledge: because thou hast rejected knowledge, I will also reject thee, that thou shalt be no priest to me: seeing thou hast forgotten the law of thy God, I will also forget thy children.

ISAIAH 29:9-14—(9) Stay yourselves, and wonder; cry ye out, and cry: they are drunken, but not with wine; they stagger, but not with strong drink. (10) For the LORD hath poured out upon you the spirit of deep sleep, and hath closed your eyes: the prophets and your rulers, the seers hath he covered. (11) And the vision of all is become unto you as the words of a book that is sealed, which men deliver to one that is learned, saying, Read this, I pray thee: and he saith, I cannot; for it is sealed: (12) And the book is delivered to him that is not learned, saying, Read this, I pray thee: and he saith, I am not learned. (13) Wherefore the Lord said, Forasmuch as this people draw near me with their mouth, and with their lips do honour me, but have removed their heart far from me, and their fear toward me is taught by the precept of men: (14) Therefore, behold, I will proceed to do a marvelous work among this people, even a marvelous work and a wonder: for the wisdom of their wise men shall perish, and the understanding of their prudent men shall be hid.

ISAIAH 1:3—The ox knoweth his owner, and the ass his master's crib: but Israel doth not know, my people doth not consider.

ISAIAH 6:9—And he said, Go, and tell this people, Hear ye indeed, but understand not; and see ye indeed, but perceive not.

MARK 4:12—That seeing they may see, and not perceive; and hearing they may hear, and not understand; lest at any time they should be converted, and their sins should be forgiven them.

LUKE 8:10—And he said, Unto you it is given to know the mysteries of the kingdom of God: but to others in parables; that seeing they might not see, and hearing they might not understand.

(Deuteronomy 29:4; Jeremiah 5:21; Ezekiel 12:2; John 12:40; Acts 8:30-31, 28:26; Romans 11:8)

ROMANS 10:3
For they being ignorant of God's righteousness, and going about to establish their own righteousness, have not submitted themselves unto the righteousness of God.

During his ministry, Messiah's main disagreements with the Pharisees and Sadducees revolved around the man-made traditions (Talmud), which they brought with them from the Babylonian captivity, traditions that contradicted TMH's laws (Torah). This led our people to walk in the flesh. Consequently, these practices ultimately caused them to seek after their own righteousness rather than TMH's righteousness, which is a circumcised heart.

ISAIAH 29:13—Wherefore the Lord said, Forasmuch as this people draw near me with their mouth, and with their lips do honor me, but have removed their heart far from me, and their fear toward me is taught by the precept of men:

MARK 7:6-9—(6) He answered and said unto them, Well hath Esaias prophesied of you hypocrites, as it is written, This people honoureth me with their lips, but their heart is far from me. (7) Howbeit in vain do they worship me, teaching for doctrines the commandments of men. (8) For laying aside the commandment of God, ye hold the tradition of men, as the washing of pots and cups: and many other such like things ye do. (9) And he said unto them, Full well ye reject the commandment of God, that ye may keep your own tradition.

LUKE 18:9-14—(9) And he spake this parable unto certain which trusted in themselves that they were righteous, and despised others: (10) Two men went up into the temple to pray; the one a Pharisee, and the other a publican. (11) The Pharisee stood and prayed thus with himself, God, I thank thee, that I am not as other men are, extortioners, unjust, adulterers, or even as this publican. (12) I fast twice in the week, I give tithes of all that I possess. (13) And the publican, standing afar off, would not lift up so much as his eyes unto heaven, but smote upon his breast, saying, God be merciful to me a sinner. (14) I tell you, this man went down to his house justified rather than the other: for every one that exalteth himself shall be abased; and he that humbleth himself shall be exalted.

JOHN 12:40—He hath blinded their eyes, and hardened their heart; that they should not see with their eyes, nor understand with their heart, and be converted, and I should heal them.

ROMANS 1:17—For therein is the righteousness of God revealed from faith to faith: as it is written, The just shall live by faith.

PHILIPPIANS 3:9—And be found in him, not having mine own righteousness, which is of the law, but that which is through the faith of Christ, the righteousness which is of God by faith.

PROVERBS 30:12—There is a generation that are pure in their own eyes, and yet is not washed from their filthiness.

COLOSSIANS 2:8—Beware lest any man spoil you through philosophy and vain deceit, after the tradition of men, after the rudiments of the world, and not after Christ.

(Matthew 6:1-6, 16-18, 23:1-12; Luke 11:37-54)

ROMANS 10:4
For Christ is the end of the law for
<u>righteousness to every one that believeth</u>.

MATTHEW 5:17—Think not that I am come to destroy the law, or the prophets: <u>I am not come to destroy, but to fulfill</u>.

HEBREWS 9:19-28—(19) For when Moses had spoken every precept to all the people according to the law, he took the blood of calves and of goats, with water, and scarlet wool, and hyssop, and sprinkled both the book, and all the people, (20) Saying, This is the blood of the testament which God hath enjoined unto you. (21) Moreover he sprinkled with blood both the tabernacle, and all the vessels of the ministry. (22) And **almost all things** are by the law purged with blood; and without shedding of blood is no remission. (23) It was therefore necessary that the patterns of things in the heavens should be purified with these; but the heavenly things themselves with better sacrifices than these. (24) For Christ is not entered into the holy places made with hands, which are the figures of the true; but into heaven itself, now to appear in the presence of God for us: (25) Nor yet that he should offer himself often, as the high priest entereth into the holy place every year with blood of others; (26) For then must he often have suffered since the foundation of the world: but now once in the end of the world hath he appeared to put away sin by the sacrifice of himself. (27) And as it is appointed unto men once to die, but after this the judgment: (28) So Christ was once offered to bear the sins of many; and unto them that look for him shall he appear the second time without sin unto salvation.

ACTS 13:38-39—(38) Be it known unto you therefore, men and brethren, that through this man is preached unto you the forgiveness of sins: (39) And by him all that believe are justified from all things, from which ye could not be justified by the law of Moses.

HEBREWS 10:1-2—(1) For the law having a shadow of good things to come, and not the very image of the things, can never with those sacrifices which they offered year by year continually make the comers thereunto perfect. (2) For then would they not have ceased to be offered? Because that the worshippers once purged should have had no more conscience of sins.

ROMANS 7:21-25—(21) I find then a law, that, when I would do good, evil is present with me. (22) For I delight in the law of God after the inward man: (23) But I see <u>another law in my members, warring against the law of my mind, and bringing me into captivity to the law of sin</u> which is in my members. (24) O wretched man that I am! Who shall deliver me from the body of this death? (25) I thank God through Jesus Christ our Lord. So then with the mind I myself serve the law of God; but with the flesh the <u>law of sin</u>.**

ROMANS 8:1-4—(1) There is therefore now no condemnation to them which are in Christ Jesus, who walk not after the flesh, but after the Spirit. (2) For the law of the Spirit of life in Christ Jesus hath made me <u>free from the law of sin and death</u>.** (3) For what the law could not do, in that it was weak through the flesh, God sending his own Son in the likeness of sinful flesh, and for sin, condemned sin in the flesh: (4) <u>That the righteousness of the law might be fulfilled in us, who walk not after the flesh, but after the Spirit.</u>

GALATIANS 3:24—Wherefore the law was our schoolmaster to bring us unto Christ<u>, that we might be justified by faith</u>.

GALATIANS 4:5—To redeem them that were under the law, <u>that we might receive the adoption of sons</u>.

(**Re: Law of sin—see Romans 7:21-23, 8:2-3 commentary on pgs.190 &193, respectively.)

ROMANS 10:5
For Moses describeth the righteousness which is of the law, that the man which doeth those things shall live by them.

LEVITICUS 18:5—Ye shall therefore keep my statutes, and my judgments: which if a man do, he shall live in them: I am the LORD.

DEUTERONOMY 4:1—Now therefore hearken, O Israel, unto the statutes and unto the judgments, which I teach you, for to do them, that ye may live, and go in and possess the land, which the LORD God of your fathers giveth you.

DEUTERONOMY 30:17-19—(17) But if thine heart turn away, so that thou wilt not hear, but shalt be drawn away, and worship other gods, and serve them; (18) I denounce unto you this day, that ye shall surely perish, and that ye shall not prolong your days upon the land, whither thou passest over Jordan to go to possess it. (19) I call heaven and earth to record this day against you, that I have set before you life and death, blessing and cursing: therefore choose life, that both thou and thy seed may live.

EZEKIEL 20:11-13—(11) And I gave them my statutes, and shewed them my judgments, which if a man do, he shall even live in them. (12) Moreover also I gave them my sabbaths, to be a sign between me and them, that they might know that I am the LORD that sanctify them. (13) But the house of Israel rebelled against me in the wilderness: they walked not in my statutes, and they despised my judgments, which if a man do, he shall even live in them; and my sabbaths they greatly polluted: then I said, I would pour out my fury upon them in the wilderness, to consume them.

GALATIANS 3:12—And the law is not of faith: but, The man that doeth them shall live in them.

ROMANS 10:6-8

(6) **But the righteousness, which is of faith, speaketh on this wise, Say not in thine heart, Who shall ascend into heaven? [that is, to bring Christ down from above:]** (7) **Or, Who shall descend into the deep? [that is, to bring up Christ again from the dead.]** (8) **But what saith it? The word is nigh thee, even in thy mouth, and in thy heart: that is, the word of faith, which we preach.**

DEUTERONOMY 30:11-14—(11) For this commandment which I command thee this day, it is not hidden from thee, neither is it far off. (12) It is not in heaven, that thou shouldest say, Who shall go up for us to heaven, and bring it unto us, that we may hear it, and do it? (13) Neither is it beyond the sea, that thou shouldest say, Who shall go over the sea for us, and bring it unto us, that we may hear it, and do it? (14) But the word is very nigh unto thee, in thy mouth, and in thy heart, that thou mayest do it.

ISAIAH 46:13—I bring near my righteousness; it shall not be far off, and my salvation shall not tarry: and I will place salvation in Zion for Israel my glory.

JEREMIAH 31:33—But this shall be the covenant that I will make with the house of Israel; After those days, saith the LORD, I will put my law in their inward parts, and write it in their hearts; and will be their God, and they shall be my people.

JOHN 14:16-17—(16) And I will pray the Father, and he shall give you another Comforter, that he may abide with you for ever; (17) even the Spirit of truth; whom the world cannot receive, because it seeth him not, neither knoweth him: but ye know him; for he dwelleth with you, and shall be in you.

EPHESIANS 2:8-10—(8) For by grace are ye saved through faith; and that not of yourselves: it is the gift of God: (9) Not of works, lest any man should boast. (10) For we are his workmanship, created in Christ Jesus unto good works, which God hath before ordained that we should walk in them.

GALATIANS 3:6—Even as Abraham believed God, and it was accounted to him for righteousness.

(John 3:13)

ROMANS 10:9-10

(9) **That if thou shalt confess with thy mouth the Lord Jesus, and shalt believe in thine heart that God hath raised him from the dead, thou shalt be saved.** (10) **For with the heart man believeth unto righteousness; and with the mouth confession is made unto salvation.**

ACTS 8:37—And Philip said, If you believe with all your heart, you may. And he answered and said, I believe that Jesus Christ is the Son of God.

MATTHEW 10:32—Whosoever therefore shall confess me before men, him will I confess also before my Father which is in heaven.

LUKE 12:8—Also I say unto you, Whosoever shall confess me before men, him shall the Son of man also confess before the angels of God

1 JOHN 4:2—Hereby know ye the Spirit of God: Every spirit that confesseth that Jesus Christ is come in the flesh is of God

JOEL 3:27, 31-32—(27) And ye shall know that I am in the midst of Israel, and that I am the LORD your God, and none else: and my people shall never be ashamed...(31) The sun shall be turned into darkness, and the moon into blood, before the great and the terrible day of the LORD come. (32) And it shall come to pass, that whosoever shall call on the name of the LORD shall be delivered: for in mount Zion and in Jerusalem shall be deliverance, as the LORD hath said, and in the remnant whom the LORD shall call.

1 CORINTHIANS 15:2-4—(2) By which also ye are saved, if ye keep in memory what I preached unto you, unless ye have believed in vain. (3) For I delivered unto you first of all that which I also received, how that Christ died for our sins according to the scriptures; (4) And that he was buried, and that he rose again the third day according to the scriptures.

ROMANS 10:11
For the scripture saith, Whosoever believeth on him shall not be ashamed.

JOEL 3:27—And ye shall know that I am in the midst of Israel, and that I am the LORD your God, and none else: and my people shall never be ashamed.

ISAIAH 28:16—Therefore thus saith the Lord GOD, Behold, I lay in Zion for a foundation a stone, a tried stone, a precious corner stone, a sure foundation: he that believeth shall not make haste.

1 PETER 2:6—Wherefore also it is contained in the scripture, Behold, I lay in Sion a chief corner stone, elect, precious: and he that believeth on him shall not be confounded.

ROMANS 9:33—As it is written, Behold, I lay in Sion a stumblingstone and rock of offence: and whosoever believeth on him shall not be ashamed.

ROMANS 10:12 [a]
For there is no difference between the Jew and the Greek [Hellēnos ('Ελληνος)]: for the same Lord over all is rich unto all that call upon him.

ACTS 15:6-9—(6) And the apostles and elders came together for to consider of this matter. (7) And when there had been much disputing, Peter rose up, and said unto them, Men and brethren, ye know how that a good while ago God made choice among us, that the Gentiles [*ethnos* (ἔθνος)] by my mouth should hear the word of the gospel, and believe.

(8) And God, which knoweth the hearts, bare them witness, giving them the Holy Ghost, even as he did unto us; (9) and put no difference between us and them, purifying their hearts by faith.

STRONG'S #1484: 'Gentiles'—*ethnos* (ἔθνος)
USAGE: a race, people, nation; the nations, heathen world, Gentiles

ROMANS 9:4—Who are Israelites; to whom pertaineth the adoption, and the glory, and the covenants, and the giving of the law, and the service of God, and the promises.

GALATIANS 4:4-5—(4) But when the fullness of the time was come, God sent forth his Son, made of a woman, made under the law, (5) To redeem them that were under the law, that we might receive the adoption of sons.

ROMANS 10:12 [b]
For there is no difference between the Jew and the Greek [*Hellēnos* (Ἕλληνος)]**: for the same Lord over all is rich unto all that call upon him.**

Prophecy That Judah Would Go Into Captivity To The Greeks

JOEL 3:6—The children also of Judah and the children of Jerusalem have ye sold unto the Grecians, that ye might remove them far from their border.

**Israelites From The House Of Judah Became
'Greek/Grecian/Gentiles *in the flesh***'

2 MACCABEES 6:1-11—(1) Not long after this the king sent an old man of Athens to compel the Jews to depart from the laws of their fathers, and not to live after the laws of God: (2) And to pollute also the temple in Jerusalem, and to call it the temple of Jupiter Olympius; and that in Garizim, of Jupiter the Defender of strangers, as they did desire that dwelt in the place. (3) The coming in of this mischief was sore and grievous to the people: (4) For the temple was filled with riot and revelling by the Gentiles, who dallied with harlots, and had to do with women within the circuit of the holy places, and besides that brought in things that were not lawful. (5) The altar also was filled with profane things, which the law forbiddeth. (6) Neither was it lawful for a man to keep sabbath days or ancient fasts, or to profess himself at all to be a Jew. (7) And in the day of the king's birth every month they were brought by bitter constraint to eat of the sacrifices; and when the fast of Bacchus was kept, the Jews were compelled to go in procession to Bacchus, carrying ivy. (8)

Moreover there went out a decree to the neighbour cities of the heathen, by the suggestion of Ptolemee, against the Jews, that they should observe the same fashions, and be partakers of their sacrifices: (9) And whoso would not conform themselves to the manners of the Gentiles should be put to death. Then might a man have seen the present misery. (10) For there were two women brought, who had circumcised their children; whom when they had openly led round about the city, the babes handing at their breasts, they cast them down headlong from the wall. (11) And others, that had run together into caves near by, to keep the Sabbath day secretly, being discovered by Philip, were all burnt together, because they made a conscience to help themselves for the honour of the most sacred day.

1 MACCABEES 1:13-15—(13) Then certain of the people were so forward herein, that they went to the king, who gave them license to do after the ordinances of the heathen (14) whereupon they built a place of exercise at Jerusalem according to the customs of the heathen: (15) And made themselves uncircumcised, and forsook the holy covenant, and joined themselves to the heathen, and were sold to do mischief...

1 MACCABEES 1:41-42—(41) Moreover king Antiochus wrote to his whole kingdom, that all should be one people, (42) and every one should leave his laws: so all the heathen agreed according to the commandment of the king.

1 MACCABEES 1:48-53—(48) That they should also leave their children uncircumcised, and make their souls abominable with all manner of uncleanness and profanation: (49) To the end they might forget the law, and change all the ordinances. (50) And whosoever would not do according to the commandment of the king, he said, he should die. (51) In the selfsame manner wrote he to his whole kingdom, and appointed overseers over all the people, commanding the cities of Juda to sacrifice, city by city. (52) Then many of the people were gathered unto them, to wit every one that forsook the law; and so they committed evils in the land; (53) And drove the Israelites into secret places, even wheresoever they could flee for succor.

Forgiveness And Reconciliation To Gentile/Greek Israelites Through Messiah's Sacrifice/The New Covenant

GALATIANS 4:4-5—(4) But when the fullness of the time was come, God sent forth his Son, made of a woman, made under the law, (5) **To redeem them that were under the law**, that we might receive the **adoption of sons**. *(Deuteronomy 29:14-15)*

ROMANS 9:4—Who are Israelites; to whom **pertaineth the adoption**, and the glory, and the covenants, and the giving of the law, and the service of God, and the promises.

JOHN 7:35—Then said the Jews among themselves, Whither will he go, that we shall not find him? Will he go unto the **dispersed** among the Gentiles, and teach the Gentiles?

JAMES 1:1—James, a servant of God and of the Lord Jesus Christ, to the twelve tribes which are **scattered** abroad, greeting.

1 PETER 1:1—Peter, an apostle of Jesus Christ, to the **strangers scattered** throughout Pontus, Galatia, Cappadocia, Asia, and Bithynia.

HEBREWS 11:13—These all died in faith, not having received the promises, but having seen them afar off, and were persuaded of them, and embraced them, and confessed that they were strangers and pilgrims on the earth.

EPHESIANS 2:11-22—(11) Wherefore remember, that ye being in time past Gentiles in the flesh, who are called Uncircumcision by that which is called the Circumcision in the flesh made by hands. (12) That at that time ye were without Christ, being aliens from the commonwealth of Israel, and strangers from the covenants of promise, having no hope, and without God in the world: (13) But now in Christ Jesus ye who sometimes were far off are made nigh by the blood of Christ. (14) For he is our peace, who hath made both one, and hath broken down the middle wall of partition between us; (15) Having abolished in his flesh the enmity, even the law of commandments contained in ordinances; for to make in himself of twain one new man, so making peace; (16) And that he might reconcile both unto God in one body by the cross, having slain the enmity thereby: (17) And came and preached peace to you which were afar off, and to them that were nigh. (18) For through him we both have access by one Spirit unto the Father. (19) Now therefore ye are no more strangers and foreigners, but fellow citizens with the saints, and of the household of God; (20) And are built upon the foundation of the apostles and prophets, Jesus Christ himself being the chief corner stone; (21) In whom all the building fitly framed together groweth unto an holy temple in the Lord: (22) In whom ye also are builded together for an habitation of God through the Spirit. *(1 Maccabees 1:15, 48)*

ROMANS 1:16—For I am not ashamed of the gospel of Christ: for it is the power of God unto salvation to every one that believeth; to the Jew first, and also to the Greek.

ROMANS 3:22, 29—(22) Even the righteousness of God, which is by faith of Jesus Christ unto all and upon all them that believe: for there is no difference...(29) Is he the God of the Jews only? Is he not also of the Gentiles? Yes, of the Gentiles also.

GALATIANS 3:28—There is neither Jew nor Greek, there is neither bond nor free, there is neither male nor female: for ye are all one in Christ Jesus.

(For a complete breakdown on Gentile/Greek Israelites, see Gentiles & Greeks, pg. 27 and The People Of Romans, pg. 53)

ROMANS 10:12 [c]
For there is no difference between <u>the Jew and the Greek</u> [Hellēnos ('Ελληνος)]: for the same Lord over all is rich unto all that call upon him.

DEUTERONOMY 29:10-15—(10) <u>Ye stand this day all of you before the LORD your God; your captains of your tribes, your elders, and your officers, with all the men of Israel</u>, (11) Your little ones, your wives, and thy stranger that is in thy camp, from the hewer of thy wood unto the drawer of thy water: (12) <u>That thou shouldest enter into covenant with the LORD thy God</u>, and into his oath, which the LORD thy God maketh with thee this day: (13) <u>That he may establish thee to day for a people unto himself, and that he may be unto thee a God</u>, as he hath said unto thee, and as he hath sworn unto thy fathers, to Abraham, to Isaac, and to Jacob. (14) <u>Neither with you only do I make this covenant and this oath; (15) But with him that standeth here with us</u> this day before the LORD our God, <u>and also with him that is not here with us this day.</u>

ACTS 5:31—Him hath God exalted with his right hand to be a Prince and a Saviour, for <u>to give repentance to Israel</u>, and forgiveness of sins.

ACTS 10:36—The word, which God sent unto <u>the children of Israel</u>, preaching peace by Jesus Christ: (<u>he is Lord of all</u>).

ACTS 15:8-9—(8) And God, which knoweth the hearts, bare them witness, giving them the Holy Ghost, even as he did unto us; (9) And put <u>no difference between us and them</u>, purifying their hearts by faith.

ROMANS 9:4—<u>Who are Israelites; to whom pertaineth the adoption, and the glory, and the covenants, and the giving of the law, and the service of God, and the promises.</u>

ROMANS 10:1—Brethren, my heart's desire and prayer to God <u>for Israel is, that they might be saved</u>.

GALATIANS 4:4-5—(4) But when the fullness of the time was come, God sent forth his Son, made of a woman, made under the law, (5) <u>To redeem them that were under the law</u>, that we might receive the adoption of sons.

1 TIMOTHY 2:5—For there is one God, and one mediator between God and men, the man Christ Jesus.

ROMANS 10:13
For whosoever shall call upon the name of the Lord shall be saved.

JOEL 2:30-32—(30) And I will shew wonders in the heavens and in the earth, blood, and fire, and pillars of smoke. (31) The sun shall be turned into darkness, and the moon into blood, before the great and the terrible day of the LORD come. (32) <u>And it shall come to pass, that **whosoever shall call on the name of the LORD shall be delivered: for in mount Zion and in Jerusalem shall be deliverance**, as the LORD hath said, and **in the remnant whom the LORD shall call**</u>.

LUKE 1:68-79—(68) Blessed be the <u>Lord God of Israel; for he hath visited and redeemed his people</u>, (69) and hath raised up an horn of salvation for us in the house of his servant David; (70) as he spake by the mouth of his holy prophets, which have been since the world began: (71) <u>that we should be saved from our enemies, and from the hand of all that hate us; (72) to perform the mercy promised to our fathers, and to remember his holy covenant;</u> (73) the oath which he sware to our father Abraham, (74) that he would grant unto us, <u>that we being delivered out of the hand of our enemies might serve him without fear, (75) in holiness and righteousness before him, all the days of our life.</u> (76) And thou, child, shalt be called the prophet of the Highest: for thou shalt go before the face of the Lord to prepare his ways; (77) <u>to give knowledge of salvation unto his people by the remission of their sins</u>, (78) through the tender mercy of our God; whereby the dayspring from on high hath visited us, (79) to give light to them that sit in darkness and in the shadow of death, to guide our feet into the way of peace.

ACTS 2:21-22—(21) And it shall come to pass, that whosoever shall call on the name of the Lord shall be saved. (22) Ye men of Israel, hear these words.

PRECEPTS FOR ROMANS

ROMANS 3:22—Even the righteousness of God, which is by faith of Jesus Christ unto all and upon all them that believe: for there is no difference.

ROMANS 9:4—Who are Israelites; to whom pertaineth the adoption, and the glory, and the covenants, and the giving of the law, and the service of God, and the promises.

GALATIANS 4:4-5—(4) But when the fullness of the time was come, God sent forth his Son, made of a woman, made under the law, (5) To redeem them that were under the law, that we might receive the adoption of sons.

2 MACCABEES 8:1-5—(1) Then Judas Maccabeus, and they that were with him, went privily into the towns, and called their kinsfolks together, and took unto them all such as continued in the Jews' religion, and assembled about six thousand men. (2) And they called upon the Lord, that he would look upon the people that was trodden down of all; and also pity the temple profaned of ungodly men; (3) And that he would have compassion upon the city, sore defaced, and ready to be made even with the ground; and hear the blood that cried unto him, (4) And remember the wicked slaughter of harmless infants, and the blasphemies committed against his name; and that he would shew his hatred against the wicked. (5) Now when Maccabeus had his company about him, he could not be withstood by the heathen: for the wrath of the Lord was turned into mercy.

ROMANS 10:14-15

(14) **How then shall they call on him in whom they have not believed? And how shall they believe in him of whom they have not heard? And how shall they hear without a preacher?** (15) **And how shall they preach, except they be sent? As it is written, How beautiful are the feet of them that preach the gospel of peace, and bring glad tidings of good things!**

ISAIAH 52:5-7—(5) Now therefore, what have I here, saith the LORD, that my people is taken away for nought? They that rule over them make them to howl, saith the LORD; and my name continually every day is blasphemed. (6) Therefore my people shall know my name: therefore they shall know in that day that I am he that doth speak: behold, it is I. (7) How beautiful upon the mountains are the feet of him that bringeth good tidings, that publisheth peace; that bringeth good tidings of good, that publisheth salvation; that saith unto Zion, Thy God reigneth!

NAHUM 1:15—Behold upon the mountains the feet of him that bringeth good tidings, that publisheth peace! O Judah, keep thy solemn feasts, perform thy vows: for the wicked shall no more pass through thee; he is utterly cut off.

ACTS 13:2—As they ministered to the Lord, and fasted, the Holy Ghost said, Separate me Barnabas and Saul for the work whereunto I have called them.

TITUS 1:3—But hath in due times manifested his word through preaching, which is committed unto me according to the commandment of God our Saviour.

ROMANS 10:16-17
(16) **But they have not all obeyed the gospel. For Esaias saith, Lord, who hath believed our report?** (17) **So then faith cometh by hearing, and hearing by the word of God.**

ISAIAH 53:1-12—(1) Who hath believed our report? And to whom is the arm of the LORD revealed? (2) For he shall grow up before him as a tender plant, and as a root out of a dry ground: he hath no form nor comeliness; and when we shall see him, there is no beauty that we should desire him. (3) He is despised and rejected of men; a man of sorrows, and acquainted with grief: and we hid as it were our faces from him; he was despised, and we esteemed him not. (4) Surely he hath borne our griefs, and carried our sorrows: yet we did esteem him stricken, smitten of God, and afflicted. (5) But he was wounded for our transgressions, he was bruised for our iniquities: the chastisement of our peace was upon him; and with his stripes we are healed. (6) All we like sheep have gone astray; we have turned every one to his own way; and the LORD hath laid on him the iniquity of us all. (7) He was oppressed, and he was afflicted, yet he opened not his mouth: he is brought as a lamb to the slaughter, and as a sheep before her shearers is dumb, so he openeth not his mouth. (8) He was taken from prison and from judgment: and who shall declare his generation? For he was cut off out of the land of the living: for the transgression of my people was he stricken. (9) And he made his grave with the wicked, and with the rich in his death; because he had done no violence, neither was any deceit in his mouth. (10) Yet it pleased the LORD to bruise him; he hath put him to grief: when thou shalt make his soul an offering for sin, he shall see his seed, he shall prolong his days, and the pleasure of the LORD shall prosper in his hand. (11) He shall see of the travail of his soul, and shall be satisfied: by his knowledge shall my righteous servant justify many; for he shall bear their iniquities. (12) Therefore will I divide him a portion with the great, and he shall divide the spoil with the strong; because he hath poured out his soul unto death: and he was numbered with the transgressors; and he bare the sin of many, and made intercession for the transgressors.

JOHN 12:38—That the saying of Esaias the prophet might be fulfilled, which he spake, Lord, who hath believed our report? And to whom hath the arm of the Lord been revealed?

1 THESSALONIANS 2:13—For this cause also thank we God without ceasing, because, when ye received the word of God which ye heard of us, ye received it not as the word of men, but as it is in truth, the word of God, which effectually worketh also in you that believe.

2 THESSALONIANS 2:15—Therefore, brethren, stand fast, and hold the traditions which ye have been taught, whether by word, or our epistle.

ROMANS 10:18
But I say, Have they not heard? Yes verily, their sound went into all the earth, and their words unto the ends of the world.

1 KINGS 18:10—As the LORD thy God liveth, there is no nation or kingdom, whither my lord hath not sent to seek thee: and when they said, He is not there; he took an oath of the kingdom and nation, that they found thee not.

PSALMS 19:4—Their line is gone out through all the earth, and their words to the end of the world. In them hath he set a tabernacle for the sun.

MATTHEW 24:14—And this gospel of the kingdom shall be preached in all the world for a witness unto all nations; and then shall the end come.

MARK 13:10—And the gospel must first be published among all nations.

(Colossians 1:6, 1:23)

ROMANS 10:19 [a]
But I say, Did not Israel know? First Moses saith, I will provoke you to jealousy by them that are no people, and by a foolish nation I will anger you.

STRONG'S # 3863: 'to provoke to jealousy'—*parazéloó* (παραζηλόω)
USAGE: make jealous, provoke to jealously, provoke to anger

ஓ௸

Without correct biblical precepts, *Romans 10:19* can be confusing. Constantine Christianity has, since its inception, misinterpreted this verse, attributing Paul's references of *"them that are no people,"* and *"a foolish nation"* to non-Israelites alone.

Though other nations are welcome to glean spiritual enlightenment, comfort, and inspiration from our scriptures, this epistle, and this scripture, in particular, was written <u>to</u> Israelites, <u>about</u> Israelites, and <u>for</u> Israelites, as was the entire bible.

In this section (*Romans 10:19 [a]*), I've provided reference scriptures for Paul's use of the word 'jealousy.' I'll unpack this (and other key points of understanding) further in *Romans 10:19 [b], [c],* and *[d]* subsections below.

DEUTERONOMY 32:21—<u>They have moved me to jealousy</u> with that which is not God; they have provoked me to anger with their vanities: and <u>I will move them to jealousy with those</u>, which are not a people; I will provoke them to anger with a foolish nation.

ROMANS 11:11—I say then, Have they stumbled that they should fall? God forbid: but rather through their fall salvation is come unto the Gentiles, for <u>to provoke them to jealousy</u>.

ROMANS 11:30-32—(30) For as ye in times past have not believed God, <u>yet have now obtained mercy through their unbelief</u>: (31) Even so have these also now not believed, that through your mercy they also may obtain mercy. (32) For God hath concluded them all in unbelief, that he might have mercy upon all.

TITUS 3:3—For we ourselves also were sometimes foolish, disobedient, deceived, serving divers lusts and pleasures, living in malice and envy, <u>hateful, and hating one another</u>.

(Luke 15:11-32; Galatians 2:11-13)

ROMANS 10:19 [b]

But I say, Did not Israel know? First Moses saith, I will provoke you to jealousy by them that are no people, and by a foolish nation [*ethnei* (ἔθνει)] I will anger you.

First, lets define 'nation' as it applies here. The Greek word, *ethnei* (ἔθνει) has a familiar root—*Ethnos*—which is used repeatedly in *John 11:47-52*. There it describes the tribe of Judah as a separate *nation* from the other tribes, despite the fact that they're all of Jacob's seed:

JOHN 11:47-52—(47) Then gathered the chief priests and the Pharisees a council, and said, What do we? For this man doeth many miracles. (48) If we let him thus alone, all men will believe on him: and the Romans shall come and take away both our place and **nation** [*Ethnos* (ἔθνος)] (49) And one of them, named Caiaphas, being the high priest that same year, said unto them, Ye know nothing at all, (50) Nor consider that it is expedient for us, that one man should die for the people, and that the whole **nation** [*Ethnos* (ἔθνος)] perish not. (51) And this spake he not of himself: but being high priest that year, he prophesied that Jesus should die for that **nation** [*Ethnous* (ἔθνους)]; (52) And not for that **nation** [*Ethnous* (ἔθνους)] only, but that also he should gather together in one the children of God that were scattered abroad.

As seen above, *Ethnos* is not only used for non-Israelites, it's also used to refer to the twelve tribes of Israel which were scattered to the four corners of the earth. In the case of *Romans 10:19-20*, Paul is discussing the Northern and Southern kingdoms, AKA the twelve tribes of Israel. Therefore, as we'll see in *Romans 10:19 [c]* below, the references to *a 'foolish nation'* and *'those who are not a people'* are speaking about the Northern Kingdom. Read on:

ROMANS 10:19 [c]
But I say, Did not Israel know? First Moses saith, I will provoke you to jealousy by them that are no people, and by a foolish nation I will anger you.

In *Romans 10:19 [c]*, we're basically seeing the parable of the Prodigal Son play out. The older son (Judah) was provoked to jealousy by his foolish younger brother (Ephraim). As a side note, we should also include the estranged remnant of Judah who were Hellenized during the Greek captivity here too.

Anyway, let's first take a look at *Deuteronomy 32:20-21*, the script Paul is pulling from, so we can understand whom he's talking about here:

DEUTERONOMY 32:20-21—(20) And he said, I will hide my face from them, I will see what their end shall be: for they are a very froward generation, children in whom is no faith. (21) They have moved me to jealousy with that which is not God; they have provoked me to anger with their vanities: and I will move them to jealousy **with those, which are not a people**; I will provoke them to anger with **a foolish nation.**

This begs the question, how can Moses be speaking about Israel being jealous of a "foolish nation," while addressing all of Israel in *Deuteronomy 32:21*? Simple. First, he was speaking prophetically, just as he did in Deuteronomy 29:27-28. A large portion of Israel would be scattered and cut off from being a part of Israel, thereby becoming strange, or Gentiles. They'd go from being a people to not being a people once they—*foolishly*—rejected TMH, their heritage, birthright, and identity. Let's begin by looking at the prophecies against The House of Israel, specifically, Ephraim (The Northern Kingdom) that show the 10 tribes losing their heritage in captivity because of idolatry:

ISAIAH 44:17-19—(17) And the residue thereof he maketh a god, even his graven image: he falleth down unto it, and worshippeth it, and prayeth unto it, and saith, Deliver me; for thou art my god. (18) They have not known nor understood: for he hath shut their eyes, that they cannot see; and their hearts, that they cannot understand. (19) And none considereth in his heart, neither is there knowledge nor understanding to say, I have burned part of it in the fire; yea, also I have baked bread upon the coals thereof; I have roasted flesh, and eaten it: and shall I make the residue thereof an abomination? Shall I fall down to the stock of a tree?

EZEKIEL 20:30-32—(30) Wherefore say unto the house of Israel, Thus saith the Lord GOD; Are ye polluted after the manner of your fathers? And commit ye whoredom after their abominations? (31) For when ye offer your gifts, when ye make your sons to pass through the fire, ye pollute yourselves with all your idols, even unto this day: and shall I be inquired of by you, O house of Israel? As I live, saith the Lord GOD, I will not be inquired of by you. (32) And that which cometh into your mind shall not be at all, that ye say, **We will be as the heathen, as the families of the countries, to serve wood and stone.**

By trading TMH's truth for dumb idols, they became the **foolish nation** Moses spoke about.

ROMANS 1:21—Because that, when they knew God, they glorified him not as God, neither were thankful; but became vain in their imaginations, **and their foolish heart was darkened.**

This is why TMH sent them packing and deemed them 'not a people.'

ISAIAH 7:8-9—(8) For the head of Syria is Damascus, and the head of Damascus is Rezin; and within threescore and five years **shall Ephraim be broken, that it be not a people.** (9) And the head of Ephraim is Samaria, and the head of Samaria is Remaliah's son. If ye will not believe, surely ye shall not be established.

HOSEA 1:6-11—(6) And she conceived again, and bare a daughter. And God said unto him, Call her name Loruhamah: for **I will no more have mercy upon the house of Israel; but I will utterly take them away.** (7) But I will have mercy upon the house of Judah, and will save them by the LORD their God, and will not save them by bow, nor by sword, nor by battle, by horses, nor by horsemen. (8) Now when she had weaned Loruhamah, she conceived, and bare a son. (9) Then said God, Call his name Loammi: **for ye are not my people, and I will not be your God**. (10) Yet the number of the children of Israel shall be as the sand of the sea, which cannot be measured nor numbered; and it shall come to pass, that **in the place where it was said unto them, Ye are not my people, there it shall be said unto them, Ye are the sons of the living God**. **(11)** **Then shall the children of Judah and the children of Israel be gathered together**, and appoint themselves one head, and they shall come up out of the land: for great shall be the day of Jezreel.

HOSEA 2:22-23—(22) And the earth shall hear the corn, and the wine, and the oil; and they shall hear Jezreel. (23) And I will sow her unto me in the earth; and I will have mercy upon her that had not obtained mercy; **and I will say to them which were not my people, Thou art my people; and they shall say, Thou art my God**.

1 PETER 2:9-10—(9) But ye are a **chosen generation**, a **royal priesthood**, an **holy nation**, a **peculiar people**; that ye should shew forth the praises of him who hath called you out of darkness into his marvelous light: (10) **Which in time past were not a people**, but are now the people of God: which **had not obtained mercy**, but now have obtained mercy.

Re: 1 Peter 2:9-10

1. Who are TMH's chosen people? *(Deuteronomy 7:3-6, 14:2; Isaiah 14:1, 43:20-21; Jeremiah 33:24; 2 Esdras 6:54-55; 2 Baruch 48:18-19; Wisdom of Solomon 4:15; Psalms 155:21 [part of the Pseudepigrapha]; The Book of Jubilees 22:9)*
2. Who are called to the royal priesthood? *(Exodus 19:6; Isaiah 61:6; Revelation 1:6; 5:8-10, 7:3-8)*
3. Who is TMH's holy nation? *(Leviticus 20:26; Deuteronomy 7:6; 14:2, 28:9; Ezra 10:9-12, 16-17; 1 Esdras 8:69-71, 8:84:85; Tobit 4:12-13; Sirach 6:13; 26:19-21; The Book of Jubilees 22:16-18; Joseph & Aseneth 7:1-7; Additions to Esther 10:9-12)*
4. Who are TMH's peculiar people? *(Deuteronomy 14:2, 26:18-19; Titus 2:13-14)*
5. Who is the nation called to sing forth TMH's praises? *(Psalms 79:13; Isaiah 43:20-21; Jeremiah 13:11)*

Therefore, the people referred to in #'s 1-5 above *(1 Peter 2:9)* are the same people spoken of in *1 Peter 2:10*, "which in time past were not a people." This is "**foolish**" Ephraim and the 10-tribe Northern Kingdom he represents. *Deuteronomy 32:20-21*, as applied by Paul in *Romans 10:19* above isn't referring to non-Israelites because non-Israelites, as a whole, have always maintained their heritage, lands, and identities. Only the

children of Israel have repeatedly lost their history and identity through captivity after captivity, over thousands of years.
.Again:

ISAIAH 7:8—For the head of Syria is Damascus, and the head of Damascus is Rezin; and within threescore and five years **shall Ephraim be broken, that it be not a people.**

ROMANS 10:19 [d]
But I say, Did not Israel know? First Moses saith, I will provoke you to jealousy by <u>them that are no people,</u> <u>and by a foolish nation I will anger you.</u>

It's said that although TMH may say something once within a scripture, He oftentimes speaks twice. In a deeper sense, *Deuteronomy 32:20-21* does have a modern-day fulfillment as does *Romans 10:19*. Those of us who've been awakened, in *this* generation—in all our sinfulness—have been provoked to jealousy by a *very* foolish nation, a nation 'which is not a people.'

Consider this:

GENESIS 9:27—God shall enlarge *[(paw-thaw' (פתה)]* Japheth, and he shall dwell in the tents of Shem; and Canaan shall be his servant.

In this verse, *'pathah' (paw-thaw')* is consistently mistranslated as 'enlarge'. However, it actually means:

STRONG'S #H6601: (פתה paw-thaw'): A primitive root; to open, that is, be (causatively make) roomy; usually figuratively (in a mental or moral sense) to be (causatively make) simple or (in a sinister way) delude: - allure, deceive, enlarge, entice, flatter, persuade, silly (one).

In order for the text to mean what they're implying (by using enlarge, AKA to expand or make big), Moses would have used the Hebrew word *'rachab'* instead:

rachab: to be or grow wide or large
Original Word: רָחַב
Part of Speech: Verb
Transliteration: rachab
Phonetic Spelling: (raw-khab')
Short Definition: enlarge

To show how far from the mark these translators landed, if you do a word search for *pathah* H6601 *(פתה paw-thaw')* you'll find that of the

28 times it appears in the OT King James, it's only translated as 'enlarge' in Genesis 9:27. Therefore, it would be better translated as:

> God shall deceive (or entice) Japheth and he shall dwell in the tents of Shem...

TMH has, in the past, sent lying spirits to individuals for His divine purposes. *(1 Kings 22:22-23; 2 Chronicles 18:21-22)* Therefore, a people who are not a people have been deceived (a foolish nation) and are dwelling in the tents of Shem.

REVELATION 3:9—Behold, I will make them of the synagogue of Satan, which say they are Jews, and are not, but do lie; behold, I will make them to come and worship before thy feet, and to know that I have loved thee.

This same *foolish nation* is also of the seed of Edom since Esau has mixed/spoiled his seed *(Jeremiah 49:10; 1 Esdras 8:69)*...literally everywhere *(Genesis 27:39)*. So *they're not a people for the simple fact that they're not the people they claim to be*. They're an admixture of many nations within Edom and Japheth.

According to TMH, both Edom/Idumea *and* their heathen conspirators have taken TMH's land. This, by default, puts them there—Japheth in the tents of Shem per *Genesis 9:27* and Edom covering the earth like dew, meaning he would be everywhere, which would include Shem's and everyone else's lands. *(Genesis 27:39)*

EZEKIEL 36:5—Therefore thus saith the Lord GOD; Surely in the fire of my jealousy have I spoken against the residue of the heathen, and against all Idumea, which have appointed my land into their possession with the joy of all their heart, with despiteful minds, to cast it out for a prey.

All this is the consequence of Israel's disobedience. This shows what happens when TMH turns His face from us. Our land gets plundered and we go into captivity: *Ezra 9:7; Isaiah 1:3, 5:13, 29:9-10; Jeremiah 29:9-10, 50:6, Lamentations 2:6, Daniel 9:7-8; Hosea 3:1-5, 4:6, Baruch 1:15; 2 Baruch 3:5-6; Book of Jubilees 1:8, 6:34-38.*

We forgot our heritage, as did the world, which according to *Psalms 83:1-4* was an international conspiracy approved by TMH God because of our disobedience. So He gave the children's bread to the other nations in order to provoke us to jealousy. Think about it. Is that not what's happening now? Doesn't the sight of seeing someone claim your heritage—something you've always longed for—hit you like a gut punch?

As an aside, even if *Romans 11:17-19* meant 'contemporary Christians' were grafted in (which is doesn't), it still doesn't work. Given the non-Israelite nation's and Christianity's track record, which includes: [1]

committing atrocities against TMH's people (hundreds of years of murder, rape, torture, slavery), [2] dividing TMH's land, [3] removing, hiding, tampering with, and destroying holy books, [4] whitewashing the patriarchs and TMH, promoting both a false messiah and [5] a false gospel, and finally, [6] using the holy scriptures to conquer and subjugate whole lands and peoples, is there *any* way all that could possibly go unpunished, especially considering the punishment TMH gave Israel? Is there any way a people guilty of doing these blasphemies would be grafted into TMH's bride, the holy nation of Israel, a people created to be His heritage, considering the entirety of the bible chronicles TMH's efforts to keep His people holy and separated from all nations? As it is written:

> **GALATIANS 1:6-9**—(6) I marvel that ye are so soon removed from him that called you into the grace of Christ unto another gospel: (7) Which is not another; but there be some that trouble you, and would pervert the gospel of Christ. (8) But though we, or an angel from heaven, preach any other gospel unto you than that which we have preached unto you, let him be accursed. (9) As we said before, so say I now again, If any man preach any other gospel unto you than that ye have received, let him be accursed.

Scripture is quite clear about what awaits the nations. Yes, nations. Just as Israel was punished as a nation, non-Israelite nations will be punished nationally as well. This isn't hate. This is truth.

> **2 ESDRAS 15:15-21**—(15) For the sword and their destruction draweth nigh, and one people shall stand up and fight against another, and swords in their hands. (16) For there shall be sedition among men, and invading one another; they shall not regard their kings nor princes, and the course of their actions shall stand in their power. (17) A man shall desire to go into a city, and shall not be able. (18) For because of their pride the cities shall be troubled, the houses shall be destroyed, and men shall be afraid. (19) A man shall have no pity upon his neighbour, but shall destroy their houses with the sword, and spoil their goods, because of the lack of bread, and for great tribulation. (20) Behold, saith God, I will call together all the kings of the earth to reverence me, which are from the rising of the sun, from the south, from the east, and Libanus; to turn themselves one against another, and repay the things that they have done to them. (21) **Like as they do yet this day unto my chosen, so will I do also, and recompense in their bosom. Thus saith the Lord God**...

This is what the Day of the Lord is all about. TMH repaying the nations for their blasphemies against Him and His children.

2 BARUCH 72:4-6—(4) Every nation, which knows not Israel and has not trodden down the seed of Jacob, shall indeed be spared. (5) And this because some out of every nation shall be subjected to your people. (6) But all those who have ruled over you, or have known you, shall be given up to the sword.

What nation hasn't known, murdered, lied to, robbed, and oppressed the children of Israel? What nation hasn't reaped the benefits of the children of Israel's downfall? What nation hasn't served themselves at the children of Israel's expense? This is why TMH said what He said in Amos:

AMOS 9:11-12—(11) In that day will I raise up the tabernacle of David that is fallen, and close up the breaches thereof; and I will raise up his ruins, and I will build it as in the days of old: (12) That they may possess the remnant of Edom, and of all the heathen, which are called by my name, saith the LORD that doeth this.

Just as repentant and humbled Egyptians who cleaved to Israel received mercy in Egypt when we left with a mixed multitude, history will repeat itself during Israel's final exodus. *(See The Strangers Among Us pg. 426)* The promises and everything else mentioned in *Romans 9:4-5* still belong to Israel and always will. Non-Israelites **will not** be grafted into our tree. That honor is saved for the scattered and lost within the 12 tribes.

Again, repentant non-Israelites are welcome to join and cleave to us, worship our God, and receive blessings per *Genesis 12:3, 27:29*, but our tree is a twelve-tribe tree and our blessings belong to us and us alone. While we were in time out, the other kids got to play, but make no mistake, we're coming off of punishment, and are more than ready for our inheritance. After all, our Daddy promised it to us.

ISAIAH 14:1-2—(1) For the LORD will have mercy on Jacob, and will yet choose Israel, and set them in their own land: and the strangers shall be joined with them, and they shall cleave to the house of Jacob, (2) and the people shall take them, and bring them to their place: and the house of Israel shall possess them in the land of the LORD for servants and handmaids: and they shall take them captive, whose captives they were; and they shall rule over their oppressors.

(Isaiah 34:4-8; Jeremiah 25:38; Ezekiel 35:9-10, 12, 14-15; Joel 3:2, Obadiah 1:16; Revelation 2:9)

ROMANS 10:20-21

(20) **But Esaias is very bold, and saith, I was found of them that sought me not; I was made manifest unto them that asked not after me.** (21) **But to Israel he saith, All day long I have stretched forth my hands unto a disobedient and gainsaying people.**

In this verse Paul paraphrases *Isaiah 65* where TMH addresses the Northern Kingdom and the fallen in Judah: those who had gone astray and forgotten about Him. They neither sought Him out, nor were they called by His name because He disowned/divorced them.

ISAIAH 65:1-11—(1) I am sought of them that asked not for me; I am found of them that sought me not: I said, Behold me, behold me, unto a nation that was not called by my name. (2) I have spread out my hands all the day unto a rebellious people, which walketh in a way that was not good, after their own thoughts...(9) And I will bring forth a seed out of Jacob, and out of Judah an inheritor of my mountains: and mine elect shall inherit it, and my servants shall dwell there. (10) And Sharon shall be a fold of flocks, and the valley of Achor a place for the herds to lie down in, for my people that have sought me. (11) But ye are they that forsake the LORD, that forget my holy mountain, that prepare a table for that troop, and that furnish the drink offering unto that number.

HOSEA 1:6-10—(6) And she conceived again, and bare a daughter. And God said unto him, Call her name Loruhamah: for I will no more have mercy upon the house of Israel; but I will utterly take them away. (7) But I will have mercy upon the house of Judah, and will save them by the LORD their God, and will not save them by bow, nor by sword, nor by battle, by horses, nor by horsemen. (8) Now when she had weaned Loruhamah, she conceived, and bare a son. (9) Then said God, Call his name Loammi: for ye are not my people, and I will not be your God. (10) Yet the number of the children of Israel shall be as the sand of the sea, which cannot be measured nor numbered; and it shall come to pass, that in the place where it was said unto them, Ye are not my people, there it shall be said unto them, Ye are the sons of the living God.

EZEKIEL 20:30-32—(30) Wherefore say unto the house of Israel, Thus saith the Lord GOD; Are ye polluted after the manner of your fathers? And commit ye whoredom after their abominations? (31) For when ye offer your gifts, when ye make your sons to pass through the fire, ye pollute yourselves with all your idols, even unto this day: and shall I be inquired of by you, O house of Israel? As I live, saith the Lord GOD, I will not be inquired of by you. (32) And that which cometh into your mind shall not be at all, that ye say, We will be as the heathen, as the families of the countries, to serve wood and stone.

ROMANS 11

ROMANS 11:1 [a]
I say then, Hath God cast away his people? God forbid. For I also am an Israelite, of the seed of Abraham, of the tribe of Benjamin.

In the last two verses *(Romans 10:20-21)* Paul paraphrased *Isaiah 65* regarding Northern and Southern kingdom rebellion. *Romans 11:1* continues the conversation, in that, despite the unfaithfulness of both houses of Israel, TMH has not, nor will He ever cast His people away.

PSALMS 94:14—For the LORD will not cast off his people, neither will he forsake his inheritance.

JEREMIAH 31:37—Thus saith the LORD; If heaven above can be measured, and the foundations of the earth searched out beneath, I will also cast off all the seed of Israel for all that they have done, saith the LORD.

1 SAMUEL 12:22—For the LORD will not forsake his people for his great name's sake: because it hath pleased the LORD to make you his people.

ISAIAH 14:1-2—(1) For the LORD will have mercy on Jacob, and will yet choose Israel, and set them in their own land: and the strangers shall be joined with them, and they shall cleave to the house of Jacob. (2) And the people shall take them, and bring them to their place: and the house of Israel shall possess them in the land of the LORD for servants and handmaids: and they shall take them captives, whose captives they were; and they shall rule over their oppressors.

ISAIAH 43:1—But now thus saith the LORD that created thee, O Jacob, and he that formed thee, O Israel, Fear not: for I have redeemed thee, I have called thee by thy name; thou art mine.

ISAIAH 44:21—Remember these, O Jacob and Israel; for thou art my servant: I have formed thee; thou art my servant: O Israel, thou shalt not be forgotten of me.

ISAIAH 49:14-16—(14) But Zion said, The LORD hath forsaken me, and my Lord hath forgotten me. (15) Can a woman forget her sucking child, that she should not have compassion on the son of her womb? yea, they may forget, yet will I not forget thee. (16) Behold, I have graven thee upon the palms of my hands; thy walls are continually before me.

ISAIAH 59:21—As for me, this is my covenant with them, saith the LORD; My spirit that is upon thee, and my words which I have put in thy mouth, shall not depart out of thy mouth, nor out of the mouth of thy seed, nor out of the mouth of thy seed's seed, saith the LORD, from henceforth and forever.

JEREMIAH 46:28—Fear thou not, O Jacob my servant, saith the LORD: for I am with thee; for I will make a full end of all the nations whither I have driven thee: but I will not make a full end of thee, but correct thee in measure; yet will I not leave thee wholly unpunished.

ROMANS 11:1 [b]
I say then, Hath God cast away his people? God forbid. <u>For I also am an Israelite, of the seed of Abraham, of the tribe of Benjamin</u>.

Paul, Mistaken For An Egyptian:

ACTS 21:38—<u>Art not thou that Egyptian</u>, which before these days madest an uproar, and leddest out into the wilderness four thousand men that were murderers?

Paul, A Roman Citizen:

ACTS 22:22-29—(22) And they gave him audience unto this word, and then lifted up their voices, and said, Away with such a fellow from the earth: for it is not fit that he should live. (23) And as they cried out, and cast off their clothes, and threw dust into the air, (24) The chief captain commanded him to be brought into the castle, and bade that he should be examined by scourging; that he might know wherefore they cried so against him. (25) And as they bound him with thongs, <u>Paul said unto the centurion that stood by, Is it lawful for you to scourge a man that is a Roman, and uncondemned</u>? (26) When the centurion heard that, he went and told the chief captain, saying, Take heed what thou doest: for this man is a Roman. (27) Then the chief captain came, and said unto him, Tell me, art thou a Roman? He said, Yea. (28) And the chief captain answered, With a great sum obtained I this freedom. And Paul said, But I was free born. (29) Then straightway they departed from him which should have examined him: and <u>the chief captain also was afraid, after he knew that he was a Roman</u>, and because he had bound him.

ACTS 23:27—This man was taken of the Jews, and should have been killed of them: then came I with an army, and rescued him, having understood that he was a Roman.

Paul, From The Tribe Of Benjamin, A Pharisee, A Hebrew And An Israelite:

2 CORINTHIANS 11:22—Are they Hebrews? So am I. Are they Israelites? So am I. Are they the seed of Abraham? So am I.

ROMANS 11:1—... For I also am an Israelite, of the seed of Abraham, of the tribe of Benjamin.

PHILIPPIANS 3:5—Circumcised the eighth day, of the stock of Israel, of the tribe of Benjamin, an Hebrew of the Hebrews; as touching the law, a Pharisee.

ROMANS 11:2-4 [a]
(2) **God hath not cast away his people, which he foreknew. Wot ye not what the scripture saith of Elias? How he maketh intercession to God against Israel, saying,** (3) **Lord, they have killed thy prophets, and digged down thine altars; and I am left alone, and they seek my life.** (4) **But what saith the answer of God unto him? I have reserved to myself seven thousand men, who have not bowed the knee to the image of Baal.**

STRONG'S #G4267: "foreknew"—*proginóskó (προγινώσκω)*
USAGE: know beforehand, foreknow.
The KJV translates Strong's G4267 in the following manner: foreknow (2x), foreordain (1x), know (1x), know before (1x)

❧

To 'foreordain' is to predestinate. The above scriptures should be read contextually. Meaning, that the same people Paul has been speaking about in this whole epistle (Northern and Southern kingdoms) are the only people as per *Romans 11:2* that TMH 'foreknew' aka 'foreordained.' The scriptures bear this out, repeatedly.

EPHESIANS 1:5—Having predestinated us unto the adoption of children by Jesus Christ to himself, according to the good pleasure of his will

ROMANS 8:29-30—(29) For whom he did foreknow, he also did predestinate [to be] conformed to the image of his Son, that he might be the firstborn among many brethren. (30) Moreover whom he did predestinate, them he also called: and whom he called, them he also justified: and whom he justified, them he also glorified.

AMOS 3:2—You only have I known of all the families of the earth: therefore I will punish you for all your iniquities.

PSALMS 147:19-20—(19) He sheweth his word unto Jacob, his statutes and his judgments unto Israel. (20) He hath not dealt so with any nation: and as for his judgments, they have not known them. Praise ye the LORD.

ROMANS 11:2-4 [b]

(2) God hath not cast away his people, which he foreknew. Wot ye not what the scripture saith of Elias? How he maketh intercession to God against Israel, saying, (3) Lord, they have killed thy prophets, and digged down thine altars; and I am left alone, and they seek my life. (4) But what saith the answer of God unto him? I have reserved to myself seven thousand men, who have not bowed the knee to the image of Baal.

Here Paul mentions Elijah, a **Northern Kingdom** prophet who lived under the tyranny of wicked King Ahab and Queen Jezebel. In *Kings* chapter 19, we see Elijah in hiding because he believes they've either killed or compromised all of the TMH prophets and devoted followers. Believing he's the last one alive, he cries out for divine help, however TMH assures him that He has 7000 men in reserve who've not bent the knee to Baal:

1 KINGS 19:10, 14, 18—(10) And he said, I have been very jealous for the LORD God of hosts: for the children of Israel have forsaken thy covenant, thrown down thine altars, and slain thy prophets with the sword; and I, even I only, am left; and they seek my life, to take it away…(14) And he said, I have been very jealous for the LORD God of hosts: because the children of Israel have forsaken thy covenant, thrown down thine altars, and slain thy prophets with the sword; and I, even I only, am left; and they seek my life, to take it away…(18) Yet I have left me seven thousand in Israel, all the knees which have not bowed unto Baal, and every mouth which hath not kissed him.

TMH will never cast away His people and always reserves a remnant.

PSALMS 94:14—For the LORD will not cast off his people, neither will he forsake his inheritance.

PRECEPTS FOR ROMANS

ISAIAH 41:8-9—(8) But thou, Israel, art my servant, Jacob whom I have chosen, the seed of Abraham my friend. (9) Thou whom I have taken from the ends of the earth, and called thee from the chief men thereof, and said unto thee, Thou art my servant; I have chosen thee, and not cast thee away.

JEREMIAH 33:23-26—(23) Moreover the word of the LORD came to Jeremiah, saying, (24) Considerest thou not what this people have spoken, saying, The two families which the LORD hath chosen, he hath even cast them off? Thus they have despised my people, that they should be no more a nation before them. (25) Thus saith the LORD; If my covenant be not with day and night, and if I have not appointed the ordinances of heaven and earth; (26) Then will I cast away the seed of Jacob, and David my servant, so that I will not take any of his seed to be rulers over the seed of Abraham, Isaac, and Jacob: for I will cause their captivity to return, and have mercy on them.

ROMANS 8:29—For whom he did foreknow, he also did predestinate to be conformed to the image of his Son, that he might be the firstborn among many brethren.

ROMANS 11:5 [a]
Even so then at this present time also there is a remnant according to the election of grace.

Just as TMH reserved a remnant during King Ahab and Jezebel's reign, He's also reserved a remnant today.

ISAIAH 10:21—The remnant shall return, even the remnant of Jacob, unto the mighty God.

ISAIAH 46:3—Hearken unto me, O house of Jacob, and all the remnant of the house of Israel, which are borne by me from the belly, which are carried from the womb.

ROMANS 11:5 [b]
Even so then at this present time also there is a remnant according to the election of grace.

GRACE

STRONG'S #G5485: "grace"—charis (χάρις)
USAGE: (a) grace, as a gift or blessing brought to man by Jesus Christ, (b) favor, (c) gratitude, thanks, (d) a favor, kindness.

ISAIAH 45:4—For Jacob my servant's sake, and Israel mine elect, I have even called thee by thy name: I have surnamed thee, though thou hast not known me.

ROMANS 9:27—Esaias also crieth concerning Israel, Though the number of the children of Israel be as the sand of the sea, a remnant shall be saved

ROMANS 11:6
And if by grace, then is it no more of works: otherwise grace is no more grace. But if it be of works, then is it no more grace: otherwise work is no more work.

ROMANS 4:4-5—(4) Now to him that worketh is the reward not reckoned of grace, but of debt. (5) But to him that worketh not, but believeth on him that justifieth the ungodly, his faith is counted for righteousness.

ROMANS 6:1-4—(1) What shall we say then? Shall we continue in sin, that grace may abound? (2) God forbid. How shall we that are dead to sin, live any longer therein? (3) Know ye not, that so many of us as were baptized into Jesus Christ were baptized into his death? (4) Therefore we are buried with him by baptism into death: that like as Christ was raised up from the dead by the glory of the Father, even so we also should walk in newness of life.

SIRACH 35:19—Till he have rendered to every man according to his deeds, and to the works of men according to their devices; till he have judged the cause of his people, and made them to rejoice in his mercy.

ROMANS 11:7 [a]
What then? Israel hath not obtained that which he seeketh for; but the election hath obtained it, and the rest were blinded

The nation of Israel, as a whole, did not obtain what it sought, because they sought it in error, a salvation through unrighteousness. Animal sacrifices don't have the power to change hearts. Messiah's sacrifice does.

LEVITICUS 16:15-16—(15) Then shall he kill the goat of the sin offering, that is for the people, and bring his blood within the veil, and do with that blood as he did with the blood of the bullock, and sprinkle it upon the mercy seat, and before the mercy seat: (16) And he shall make an atonement for the holy place, because of the uncleanness of the children of Israel, and because of their transgressions in all their sins: and so shall he do for the tabernacle of the congregation, that remaineth among them in the midst of their uncleanness.

HEBREWS 10:3-4—(3) But in those sacrifices there is a remembrance again made of sins every year. (4) For it is not possible that the blood of bulls and of goats should take away sins.

MATTHEW 22:11-14—(11) And when the king came in to see the guests, he saw there a man which had not on a wedding garment: (12) and he saith unto him, Friend, how camest thou in hither not having a wedding garment? And he was speechless. (13) Then said the king to the servants, Bind him hand and foot, and take him away, and cast him into outer darkness; there shall be weeping and gnashing of teeth. (14) For many are called, but few are chosen.

ROMANS 4:14—For if they which are of the law be heirs, faith is made void, and the promise made of none effect.

ROMANS 11:7 [b]
What then? Israel hath not obtained that which he seeketh for; but the election hath obtained it, and the rest were blinded

A portion of Israel did obtain righteousness through faith in the Messiah and His sacrifice—both Northern and Southern kingdom Israelites (Circumcision and Uncircumcision). These are the elect within TMH's children because they're not all Israel that are of Israel. *(Romans 9:6)*

ROMANS 1:17—For therein is the righteousness of God revealed from faith to faith: as it is written, The just shall live by faith.

ROMANS 9:30—What shall we say then? That the Gentiles, which followed not after righteousness, have attained to righteousness, even the righteousness, which is of faith.

HEBREWS 7:27—Who needeth not daily, as those high priests, to offer up sacrifice, first for his own sins, and then for the people's: for this he did once, when he offered up himself.

HEBREWS 9:12-14—(12) Neither by the blood of goats and calves, but by his own blood he entered in once into the holy place, having obtained eternal redemption for us. (13) For if the blood of bulls and of goats, and the ashes of an heifer sprinkling the unclean, sanctifieth to the purifying of the flesh: (14) How much more shall the blood of Christ, who through the eternal Spirit offered himself without spot to God, purge your conscience from dead works to serve the living God?

HEBREWS 10:5-18—(5) Therefore when he comes into the world, he says, Sacrifice and offering you desired not, but a body have you prepared me: (6) In burnt offerings and sacrifices for sin you have had no pleasure. (7) Then said I, Lo, I come (in the volume of the book it is written of me,) to do your will, O God. (8) Above when he said, Sacrifice and offering and burnt offerings and offering for sin you desired not, neither had pleasure in them; which are offered by the law; (9) Then said he, Lo, I come to do your will, O God. He takes away the first, that he may establish the second. (10) By the which will we are sanctified through the offering of the body of Jesus Christ once for all. (11) And every priest stands daily ministering and offering frequently the same sacrifices, which can never take away sins: (12) But this man, after he had offered one sacrifice for sins forever, sat down on the right hand of God; (13) From then on waiting till his enemies be made his footstool. (14) For by one offering he has perfected forever them that are sanctified. (15) The Holy Spirit also is a witness to us: for after this he had said before, (16) This is the covenant that I will make with them after those days, says the Lord, I will put my laws into their hearts, and in their minds will I write them; (17) And their sins and iniquities will I remember no more. (18) Now where remission of these is, there is no more offering for sin.

ROMANS 11:7 [c]
What then? Israel hath not obtained that which he seeketh for; but the election hath obtained it, <u>and the rest were blinded</u>

Those blinded within Israel were the Scribes, Pharisees and their loyalists as well as Israelites caught up in Greek philosophies. *(1 Corinthians 1:22-24)* The same is true today. Many within Christian churches blindly follow pastors, spiritual leaders, and their own vain philosophies rather than read the bible for themselves to discover the truth. Others are blinded because they refuse to leave spiritual Babylon. *(Revelation 18:4)*

2 CORINTHIANS 3:14—But their minds were blinded: for until this day remaineth the same veil untaken away in the reading of the old testament; which veil is done away in Christ. *(Isaiah 45:4)*

JOHN 12:40—He hath blinded their eyes, and hardened their heart; that they should not see with their eyes, nor understand with their heart, and be converted, and I should heal them.

ROMANS 9:31-32—(31) But Israel, which followed after the law of righteousness, hath not attained to the law of righteousness. (32)

Wherefore? Because they sought it not by faith, but as it were by the works of the law. For they stumbled at that stumblingstone.

ISAIAH 30:12-13—(12) Wherefore thus saith the Holy One of Israel, Because ye despise this word, and trust in oppression and perverseness, and stay thereon: (13) Therefore this iniquity shall be to you as a breach ready to fall, swelling out in a high wall, whose breaking cometh suddenly at an instant.

MATTHEW 23:15-16, 24—(15) Woe unto you, scribes and Pharisees, hypocrites! For ye compass sea and land to make one proselyte, and when he is made, ye make him twofold more the child of hell than yourselves. (16) Woe unto you, ye blind guides, which say, Whosoever shall swear by the temple, it is nothing; but whosoever shall swear by the gold of the temple, he is a debtor!...(24) Ye blind guides, which strain at a gnat, and swallow a camel.

ROMANS 10:2—For I bear them record that they have a zeal of God, but not according to knowledge.

ROMANS 11:8
According as it is written, God hath given them the spirit of slumber, eyes that they should not see, and ears that they should not hear; unto this day.

DEUTERONOMY 29:4—Yet the LORD hath not given you an heart to perceive, and eyes to see, and ears to hear, unto this day.

ISAIAH 6:9-13—(9) And he said, Go, and tell this people, Hear ye indeed, but understand not; and see ye indeed, but perceive not. (10) Make the heart of this people fat, and make their ears heavy, and shut their eyes; lest they see with their eyes, and hear with their ears, and understand with their heart, and convert, and be healed. (11) Then said I, Lord, how long? And he answered, Until the cities be wasted without inhabitant, and the houses without man, and the land be utterly desolate, (12) And the LORD have removed men far away, and [there be] a great forsaking in the midst of the land. (13) But yet in it shall be a tenth, and it shall return, and shall be eaten: as a teil tree, and as an oak, whose substance is in them, when they cast their leaves: so the holy seed shall be the substance thereof.

JEREMIAH 5:19-21—(19) And it shall come to pass, when ye shall say, Wherefore doeth the LORD our God all these things unto us? Then shalt thou answer them, Like as ye have forsaken me, and served strange gods in your land, so shall ye serve strangers in a land that is not yours.

(20) Declare this in the house of Jacob, and publish it in Judah, saying, (21) Hear now this, O foolish people, and without understanding; which have eyes, and see not; which have ears, and hear not.

MATTHEW 13:14—And in them is fulfilled the prophecy of Esaias, which saith, By hearing ye shall hear, and shall not understand; and seeing ye shall see, and shall not perceive.

ACTS 28:26-27—(26) Saying, Go unto this people, and say, Hearing ye shall hear, and shall not understand; and seeing ye shall see, and not perceive: (27) For the heart of this people is waxed gross, and their ears are dull of hearing, and their eyes have they closed; lest they should see with [their] eyes, and hear with [their] ears, and understand with their heart, and should be converted, and I should heal them.

2 BARUCH 51:4-6—(4) For over this above all shall those who come then lament, that they rejected My law, and stopped their ears that they might not hear wisdom or receive understanding. (5) When therefore they see those, over whom they are now exalted, (but) who shall then be exalted and glorified more than they, they shall respectively be transformed, the latter into the splendor of angels, and the former shall yet more waste away in wonder at the visions and in the beholding of the forms. (6) For they shall first behold and afterwards depart to be tormented.

ROMANS 11:9 [a]
And David saith, Let their <u>table</u> be made a snare, and a trap, and a stumbling block, and a recompence unto them:

Tables are tablets which TMH's word is written upon.

HABAKKUK 2:2—And the LORD answered me, and said, Write the vision, and make it plain upon tables, that he may run that readeth it.

ROMANS 11:9 [b]
And David saith, Let their table be made <u>a snare, and a trap, and a stumbling block, and a recompence</u> unto them:

PSALMS 69:22-23—(22) Let their table become a snare before them: and that which should have been for their welfare, let it become a trap. (23) Let their eyes be darkened, that they see not; and make their loins continually to shake.

ISAIAH 8:14-18—(14) And he shall be for a sanctuary; but for a stone of stumbling and for a rock of offence to both the houses of Israel, for a gin and for a snare to the inhabitants of Jerusalem. (15) And many among them shall stumble, and fall, and be broken, and be snared, and be taken. (16) Bind up the testimony, seal the law among my disciples. (17) And I will wait upon the LORD, that hideth his face from the house of Jacob, and I will look for him. (18) Behold, I and the children whom the LORD hath given me are for signs and for wonders in Israel from the LORD of hosts, which dwelleth in mount Zion.

ROMANS 11:10
Let their eyes be darkened, that they may not see, and bow down their back always.

ISAIAH 29:10-13—(10) For the LORD hath poured out upon you the spirit of deep sleep, and hath closed your eyes: the prophets and your rulers, the seers hath he covered. (11) And the vision of all is become unto you as the words of a book that is sealed, which [men] deliver to one that is learned, saying, Read this, I pray thee: and he saith, I cannot; for it is sealed: (12) And the book is delivered to him that is not learned, saying, Read this, I pray thee: and he saith, I am not learned. (13) Wherefore the Lord said, Forasmuch as this people draw near [me] with their mouth, and with their lips do honour me, but have removed their heart far from me, and their fear toward me is taught by the precept of men:

ROMANS 9:31—But Israel, which followed after the law of righteousness, hath not attained to the law of righteousness.

ROMANS 10:3—For they being ignorant of God's righteousness, and going about to establish their own righteousness, have not submitted themselves unto the righteousness of God.

(Deuteronomy 29:4; Isaiah 6:9-13; Jeremiah 5:19-21; 2 Baruch 51:4-6; Matthew 13:14; Matthew 23:15-16, 24; John 12:40; Acts 28:26-27)

ROMANS 11:11 [a]
I say then, have they stumbled that they should fall? God forbid: but rather through their fall salvation is come unto the Gentiles, for to provoke them to jealousy.

Though they stumbled, those of the election of grace, were prophesied to be reconciled to TMH in the knowledge of the truth.

LUKE 2:34—And Simeon blessed them, and said unto Mary his mother, Behold, this child is set for the **fall and rising again** of many in Israel; and for a sign which shall be spoken against.

(Isaiah 8:14, Matthew 21:43-45)

ROMANS 11:11 [b]
I say then, have they stumbled that they should fall? God forbid: but rather through their fall salvation is come unto the Gentiles, for to provoke them to jealousy.

We've already established that there are two kinds of Gentiles within scripture: Israelite and non-Israelite. Biblical history, prophetic precedence as well as the overall context of this epistle, tells us the Gentiles in *Romans 11:11* are the House of Israel, i.e. Northern Kingdom Israelites *and* Greek Israelites who, as a result of idolatry, fell away.

EZEKIEL 20:30-32—(30) Wherefore say unto the house of Israel, Thus saith the Lord GOD; Are ye polluted after the manner of your fathers? And commit ye whoredom after their abominations? (31) For when ye offer your gifts, when ye make your sons to pass through the fire, ye pollute yourselves with all your idols, even unto this day: and shall I be inquired of by you, O house of Israel? As I live, saith the Lord GOD, I will not be inquired of by you. (32) And that which cometh into your mind shall not be at all, that ye say, We will be as the heathen, as the families of the countries, to serve wood and stone.

EZEKIEL 34:12—As a shepherd seeketh out his flock in the day that he is among his sheep that are scattered; so will I seek out my sheep, and will deliver them out of all places where they have been scattered in the cloudy and dark day.

MATTHEW 18:12-14—(12) How think ye? If a man have an hundred sheep, and one of them be gone astray, doth he not leave the ninety and nine, and goeth into the mountains, and seeketh that which is gone astray? (13) And if so be that he find it, verily I say unto you, he rejoiceth more of that sheep, than of the ninety and nine which went not astray. (14) Even so it is not the will of your Father, which is in heaven, that one of these little ones should perish.

LUKE 15:31-32—(31) And he said unto him, Son, thou art ever with me, and all that I have is thine. (32) It was meet that we should make merry, and be glad: for this thy brother was dead, and is alive again; and was lost, and is found.

JOHN 10:16—And other sheep I have, which are not of this fold: them also I must bring, and they shall hear my voice; and there shall be one fold, and one shepherd

ACTS 10:11-16—(11) And saw heaven opened, and a certain vessel descending unto him, as it had been a great sheet knit at the four corners,* and let down to the earth. (12) Wherein were all manner of four-footed beasts of the earth, and wild beasts, and creeping things, and fowls of the air. (13) And there came a voice to him, Rise, Peter; kill, and eat. (14) But Peter said, Not so, Lord; for I have never eaten any thing that is common or unclean. (15) And the voice spake unto him again the second time, What God hath cleansed, that call not thou common. (16) This was done thrice: and the vessel was received up again into heaven.

ISAIAH 42:6-7—(6) I the LORD have called thee in righteousness, and will hold thine hand, and will keep thee, and give thee for a covenant of the people, for a light of the Gentiles; (7) To open the blind eyes, to bring out the prisoners from the prison, and them that sit in darkness out of the prison house.

ISAIAH 61:1—The Spirit of the Lord GOD is upon me; because the LORD hath anointed me to preach good tidings unto the meek; he hath sent me to bind up the brokenhearted, to proclaim liberty to the captives, and the opening of the prison to them that are bound.

(Jeremiah 23:3, 31:10; Luke 4:16-21, 19:10)

ROMANS 11:11 [c]
I say then, have they stumbled that they should fall? God forbid: but rather through their fall salvation is come unto the Gentiles, for <u>to provoke them to jealousy</u>.

Jealousy: (n) jealousy, green-eyed monster; a feeling of jealous envy, especially of a rival

As noted previously, this sentiment of jealousy is the essence of the Parable of the Prodigal Son. *(Luke 15:11-32)* Two sons and one loving father. The eldest son (Judah/Southern Kingdom) remained behind to work the father's land while the other (Ephraim/Northern Kingdom) ran off and squandered his inheritance, living a life of debauchery (transgressing the law). Once he hit rock bottom, the younger son "joined himself to a citizen" of a foreign country (became a gentile) and got a job feeding pigs, eating the same slop they did.

But when he came to himself and realized how far he'd fallen into sin, and that even his father's servants ate better than he did now, he returned home, hat in hand, humbled, disgraced and apologetic (Repentance), telling his father that he didn't even deserve to be called his son anymore.

---

* *Deuteronomy 32:26; Isaiah 11:12, Zechariah 2:6-7; Matthew 24:31; Mark 13:26-27; Words of Gad The Seer 2:66-68*

Yet to his surprise, his father not only welcomed him with open arms, he elevated him to the station he was at before (Redemption). However, when the man's older son learned that his aimless brother had returned, and his father had thrown a lavish party to welcome him back, he burned hot with anger (Jealousy)*

LUKE 15:29-32—(29) And he answering said to his father, Lo, these many years do I serve thee, neither transgressed I at any time thy commandment: and yet thou never gavest me a kid, that I might make merry with my friends: (30) But as soon as this thy son was come, which hath devoured thy living with harlots, thou hast killed for him the fatted calf. (31) And he said unto him, Son, thou art ever with me, and all that I have is thine. (32) It was meet that we should make merry, and be glad: for this thy brother was dead, and is alive again; and was lost, and is found.

(*Compare this with commentaries for Romans 11:13 and 11:14, pgs. 313-319)

MATTHEW 18:12-14—(12) How think ye? If a man have an hundred sheep, and one of them be gone astray, doth he not leave the ninety and nine, and goeth into the mountains, and seeketh that which is gone astray? (13) And if so be that he find it, verily I say unto you, he rejoiceth more of that sheep, than of the ninety and nine which went not astray. (14) Even so it is not the will of your Father, which is in heaven that one of these little ones should perish.

ACTS 13:45-46—(45) But when the Jews saw the multitudes, they were filled with envy, and spake against those things, which were spoken by Paul, contradicting and blaspheming. (46) Then Paul and Barnabas waxed bold, and said, It was necessary that the word of God should first have been spoken to you: but seeing ye put it from you, and judge yourselves unworthy of everlasting life, lo, we turn to the Gentiles.

ACTS 28:28—Be it known therefore unto you, that the salvation of God is sent unto the Gentiles, and that they will hear it.

ROMANS 10:19—But I say, Did not Israel know? First Moses saith, I will provoke you to jealousy by them that are no people, and by a foolish nation I will anger you.

ROMANS 11:13-14—(13) For I speak to you Gentiles, inasmuch as I am the apostle of the Gentiles, I magnify mine office: (14) If by any means I may provoke to emulation them which are my flesh, and might save some of them.

(Deuteronomy 32:21-36; Isaiah 11:13; See also Romans 10:19 commentary, pgs. 279-287)

ROMANS 11:12 [a]
Now if the fall of them be <u>the riches of the world,</u> and the diminishing of them the riches of the Gentiles; How much more their fullness?

Since scripture defines scripture, what riches of the world is Paul referring to? *Deuteronomy, Ephesians, Romans,* and *Colossians* provide the answer:

DEUTERONOMY 29:29—<u>The secret things belong unto the LORD our God: but those things which are revealed belong unto us and to our children forever, that we may do all the words of this law.</u>

EPHESIANS 1:15-19—(15) Wherefore I also, after I heard of your faith in the Lord Jesus, and love unto all the saints, (16) Cease not to give thanks for you, making mention of you in my prayers; (17) That the God of our Lord Jesus Christ<u>, the Father of glory, may give unto you the spirit of wisdom and revelation in the knowledge of him: (18) The eyes of your understanding being enlightened; that ye may know what is the hope of his calling, and what the riches of the glory of his inheritance in the saints,</u> (19) And what is the exceeding greatness of his power to us-ward who believe, according to the working of his mighty power.

ROMANS 11:33—O the depth of the <u>riches both of the wisdom and knowledge of God!</u> How unsearchable are his judgments, and His ways past finding out!

COLOSSIANS 1:23-29—(23) If ye continue in the faith grounded and settled, and be not moved away from the hope of the gospel, which ye have heard, and which was preached to every creature which is under heaven; whereof I Paul am made a minister; (24) Who now rejoice in my sufferings for you, and fill up that which is behind of the afflictions of Christ in my flesh for his body's sake, which is the church: (25) Whereof I am made a minister, according to the dispensation of God which is given to me for you, to fulfill the word of God; (26) <u>Even the mystery which hath been hid from ages and from generations, but now is made manifest to his saints: (27) To whom God would make known what is the riches of the glory of this mystery among the Gentiles; which is Christ in you</u>, the hope of glory: (28) Whom we preach, warning every man, and teaching every man in all wisdom; that we may present every man perfect in Christ Jesus: (29) Whereunto I also labor, striving according to his working, which worketh in me mightily.

Although Israel lost those riches at the fall, the nations (non-Israelites) *did not* receive these riches (wisdom and knowledge of TMH, faith of the Messiah, and the Law written on the heart). History can attest to this. The fall of Israel enabled them to destroy the children of Israel *and* to deceive and control the entire world by misusing the Israelite's holy book:

JOB 9:24—The earth is given into the hand of the wicked: he covereth the faces of the judges thereof; if not, where, *and* who *is* he?

Still in doubt? Well, consider the following:

1. Creation of another gospel * another Messiah, (a European messiah, whom the world calls 'Jesus'):

JOHN 5:43—I am come in my Father's name, and ye receive me not: if another shall come in his own name, him ye will receive.

GALATIANS 1:8-9—(8) But though we, or an angel from heaven, preach any other gospel unto you than that which we have preached unto you, let him be accursed. (9) As we said before, so say I now again, if any man preach any other gospel unto you than that ye have received, let him be accursed.

1 THESSALONIANS 2:11-12—(11) And for this cause God shall send them strong delusion, that they should believe a lie: (12) that they all might be damned who believed not the truth, but had pleasure in unrighteousness.

ODES OF SOLOMON 38:7-15—(7) But Truth was proceeding on the upright way, and whatever I did not understand He exhibited to me: (8) All the poisons of error, and pains of death, which are considered sweetness. (9) And the corrupting of the Corruptor, I saw when the bride who was corrupting was adorned, and the bridegroom who corrupts and is corrupted. (10) And I asked the Truth, Who are these? And He said to me: This is the Deceiver and the Error. (11) And they imitate the Beloved and His Bride, and they cause the world to err and corrupt it. (12) And they invite many to the wedding feast, and allow them to drink the wine of their intoxication; (13) So they cause them to vomit up their wisdom and their knowledge, and prepare for them mindlessness. (14) Then they abandon them; and so they stumble about like mad and corrupted men. (15) Since there is no understanding in them, neither do they seek it.

ODES OF SOLOMON 41:8-10—All those who see Me will be amazed because I am from another race. For the Father of Truth remembered

Me: He who possessed Me from the beginning. For His riches begat Me, and the thought of His heart.

2. Oppression, Murder And, Enslavement Of TMH's Chosen People

2 ESDRAS 15:20-23—(20) Behold, saith God, I will call together all the kings of the earth to reverence me, which are from the rising of the sun, from the south, from the east, and Libanus; to turn themselves one against another, and repay the things that they have done to them. (21) Like as they do yet this day unto my chosen, so will I do also, and recompense in their bosom. Thus saith the Lord God; (22) My right hand shall not spare the sinners, and my sword shall not cease over them that shed innocent blood upon the earth. (23) The fire is gone forth from his wrath, and hath consumed the foundations of the earth, and the sinners, like the straw that is kindled.

JEREMIAH 51:4-6—(4) Thus the slain shall fall in the land of the Chaldeans, and they that are thrust through in her streets. (5) For Israel hath not been forsaken, nor Judah of his God, of the LORD of hosts; though their land was filled with sin against the Holy One of Israel. (6) Flee out of the midst of Babylon, and deliver every man his soul: be not cut off in her iniquity; for this is the time of the LORD'S vengeance; he will render unto her a recompense.

JEREMIAH 51:35-36—(35) The violence done to me and to my flesh *be* upon Babylon, shall the inhabitant of Zion say; and my blood upon the inhabitants of Chaldea, shall Jerusalem say. (36) Therefore thus saith the LORD; Behold, I will plead thy cause, and take vengeance for thee; and I will dry up her sea, and make her springs dry.

JEREMIAH 51:49—As Babylon *hath caused* the slain of Israel to fall, so at Babylon shall fall the slain of all the earth.

AMOS 1:9—Thus saith the LORD; For three transgressions of Tyrus, and for four, I will not turn away the punishment thereof; because they delivered up the whole captivity to Edom, and remembered not the brotherly covenant:

ZECHARIAH 2:8-9—(8) For thus saith the LORD of hosts; After the glory hath he sent me unto the nations which spoiled you: for he that toucheth you toucheth the apple of his eye. (9) For, behold, I will shake mine hand upon them, and they shall be a spoil to their servants: and ye shall know that the LORD of hosts hath sent me.

JOEL 3:2-4—(2) I will also gather all nations, and will bring them down into the valley of Jehoshaphat, and will plead with them there for my people and for my heritage Israel, whom they have scattered among the nations, and parted my land. (3) And they have cast lots for my people; and have given a boy for an harlot, and sold a girl for wine, that they might drink. (4) Yea, and what have ye to do with me, O Tyre, and Zidon, and all the coasts of Palestine? Will ye render me a recompense? And if ye recompense me, swiftly *and* speedily will I return your recompense upon your own head...

JOEL 3:7-12—(7) Behold, I will raise them out of the place whither ye have sold them, and will return your recompence upon your own head: (8) And I will sell your sons and your daughters into the hand of the children of Judah, and they shall sell them to the Sabeans, to a people far off: for the LORD hath spoken it. (9) Proclaim ye this among the Gentiles; Prepare war, wake up the mighty men, let all the men of war draw near; let them come up. (10) Beat your plowshares into swords, and your pruning hooks into spears: let the weak say, I am strong. (11) Assemble yourselves, and come, all ye heathen, and gather yourselves together round about: thither cause thy mighty ones to come down, O LORD. (12) Let the heathen be wakened, and come up to the valley of Jehoshaphat: for there will I sit to judge all the heathen round about.

JOEL 3:19—Egypt shall be a desolation, and Edom shall be a desolate wilderness, for the violence against the children of Judah, because they have shed innocent blood in their land.

PSALMS 137:7—Remember, O LORD, the children of Edom in the day of Jerusalem; who said, Rase it, rase it, even to the foundation thereof.

OBADIAH 1:10-14—(10) For thy violence against thy brother Jacob shame shall cover thee, and thou shalt be cut off forever. (11) In the day that thou stoodest on the other side, in the day that the strangers carried away captive his forces, and foreigners entered into his gates, and cast lots upon Jerusalem, even thou wast as one of them. (12) But thou shouldest not have looked on the day of thy brother in the day that he became a stranger; neither shouldest thou have rejoiced over the children of Judah in the day of their destruction; neither shouldest thou have spoken proudly in the day of distress. (13) Thou shouldest not have entered into the gate of my people in the day of their calamity; yea, thou shouldest not have looked on their affliction in the day of their calamity, nor have laid hands on their substance in the day of their calamity; (14) Neither shouldest thou have stood in the crossway, to cut off those of his that did escape; neither shouldest thou have delivered up those of his that did remain in the day of distress.

EZEKIEL 25:12-14—(12) Thus saith the Lord GOD; Because that Edom hath dealt against the house of Judah by taking vengeance, and hath greatly offended, and revenged himself upon them; (13) Therefore thus saith the Lord GOD; I will also stretch out mine hand upon Edom, and will cut off man and beast from it; and I will make it desolate from Teman; and they of Dedan shall fall by the sword. (14) And I will lay my vengeance upon Edom by the hand of my people Israel: and they shall do in Edom according to mine anger and according to my fury; and they shall know my vengeance, saith the Lord GOD.

EZEKIEL 35:5-9—(5) Because thou hast had a perpetual hatred, and hast shed the blood of the children of Israel by the force of the sword in the time of their calamity, in the time that their iniquity had an end: (6) Therefore, as I live, saith the Lord GOD, I will prepare thee unto blood, and blood shall pursue thee: sith thou hast not hated blood, even blood shall pursue thee. (7) Thus will I make mount Seir most desolate, and cut off from it him that passeth out and him that returneth. (8) And I will fill his mountains with his slain men: in thy hills, and in thy valleys, and in all thy rivers, shall they fall that are slain with the sword. (9) I will make thee perpetual desolations, and thy cities shall not return: and ye shall know that I am the LORD.

ISAIAH 51:22-23—(22) Thus saith thy Lord the LORD, and thy God *that* pleadeth the cause of his people, Behold, I have taken out of thine hand the cup of trembling, *even* the dregs of the cup of my fury; thou shalt no more drink it again: (23) But I will put it into the hand of them that afflict thee; which have said to thy soul, Bow down, that we may go over: and thou hast laid thy body as the ground, and as the street, to them that went over.

THE LADDER OF JACOB 6 (Rec 1)—And know thou, Jacob, that thy seed shall be strangers in a strange land, and men will ill-treat them with bondage and lay blows on them daily: but the people whom they serve will the Lord judge. When a king ariseth and fightest, then will there be to that place (al. when the Most High giveth his judgment to that place, he will lead forth) then will thy seed, even Israel, go forth out of bondage of the heathen who ruled over them with violence, and will be set free from all reproach of their enemies. For this kings is the head of every revenge and retribution of them that make attacks on thee, Israel. And (at the) end of the age. For the miserable will rise and cry, and the Lord heareth them, and will be softened, and the mighty letteth himself pity their sufferings, because the angels and archangels pour out their prayers for the saving of thy race. Then will their women bear much fruit, and then will the Lord fight for thy race. *The Lost Apocrypha of the Old Testament, Their Titles And Fragments, pg. 99-100*

3. Stolen Holy Land

EZEKIEL 36:5—Therefore thus saith the Lord GOD; Surely in the fire of my jealousy have I spoken against the residue of the heathen, and against all Idumea, which have appointed my land into their possession with the joy of all their heart, with despiteful minds, to cast it out for a prey.

EZEKIEL 35:9-10,12, 14-15—(9) I will make thee perpetual desolations, and thy cities shall not return: and ye shall know that I am the LORD. (10) Because thou hast said, These two nations and these two countries shall be mine, and we will possess it; whereas the LORD was there...(12) And thou shalt know that I am the LORD, and that I have heard all thy blasphemies which thou hast spoken against the mountains of Israel, saying, They are laid desolate, they are given us to consume...(14) Thus saith the Lord GOD; When the whole earth rejoiceth, I will make thee desolate. (15) As thou didst rejoice at the inheritance of the house of Israel, because it was desolate, so will I do unto thee: thou shalt be desolate, O mount Seir, and all Idumea, even all of it: and they shall know that I am the LORD.

ISAIAH 34:4-8—(4) And all the host of heaven shall be dissolved, and the heavens shall be rolled together as a scroll: and all their host shall fall down, as the leaf falleth off from the vine, and as a falling fig from the fig tree. (5) For my sword shall be bathed in heaven: behold, it shall come down upon Idumea, and upon the people of my curse, to judgment. (6) The sword of the LORD is filled with blood, it is made fat with fatness, and with the blood of lambs and goats, with the fat of the kidneys of rams: for the LORD hath a sacrifice in Bozrah, and a great slaughter in the land of Idumea. (7) And the unicorns shall come down with them, and the bullocks with the bulls; and their land shall be soaked with blood, and their dust made fat with fatness. (8) For it is the day of the LORD'S vengeance, and the year of recompenses for the controversy of Zion.

JOEL 3:2—I will also gather all nations, and will bring them down into the valley of Jehoshaphat, and will plead with them there for my people and for my heritage Israel, whom they have scattered among the nations, and parted my land.

OBADIAH 1:16—For as ye have drunk upon my holy mountain, so shall all the heathen drink continually, yea, they shall drink, and they shall swallow down, and they shall be as though they had not been.

4. All these wicked deeds were the antithesis of TMH's riches of wisdom and knowledge, faith in the true Messiah, and the holy Law written on the heart. Prophecy predicted the nations would be confederate against Israel and would turn the truth into lies.

PSALMS 83:4-12—(4) They have said, Come, and let us cut them off from being a nation; that the name of Israel may be no more in remembrance. (5) For they have consulted together with one consent: they are confederate against thee: (6) The tabernacles of Edom, and the Ishmaelites; of Moab, and the Hagarenes; (7) Gebal, and Ammon, and Amalek; the Philistines with the inhabitants of Tyre; (8) Assur also is joined with them: they have holpen the children of Lot. Selah. (9) Do unto them as unto the Midianites; as to Sisera, as to Jabin, at the brook of Kison: (10) Which perished at Endor: they became as dung for the earth. (11) Make their nobles like Oreb, and like Zeeb: yea, all their princes as Zebah, and as Zalmunna: (12) Who said, Let us take to ourselves the houses of God in possession.

1 MACCABEES 3:46-51—(46) Wherefore the Israelites assembled themselves together, and came to Maspha, over against Jerusalem; for in Maspha was the place where they prayed aforetime in Israel. (47) Then they fasted that day, and put on sackcloth, and cast ashes upon their heads, and rent their clothes, (48) And laid open the book of the law, wherein the heathen had sought to paint the likeness of their images. (49) They brought also the priests' garments, and the firstfruits, and the tithes: and the Nazarites they stirred up, who had accomplished their days. (50) Then cried they with a loud voice toward heaven, saying, What shall we do with these, and whither shall we carry them away? (51) For thy sanctuary is trodden down and profaned, and thy priests are in heaviness, and brought low.

PSALMS 50:16-19—(16) But unto the wicked God saith, What hast thou to do to declare my statutes, or that thou shouldest take my covenant in thy mouth (17) seeing thou hatest instruction, and castest my words behind thee. (18) When thou sawest a thief, then thou consentedst with him, and hast been partaker with adulterers. (19) Thou givest thy mouth to evil, and thy tongue frameth deceit.

REVELATION 2:9—I know thy works, and tribulation, and poverty, (but thou art rich) and I know the blasphemy of them which say they are Jews, and are not, but are the synagogue of Satan.

REVELATION 3:9—Behold, I will make them of the synagogue of Satan, which say they are Jews, and are not, but do lie; behold, I will make them to come and worship before thy feet, and to know that I have loved thee

2 BARUCH 39:5-7—(5) And after these things a fourth kingdom will arise, whose power will be harsh and evil far beyond those which were before it, and it will rule many times as the forests on the plain, and it will hold fast for times, and will exalt itself more than the cedars of Lebanon. (6) And by it the truth will be hidden, and all those who are polluted with iniquity will flee to it, as evil beasts flee and creep into the forest. (7) And it will come to pass when the time of its consummation that it should fall has approached, then the principate of My Messiah will be revealed....

DANIEL 7:25—And he shall speak great words against the most High, and shall wear out the saints of the most High, and think to change times and laws: and they shall be given into his hand until a time and times and the dividing of time.

JEREMIAH 16:19—O LORD, my strength, and my fortress, and my refuge in the day of affliction, the Gentiles shall come unto thee from the ends of the earth, and shall say, Surely our fathers have inherited lies, vanity, and things wherein there is no profit.

WISDOM OF SOLOMON 5:6-7—(6) Therefore have we erred from the way of truth, and the light of righteousness hath not shined unto us, and the sun of righteousness rose not upon us. (7) We wearied ourselves in the way of wickedness and destruction: yea, we have gone through deserts, where there lay no way: but as for the way of the Lord, we have not known it.

WORDS OF GAD THE SEER 1:5-11—(5) And it came to pass when I finished calling that cry, I opened my eyes and saw a yoke of oxen led by a donkey and a camel, coming up from the stream of Kidron, the donkey on the right of the yoke and the camel on the left. (6) And a great voice was going before them like the rolling thunder, crying in a bitter voice, saying: (7) See, Seer, Seer, these are four mixtures that confuse the people of the Lord. (8) For the impure and the pure have been mixed, and purity had been put under the hand of impurity; a mixture from Edom to rule over them, (9) to increase power over a righteous doer and therefore, to betray, (10) to destroy holiness, to crown wickedness, to set up matters of impurity in the guise of purity. (11) And after the voice came, a great shock shook over the impurity and blew away the donkey and the camel into the moon with a bitter wind.

WORDS OF GAD THE SEER 2:78-81—(78) Woe to you, O Edom that sits in the land of Kittim in the north of the sea. (79) For your destroyers will emerge from a terrible nation not leaving you a remnant. (80) For you said: On high is my seat, and I have knowledge of the god of gods, for the Lord chose me instead of His holy people, for He loathed them. (81)

And His former people, despised and rejected, did not know the Lord or His image.

BOOK OF ENOCH 103-6-10—(6) And be assured by me, that light and darkness, day and night, behold all your transgressions. Be not impious in your thoughts; lie not; surrender not the word of uprightness; lie not against the word of the holy and the mighty One; glorify not your idols; for all your lying and all your impiety is not for righteousness, but for great crime. (7) Now will I point out a mystery: Many sinners shall turn and transgress against the word of uprightness. (8) They shall speak evil things; they shall utter falsehood; execute great undertakings; and compose books in their own words. But when they shall write all my words correctly in their own languages, (9) they shall neither change or diminish them; but shall write them all correctly; all which from the first I have uttered concerning them. (10) Another mystery also I point out. To the righteous and the wise shall be given books of joy, of integrity, and of great wisdom. To them shall books be given, in which they shall believe;

ROMANS 11:12 [b]
Now if the fall of them be the riches of the world [kosmou (κόσμου)], and the diminishing of them the riches of the Gentiles; How much more their fullness?

The "world" referenced here [kosmou (κόσμου)] isn't the whole world and its inhabitants as in Oikoumenēs" (οἰκουμένης). The world of Romans 11:12 is the world of Israel. *(See Romans 11:15 [c] commentary for a full breakdown, pg. 322)*

As noted in the commentary of Romans 11:12 [a], the riches of Israel's world include the wisdom and knowledge of TMH. By rejecting the Messiah, many within the house of Judah's leadership and their followers fell into darkness, relinquishing the riches of the world. As a result of their fall (i.e. their diminishing) the lost sheep of the tribes of Israel were able to partake in this aforementioned spiritual wealth.

Touting their own self-righteousness, the leadership within Judah and their followers became stumbling blocks to others:

MATTHEW 23:15—Woe to you, scribes and Pharisees, you hypocrites! You traverse land and sea to win a single convert, and when he becomes one, you make him twice as much a son of hell as you are.

1 THESSALONIANS 2:14-16—(14) For ye, brethren, became followers of the churches of God which in Judaea are in Christ Jesus: for ye also have suffered like things of your own countrymen, even as they have of the Jews: (15) who both killed the Lord Jesus, and their own prophets, and have persecuted us; and they please not God, and are contrary to all men: (16) Forbidding us to speak to the Gentiles that they might be saved, to fill up their sins always: for the wrath is come upon them to the uttermost.

So their fall was necessary, if to only allow **Israelite Gentiles** easy access to Messiah's saving blood. **These are the Gentiles who received the riches, which is the wisdom and knowledge of TMH, the same riches the 'Circumcision' lost when they rejected Messiah.**

ISAIAH 45:17—But Israel shall be saved in the LORD with an everlasting salvation: ye shall not be ashamed nor confounded world without end.

JOHN 3:16—For God so loved the world, that he gave his only begotten Son, that whosoever believeth in him should not perish, but have everlasting life.

ROMANS 11:12 [c]
Now if the fall of them be the riches of the world, and the diminishing of them the riches of the Gentiles; How much more their fullness? [plērōmadoes (πλήρωμα)]

Paul's use of 'fullness' in this context, means the restoration and return of the fallen House of Judah—leaders and followers—once they repent and accept the Messiah's sacrifice. He uses the same word in Romans 11:25 [Fullness—'plērōmadoes' (πλήρωμα)] when speaking about the in-gathering of the remaining Israelite Gentiles.

ROMANS 11:25—For I would not, brethren, that ye should be ignorant of this mystery, lest ye should be wise in your own conceits; that blindness in part is happened to Israel, until the fullness of the Gentiles be come in.

HOSEA 1:10—Yet the number of the children of Israel shall be as the sand of the sea, which cannot be measured nor numbered; and it shall come to pass, that in the place where it was said unto them, Ye are not my people, there it shall be said unto them, Ye are the sons of the living God.

HOSEA 2:23—And I will sow her unto me in the earth; and I will have mercy upon her that had not obtained mercy; and I will say to them which were not my people, Thou art my people; and they shall say, Thou art my God.

ROMANS 11:33—O the depth of the riches both of the wisdom and knowledge of God! How unsearchable are his judgments, and his ways past finding out!

ROMANS 11:13
For I speak to you Gentiles, inasmuch as I am the apostle of the Gentiles, I magnify mine office:

ACTS 13:14, 16, 47-48—(14) But when they departed from Perga, they came to Antioch in Pisidia, and went into the synagogue on the Sabbath day, and sat down...(16) Then Paul stood up, and beckoning with his hand said, Men of Israel, and ye that fear God, give audience...(47) For so hath the Lord commanded us, saying, I have set thee to be a light of the Gentiles, that thou shouldest be for salvation unto the ends of the earth. (48) And when the Gentiles heard this, they were glad, and glorified the word of the Lord: and as many as were ordained to eternal life believed.

ACTS 22:21—And he said unto me, Depart: for I will send thee far hence unto the Gentiles.

ROMANS 15:16—That I should be the minister of Jesus Christ to the Gentiles, ministering the gospel of God, that the offering up of the Gentiles might be acceptable, being sanctified by the Holy Ghost.

1 CORINTHIANS 9:22—To the weak became I as weak, that I might gain the weak: I am made all things to all men, that I might by all means save some.

ROMANS 11:14 [a]
... if by any means I may provoke to emulation them which are my flesh, and might save some of them.

Emulate: (v) (1) strive to equal or match, especially by imitating (2) compete with successfully; approach or reach equality with

1 CORINTHIANS 11:1-2—(1) Be imitators of me, even as I also am of Christ. (2) Now I praise you, brothers, that you remember me in all things, and hold firm the traditions, even as I delivered them to you. (WEB)

ACTS 13:43—Now when the congregation was broken up, many of the Jews and religious proselytes followed Paul and Barnabas: who, speaking to them, persuaded them to continue in the grace of God.

1 TIMOTHY 4:16—Take heed unto thyself, and unto the doctrine; continue in them: for in doing this thou shalt both save thyself, and them that hear thee.

JAMES 5:20—Let him know, that he which converteth the sinner from the error of his way shall save a soul from death, and shall hide a multitude of sins.

ROMANS 11:14 [b]
... if by any means I may provoke to emulation them which are my flesh, and might save some of them.

Before we delve into this verse, let's get some background. The House of Judah was considered a separate nation, *(John 11:47-52)*, since the split. *(1 Kings 12:13-20)* Consequently, Ephraim (aka The House of Israel) mixed (its seed) with the heathen nations, which resulted in TMH disowning them *(Hosea 1:1-8)*. This is why they're referred to as wild olives trees *(Romans 11:24)*. It got so bad that the scriptures quote TMH as saying that He (TMH) had '*polluted*' His own inheritance by scattering His people amongst the heathen. This is how the holy seed became 'mixed' and 'spoiled' through intermarriage and idolatry.

HOSEA 7:8—Ephraim, he hath mixed himself among the people; Ephraim is a cake not turned.

ISAIAH 47:6—I was wroth with my people, I have polluted mine inheritance, and given them into thine hand: thou didst shew them no mercy; upon the ancient hast thou very heavily laid thy yoke

Therefore, in *Romans 11:14*, where Paul says *"provoke to emulation them which are my flesh,"* he's referring to the Circumcision within the House/NATION *(John 11:47-52)* of Judah who rejected the Messiah, mainly those of the leadership (of which Paul was a member) just as Messiah predicted. Let's examine this further:

JOHN 1:11-13—(11) He came unto his own, and his own received him not. (12) But as many as received him, to them gave he power to become the sons of God, even to them that believe on his name: (13) Which were born, not of blood, nor of the will of the flesh, nor of the will of man, but of God.

> **QUESTION: Did all of Judah reject Messiah?**
>
> **ANSWER: Absolutely not.** See *John 7:31, 8:28-32, 10:40-42, 11:45-48, 12:9-11; Acts 9:40-42; Matthew 21:43-46; Mark 14:1-2.*

JOHN 7:31—And many of the people believed on him, and said, When Christ cometh, will he do more miracles than these which this man hath done.

JOHN 8:28-31—(28) Then said Jesus unto them, When ye have lifted up the Son of man, then shall ye know that I am he, and that I do nothing of myself; but as my Father hath taught me, I speak these things. (29) And he that sent me is with me: the Father hath not left me alone; for I do always those things that please him. (30) As he spake these words, many believed on him. (31) Then said Jesus to those Jews which believed on him, If ye continue in my word, [then] are ye my disciples indeed; (32) And ye shall know the truth, and the truth shall make you free

JOHN 10:40-42—(40) And went away again beyond Jordan into the place where John at first baptized; and there he abode. 41And many resorted unto him, and said, John did no miracle: but all things that John spake of this man were true. (42) And many believed on him there.

JOHN 12:9-11—(9) Much people of the Jews therefore knew that he was there: and they came not for Jesus' sake only, but that they might see Lazarus also, whom he had raised from the dead. (10) But the chief priests consulted that they might put Lazarus also to death; (11) Because that by reason of him many of the Jews went away, and believed on Jesus.

ACTS 9:40-42—(40) But Peter put them all forth, and kneeled down, and prayed; and turning him to the body said, Tabitha, arise. And she opened her eyes: and when she saw Peter, she sat up. (41) And he gave her his hand, and lifted her up, and when he had called the saints and widows, presented her alive. (42) And it was known throughout all Joppa; and many believed in the Lord.

MATTHEW 21:43-46—(43) Therefore say I unto you, The kingdom of God shall be taken from you, and given to a nation bringing forth the fruits thereof. (44) And whosoever shall fall on this stone shall be broken: but on whomsoever it shall fall, it will grind him to powder. (45) And when the chief priests and Pharisees had heard his parables, they perceived that he spake of them. (46) But when they sought to lay hands on him, they feared **the multitude**, because they **took him for a prophet**.

MARK 14:1-2—(1) After two days was the feast of the Passover, and of unleavened bread: and the chief priests and the scribes sought how they might take him by craft, and put him to death. (2) But they said, Not on the feast day, **lest there be an uproar of the people**.

JOHN 11:45-48—(45) Then **many of the Jews** which came to Mary, and had seen the things which Jesus did, **believed on him**. (46) But some of them went their ways to the Pharisees, and told them what things Jesus had done. (47) Then gathered the chief priests and the Pharisees a council, and said, What do we? for this man doeth many miracles. (48) **If we let him thus alone, all men will believe on him**: and the Romans shall come and take away both our place and nation.

There were even some within the Judean leadership who believed on Messiah, but followed Him in secret:

JOHN 3:1-2—(1) There was a man of the Pharisees, named Nicodemus, a ruler of the Jews: (2) The same came to Jesus by night, and said unto him, Rabbi, we know that thou art a teacher come from God: for no man can do these miracles that thou doest, except God be with him.

JOHN 7:50-53—(50) Nicodemus saith unto them, (he that came to Jesus by night, being one of them,) (51) Doth our law judge any man, before it hear him, and know what he doeth? (52) They answered and said unto him, Art thou also of Galilee? Search, and look: for out of Galilee ariseth no prophet. (53) And every man went unto his own house.

JOHN 12:42-43—(42) Nevertheless among the chief rulers also many believed on him; but because of the Pharisees they did not confess him, lest they should be put out of the synagogue: (43) For they loved the praise of men more than the praise of God.

JOHN 19:38-39—(38) And after this Joseph of Arimathaea, being a disciple of Jesus, but secretly for fear of the Jews, besought Pilate that he might take away the body of Jesus: and Pilate gave him leave. He came therefore, and took the body of Jesus. (39) And there came also Nicodemus, which at the first came to Jesus by night, and brought a mixture of myrrh and aloes, about an hundred pound weight.

MARK 15:43—Joseph of Arimathaea, an honorable counselor, which also waited for the kingdom of God, came, and went in boldly unto Pilate, and craved the body of Jesus.

MATTHEW 27:57-60—(57) When the even was come, there came a rich man of Arimathaea, named Joseph, who also himself was Jesus' disciple: (58) He went to Pilate, and begged the body of Jesus. Then Pilate commanded the body to be delivered. (59) And when Joseph had taken the body, he wrapped it in a clean linen cloth, (60) And laid it in his own new tomb, which he had hewn out in the rock: and he rolled a great stone to the door of the sepulcher, and departed.

Yes, many became fearful and fled when the Romans seized, and ultimately crucified the Messiah, *(Zechariah 13:7)* but believers regained their courage and faith when He came back from the dead! *(The Book of Acts)*

So, as we've seen, everyone didn't reject the Messiah. So who did? Who are those whom *John 1:11-13* referred to as "his own" that "received him not"? Messiah tells us in *Mark* and *Luke*:

MARK 8:27-31—(27) And Jesus went out, and his disciples, into the towns of Caesarea Philippi: and by the way he asked his disciples, saying unto them, Whom do men say that I am? (28) And they answered, John the Baptist: but some say, Elias; and others, One of the prophets. (29) And he saith unto them, But whom say ye that I am? And Peter answereth and saith unto him, Thou art the Christ. (30) And he charged them that they should tell no man of him. (31) And he began to teach them, that the Son of man must suffer many things, **and be rejected of the elders, and of the chief priests, and scribes**, and be killed, and after three days rise again.

LUKE 9:18-22—(18) And it came to pass, as he was alone praying, his disciples were with him: and he asked them, saying, Whom say the people that I am? (19) They answering said, John the Baptist; but some say, Elias; and others say, that one of the old prophets is risen again. (20) He said unto them, But whom say ye that I am? Peter answering said, The Christ of God. (21) And he straightly charged them, and commanded them to tell no man that thing; (22) Saying, The Son of man must suffer many things, **and be rejected of the elders and chief priests and scribes**, and be slain, and be raised the third day.

His own were the elders, priests, and scribes—fellow leaders and teachers of the Torah, along with their devotees. They and many others who heedlessly followed them could not see the light for the blinding darkness.

ISAIAH 28:14-17—(14) Wherefore hear the word of the LORD, ye scornful men, that rule this people which [is] in Jerusalem. (15) Because ye have said, We have made a covenant with death, and with hell are we at agreement; when the overflowing scourge shall pass through, it shall not come unto us: for we have made lies our refuge, and under falsehood have we hid ourselves: (16) Therefore thus saith the Lord GOD, Behold, I lay in Zion for a foundation a stone, a tried stone, a precious corner [stone], a sure foundation: he that believeth shall not make haste. (17) Judgment also will I lay to the line, and righteousness to the plummet: and the hail shall sweep away the refuge of lies, and the waters shall overflow the hiding place.

ISAIAH 53:1—Who hath believed our report? And to whom is the arm of the LORD revealed?

MATTHEW 21:33-46—(33) Hear another parable: There was a certain householder, which planted a vineyard, and hedged it round about, and digged a winepress in it, and built a tower, and let it out to husbandmen, and went into a far country: (34) And when the time of the fruit drew near, he sent his servants to the husbandmen, that they might receive the fruits of it. (35) And the husbandmen took his servants, and beat one, and killed another, and stoned another. (36) Again, he sent other servants more than the first: and they did unto them likewise. (37) But last of all he sent unto them his son, saying, They will reverence my son. (38) But when the husbandmen saw the son, they said among themselves, This is the heir; come, let us kill him, and let us seize on his inheritance. (39) And they caught him, and cast him out of the vineyard, and slew him. (40) When the lord therefore of the vineyard cometh, what will he do unto those husbandmen? (41) They say unto him, He will miserably destroy those wicked men, and will let out [his] vineyard unto other husbandmen, which shall render him the fruits in their seasons. (42) Jesus saith unto them, Did ye never read in the scriptures, The stone which the builders rejected, the same is become the head of the corner: this is the Lord's doing, and it is marvelous in our eyes? (43) Therefore say I unto you, The kingdom of God shall be taken from you, and given to a nation bringing forth the fruits thereof. (44) And whosoever shall fall on this stone shall be broken: but on whomsoever it shall fall, it will grind him to powder. (45) And when the chief priests and Pharisees had heard his parables, they perceived that he spake of them. (46) But when they sought to lay hands on him, they feared the multitude, because they took him for a prophet.

JOHN 12:37-43—(37) But though he had done so many miracles before them, yet they believed not on him: (38) That the saying of Esaias the prophet might be fulfilled, which he spake, Lord, who hath believed our report? And to whom hath the arm of the Lord been revealed? (39) Therefore they could not believe, because that Esaias said again, (40) He hath blinded their eyes, and hardened their heart; that they should not see with their eyes, nor understand with their heart, and be converted, and I should heal them. (41) These things said Esaias, when he saw his glory, and spake of him. (42) Nevertheless among the chief rulers also many believed on him; but because of the Pharisees they did not confess him, lest they should be put out of the synagogue: (43) For they loved the praise of men more than the praise of God.

JOHN 11:47-52—(47) Then gathered the chief priests and the Pharisees a council, and said, What do we? for this man doeth many miracles. (48) If we let him thus alone, all [men] will believe on him: and the Romans shall come and take away both our place and nation. (49) And one of them, [named] Caiaphas, being the high priest that same year, said unto them, Ye know nothing at all, (50) Nor consider that it is expedient for us, that one man should die for the people, and that the whole nation perish not. (51) And this spake he not of himself: but being high priest that year, he prophesied that Jesus should die for that nation; (52) And not for that nation only, but that also he should gather together in one the children of God that were scattered abroad.

Those who rejected Messiah chose to rely on the works of the flesh as outlined in the Old Covenant. However, Paul makes a distinction in *Philippians* between works of the spirit and works of the flesh. It's these works of the spirit, which he hoped would provoke the rebellious Circumcision (leadership and their followers) within the House of Judah to emulate him.

It should be noted that Paul, more than anyone during that time period, could boast in his flesh. He was a "Hebrew of Hebrews" as pertaining to the Law of Moses. However, he rightfully proclaimed that in Messiah, there was no cause to boast. This is what he hoped the Circumcision would someday come to understand:

PHILIPPIANS 3:1-16—(1) Finally, my brethren, rejoice in the Lord. To write the same things to you, to me indeed is not grievous, but for you it is safe. (2) Beware of dogs, beware of evil workers, beware of the concision. (3) For we are the circumcision, which worship God in the spirit, and rejoice in Christ Jesus, and have no confidence in the flesh. (4) Though I might also have confidence in the flesh. If any other man thinketh that he hath whereof he might trust in the flesh, I more: (5) Circumcised the eighth day, of the stock of Israel, of the tribe of Benjamin, an Hebrew of the Hebrews; as touching the law, a Pharisee; (6) Concerning zeal, persecuting the church; touching the righteousness which is in the law, blameless. (7) But what things were gain to me, those I counted loss for Christ. (8) Yea doubtless, and I count all things but loss for the excellency of the knowledge of Christ Jesus my Lord: for whom I have suffered the loss of all things, and do count them but dung, that I may win Christ, (9) And be found in him, not having mine own righteousness, which is of the law, but that which is through the faith of Christ, the righteousness which is of God by faith: (10) That I may know him, and the power of his resurrection, and the fellowship of his sufferings, being made conformable unto his death; (11) If by any means I might attain unto the resurrection of the dead. (12) Not as though I had already attained, either were already perfect: but I follow after, if that I may apprehend that for which also I am apprehended of Christ Jesus. (13) Brethren, I count not myself to have apprehended: but this one thing I do, forgetting those things which are behind, and reaching forth unto those things which are before, (14) I press toward the mark for the prize of the high calling of God in Christ Jesus. (15) Let us therefore, as many as be perfect, be thus minded: and if in any thing ye be otherwise minded, God shall reveal even this unto you. (16) Nevertheless, whereto we have already attained, let us walk by the same rule, let us mind the same thing.

ROMANS 11:15 [a]

For if the <u>casting away of them</u> be the reconciling of the world, what shall the receiving of them be, but life from the dead?

The 'them' here are the same 'them' of verse 14 above, the blind, unbelieving, rebellious Circumcision (Pharisees, Sadducees, Scribes and their followers) within the House of Judah.

MARK 12:9-12—(9) What shall therefore the lord of the vineyard do? He will come and destroy the husbandmen, and will give the vineyard unto others. (10) And have ye not read this scripture; the stone which the builders rejected is become the head of the corner: (11) This was the Lord's doing, and it is marvelous in our eyes? (12) And they sought to lay hold on him, but feared the people: for they knew that he had spoken the parable against them: and they left him, and went their way.

ISAIAH 8:14—And he shall be for a sanctuary; but for a stone of stumbling and for a rock of offence to both the houses of Israel, for a gin and for a snare to the inhabitants of Jerusalem.

LUKE 2:34—And Simeon blessed them, and said unto Mary his mother, Behold, this child is set for the fall and rising again of many in Israel; and for a sign which shall be spoken against.

ACTS 13:46—Then Paul and Barnabas waxed bold, and said, It was necessary that the word of God should first have been spoken to you: but seeing ye put it from you, and judge yourselves unworthy of everlasting life, lo, we turn to the Gentiles.

ACTS 18:6—And when they opposed themselves, and blasphemed, he shook his raiment, and said unto them, Your blood be upon your own heads; I am clean: from henceforth I will go unto the Gentiles

ACTS 28:24-29—(24) And some believed the things, which were spoken, and some believed not. (25) And when they agreed not among themselves, they departed, after that Paul had spoken one word, Well spake the Holy Ghost by Esaias the prophet unto our fathers, (26) Saying, Go unto this people, and say, Hearing ye shall hear, and shall not understand; and seeing ye shall see, and not perceive: (27) For the heart of this people is waxed gross, and their ears are dull of hearing, and their eyes have they closed; lest they should see with their eyes, and hear with their ears, and understand with their heart, and should be converted, and I should heal them. (28) Be it known therefore unto you, that the salvation of God is sent unto the Gentiles, and that they will hear it. (29) And when he had said these words, the Jews departed, and had great reasoning among themselves.

ROMANS 11:15 [b]
For if the casting away of them be the <u>reconciling</u> of the world, what shall the receiving of them be, but life from the dead?

Reconcile: (1) To reestablish a relationship between opposing parties. (2) To reestablish a marital relationship.

Contextually, the word 'reconcile' here, implies a *prior* relationship, a prior covenant *(Deuteronomy 7:7-8; 32:8-9; 2 Samuel 7:23-24; Isaiah 49:13-16; Malachi 1:2)* a relationship that was severed; *(Isaiah 50:1, Hosea 1:9, 4:6)* hence the need for reconciliation. *(2 Chronicles 6:38-39; Hosea 1:10; Malachi 3:7; Matthew 10:6)*

The central relationship in the bible is TMH's covenant relationship with His people. More specifically, a covenant relationship that ended when Israel, TMH's wife, cheated on Him. *(Jeremiah 3:1-14; 5:7; Ezekiel 16:30-33)*

Per the law, a sacrifice was always needed for reconciliation. In the past, the blood of bulls sufficed, however TMH, by sending His son as the ultimate sacrifice, did away with the law of sacrifice with <u>one</u> ultimate sacrifice. Therefore, animal sacrifices were no longer necessary.

2 CHRONICLES 29:23-24—(23) And they brought forth the he goats for the sin offering before the king and the congregation; and they laid their hands upon them: (24) And the priests killed them, and they made reconciliation with their blood upon the altar, to make an atonement for all Israel: for the king commanded [that] the burnt offering and the sin offering should be made for all Israel.

ROMANS 5:10—For if, when we were enemies, we were reconciled to God by the death of his Son, much more, being reconciled, we shall be saved by his life.

TMH's chosen people needed reconciliation with the God they forsook. This is why the bible is chock-full of prophecies foretelling Israel's redemption. *(Psalms 14:7, 25:22, 130:8; Ezekiel 36:24-27; Jeremiah 30:17-24; Matthew 1:21)*

After Rome destroyed Jerusalem, killing and scattering TMH's people, Roman Catholicism (and later Protestantism) created their own doctrines, hid/burned books, and mistranslated the scriptures. So there has *never* been any **covenant relationship** between the heathen world and TMH. They profane His commandments, *(Psalms 50:16-21)* created a false messiah (John 5:43, 2 Corinthians 11:4), enslaved, *(Psalms 83; Lamentations 4:22; Joel 3:6; Deuteronomy 28:68)* and abused TMH's people, *(Ezekiel 25:12; Micah 2:2)* as well as deceived the entire world *(Jeremiah 16:19; 1 Maccabees 3:46-51; 2 Thessalonians 2:11).*

ROMANS 11:15 [c]
For if the casting away of them be the reconciling of the world, *[Kosmos (κόσμος)]* what shall the receiving of them be, but life from the dead?

1 John 2:15 tells us love not the world or the things of the world, and in *John 17:8-20* Messiah says He's not praying for the world. *John 3:16* tells us God so loved the world that He gave His only begotten son. And *Matthew 1:21, 15:24;* and *Luke 1:76-77* tell us Messiah died for the sins of Israel. So which is it? Does TMH love the world or not? If not, why is He trying to reconcile it?

First, we need to recognize there are many definitions of the word 'world,' even in the Greek. World can mean (1) the earth, (2) a timeframe, (3) the entire inhabited earth, or (4) a structured society/organization.

"Gē" (γῆ)—soil, earth, land, inhabitants of a region or country. *(Matthew 2:20-21; Mark 9:20; Luke 5:24; John 12:32; Hebrews 11:9; Rev 13:3, 8)*

"Aiōna" (αἰῶνα)—measure of time, age, cycle, or timeframe *(Matthew 13:40; Luke 1:33; 20:34; Acts 15:18, Ephesians 1:21; 2 Timothy 4:10; Hebrews 1:2)*

"Oikoumenēs" (οἰκουμένης)—the inhabited world *(Matthew 24:14; Luke 21:26; Acts 11:28; Hebrews 2:5; Revelation 3:10; 12:9, 16:14)*

"Kosmos" (κόσμος)—systematic universe, decoration, structured world, group, society or organization *(John 1:10, 29, 3:16, 17:9, 14;* **Romans 11:15**; *James 3:6; 1 John 2:15, 4:5)*

The *"reconciling of the world"* in Romans 11:15 applies to the world of Israel. We can be sure of this because:

a) Paul (and John in *John 3:16*) could have used *"Oikoumenēs"* (the inhabited world), but they both chose "Kosmou" (structured world or organization). In this case, the implied meaning here is reconciliation of a specific audience.
b) Israel is called a 'world without end.' *(Isaiah 45:17)*
c) Messiah said in *John 18:20*: *"I spake openly to the world; I ever taught in the synagogue, and in the temple, whither the Jews always resort; and in secret have I said nothing."* He was not talking about the whole world. He outlined exactly the world He was referring to—the world that had temples and synagogues, and wherever else the Jews "resorted." **That would be ISRAEL.** Incidentally, the Greek word used there for 'world' is also *kosmō (κόσμῳ)*.

d) The context of this chapter, the entirety of Paul's epistle *(See commentary on Romans 1:7 pgs. 85-89)*, and the bible as a whole, is the reconciliation of Israel to her God.

e) There is no teaching of TMH reconciling Himself to the non-Israelite world in scripture. It's always been about Israel. This is not to say that non-Israelites aren't welcome to worship TMH and cleave to Israel as Rahab and other strangers have, for which some escaped wrath. *(Joshua 6:25, Leviticus 19:34)* That's a totally different topic. Here, we're speaking about *reconciliation* of TMH and His chosen people, which is the central theme of the bible.

However, while *Romans 11:15* pertains to the world of Israel, *reconciliation* does *not* include all of Israel:

JOHN 17:9—I pray not for the world *(kosmou)*, but for them which thou hast given me; for they are thine.

Many are called within Israel, but few are chosen *(Matthew 22:14)* since not all Israel is Israel. *(Romans 9:6)*

ROMANS 11:15 [d]
For if the casting away of them be the reconciling of the world, what shall <u>the receiving of them be, but life from the dead</u>?

The 'them' in this verse are the same 'them' Paul has been speaking about in the previous verses: the blind leadership and followers of the Circumcision. All outside of Messiah are considered dead.

EPHESIANS 2:1-5—(1) And you hath he quickened, who were dead in trespasses and sins; (2) Wherein in time past ye walked according to the course of this world, according to the prince of the power of the air, the spirit that now worketh in the children of disobedience (3) Among whom also we all had our conversation in times past in the lusts of our flesh, fulfilling the desires of the flesh and of the mind; and were by nature the children of wrath, even as others. (4) But God, who is rich in mercy, for his great love wherewith he loved us, (5) Even when we were dead in sins, hath quickened us together with Christ, (by grace ye are saved).

LUKE 15:29-32—(29) And he answering said to his father, Lo, these many years do I serve thee, neither transgressed I at any time thy commandment: and yet thou never gavest me a kid, that I might make merry with my friends: (30) But as soon as this thy son was come, which hath devoured thy living with harlots, thou hast killed for him the fatted calf. (31) And he said unto him, Son, thou art ever with me, and all that I have is thine. (32) It was meet that we should make merry, and be glad: for this thy brother was dead, and is alive again; and was lost, and is found.

COLOSSIANS 2:13—And you, being dead in your sins and the uncircumcision of your flesh, hath he quickened together with him, having forgiven you all trespasses.

EZEKIEL 37:1, 10-13—(1) The hand of the LORD was upon me, and carried me out in the spirit of the LORD, and set me down in the midst of the valley which was full of bones...(10) So I prophesied as he commanded me, and the breath came into them, and they lived, and stood up upon their feet, an exceeding great army. (11) Then he said unto me, Son of man, these bones are the whole house of Israel: behold, they say, Our bones are dried, and our hope is lost: we are cut off for our parts. (12) Therefore prophesy and say unto them, Thus saith the Lord GOD; Behold, O my people, I will open your graves, and cause you to come up out of your graves, and bring you into the land of Israel. (13) And ye shall know that I am the LORD, when I have opened your graves, O my people, and brought you up out of your graves...

ISAIAH 26:16-19—(16) LORD, in trouble have they visited thee, they poured out a prayer when thy chastening was upon them. (17) Like as a woman with child, that draweth near the time of her delivery, is in pain, and crieth out in her pangs; so have we been in thy sight, O LORD. (18) We have been with child, we have been in pain, we have as it were brought forth wind; we have not wrought any deliverance in the earth; neither have the inhabitants of the world fallen. (19) Thy dead men shall live, together with my dead body shall they arise. Awake and sing, ye that dwell in dust: for thy dew is as the dew of herbs, and the earth shall cast out the dead.

REVELATION 11:10-11—(10) And they that dwell upon the earth shall rejoice over them, and make merry, and shall send gifts one to another; because these two prophets tormented them that dwelt on the earth. (11) And after three days and an half the Spirit of life from God entered into them, and they stood upon their feet; and great fear fell upon them which saw them.

PROVERBS 21:16—The man that wandereth out of the way of understanding shall remain in the congregation of the dead.

(John 5:25-30)

ROMANS 11:16
For if the firstfruit be holy, the lump is also holy: and if the root be holy, so are the branches.

First Fruit

1 CORINTHIANS 15:20-23—(20) But now is Christ risen from the dead, and become the firstfruits of them that slept. (21) For since by man came death, by man came also the resurrection of the dead. (22) For as in Adam all die, even so in Christ shall all be made alive. (23) But every man in his own order: Christ the firstfruits; afterward they that are Christ's at his coming.

JAMES 1:18—Of his own will begat he us with the word of truth, that we should be a kind of firstfruits of his creatures.

(Jeremiah 2:3)

Lump

1 CORINTHIANS 5:7—Purge out therefore the old leaven, that ye may be a new lump, as ye are unleavened. For even Christ our Passover is sacrificed for us

Root

ROMANS 15:12—And again, Esaias saith, There shall be a root of Jesse, and he that shall rise to reign over the Gentiles; in him shall the Gentiles trust.

REVELATION 5:5—And one of the elders saith unto me, Weep not: behold, the Lion of the tribe of Judah, the Root of David, hath prevailed to open the book, and to loose the seven seals thereof.

REVELATION 22:16—I Jesus have sent mine angel to testify unto you these things in the churches. I am the root and the offspring of David, and the bright and morning star.

Branches

JOHN 15:5—I am the vine, ye are the branches: He that abideth in me, and I in him, the same bringeth forth much fruit: for without me ye can do nothing.

(Leviticus 23:10; Numbers 15:19-20)

ROMANS 11:17 [a]
And if some of the branches be broken off, and thou, being a wild olive tree, wert graffed in among them, and with them partakest of the root and fatness of the olive tree

The children of Israel make up the tree, and Messiah is the root. Elsewhere in scripture, Israel is also likened to olive plants, trees, figs, and grapes.

JEREMIAH 24:3-7—(3) Then said the LORD unto me, What seest thou, Jeremiah? And I said, Figs; the good figs, very good; and the evil, very evil, that cannot be eaten, they are so evil. (4) Again the word of the LORD came unto me, saying, (5) Thus saith the LORD, the God of Israel; Like these good figs, so will I acknowledge them that are carried away captive of Judah, whom I have sent out of this place into the land of the Chaldeans for their good. (6) 'For I will set mine eyes upon them for good, and I will bring them again to this land: and I will build them, and not pull them down; and I will plant them, and not pluck them up. (7) 'And I will give them an heart to know me, that I am the LORD: and they shall be my people, and I will be their God: for they shall return unto me with their whole heart.'

PSALMS 128:3—Thy wife shall be as a fruitful vine by the sides of thine house: thy children like olive plants round about thy table.

HOSEA 9:10—I found Israel like grapes in the wilderness; I saw your fathers as the firstfruits on the fig tree in its first season. But they went to Baal Peor, and separated themselves to that shame; they became an abomination like the thing they loved.

HOSEA 14:1-8—(1) O Israel, return unto the LORD thy God; for thou hast fallen by thine iniquity. (2) Take with you words, and turn to the LORD: say unto him, Take away all iniquity, and receive us graciously: so will we render the calves of our lips. (3) Asshur shall not save us; we will not ride upon horses: neither will we say any more to the work of our hands, Ye are our gods: for in thee the fatherless findeth mercy. (4) I will heal their backsliding, I will love them freely: for mine anger is turned away from him. (5) I will be as the dew unto Israel: he shall grow as the lily, and cast forth his roots as Lebanon. (6) His branches shall spread, and his beauty shall be as the olive tree, and his smell as Lebanon. (7) They that dwell under his shadow shall return; they shall revive as the corn, and grow as the vine: the scent thereof shall be as the wine of Lebanon. (8) Ephraim shall say, What have I to do any more with idols? I have heard him, and observed him: I am like a green fir tree. From me is thy fruit found.

SONG OF SOLOMON 2:13—The fig tree putteth forth her green figs, and the vines with the tender grape give a good smell. Arise, my love, my fair one, and come away.

MATTHEW 24:32-33—(32) Now learn a parable of the fig tree; When his branch is yet tender, and putteth forth leaves, ye know that summer is nigh: (33) So likewise ye, when ye shall see all these things, know that it is near, even at the doors.

LUKE 21:29-31—(29) And he spake to them a parable; Behold the fig tree, and all the trees; (30) When they now shoot forth, ye see and know of your own selves that summer is now nigh at hand. (31) So likewise ye, when ye see these things come to pass, know ye that the kingdom of God is nigh at hand.

JOHN 15:5—I am the vine, ye are the branches: He that abideth in me, and I in him, the same bringeth forth much fruit: for without me ye can do nothing.

(Jeremiah 24:3)

ROMANS 11:17 [b]
And if <u>some of the branches be broken off</u>, and thou, being a wild olive tree, wert graffed in among them, and with them partakest of the root and fatness of the olive tree

The children of Israel make up the tree to which the <u>broken branches</u> belong:

JEREMIAH 11:16-17—(16) The LORD called thy name, a green olive tree, fair, and of goodly fruit: with the noise of a great tumult he hath kindled fire upon it, <u>and the branches of it are broken</u>. (17) For the LORD of hosts, that planted thee, hath pronounced evil against thee, for the evil of the house of Israel and of the house of Judah, which they have done against themselves to provoke me to anger in offering incense unto Baal.

JOHN 15:2-6—(2) <u>Every branch in me that beareth not fruit he taketh away</u>: and every branch that beareth fruit, he purgeth it, that it may bring forth more fruit. (3) Now ye are clean through the word, which I have spoken unto you. (4) Abide in me, and I in you. As the branch cannot bear fruit of itself, except it abide in the vine; no more can ye, except ye abide in me. (5) I am the vine, ye are the branches: He that abideth in me, and I in him, the same bringeth forth much fruit: for without me ye can do nothing. (6) If a man abide not in me, he is cast forth as a branch, and is withered; and men gather them, and cast them into the fire, and they are burned.

WISDOM OF SOLOMON 4:4-5—(4) For though they flourish in branches for a time; yet standing not last, they shall be shaken with the wind, and through the force of winds they shall be rooted out. (5) The imperfect branches shall be broken off, their fruit unprofitable, not ripe to eat, yea, meet for nothing.

JEREMIAH 24:8-10—(8) And as the evil figs, which cannot be eaten, they are so evil; surely thus saith the LORD, So will I give Zedekiah the king of Judah, and his princes, and the residue of Jerusalem, that remain in this land, and them that dwell in the land of Egypt: (9) And I will deliver them to be removed into all the kingdoms of the earth for their hurt, to be a reproach and a proverb, a taunt and a curse, in all places whither I shall drive them. (10) And I will send the sword, the famine, and the pestilence, among them, till they be consumed from off the land that I gave unto them and to their fathers.

MATTHEW 3:10—And now also the axe is laid unto the root of the trees: therefore every tree, which bringeth not forth good fruit, is hewn down, and cast into the fire.

MATTHEW 7:9—Every tree that bringeth not forth good fruit is hewn down, and cast into the fire.

MATTHEW 21:19—And when he saw a fig tree in the way, he came to it, and found nothing thereon, but leaves only, and said unto it, Let no fruit grow on thee henceforward for ever. And presently the fig tree withered away.

MARK 11:11-14—(13) And seeing a fig tree afar off having leaves, he came, if haply he might find any thing thereon: and when he came to it, he found nothing but leaves; for the time of figs was not yet. (14) And Jesus answered and said unto it, No man eat fruit of thee hereafter forever. And his disciples heard it.

MATTHEW 25:26-30—(26) His lord answered and said unto him, Thou wicked and slothful servant, thou knewest that I reap where I sowed not, and gather where I have not strawed: (27) Thou oughtest therefore to have put my money to the exchangers, and then at my coming I should have received mine own with usury. (28) Take therefore the talent from him, and give it unto him which hath ten talents. (29) For unto every one that hath shall be given, and he shall have abundance: but from him that hath not shall be taken away even that which he hath. (30) And cast ye the unprofitable servant into outer darkness: there shall be weeping and gnashing of teeth.

ROMANS 11:17 [c]
And if some of the branches be broken off, and thou, being a <u>wild olive tree</u>, wert graffed in among them, and with them partakest of the root and fatness of the olive tree

Here Paul is speaking to Gentile Israelites who he likened to a wild olive tree. They, who were once a good tree with good fruit, became wild because of idolatry and wickedness.

ISAIAH 5:1-7—(1) Now will I sing to my well-beloved a song of my beloved touching his vineyard. My well-beloved hath a vineyard in a very fruitful hill: (2) And he fenced it, and gathered out the stones thereof, and planted it with the choicest vine, and built a tower in the midst of it, and also made a winepress therein: and he looked that it should bring forth grapes, and it brought forth wild grapes. (3) And now, O inhabitants of Jerusalem, and men of Judah, judge, I pray you, betwixt me and my vineyard. (4) What could have been done more to my vineyard, that I have not done in it? Wherefore, when I looked that it should bring forth grapes, brought it forth wild grapes? (5) And now go to; I will tell you what I will do to my vineyard: I will take away the hedge thereof, and it shall be eaten up; and break down the wall thereof, and it shall be trodden down: (6) And I will lay it waste: it shall not be pruned, nor digged; but there shall come up briers and thorns: I will also command the clouds that they rain no rain upon it. (7) For the vineyard of the LORD of hosts is the house of Israel, and the men of Judah his pleasant plant: and he looked for judgment, but behold oppression; for righteousness, but behold a cry.

JEREMIAH 11:16-17—(16) The LORD called thy name, A green olive tree, fair, and of goodly fruit: with the noise of a great tumult he hath kindled fire upon it, and the branches of it are broken. (17) For the LORD of hosts, that planted thee, hath pronounced evil against thee, for the evil of the house of Israel and of the house of Judah, which they have done against themselves to provoke me to anger in offering incense unto Baal.

ZECHARIAH 4:2-14—(2) And said unto me, What seest thou? And I said, I have looked, and behold a candlestick all [of] gold, with a bowl upon the top of it, and his seven lamps thereon, and seven pipes to the seven lamps, which [are] upon the top thereof: (3) And two olive trees by it, one upon the right [side] of the bowl, and the other upon the left [side] thereof. (4) So I answered and spake to the angel that talked with me, saying, What [are] these, my lord? (5) Then the angel that talked with me answered and said unto me, Knowest thou not what these be? And I said, No, my lord. (6) Then he answered and spake unto me, saying, This is the word of the LORD unto Zerubbabel, saying, Not by might, nor by power, but by my spirit, saith the LORD of hosts. (7) Who art thou, O great mountain? before Zerubbabel [thou shalt become] a plain: and he shall bring forth the headstone [thereof with] shoutings, [crying], Grace, grace unto it. (8) Moreover the word of the LORD came unto me, saying, (9) The hands of Zerubbabel have laid the foundation of this house; his hands shall also finish it; and thou shalt know that the LORD of hosts hath sent me unto you. (10) For who hath despised the day of small things? For they shall rejoice, and shall see the plummet in the hand of Zerubbabel with those seven; they [are] the eyes of the LORD, which run to and fro through the whole earth. (11) Then answered I, and said unto him, What are these two olive trees upon the right [side] of the candlestick and upon the left side thereof? (12) And I answered again, and said unto him, What be these two olive branches which through the two golden pipes empty the golden oil out of themselves? (13) And he answered me and said, Knowest thou not what these be? And I said, No, my lord. (14) Then said he, These are the two anointed ones, that stand by the Lord of the whole earth.

(Deuteronomy 22:9, Hosea 14:1-8)

ROMANS 11:17 [d]
And if some of the branches be broken off, <u>and thou</u>, being a wild olive tree, <u>wert graffed in among them</u>, and with them partakest of the root and fatness of the olive tree

This grafting in or rejoining of the two houses of Israel was first prophesied in Ezekiel and elsewhere.

EZEKIEL 37:15-22—(15) The word of the LORD came again unto me, saying, (16) Moreover, thou son of man, take thee one stick, and write upon it, For Judah, and for the children of Israel his companions: then take another stick, and write upon it, For Joseph, the stick of Ephraim, and for all the house of Israel his companions: (17) And join them one to another into one stick; and they shall become one in thine hand. (18) And when the children of thy people shall speak unto thee, saying, Wilt thou not shew us what thou meanest by these? (19) Say unto them, Thus saith the Lord GOD; Behold, I will take the stick of Joseph, which is in the hand of Ephraim, and the tribes of Israel his fellows, and will put them with him, even with the stick of Judah, and make them one stick, and they shall be one in mine hand. (20) And the sticks whereon thou writest shall be in thine hand before their eyes. (21) And say unto them, Thus saith the Lord GOD; Behold, I will take the children of Israel from among the heathen, whither they be gone, and will gather them on every side, and bring them into their own land: (22) And I will make them one nation in the land upon the mountains of Israel; and one king shall be king to them all: and they shall be no more two nations, neither shall they be divided into two kingdoms any more at all.

HOSEA 1:11—Then shall the children of Judah and the children of Israel be gathered together, and appoint themselves one head, and they shall come up out of the land: for great shall be the day of Jezreel.

JEREMIAH 50:4—In those days, and in that time, saith the LORD, the children of Israel shall come, they and the children of Judah together, going and weeping: they shall go, and seek the LORD their God.

JOHN 10:16—And other sheep I have, which are not of this fold: them also I must bring, and they shall hear my voice; and there shall be one fold, and one shepherd.

ROMANS 11:17 [e]
And if some of the branches be broken off, and thou, being a wild olive tree, wert graffed in among them, and with them partakest of <u>the root and fatness of the olive tree</u>

Messiah is the root that nourishes the whole tree.

ISAIAH 53:2—For he shall grow up before him as a tender plant, and as a root out of a dry ground: he hath no form nor comeliness; and when we shall see him, there is no beauty that we should desire him.

ROMANS 15:12—And again, Esaias saith, There shall be a root of Jesse, and he that shall rise to reign over the Gentiles; in him shall the Gentiles trust.

REVELATION 22:16—I Jesus have sent mine angel to testify unto you these things in the churches. I am the root and the offspring of David, and the bright and morning star.

JOHN 15:1-6—(1) I am the true vine, and my Father is the husbandman. (2) Every branch in me that beareth not fruit he taketh away: and every branch that beareth fruit, he purgeth it, that it may bring forth more fruit. (3) Now ye are clean through the word, which I have spoken unto you. (4) Abide in me, and I in you. As the branch cannot bear fruit of itself, except it abide in the vine; no more can ye, except ye abide in me. (5) I am the vine, ye are the branches: He that abideth in me, and I in him, the same bringeth forth much fruit: for without me ye can do nothing. (6) If a man abide not in me, he is cast forth as a branch, and is withered; and men gather them, and cast them into the fire, and they are burned.

REVELATION 5:5—And one of the elders saith unto me, Weep not: behold, the Lion of the tribe of Judah, the Root of David, hath prevailed to open the book, and to loose the seven seals thereof.

ROMANS 11:18
Boast not against the branches. But if thou boast, thou bearest not the root, but the root thee.

JOHN 15:5—I am the vine, you are the branches. He who abides in Me, and I in him, bears much fruit; for without Me you can do nothing.

1 CORINTHIANS 10:12—Wherefore let him that thinketh he standeth take heed lest he fall.

PHILIPPIANS 2:12-13—(12) Wherefore, my beloved, as ye have always obeyed, not as in my presence only, but now much more in my absence, work out your own salvation with fear and trembling (13) for it is God which worketh in you both to will and to do of his good pleasure.

(Proverbs 16:18, 18:12)

ROMANS 11:19-21
(19) Thou wilt say then, The branches were broken off, that I might be graffed in. (20) Well; because of unbelief they were broken off, and thou standest by faith. Be not high-minded, but fear: (21) For if God spared not the natural branches, take heed lest he also spare not thee.

Paul warns Gentile Israelites not to get high-minded since they were once in full rebellion, living wickedly and worshipping idols. So if TMH didn't spare the spiritually blind leaders of the Circumcision within Judah who remained with Him for hundreds of years, why would He spare puffed up Israelite Gentiles who've been living like heathens for just as long?

1 CORINTHIANS 10:12—Wherefore let him that thinketh he standeth take heed lest he fall.

LUKE 8:18—Take heed therefore how ye hear: for whosoever hath, to him shall be given; and whosoever hath not, from him shall be taken even that which he seemeth to have.

2 PETER 3:17—Ye therefore, beloved, seeing ye know these things before, beware lest ye also, being led away with the error of the wicked, fall from your own steadfastness.

ISAIAH 5:1-13—(1) Now will I sing to my well-beloved a song of my beloved touching his vineyard. My well-beloved hath a vineyard in a very fruitful hill: (2) And he fenced it, and gathered out the stones thereof, and planted it with the choicest vine, and built a tower in the midst of it, and also made a winepress therein: and he looked that it should bring forth grapes, and it brought forth wild grapes. (3) And now, O inhabitants of Jerusalem, and men of Judah, judge, I pray you, betwixt me and my vineyard. (4) What could have been done more to my vineyard, that I have not done in it? Wherefore, when I looked that it should bring forth grapes, brought it forth wild grapes? (5) And now go to; I will tell you what I will do to my vineyard: I will take away the hedge thereof, and it shall be eaten up; and break down the wall thereof, and it shall be trodden down: (6) And I will lay it waste: it shall not be pruned, nor digged; but there shall come up briers and thorns: I will also command the clouds that they rain no rain upon it. (7) For the vineyard of the LORD of hosts is the house of Israel, and the men of Judah his pleasant plant: and he looked for judgment, but behold oppression; for righteousness, but behold a cry. (8) Woe unto them that join house to house, [that] lay field to field, till [there be] no place, that they may be placed alone in the midst of the earth! (9) In mine ears said the LORD of hosts, of a truth many houses shall be desolate, even great and fair, without inhabitant. (10) Yea, ten acres of vineyard shall yield one bath, and the seed of an homer shall yield an ephah. (11) Woe unto them that rise up early in the morning, that they may follow strong drink; that continue until night, till wine inflame them! (12) And the harp, and the viol, the tabret, and pipe, and wine, are in their feasts: but they regard not the work of the LORD, neither consider the operation of his hands. (13) Therefore my people are gone into captivity, because [they have] no knowledge: and their honorable men are famished, and their multitude dried up with thirst.

JEREMIAH 11:15-17—(15) What hath my beloved to do in mine house, seeing she hath wrought lewdness with many, and the holy flesh is passed from thee? When thou doest evil, then thou rejoicest. (16) The LORD called thy name, A green olive tree, fair, and of goodly fruit: with the noise of a great tumult he hath kindled fire upon it, and the branches of it are broken. (17) For the LORD of hosts, that planted thee, hath pronounced evil against thee, for the evil of the house of Israel and of the house of Judah, which they have done against themselves to provoke me to anger in offering incense unto Baal.

MARK 16:16—He that believeth and is baptized shall be saved; but he that believeth not shall be damned.

JOHN 3:18—He that believeth on him is not condemned: but he that believeth not is condemned already, because he hath not believed in the name of the only begotten Son of God.

JOHN 3:36—He that believeth on the Son hath everlasting life: and he that believeth not the Son shall not see life; but the wrath of God abideth on him.

HEBREWS 3:19—So we see that they could not enter in because of unbelief.

ROMANS 11:22
Behold therefore the goodness and severity of God: on them which fell, severity; but toward thee, goodness, if thou continue in his goodness: otherwise thou also shalt be cut off.

JOHN 15:2—Every branch in me that beareth not fruit he taketh away: and every branch that beareth fruit, he purgeth it, that it may bring forth more fruit.

1 CORINTHIANS 15:2—By which also ye are saved, if ye keep in memory what I preached unto you, unless ye have believed in vain.

MATTHEW 10:22—And ye shall be hated of all men for my name's sake: but he that endureth to the end shall be saved.

PROVERBS 2:21-22—(21) For the upright shall dwell in the land, and the perfect shall remain in it. (22) But the wicked shall be cut off from the earth, and the transgressors shall be rooted out of it.

ROMANS 11:23
And they also, if they abide not still in unbelief, shall be graffed in: for God is able to graft them in again.

The "they" here are the unbelieving within the House of Judah/Southern Kingdom (and the remnant of Northerners who remained with Judah). This contrasts with *Romans 11:22*, which concerns Greek Israelites and Israelite Gentiles who TMH sent Paul to.

ISAIAH 55:7—Let the wicked forsake his way, and the unrighteous man his thoughts: and let him return unto the LORD, and he will have mercy upon him; and to our God, for he will abundantly pardon.

LUKE 15:8-10—(8) Either what woman having ten pieces of silver, if she lose one piece, doth not light a candle, and sweep the house, and seek diligently till she find it? (9) And when she hath found it, she calleth her friends and her neighbors together, saying, Rejoice with me; for I have found the piece, which I had lost. (10) Likewise, I say unto you, there is joy in the presence of the angels of God over one sinner that repenteth.

LUKE 15:32—It was meet that we should make merry, and be glad: for this thy brother was dead, and is alive again; and was lost, and is found.

2 PETER 3:9—The Lord is not slack concerning his promise, as some men count slackness; but is longsuffering to us-ward, not willing that any should perish, but that all should come to repentance

ROMANS 11:24
For if thou wert cut out of the olive tree, which is wild by nature, and wert graffed contrary to nature into a good olive tree: how much more shall these, which be the natural branches, be graffed into their own olive tree?

JEREMIAH 2:21—Yet I had planted thee a noble vine, wholly a right seed: how then art thou turned into the degenerate plant of a strange vine unto me?

JEREMIAH 11:15-17—(15) What hath my beloved to do in mine house, seeing she hath wrought lewdness with many, and the holy flesh is passed from thee? when thou doest evil, then thou rejoicest. (16) The LORD called thy name, A green olive tree, fair, and of goodly fruit: with the noise of a great tumult he hath kindled fire upon it, and the branches of it are broken. (17) For the LORD of hosts, that planted thee, hath pronounced evil against thee, for the evil of the house of Israel and of the house of Judah, which they have done against themselves to provoke me to anger in offering incense unto Baal.

ISAIAH 5:3-7—(3) And now, O inhabitants of Jerusalem, and men of Judah, judge, I pray you, betwixt me and my vineyard. (4) What could have been done more to my vineyard, that I have not done in it? Wherefore, when I looked that it should bring forth grapes, brought it forth wild grapes? (5) And now go to; I will tell you what I will do to my vineyard: I will take away the hedge thereof, and it shall be eaten up; and break down the wall thereof, and it shall be trodden down: (6) And I will lay it waste: it shall not be pruned, nor digged; but there shall come up briers and thorns: I will also command the clouds that they rain no rain upon it. (7) For the vineyard of the LORD of hosts is the house of Israel, and the men of Judah his pleasant plant: and he looked for judgment, but behold oppression; for righteousness, but behold a cry.

ROMANS 11:25 [a]

For I would not, brethren, that ye should be ignorant of this mystery, <u>lest ye should be wise in your own conceits</u>; that blindness in part is happened to Israel, until the fullness of the Gentiles be come in.

PROVERBS 3:7—Be not wise in thine own eyes: fear the LORD, and depart from evil.

ISAIAH 5:21—Woe unto them that are wise in their own eyes, and prudent in their own sight!

ROMANS 12:16—Be of the same mind one toward another. Mind not high things, but condescend to men of low estate. Be not wise in your own conceits.

ROMANS 11:25 [b]

For I would not, brethren, that ye should be ignorant of this mystery, lest ye should be wise in your own conceits; <u>that blindness in part is happened to Israel</u>, until the fullness of the Gentiles be come in.

QUESTION: Was all Israel blinded?

ANSWER: No. *See John 3:1-2, 7:31, 50-53, 8:28-30, 10:40-42, 11:45-48; 12:42, 19:38-39; Acts 9:40-42; Matthew 21:43-46, 57-60; Mark 14:1-2, 15:43.*

QUESTION: Who in Israel did TMH blind?

ANSWER: The leadership within the Circumcision of the House of Judah and their followers. *(Mark 8:27:31, Luke 9:18:22, John 12:37-43; Romans 11:7-12)* **They fell because they rejected the Messiah.**

2 CORINTHIANS 3:14—But their minds were blinded: for until this day remaineth the same veil untaken away in the reading of the old testament; which veil is done away in Christ.

ISAIAH 29:9-10—(9) Stay yourselves, and wonder; cry ye out, and cry: they are drunken, but not with wine; they stagger, but not with strong drink. (10) For the LORD hath poured out upon you the spirit of deep sleep, and hath closed your eyes: the prophets and your rulers, the seers hath he covered.

ISAIAH 1:3—The ox knoweth his owner, and the ass his master's crib: but Israel doth not know, my people doth not consider.

ISAIAH 5:13—Therefore my people are gone into captivity, because they have no knowledge: and their honorable men are famished, and their multitude dried up with thirst.

JEREMIAH 2:32—Can a maid forget her ornaments, or a bride her attire? yet my people have forgotten me days without number.

JEREMIAH 13:25—This is thy lot, the portion of thy measures from me, saith the LORD; because thou hast forgotten me, and trusted in falsehood.

JEREMIAH 50:6—My people hath been lost sheep: their shepherds have caused them to go astray, they have turned them away on the mountains: they have gone from mountain to hill, they have forgotten their resting place.

LAMENTATIONS 2:6—And he hath violently taken away his tabernacle, as if it were of a garden: he hath destroyed his places of the assembly: the LORD hath caused the solemn feasts and sabbaths to be forgotten in Zion, and hath despised in the indignation of his anger the king and the priest.

DANIEL 9:7-8—(7) O Lord, righteousness belongeth unto thee, but unto us confusion of faces, as at this day; to the men of Judah, and to the inhabitants of Jerusalem, and unto all Israel, that are near, and that are far off, through all the countries whither thou hast driven them, because of their trespass that they have trespassed against thee. (8) O Lord, to us [belongeth] confusion of face, to our kings, to our princes, and to our fathers, because we have sinned against thee.

HOSEA 4:6—My people are destroyed for lack of knowledge: because thou hast rejected knowledge, I will also reject thee, that thou shalt be no priest to me: seeing thou hast forgotten the law of thy God, I will also forget thy children.

BARUCH 1:15—And ye shall say, To the Lord our God belongeth righteousness, but unto us the confusion of faces, as it is come to pass this day, unto them of Judah, and to the inhabitants of Jerusalem

---

ROMANS 11:25 [c]

For I would not, brethren, that ye should be ignorant of this mystery, lest ye should be wise in your own conceits; that blindness in part is happened to Israel, until the fullness of the Gentiles [ethnōn (ἐθνῶν)] be come in.

The 'fullness of the Gentiles' (ethnōn) coming in means the complete salvation of Israelite Gentiles. In other words, the Gentiles Paul is writing to in this epistle only represent part of Israelite Gentiles, while the fullness of the Gentiles coming in, as quoted in the scripture, means the remainder of Israelite Gentiles coming into salvation. Paul is saying here that once the fullness (or totality) of Israelite Gentiles come into the fold, blindness will be lifted off Israel's unbelieving Circumcision. This is why the apostle summarizes his thought in verse 26 with: 'therefore all Israel will be saved.'

How else can we be sure these Gentiles (ethnōn) are Israelites?

1. The apostle is still addressing the same people from Chapter 1, those he referred to as:

    a. 'The called,' which only applies to Israel *(Isaiah 48:12)*
    b. 'Called to be saints,' which only applies to Israel *(Psalms 50:5, 148:14, 147:19, 149:1-5)*

2. The House of Judah only represents two tribes (and a fraction of a third). Therefore, if all Israel will be saved, what of the other tribes *(the Northern Kingdom)*? TMH said He had not cast away His people, so where is His plan for the other scattered tribes if the Gentiles here aren't Northern Kingdom Israelites since "all Israel" will be saved? This 'coming together' was prophesied in Ezekiel 37:15-22.

3. The name 'Israel' is generally used to describe the entire nation *(Joshua 24:1; Isaiah 45:17; Jeremiah 46:27)*, while the Northern Kingdom is sometimes called Ephraim *(Hosea 4:17, 14:8; Jeremiah 31:6; Zechariah 9:13)* and The House of Israel. *(2 Samuel 12:8; Jeremiah 31:31)* Contrast this with the House of Judah (Jeremiah 21:11; Hosea 5:12; Isaiah 37:31; Zechariah 8:13). So in this instance 'all Israel' being saved refers to all twelve tribes—with the Gentiles in this epistle being the scattered Northern Kingdom tribes as well as the remainder of the scattered within the House of Judah who were also living as Gentiles. The scripture quoted in Romans 11:26 *(Isaiah 59:16-21)* supports this.

Therefore, '*The Fullness Of The Gentiles*' is in fact speaking about Israelite Gentiles and prophecy bears this out.

Let's take a look at *Genesis 48:17-20* below:

GENESIS 48:17-20—(17) And when Joseph saw that his father laid his right hand upon the head of Ephraim, it displeased him: and he held up his father's hand, to remove it from **Ephraim**'s head unto Manasseh's head. (18) And Joseph said unto his father, Not so, my father: for this is the firstborn; put thy right hand upon his head. (19) And his father refused, and said, I know it, my son, I know it: he also shall become a people, and he also shall be great: but truly his younger brother shall be greater than he, **and his seed shall become a multitude of nations**. (20) And he blessed them that day, saying, In thee shall Israel bless, saying, God make thee as Ephraim and as Manasseh: and he set Ephraim before Manasseh.

"A multitude": **"mə-lō-"** (**־מְלֹא**) – root word transliteration: **"Melo,"** which means **"fullness, that which fills"**

"Of nations": "hag-gō-w-yim" (הַגּוֹיִם:) – root word transliteration: "Goy" which means a nation, gentiles, heathen, or a people.

THIS IS VERY IMPORTANT: 'Goy' is often used to describe non-Israelites, but in *Genesis 48:19* it's applied to Ephraim, meaning "nation." Also note that "Multitude" or *Melo* in the Hebrew, means '**fullness**.' **This indicates that Paul was quoting *Genesis 48:19* in Romans 11:25:**

"...*until the fullness of the Gentiles be come in.*"

For comparison's sake, let's look a few verses above *Genesis 48:19* to verse 16 where Jacob begins the blessing:

GENESIS 48:16—The Angel which redeemed me from all evil, bless the lads; and let my name be named on them, and the name of my fathers Abraham and Isaac; and let them grow **into a multitude** in the midst of the earth.

The Hebrew word for 'multitude' here in *Genesis 48:16* is not the same word translated as 'multitude' in *Genesis 48:19*. The word here in verse 16 is *"lā-rōḇ" (לָרֹב)*, which means "multitude, abundance, or greatness." This is the meaning translators sought to imply for *Genesis 48:19*. There, in verse 19 instead of translating **"mə-lō-" (־מְלֹא)** as 'fullness,' (which is what it means) they translated it as 'multitude.' So what's the big deal? By translating *Genesis 48:19* as *'multitude'* instead of *'fullness,'* you sever its connection to *Romans 11:25*. **This in turn hides the fact that the Apostle Paul was quoting Jacob's prophecy about Ephraim!**

Therefore, all ten scattered tribes under Ephraim, *(the lead tribe of the Northern Kingdom)*, who began living as Gentiles in the dispersion, represent the 'fullness of the Gentiles.' The Greek word *'fullness' in Romans 11:25 plērōmadoes (πλήρωμα)* does double-duty since it also implies Ephraim's return and restoration. Paul used the same Greek word in *Romans 11:12* regarding The House of Judah's leadership and followers.

Now if the fall of them be the riches of the world, and the diminishing of them the riches of the Gentiles; how much more their fullness?

As an aside, in many bible translations, the precept printed for *Romans 11:25's* 'fullness of the gentiles' is *Luke 21:24*:

LUKE 21:24—And they shall fall by the edge of the sword, and shall be led away captive into all nations: and Jerusalem shall be trodden down of the Gentiles, until the times of the Gentiles be fulfilled.

This is a **huge** error. *Luke 21:24* has little, if anything to do with *Romans 11:25*. As we've seen, the latter scripture deals with Israel's salvation, while *Luke 21:24*, specifically the phrase, "times of the gentiles" pertains to end-time judgment of the non-Israelite world by TMH, i.e., the end of *this* world as we know it:

EZEKIEL 30:3—For the day is near, even the day of the LORD is near, a cloudy day; it shall be the time of the heathen.

Again, the word for 'heathen' [(root word "*goy*") *gō-w-yim*, (גוֹיִם)] can be translated as a nation, gentiles, heathen, or a people. As always, context is key. Some bible translations that use 'gentile' instead of heathen in *Ezekiel 30:3* include the New King James Version, and the Jubilee Bible.

However, the International Standard Version *completely* connects *Ezekiel 30:3's* prophecy with *Luke 21:24* by rendering the end of *Ezekiel 30:3* as '*the time of the gentiles is fulfilled.*'

Therefore, the children of Israel will remain scattered, and will be held captive and oppressed until TMH's day of vengeance on the nations. But they will not be kept blind and stumbling in the dark as the *Luke 21:24* Christian misapplication implies. If anything, TMH is waking His people up now so they can escape the judgment of the nations. *(Jeremiah 51:45; Revelation 18:4)*

2 ESDRAS 4:37-42—(37) By measure hath he measured the times; and by number hath he numbered the times; and he doth not move nor stir them, until the said measure be fulfilled. (38) Then answered I and said, O Lord that bearest rule, even we all are full of impiety. (39) And for our sakes peradventure it is that the floors of the righteous are not filled, because of the sins of them that dwell upon the earth. (40) So he answered me, and said, Go thy way to a woman with child, and ask of her when she hath fulfilled her nine months, if her womb may keep the birth any longer within her. (41) Then said I, No, Lord, that can she not. And he said unto me, In the grave the chambers of souls are like the womb of a woman: (42) For like as a woman that travaileth maketh haste to escape the necessity of the travail: even so do these places haste to deliver those things that are committed unto them.

ROMANS 11:26
And so all Israel shall be saved: as it is written, There shall come out of Sion the Deliverer, and shall turn away ungodliness from Jacob:

This verse ties *Romans 11:1-25* together, letting the reader know that the subject from the beginning—the broken branches and those that were grafted in contrary to nature—refers to 'Israel.' These two groups of branches are TMH's chosen people whom He foreknew and set apart for Himself. Those whom He swore to never cast off. *(For more information on Israelite Gentiles see The People Of Romans, pg. 53 and Gentiles & Greeks, pg. 27)*

ISAIAH 59:20-21—(20) And the Redeemer shall come to Zion, and unto them that turn from transgression in Jacob, saith the LORD. (21) As for me, this is my covenant with them, saith the LORD; My spirit that is upon thee, and my words which I have put in thy mouth, shall not depart out of thy mouth, nor out of the mouth of thy seed, nor out of the mouth of thy seed's seed, saith the LORD, from henceforth and for ever.

JOEL 2:32—And it shall come to pass, that whosoever shall call on the name of the LORD shall be delivered: for in mount Zion and in Jerusalem shall be deliverance, as the LORD hath said, and in the remnant whom the LORD shall call.

OBADIAH 1:17—But upon mount Zion shall be deliverance, and there shall be holiness; and the house of Jacob shall possess their possessions

---

ROMANS 11:27
For this is my covenant unto them, when I shall take away their sins.

> **QUESTION: Who are the 'them' referenced in the above verse?**
>
> **ANSWER: Israel**
>
> **QUESTION: Who does the covenant pertain to?**
>
> **ANSWER: Israel**

MATTHEW 1:11—And she shall bring forth a son, and thou shalt call his name JESUS: for he shall save his people from their sins.

ACTS 5:29-31—(29) Then Peter and the other apostles answered and said, We ought to obey God rather than men. (30) The God of our fathers raised up Jesus, whom ye slew and hanged on a tree. (31) Him hath God exalted with his right hand to be a Prince and a Saviour, for to give repentance to Israel, and forgiveness of sins.

ROMANS 9:4-5—(4) Who are Israelites; to whom pertaineth the adoption, and the glory, and the covenants, and the giving of the law, and the service of God, and the promises; (5) Whose are the fathers, and of whom as concerning the flesh Christ came, who is over all, God blessed for ever. Amen.

HEBREWS 8:8-13—(8) For finding fault with them, he saith, Behold, the days come, saith the Lord, when I will make a new covenant with the house of Israel and with the house of Judah: (9) Not according to the covenant that I made with their fathers in the day when I took them by the hand to lead them out of the land of Egypt; because they continued not in my covenant, and I regarded them not, saith the Lord. (10) For this [is] the covenant that I will make with the house of Israel after those days, saith the Lord; I will put my laws into their mind, and write them in their hearts: and I will be to them a God, and they shall be to me a people: (11) And they shall not teach every man his neighbour, and every man his brother, saying, Know the Lord: for all shall know me, from the least to the greatest. (12) For I will be merciful to their unrighteousness, and their sins and their iniquities will I remember no more. (13) In that he saith, A new [covenant], he hath made the first old. Now that which decayeth and waxeth old is ready to vanish away.

ROMANS 11:28 [a]
As concerning the gospel, they are enemies for your sakes: but as touching the election, they are beloved for the fathers' sakes.

Within the House of Judah, many of the Circumcision leadership and their followers became enemies when they rejected the Messiah. The Gospel is the New Covenant, which TMH promised to make with the children of Israel via the Messiah's sacrifice. The Circumcision became enemies for the sake of those who believe, but TMH did not give up on them, just as He never gave up on Ephraim.

ISAIAH 53:1-6—(1) Who hath believed our report? And to whom is the arm of the LORD revealed? (2) For he shall grow up before him as a tender plant, and as a root out of a dry ground: he hath no form nor comeliness; and when we shall see him, there is no beauty that we should desire him. (3) He is despised and rejected of men; a man of sorrows, and acquainted with grief: and we hid as it were our faces from him; he was despised, and we esteemed him not. (4) Surely he hath borne our griefs, and carried our sorrows: yet we did esteem him stricken, smitten of God, and afflicted. (5) But he was wounded for our transgressions, he was bruised for our iniquities: the chastisement of our peace was upon him; and with his stripes we are healed. (6) All we like sheep have gone astray; we have turned every one to his own way; and the LORD hath laid on him the iniquity of us all.

JEREMIAH 31:31-34—(31) Behold, the days come, saith the LORD, that I will make a new covenant with the house of Israel, and with the house of Judah: (32) Not according to the covenant that I made with their fathers in the day that I took them by the hand to bring them out of the land of Egypt; which my covenant they brake, although I was an husband unto them, saith the LORD: (33) But this shall be the covenant that I will make with the house of Israel; After those days, saith the LORD, I will put my law in their inward parts, and write it in their hearts; and will be their God, and they shall be my people. (34) And they shall teach no more every man his neighbour, and every man his brother, saying, Know the LORD: for they shall all know me, from the least of them unto the greatest of them, saith the LORD: for I will forgive their iniquity, and I will remember their sin no more.

MATTHEW 1:21—And she shall bring forth a son, and thou shalt call his name JESUS: for he shall save his people from their sins.

LUKE 1:68-79—(68) Blessed be the Lord God of Israel; for he hath visited and redeemed his people, (69) And hath raised up an horn of salvation for us in the house of his servant David; (70) As he spake by the mouth of his holy prophets, which have been since the world began: (71) That we should be saved from our enemies, and from the hand of all that hate us; (72) To perform the mercy promised to our fathers, and to remember his holy covenant; (73) The oath which he sware to our father Abraham, (74) That he would grant unto us, that we being delivered out of the hand of our enemies might serve him without fear, (75) In holiness and righteousness before him, all the days of our life. (76) And thou, child, shalt be called the prophet of the Highest: for thou shalt go before the face of the Lord to prepare his ways; (77) To give knowledge of salvation unto his people by the remission of their sins, (78) Through the tender mercy of our God; whereby the dayspring from on high hath visited us, (79) To give light to them that sit in darkness and in the shadow of death, to guide our feet into the way of peace.

1 CORINTHIANS 15:3-4—(3) For I delivered unto you first of all that which I also received, how that Christ died for our sins according to the scriptures; (4) And that he was buried, and that he rose again the third day according to the scriptures

(Isaiah 61; Hebrews 9:8-12)

ROMANS 11:28 [b]
As concerning the gospel, they are enemies for your sakes: but as <u>touching the election</u>, they are beloved for the fathers' sakes.

ISAIAH 45:4—For Jacob my servant's sake, and Israel mine elect, I have even called thee by thy name: I have surnamed thee, though thou hast not known me.

ISAIAH 65:22—They shall not build, and another inhabit; they shall not plant, and another eat: for as the days of a tree are the days of my people, and mine elect shall long enjoy the work of their hands.

MATTHEW 24:22, 24, 31—(22) And except those days should be shortened, there should no flesh be saved: but for the elect's sake those days shall be shortened...(24) For there shall arise false Christs, and false prophets, and shall shew great signs and wonders; insomuch that, if it were possible, they shall deceive the very elect...(31) And he shall send his angels with a great sound of a trumpet, and they shall gather together his elect from the four winds, from one end of heaven to the other.

LUKE 18:7—And shall not God avenge his own elect, which cry day and night unto him, though he bear long with them?

WISDOM OF SOLOMON 3:9—They that put their trust in him shall understand the truth: and such as be faithful in love shall abide with him: for grace and mercy is to his saints, and he hath care for his elect.

SIRACH 46:1—Jesus the son a Nave was valiant in the wars, and was the successor of Moses in prophecies, who according to his name was made great for the saving of the elect of God, and taking vengeance of the enemies that rose up against them, that he might set Israel in their inheritance.

SIRACH 47:22—But the Lord will never leave off his mercy, neither shall any of his works perish, neither will he abolish the posterity of his elect, and the seed of him that loveth him he will not take away: wherefore he gave a remnant unto Jacob, and out of him a root unto David.

PSALMS 155:21—Deliver Israel, your elect one; and those of the house of Jacob, your chosen one.

ROMANS 11:28 [c]
As concerning the gospel, they are enemies for your sakes: but as touching the election, <u>they are beloved for the fathers' sakes.</u>

DEUTERONOMY 7:8—But because the LORD loved you, and because he would keep the oath which he had sworn unto your fathers, hath the LORD brought you out with a mighty hand, and redeemed you out of the house of bondmen, from the hand of Pharaoh king of Egypt.

DEUTERONOMY 10:15—Only the LORD had a delight in thy fathers to love them, and he chose their seed after them, even you above all people, as it is this day.

ISAIAH 41:8—But thou, Israel, art my servant, Jacob whom I have chosen, the seed of Abraham my friend.

2 ESDRAS 3:12-15—(12) And it happened, that when they that dwelt upon the earth began to multiply, and had gotten them many children, and were a great people, they began again to be more ungodly than the first. (13) Now when they lived so wickedly before thee, thou didst choose thee a man from among them, whose name was Abraham. (14) Him thou lovedst, and unto him only thou shewedst thy will: (15) And madest an everlasting covenant with him, promising him that thou wouldest never forsake his seed.

SIRACH 44:19-21—(19) Abraham was a great father of many people: in glory was there none like unto him; (20) Who kept the law of the most High, and was in covenant with him: he established the covenant in his flesh; and when he was proved, he was found faithful. (21) Therefore he assured him by an oath, that he would bless the nations in his seed, and that he would multiply him as the dust of the earth, and exalt his seed as the stars, and cause them to inherit from sea to sea, and from the river unto the utmost part of the land....

GALATIANS 3:16—Now to Abraham and his seed were the promises made. He saith not, And to seeds, as of many; but as of one, and to thy seed, which is Christ.

ROMANS 11:29
For the gifts and calling of God are without repentance.

NUMBERS 23:19—God is not a man, that he should lie; neither the son of man, that he should repent: hath he said, and shall he not do it? Or hath he spoken, and shall he not make it good.

ISAIAH 40:8—The grass withereth, the flower fadeth: but the word of our God shall stand forever.

MALACHI 3:6—For I am the LORD, I change not; therefore ye sons of Jacob are not consumed

1 CORINTHIANS 2:9—But as it is written, Eye hath not seen, nor ear heard, neither have entered into the heart of man, the things which God hath prepared for them that love him

2 TIMOTHY 2:14—If we believe not, yet he abideth faithful: he cannot deny himself.

HEBREWS 6:13-18—(13) For when God made promise to Abraham, because he could swear by no greater, he sware by himself, (14) Saying, Surely blessing I will bless thee, and multiplying I will multiply thee. (15) And so, after he had patiently endured, he obtained the promise. (16) For men verily swear by the greater: and an oath for confirmation is to them an end of all strife. (17) Wherein God, willing more abundantly to shew unto the heirs of promise the immutability of his counsel, confirmed it by an oath: (18) That by two immutable things, in which it was impossible for God to lie, we might have a strong consolation, who have fled for refuge to lay hold upon the hope set before us.

JAMES 1:17—Every good gift and every perfect gift is from above, and cometh down from the Father of lights, with whom is no variableness, neither shadow of turning.

ROMANS 11:30-31

(30) For as ye in times past have not believed God, yet have now obtained mercy through their unbelief: (31) Even so have these also now not believed, that through your mercy they also may obtain mercy.

HOSEA 6:10—I have seen an horrible thing in the house of Israel: there is the whoredom of Ephraim, Israel is defiled.

HOSEA 14:17—Ephraim is joined to idols: let him alone.

JEREMIAH 2:21—Yet I had planted thee a noble vine, wholly a right seed: how then art thou turned into the degenerate plant of a strange vine unto me?

EPHESIANS 2:2—Wherein in time past ye walked according to the course of this world, according to the prince of the power of the air, the spirit that now worketh in the children of disobedience.

1 CORINTHIANS 12:2—Ye know that ye were Gentiles, *carried away unto these dumb idols*, even as ye were led. **

Note that when Paul wrote they were 'carried away unto these dumb idols**' he was making a direct connection to what actually happened to Ephraim/The House of Israel. They were '*carried away*' into captivity to worship and defile themselves with the Assyrian's dumb idols:

2 KINGS 17:6—In the ninth year of Hoshea the king of Assyria took Samaria, **and carried Israel away** into Assyria, and placed them in Halah and in Habor by the river of Gozan, and in the cities of the Medes.

ROMANS 11:32 [a]
For God hath concluded them all in unbelief, that he might have mercy upon all.

JEREMIAH 11:10—They are turned back to the iniquities of their forefathers, which refused to hear my words; and they went after other gods to serve them: the house of Israel and the house of Judah have broken my covenant which I made with their fathers.

JEREMIAH 11:16-17—(16) The LORD called thy name, a green olive tree, fair, and of goodly fruit: with the noise of a great tumult he hath kindled fire upon it, and the branches of it are broken. (17) For the LORD of hosts, that planted thee, hath pronounced evil against thee, for the evil of the house of Israel and of the house of Judah, which they have done against themselves to provoke me to anger in offering incense unto Baal.

ROMANS 3:9—What then? Are we better than they? No, in no wise: for we have before proved both Jews and Gentiles, that they are all under sin

ROMANS 3:23—For all have sinned, and come short of the glory of God.

ECCLESIASTES 7:20—For there is not a just man upon earth, that doeth good, and sinneth not.

1 JOHN 1:8—If we say that we have no sin, we are deceiving ourselves and the truth is not in us

ROMANS 11:32 [b]
For God hath concluded them all in unbelief, that he might have mercy upon all.

HOSEA 14:4-6—(4) I will heal their backsliding, I will love them freely: for mine anger is turned away from him. (5) I will be as the dew unto Israel: he shall grow as the lily, and cast forth his roots as Lebanon. (6) His branches shall spread, and his beauty shall be as the olive tree, and his smell as Lebanon.

ROMANS 5:19—For as by one man's disobedience many were made sinners, so by the obedience of one shall many be made righteous.

GALATIANS 3:22—But the scripture hath concluded all under sin, that the promise by faith of Jesus Christ might be given to them that believe.

ROMANS 11:33
O the depth of the riches both of the wisdom and knowledge of God! How unsearchable are his judgments, and his ways past finding out!

DEUTERONOMY 29:29—The secret things belong unto the LORD our God: but those things, which are revealed, belong unto us and to our children forever, that we may do all the words of this law.

JOB 11:7—Canst thou by searching find out God? Canst thou find out the Almighty unto perfection?

PSALMS 36:6—Thy righteousness is like the great mountains; thy judgments are a great deep: O LORD, thou preservest man and beast.

ROMANS 11:34
For who hath known the mind of the Lord? Or who hath been his counselor?

JOB 15:8—Hast thou heard the secret of God? And dost thou restrain wisdom to thyself?

JOB 36:22—Behold, God exalteth by his power: who teacheth like him?

ISAIAH 40:13—Who hath directed the Spirit of the LORD, or being his counselor hath taught him?

ISAIAH 44:24-25—(24) Thus saith the LORD, thy redeemer, and he that formed thee from the womb, I am the LORD that maketh all things; that stretcheth forth the heavens alone; that spreadeth abroad the earth by myself; (25)That frustrateth the tokens of the liars, and maketh diviners mad; that turneth wise men backward, and maketh their knowledge foolish.

JEREMIAH 23:18—For who hath stood in the counsel of the LORD, and hath perceived and heard his word? Who hath marked his word, and heard it?

WISDOM OF SOLOMON 9:13—For what man is he that can know the counsel of God? Or who can think what the will of the Lord is?

ROMANS 11:35-36
(35) Or who hath first given to him, and it shall be recompensed unto him again? (36) For of him, and through him, and to him, are all things: to whom be glory for ever. Amen.

JOB 41:11—Who hath prevented me that I should repay him? Whatsoever is under the whole heaven is mine.

PSALMS 50:5-13—(5) Gather my saints together unto me; those that have made a covenant with me by sacrifice. (6) And the heavens shall declare his righteousness: for God is judge himself. Selah. (7) Hear, O my people, and I will speak; O Israel, and I will testify against thee: I am God, even thy God. (8) I will not reprove thee for thy sacrifices or thy burnt offerings, to have been continually before me. (9) I will take no bullock out of thy house, nor he goats out of thy folds. (10) For every beast of the forest is mine, and the cattle upon a thousand hills. (11) I know all the fowls of the mountains: and the wild beasts of the field are mine. (12) If I were hungry, I would not tell thee: for the world is mine, and the fullness thereof. (13) Will I eat the flesh of bulls, or drink the blood of goats?

1 CORINTHIANS 8:6—But to us there is but one God, the Father, of whom are all things, and we in him; and one Lord Jesus Christ, by whom are all things, and we by him.

COLOSSIANS 1:16—For by him were all things created, that are in heaven, and that are in earth, visible and invisible, whether they be thrones, or dominions, or principalities, or powers: all things were created by him, and for him.

HEBREWS 2:10—For it became him, for whom are all things, and by whom are all things, in bringing many sons unto glory, to make the captain of their salvation perfect through sufferings.

2 TIMOTHY 4:18—And the Lord shall deliver me from every evil work, and will preserve me unto his heavenly kingdom: to whom be glory for ever and ever. Amen.

ROMANS 12

ROMANS 12:1
I beseech you therefore, brethren, by the mercies of God, that ye present your <u>bodies a living sacrifice</u>, <u>holy</u>, acceptable unto God, which is your reasonable <u>service</u>.

DEUTERONOMY 14:2—For thou art an <u>holy people</u> unto the LORD thy God, and the LORD hath <u>chosen thee to be a peculiar people</u> unto himself, <u>above all the nations</u> that are upon the earth.

ROMANS 9:4-5—(4) Who are Israelites; to whom pertaineth the adoption, and the glory, and the covenants, and the giving of the law, and <u>the service of God</u>, and the promises; (5) Whose are the fathers, and of whom as concerning the flesh Christ came, who is over all, God blessed for ever. Amen.

ROMANS 6:12-16—(12) Let not sin therefore reign in your mortal body, that ye should obey it in the lusts thereof. (13) Neither yield ye your members as instruments of unrighteousness unto sin: but <u>yield yourselves unto God, as those that are alive from the dead, and your members as instruments of righteousness unto God. (14) For sin shall not have dominion over you: for ye are not under the law, but under grace.</u> (15) What then? Shall we sin, because we are not under the law, but under grace? God forbid. (16) Know ye not, that to whom ye yield yourselves <u>servants</u> to obey, <u>his servants</u> ye are to whom ye obey; whether of sin unto death, or of obedience unto righteousness?

1 CORINTHIANS 6:18-20—(18) Flee fornication. Every sin that a man doeth is without the body; but he that committeth fornication sinneth against his own body. (19) What? Know ye not that <u>your body is the temple of the Holy Ghost which is in you</u>, which ye have of God, and ye are not your own? (20) For ye are bought with a price: therefore <u>glorify God in your body</u>, and in your spirit, which are God's.

1 PETER 2:4-5, 9-10—(4) To whom coming, as unto a living stone, disallowed indeed of men, but <u>chosen of God</u>, and precious, (5) Ye also, as lively stones, are built up a spiritual house, <u>an holy priesthood</u>, to offer up spiritual sacrifices, acceptable to God by Jesus Christ...(9) But ye are <u>a chosen generation, a royal priesthood, an holy nation, a peculiar people</u>; that ye should shew forth the praises of him who hath called you out of darkness into his marvelous light: (10) Which in time past were not a people, but are now the people of God: which had not obtained mercy, but now have obtained mercy.

ACTS 20:28—Take heed therefore unto yourselves, and to all the flock, over the which the Holy Ghost hath made you overseers, to feed the church of God, which he hath purchased with his own blood.

ROMANS 12:2
And be not conformed to this world: but be ye transformed by the renewing of your mind, that ye may prove what is that good, and acceptable, and perfect, will of God.

EPHESIANS 4:23—And be renewed in the spirit of your mind.

EPHESIANS 5:10, 17—(10) Proving what is acceptable unto the Lord...(17) Wherefore be ye not unwise, but understanding what the will of the Lord is.

JOHN 3:3-8—(3) Jesus answered and said unto him, Verily, verily, I say unto thee, Except a man be born again, he cannot see the kingdom of God. (4) Nicodemus saith unto him, How can a man be born when he is old? can he enter the second time into his mother's womb, and be born? (5) Jesus answered, Verily, verily, I say unto thee, Except a man be born of water and of the Spirit, he cannot enter into the kingdom of God. (6) That which is born of the flesh is flesh; and that which is born of the Spirit is spirit. (7) Marvel not that I said unto thee, Ye must be born again. (8) The wind bloweth where it listeth, and thou hearest the sound thereof, but canst not tell whence it cometh, and whither it goeth: so is every one that is born of the Spirit.

1 PETER 1:22-23—(22) Seeing ye have purified your souls in obeying the truth through the Spirit unto unfeigned love of the brethren, see that ye love one another with a pure heart fervently: (23) Being born again, not of corruptible seed, but of incorruptible, by the word of God, which liveth and abideth for ever.

JOHN 17:13-19—(13) And now come I to thee; and these things I speak in the world, that they might have my joy fulfilled in themselves. (14) I have given them thy word; and the world hath hated them, because they are not of the world, even as I am not of the world. (15) I pray not that thou shouldest take them out of the world, but that thou shouldest keep them from the evil. (16) They are not of the world, even as I am not of the world. (17) Sanctify them through thy truth: thy word is truth. (18) As thou hast sent me into the world, even so have I also sent them into the world.

(19) And for their sakes I sanctify myself, that they also might be sanctified through the truth.

TITUS 3:5—Not by works of righteousness which we have done, but according to his mercy he saved us, by the washing of regeneration, and renewing of the Holy Ghost.

1 JOHN 2:15—Love not the world, neither the things that are in the world. If any man love the world, the love of the Father is not in him.

1 THESSALONIANS 4:3—For this is the will of God, even your sanctification, that ye should abstain from fornication.

1 PETER 1:14—As obedient children, not fashioning yourselves according to the former lusts in your ignorance

ROMANS 12:3
For I say, through the grace given unto me, to every man that is among you, not to think of himself more highly than he ought to think; but to think soberly, according as God hath dealt to every man the measure of faith.

EPHESIANS 4:7—But unto every one of us is given grace according to the measure of the gift of Christ.

PSALMS 138:6—Though the LORD is on high, Yet He regards the lowly; But the proud He knows from afar.

LUKE 14:7-11—(7) And he put forth a parable to those which were bidden, when he marked how they chose out the chief rooms; saying unto them, (8) When thou art bidden of any man to a wedding, sit not down in the highest room; lest a more honorable man than thou be bidden of him; (9) And he that bade thee and him come and say to thee, Give this man place; and thou begin with shame to take the lowest room. (10) But when thou art bidden, go and sit down in the lowest room; that when he that bade thee cometh, he may say unto thee, Friend, go up higher: then shalt thou have worship in the presence of them that sit at meat with thee. (11) For whosoever exalteth himself shall be abased; and he that humbleth himself shall be exalted.

1 CORINTHIANS 4:6—And these things, brethren, I have in a figure transferred to myself and to Apollos for your sakes; that ye might learn in us not to think of men above that which is written, that no one of you be puffed up for one against another.

1 CORINTHIANS 7:17-20—(17) But as God hath distributed to every man, as the Lord hath called every one, so let him walk. And so ordain I in all churches. (18) Is any man called being circumcised? Let him not become uncircumcised. Is any called in uncircumcision? Let him not be circumcised. (19) Circumcision is nothing, and uncircumcision is nothing, but the keeping of the commandments of God. (20) Let every man abide in the same calling wherein he was called.

1 CORINTHIANS 12:11—But all these worketh that one and the selfsame Spirit, dividing to every man severally as he will.

ISAIAH 57:15—For thus saith the high and lofty One that inhabiteth eternity, whose name is Holy; I dwell in the high and holy place, with him also that is of a contrite and humble spirit, to revive the spirit of the humble, and to revive the heart of the contrite ones.

ROMANS 12:4-5
(4) For as we have many members in one body, and all members have not the same office: (5) So we, being many, are one body in Christ, and every one members one of another.

1 CORINTHIANS 12:12-14—(12) For as the body is one, and hath many members, and all the members of that one body, being many, are one body: so also is Christ. (13) For by one Spirit are we all baptized into one body, whether we be Jews or Gentiles, whether we be bond or free; and have been all made to drink into one Spirit. (14) For the body is not one member, but many.

EPHESIANS 4:16—From whom the whole body fitly joined together and compacted by that which every joint supplieth, according to the effectual working in the measure of every part, maketh increase of the body unto the edifying of itself in love.

1 CORINTHIANS 10:17—For we being many are one bread, and one body: for we are all partakers of that one bread.

EPHESIANS 4:4—There is one body, and one Spirit, even as ye are called in one hope of your calling.

JOHN 17:21—That they all may be one; as thou, Father, art in me, and I in thee, that they also may be one in us: that the world may believe that thou hast sent me.

EPHESIANS 4:25—Wherefore putting away lying, speak every man truth with his neighbour: for we are members one of another.

ROMANS 12:6-8

(6) Having then gifts differing according to the grace that is given to us, whether prophecy, let us prophesy according to the proportion of faith; (7) or ministry, let us wait on our ministering: or he that teacheth, on teaching; (8) or he that exhorteth, on exhortation: he that giveth, let him do it with simplicity; he that ruleth, with diligence; he that sheweth mercy, with cheerfulness.

EPHESIANS 4:11—And he gave some, apostles; and some, prophets; and some, evangelists; and some, pastors and teachers.

ACTS 2:18—And on my servants and on my handmaidens I will pour out in those days of my Spirit; and they shall prophesy

MATTHEW 25:24-30—(24) Then he which had received the one talent came and said, Lord, I knew thee that thou art an hard man, reaping where thou hast not sown, and gathering where thou hast not strawed: (25) And I was afraid, and went and hid thy talent in the earth: lo, there thou hast that is thine. (26) His lord answered and said unto him, Thou wicked and slothful servant, thou knewest that I reap where I sowed not, and gather where I have not strawed: (27) Thou oughtest therefore to have put my money to the exchangers, and then at my coming I should have received mine own with usury. (28) Take therefore the talent from him, and give it unto him which hath ten talents. (29) For unto every one that hath shall be given, and he shall have abundance: but from him that hath not shall be taken away even that which he hath. (30) And cast ye the unprofitable servant into outer darkness: there shall be weeping and gnashing of teeth.

1 CORINTHIANS 12:4—Now there are diversities of gifts, but the same Spirit.

MATTHEW 24:42-51—(42) Watch therefore: for ye know not what hour your Lord doth come. (43) But know this, that if the goodman of the house had known in what watch the thief would come, he would have watched, and would not have suffered his house to be broken up. (44) Therefore be ye also ready: for in such an hour as ye think not the Son of man cometh. (45) Who then is a faithful and wise servant, whom his lord hath made ruler over his household, to give them meat in due season? (46) Blessed is that servant, whom his lord when he cometh shall find so doing. (47) Verily I say unto you, That he shall make him ruler over all his goods. (48) But and if that evil servant shall say in his heart, My lord delayeth his coming; (49) And shall begin to smite his fellowservants, and to eat and drink with the drunken; (50) The lord of that servant shall come in a day when he looketh not for him, and in an hour that he is not aware of, (51) And shall cut him asunder, and appoint him his portion with the hypocrites: there shall be weeping and gnashing of teeth.

ACTS 20:28—Take heed therefore unto yourselves, and to all the flock, over the which the Holy Ghost hath made you overseers, to feed the church of God, which he hath purchased with his own blood.

2 CORINTHIANS 9:7—Every man according as he purposeth in his heart, so let him give; not grudgingly, or of necessity: for God loveth a cheerful giver.

JOHN 3:27—John answered and said, A man can receive nothing, except it be given him from heaven.

ROMANS 12:9
Let love be without dissimulation. Abhor that which is evil; cleave to that which is good.

PSALMS 97:10—Ye that love the LORD, hate evil: he preserveth the souls of his saints; he delivereth them out of the hand of the wicked

AMOS 5:15—Hate the evil, and love the good, and establish judgment in the gate: it may be that the LORD God of hosts will be gracious unto the remnant of Joseph.

PSALMS 34:14—Depart from evil, and do good; seek peace, and pursue it.

1 THESSALONIANS 5:13—See that none render evil for evil unto any man; but ever follow that which is good, both among yourselves, and to all men

1 TIMOTHY 1:5—Now the end of the commandment is charity out of a pure heart, and of a good conscience, and of faith unfeigned.

ROMANS 12:10
Be kindly affectioned one to another with brotherly love; in honour preferring one another

HEBREWS 13:1—Let brotherly love continue.

JOHN 13:34-35—(34) A new commandment I give unto you, That ye love one another; as I have loved you, that ye also love one another. (35) By this shall all men know that ye are my disciples, if ye have love one to another.

EPHESIANS 4:3—Endeavoring to keep the unity of the Spirit in the bond of peace.

MATTHEW 6:14-15—(14) For if ye forgive men their trespasses, your heavenly Father will also forgive you: (15) But if ye forgive not men their trespasses, neither will your Father forgive your trespasses.

LUKE 17:3-4—(3) Take heed to yourselves: If thy brother trespass against thee, rebuke him; and if he repent, forgive him. (4) And if he trespass against thee seven times in a day, and seven times in a day turn again to thee, saying, I repent; thou shalt forgive him.

COLOSSIANS 3:13—Forbearing one another, and forgiving one another, if any man have a quarrel against any: even as Christ forgave you, so also do ye.

PSALMS 152:4-8—(4) Gather yourselves together to make known His strength; and be not slow in showing forth His deliverance and His strength and His glory to all babes. (5) That the honour of the Lord may be known, wisdom hath been given; and to tell of His works it hath been made known to men: (6) to make known unto babes His strength, and to make them that lack understanding (literally, heart) to comprehend His glory; (7) who are far from His entrances and distant from His gates: (8) because the Lord of Jacob is exalted, and His glory is upon all His works.

ZEPHANIAH 2:1-3—(1) Gather yourselves together, yea, gather together, O nation not desired; (2) Before the decree bring forth, before the day pass as the chaff, before the fierce anger of the LORD come upon you, before the day of the LORD'S anger come upon you. (3) Seek ye the LORD, all ye meek of the earth, which have wrought his judgment; seek righteousness, seek meekness: it may be ye shall be hid in the day of the LORD'S anger.

ROMANS 12:11
Not slothful in business; fervent in spirit; serving the Lord;

PROVERBS 13:4—The soul of the sluggard desireth, and hath nothing: but the soul of the diligent shall be made fat

HEBREWS 6:12—That ye be not slothful, but followers of them who through faith and patience inherit the promises.

PROVERBS 6:6-11—(6) Go to the ant, thou sluggard; consider her ways, and be wise: (7) Which having no guide, overseer, or ruler, (8) Provideth her meat in the summer, and gathereth her food in the harvest. (9) How long wilt thou sleep, O sluggard? When wilt thou arise out of thy sleep? (10) Yet a little sleep, a little slumber, a little folding of the hands to sleep: (11) So shall thy poverty come as one that travelleth, and thy want as an armed man.

PROVERBS 10:4—He becometh poor that dealeth with a slack hand: but the hand of the diligent maketh rich.

PROVERBS 12:27—The slothful man roasteth not that which he took in hunting: but the substance of a diligent man is precious.

HEBREWS 12:1—Wherefore seeing we also are compassed about with so great a cloud of witnesses, let us lay aside every weight, and the sin which doth so easily beset us, and let us run with patience the race that is set before us

ROMANS 12:12
Rejoicing in hope; patient in tribulation; continuing instant in prayer;

PHILIPPIANS 4:10-13—(10) But I rejoiced in the Lord greatly, that now at the last your care of me hath flourished again; wherein ye were also careful, but ye lacked opportunity. (11) Not that I speak in respect of want: for I have learned, in whatsoever state I am, therewith to be content. (12) I know both how to be abased, and I know how to abound: everywhere and in all things I am instructed both to be full and to be hungry, both to abound and to suffer need. (13) I can do all things through Christ, which strengtheneth me.

THESSALONIANS 5:16-18—(16) Rejoice evermore. (17) Pray without ceasing. (18) In every thing give thanks: for this is the will of God in Christ Jesus concerning you.

LUKE 21:19—In your patience possess ye your souls.

LUKE 10:20—Notwithstanding in this rejoice not, that the spirits are subject unto you; but rather rejoice, because your names are written in heaven.

LUKE 18:1—And he spake a parable unto them to this end, that men ought always to pray, and not to faint.

1 PETER 4:12-19—(12) Beloved, think it not strange concerning the fiery trial which is to try you, as though some strange thing happened unto you: (13) But rejoice, inasmuch as ye are partakers of Christ's sufferings; that, when his glory shall be revealed, ye may be glad also with exceeding joy. (14) If ye be reproached for the name of Christ, happy are ye; for the spirit of glory and of God resteth upon you: on their part he is evil spoken of, but on your part he is glorified. (15) But let none of you suffer as a murderer, or as a thief, or as an evildoer, or as a busybody in other men's matters. (16) Yet if any man suffer as a Christian, let him not be ashamed; but let him glorify God on this behalf. (17) For the time is come that judgment must begin at the house of God: and if it first begin at us, what shall the end be of them that obey not the gospel of God? (18) And if the righteous scarcely be saved, where shall the ungodly and the sinner appear? (19) Wherefore let them that suffer according to the will of God commit the keeping of their souls to him in well doing, as unto a faithful Creator.

ROMANS 12:13-14
(13) Distributing to the necessity of saints; given to hospitality (14) bless them which persecute you: bless, and curse not.

LUKE 5:38-48—(38) Ye have heard that it hath been said, An eye for an eye, and a tooth for a tooth: (39) But I say unto you, That ye resist not evil: but whosoever shall smite thee on thy right cheek, turn to him the other also. (40) And if any man will sue thee at the law, and take away thy coat, let him have thy cloak also. (41) And whosoever shall compel thee to go a mile, go with him twain. (42) Give to him that asketh thee, and from him that would borrow of thee turn not thou away. (43) Ye have heard that it hath been said, Thou shalt love thy neighbour, and hate thine enemy. (44) But I say unto you, Love your enemies, bless them that curse you, do good to them that hate you, and pray for them which despitefully use you, and persecute you; (45) That ye may be the children of your Father which is in heaven: for he maketh his sun to rise on the evil and on the good, and sendeth rain on the just and on the unjust. (46) For if ye love them which love you, what reward have ye? Do not even the publicans the same? (47) And if ye salute your brethren only, what do ye more than others? do not even the publicans so? (48) Be ye therefore perfect, even as your Father which is in heaven is perfect.

MATTHEW 5:44—But I say unto you, Love your enemies, bless them that curse you, do good to them that hate you, and pray for them which despitefully use you, and persecute you.

GALATIANS 2:10—Only they would that we should remember the poor; the same which I also was forward to do.

HEBREWS 13:2—Be not forgetful to entertain strangers: for thereby some have entertained angels unawares.

1 PETER 4:9—Use hospitality one to another without grudging.

2 CORINTHIANS 9:1, 12—(1) For as touching the ministering to the saints, it is superfluous for me to write to you...(12) For the administration of this service not only supplieth the want of the saints, but is abundant also by many thanksgivings unto God;

ROMANS 12:15-16
(15) Rejoice with them that do rejoice, and weep with them that weep. (16) Be of the same mind one toward another. Mind not high things, but condescend to men of low estate. Be not wise in your own conceits.

1 CORINTHIANS 12:26—And whether one member suffer, all the members suffer with it; or one member be honored, all the members rejoice with it.

PROVERBS 3:7—Be not wise in thine own eyes: fear the LORD, and depart from evil.

ROMANS 15:5—Now the God of patience and consolation grant you to be likeminded one toward another according to Christ Jesus.

PHILIPPIANS 2:2—Fulfill ye my joy, that ye be likeminded, having the same love, being of one accord, of one mind.

PSALMS 131:1—LORD, my heart is not haughty, nor mine eyes lofty: neither do I exercise myself in great matters, or in things too high for me.

ROMANS 12:17-18
(17) Recompense to no man evil for evil. Provide things honest in the sight of all men. (18) If it be possible, as much as lieth in you, live peaceably with all men.

MATTHEW 5:39-41—(39) But I say unto you, That ye resist not evil: but whosoever shall smite thee on thy right cheek, turn to him the other also. (40) And if any man will sue thee at the law, and take away thy coat, let him have thy cloak also. (41) And whosoever shall compel thee to go a mile, go with him twain.

HEBREWS 12:14—Follow peace with all men, and holiness, without which no man shall see the Lord.

PROVERBS 16:10—When a man's ways please the LORD, he maketh even his enemies to be at peace with him

2 CORINTHIANS 8:21—Providing for honest things, not only in the sight of the Lord, but also in the sight of men.

ROMANS 12:19
Dearly beloved, avenge not yourselves, but rather give place unto wrath: for it is written, Vengeance is mine; I will repay, saith the Lord.

LEVITICUS 19:18—Thou shalt not avenge, nor bear any grudge against the children of thy people, but thou shalt love thy neighbour as thyself: I am the LORD.

DEUTERONOMY 32:35—To me belongeth vengeance, and recompence; their foot shall slide in due time: for the day of their calamity is at hand, and the things that shall come upon them make haste.

SIRACH 28:1—He that revengeth shall find vengeance from the Lord, and he will surely keep his sins in remembrance.

MATTHEW 5:39—But I say unto you, That ye resist not evil: but whosoever shall smite thee on thy right cheek, turn to him the other also.

HEBREWS 10:30—For we know him that hath said, Vengeance belongeth unto me, I will recompense, saith the Lord. And again, The Lord shall judge his people.

ROMANS 12:20-21
(20) Therefore if thine enemy hunger, feed him; if he thirst, give him drink: for in so doing thou shalt heap coals of fire on his head. (21) Be not overcome of evil, but overcome evil with good.

PROVERBS 25:21-22—(21) If thine enemy be hungry, give him bread to eat; and if he be thirsty, give him water to drink: (22) For thou shalt heap coals of fire upon his head, and the LORD shall reward thee.

LEVITICUS 19:18—Thou shalt not avenge, nor bear any grudge against the children of thy people, but thou shalt love thy neighbour as thyself: I am the LORD.

PROVERBS 20:22—Say not thou, I will recompense evil; but wait on the LORD, and he shall save thee

MATTHEW 5:39-41—(39) But I say unto you, That ye resist not evil: but whosoever shall smite thee on thy right cheek, turn to him the other also. (40) And if any man will sue thee at the law, and take away thy coat, let him have thy cloak also. (41) And whosoever shall compel thee to go a mile, go with him twain.

ROMANS 12:1-2—(1) I beseech you therefore, brethren, by the mercies of God, that ye present your bodies a living sacrifice, holy, acceptable unto God, which is your reasonable service. (2) And be not conformed to this world: but be ye transformed by the renewing of your mind, that ye may prove what is that good, and acceptable, and perfect, will of God.

1 THESSALONIANS 5:15—See that none render evil for evil unto any man; but ever follow that which is good, both among yourselves, and to all men.

1 PETER 3:8-9—(8) Finally, be ye all of one mind, having compassion one of another, love as brethren, be pitiful, be courteous: (9) Not rendering evil for evil, or railing for railing: but contrariwise blessing; knowing that ye are thereunto called, that ye should inherit a blessing.

ROMANS 13

ROMANS 13:1
Let every soul be subject unto the higher powers. For there is no power but of God: the powers that be are ordained of God.

TITUS 3:1—Put them in mind to be subject to principalities and powers, to obey magistrates, to be ready to every good work.

1 PETER 2:13—Submit yourselves to every ordinance of man for the Lord's sake: whether it be to the king, as supreme.

LUKE 20:21-26—(21) And they asked him, saying, Master, we know that thou sayest and teachest rightly, neither acceptest thou the person of any, but teachest the way of God truly: (22) Is it lawful for us to give tribute unto Caesar, or no? (23) But he perceived their craftiness, and said unto them, Why tempt ye me? (24) Shew me a penny. Whose image and superscription hath it? They answered and said, Caesar's. (25) And he said unto them, Render therefore unto Caesar the things which be Caesar's, and unto God the things which be God's. (26) And they could not take hold of his words before the people: and they marveled at his answer, and held their peace.

PROVERBS 24:21—My son, fear thou the LORD and the king: and meddle not with them that are given to change.

ROMANS 13:2-3
(2) Whosoever therefore resisteth the power, resisteth the ordinance of God: and they that resist shall receive to themselves damnation. (3) For rulers are not a terror to good works, but to the evil. Wilt thou then not be afraid of the power? Do that which is good, and thou shalt have praise of the same:

PROVERBS 16:7—When a man's ways please the LORD, he maketh even his enemies to be at peace with him.

TITUS 3:1—Put them in mind to be subject to principalities and powers, to obey magistrates, to be ready to every good work

1 PETER 2:14—Or unto governors, as unto them that are sent by him for the punishment of evildoers, and for the praise of them that do well.

ROMANS 8:31—What shall we then say to these things? If God be for us, who can be against us?

ROMANS 13:4-5

(4) For he is the minister of God to thee for good. But if thou do that which is evil, be afraid; for he beareth not the sword in vain: for he is the minister of God, a revenger to execute wrath upon him that doeth evil. (5) Wherefore ye must needs be subject, not only for wrath, but also for conscience sake.

1 PETER 2:13-14—(13) Submit yourselves to every ordinance of man for the Lord's sake: whether it be to the king, as supreme (14) or unto governors, as unto them that are sent by him for the punishment of evildoers, and for the praise of them that do well.

TITUS 3:1—Put them in mind to be subject to principalities and powers, to obey magistrates, to be ready to every good work

ECCLESIASTES 8:2—I counsel thee to keep the king's commandment, and that in regard of the oath of God.

1 PETER 2:19—For this is thankworthy, if a man for conscience toward God endure grief, suffering wrongfully.

ROMANS 13:3—For rulers are not a terror to good works, but to the evil. Wilt thou then not be afraid of the power? Do that which is good, and thou shalt have praise of the same.

ROMANS 13:6-7

(6) For this cause pay ye tribute also: for they are God's ministers, attending continually upon this very thing. (7) Render therefore to all their dues: tribute to whom tribute is due; custom to whom custom; fear to whom fear; honour to whom honour.

1 CORINTHIANS 9:9-14—(9) For it is written in the law of Moses, Thou shalt not muzzle the mouth of the ox that treadeth out the corn. Doth God take care for oxen? (10) Or saith he it altogether for our sakes? For our sakes, no doubt, this is written: that he that ploweth should plow in hope;

and that he that thresheth in hope should be partaker of his hope. (11) If we have sown unto you spiritual things, is it a great thing if we shall reap your carnal things? (12) If others be partakers of this power over you, are not we rather? Nevertheless we have not used this power; but suffer all things, lest we should hinder the gospel of Christ. (13) Do ye not know that they which minister about holy things live of the things of the temple? and they which wait at the altar are partakers with the altar? (14) Even so hath the Lord ordained that they which preach the gospel should live of the gospel.

1 TIMOTHY 5:17-20—(17) Let the elders that rule well be counted worthy of double honour, especially they who labor in the word and doctrine. (18) For the scripture saith, Thou shalt not muzzle the ox that treadeth out the corn. And, The laborer is worthy of his reward. (19) Against an elder receive not an accusation, but before two or three witnesses. (20) Them that sin rebuke before all that others also may fear.

LUKE 10:7—And in the same house remain, eating and drinking such things as they give: for the laborer is worthy of his hire. Go not from house to house.

MATTHEW 22:15-21—(15) Then went the Pharisees, and took counsel how they might entangle him in his talk. (16) And they sent out unto him their disciples with the Herodians, saying, Master, we know that thou art true, and teachest the way of God in truth, neither carest thou for any man: for thou regardest not the person of men. (17) Tell us therefore, What thinkest thou? Is it lawful to give tribute unto Caesar, or not? (18) But Jesus perceived their wickedness, and said, Why tempt ye me, ye hypocrites? (19) Shew me the tribute money. And they brought unto him a penny. (20) And he saith unto them, Whose is this image and superscription? (21) They say unto him, Caesar's. Then saith he unto them, Render therefore unto Caesar the things which are Caesar's; and unto God the things that are God's.

1 PETER 2:17—Honour all men. Love the brotherhood. Fear God. Honour the king

LUKE 20:21-26—(21) And they asked him, saying, Master, we know that thou sayest and teachest rightly, neither acceptest thou the person of any, but teachest the way of God truly: (22) Is it lawful for us to give tribute unto Caesar, or no? (23) But he perceived their craftiness, and said unto them, Why tempt ye me? (24) Shew me a penny. Whose image and superscription hath it? They answered and said, Caesar's. (25) And he said unto them, Render therefore unto Caesar the things which be Caesar's, and unto God the things which be God's. (26) And they could not take hold of his words before the people: and they marveled at his answer, and held their peace.

ROMANS 13:8
Owe no man any thing, but to love one another: for he that loveth another hath fulfilled the law.

JOHN 13:34—A new commandment I give unto you, That ye love one another; as I have loved you, that ye also love one another.

GALATIANS 5:13-14—(13) For brethren, ye have been called unto liberty; only use not liberty for an occasion to the flesh, but by love serve one another. (14) For all the law is fulfilled in one word, even in this; Thou shalt love thy neighbour as thyself.

GALATIANS 6:2—Bear ye one another's burdens, and so fulfill the law of Christ.

COLOSSIANS 3:14—And above all these things put on charity, which is the bond of perfectness.

1 TIMOTHY 1:5—Now the end of the commandment is charity out of a pure heart, and of a good conscience, and of faith unfeigned.

ROMANS 13:9-10
(9) For this, Thou shalt not commit adultery, Thou shalt not kill, Thou shalt not steal, Thou shalt not bear false witness, Thou shalt not covet; and if there be any other commandment, it is briefly comprehended in this saying, namely, Thou shalt love thy neighbour as thyself. (10) Love worketh no ill to his neighbour: therefore love is the fulfilling of the law.

EXODUS 20:13-17—(13) Thou shalt not kill. (14) Thou shalt not commit adultery. (15) Thou shalt not steal. (16) Thou shalt not bear false witness against thy neighbour. (17) Thou shalt not covet thy neighbor's house, thou shalt not covet thy neighbor's wife, nor his manservant, nor his maidservant, nor his ox, nor his ass, nor any thing that is thy neighbor's.

LEVITICUS 19:18—Thou shalt not avenge, nor bear any grudge against the children of thy people, but thou shalt love thy neighbour as thyself: I am the LORD.

DEUTERONOMY 5:17-21—(17) Thou shalt not kill. (18) Neither shalt thou commit adultery. (19) Neither shalt thou steal. (20) Neither shalt thou bear false witness against thy neighbour. (21) Neither shalt thou desire thy neighbor's wife, neither shalt thou covet thy neighbor's house, his field, or his manservant, or his maidservant, his ox, or his ass, or any thing that [is] thy neighbor's.

MATTHEW 7:12—Therefore all things whatsoever ye would that men should do to you, do ye even so to them: for this is the law and the prophets.

MATTHEW 19:18-19—(18) He saith unto him, Which? Jesus said, Thou shalt do no murder, Thou shalt not commit adultery, Thou shalt not steal, Thou shalt not bear false witness, (19) Honour thy father and thy mother: and, Thou shalt love thy neighbour as thyself.

MATTHEW 22:39-40—(39) And the second is like unto it, Thou shalt love thy neighbour as thyself. (40) On these two commandments hang all the law and the prophets.

MARK 12:31—And the second is like, namely this, Thou shalt love thy neighbour as thyself. There is none other commandment greater than these.

GALATIANS 5:14—For all the law is fulfilled in one word, even in this; Thou shalt love thy neighbour as thyself.

JAMES 2:8—If ye fulfill the royal law according to the scripture, Thou shalt love thy neighbour as thyself, ye do well.

ROMANS 13:11-12

(11) **And that, knowing the time, that now it is high time to awake out of sleep: for now is our salvation nearer than when we believed.** (12) **The night is far spent, the day is at hand: let us therefore cast off the works of darkness, and let us put on the armor of light.**

JOHN 9:4—I must work the works of him that sent me, while it is day: the night cometh, when no man can work.

EPHESIANS 6:11-13—(11) Put on the whole armor of God, that ye may be able to stand against the wiles of the devil. (12) For we wrestle not against flesh and blood, but against principalities, against powers, against the rulers of the darkness of this world, against spiritual wickedness in high places. (13) Wherefore take unto you the whole armor of God, that ye may be able to withstand in the evil day, and having done all, to stand.

1 THESSALONIANS 5:5-8—(5) Ye are all the children of light, and the children of the day: we are not of the night, nor of darkness. (6) Therefore let us not sleep, as do others; but let us watch and be sober. (7) For they that sleep sleep in the night; and they that be drunken are drunken in the night. (8) But let us, who are of the day, be sober, putting on the breastplate of faith and love; and for an helmet, the hope of salvation.

1 CORINTHIANS 15:34—Awake to righteousness, and sin not; for some have not the knowledge of God: I speak this to your shame.

2 CORINTHIANS 6:7—By the word of truth, by the power of God, by the armor of righteousness on the right hand and on the left

EPHESIANS 5:11-14—(11) And have no fellowship with the unfruitful works of darkness, but rather reprove them. (12) For it is a shame even to speak of those things which are done of them in secret. (13) But all things that are reproved are made manifest by the light: for whatsoever doth make manifest is light. (14) Wherefore he saith, Awake thou that sleepest, and arise from the dead, and Christ shall give thee light.

ROMANS 13:13-14

(13) Let us walk honestly, as in the day; not in rioting and drunkenness, not in chambering and wantonness, not in strife and envying. (14) But put ye on the Lord Jesus Christ, and make not provision for the flesh, to fulfill the lusts thereof.

GALATIANS 3:27—For as many of you as have been baptized into Christ have put on Christ.

LUKE 21:34— And take heed to yourselves, lest at any time your hearts be overcharged with surfeiting, and drunkenness, and cares of this life, and so that day come upon you unawares.

PROVERBS 23:20—Be not among winebibbers; among riotous eaters of flesh

1 CORINTHIANS 6:9-11—(9) Know ye not that the unrighteous shall not inherit the kingdom of God? Be not deceived: neither fornicators, nor idolaters, nor adulterers, nor effeminate, nor abusers of themselves with mankind. (10) Nor thieves, nor covetous, nor drunkards, nor revilers, nor extortioners, shall inherit the kingdom of God. (11) And such were some of you: but ye are washed, but ye are sanctified, but ye are justified in the name of the Lord Jesus, and by the Spirit of our God.

GALATIANS 5:16—This I say then, Walk in the Spirit, and ye shall not fulfill the lust of the flesh.

EPHESIANS 4:24—And that ye put on the new man, which after God is created in righteousness and true holiness.

PHILIPPIANS 4:8—Finally, brethren, whatsoever things are true, whatsoever things are honest, whatsoever things are just, whatsoever things are pure, whatsoever things are lovely, whatsoever things are of good report; if there be any virtue, and if there be any praise, think on these things.

JAMES 3:14—But if ye have bitter envying and strife in your hearts, glory not, and lie not against the truth.

1 PETER 2:11—Dearly beloved, I beseech you as strangers and pilgrims, abstain from fleshly lusts, which war against the soul.

ROMANS 14

ROMANS 14:1
Him that is weak in the faith receive ye, but not to doubtful disputations.

Chapter 14 begins by contrasting strong vs. weak believers within the Circumcision and Non-Circumcision community: those who knew idols held no power, though men sacrificed animals to them vs. those who struggled with their own spiritual liberty.

As believers we are to avoid food sacrificed to idols, *(Acts 15:29)* but what if one is unsure about the origin of their meal? Should the brother who eats anyway *(1 Corinthians 10:27-33)* ridicule the one who abstains? Or vice versa? In either case, these believers are to be respected. Not ridiculed or judged, hence the admonition to avoid "doubtful disputations,' i.e. pointless arguments that are neither productive nor edifying.

2 TIMOTHY 2:23-26—(23) But foolish and unlearned questions avoid, knowing that they do gender strifes. (24) And the servant of the Lord must not strive; but be gentle unto all men, apt to teach, patient, (25) In meekness instructing those that oppose themselves; if God peradventure will give them repentance to the acknowledging of the truth; (26) And that they may recover themselves out of the snare of the devil, who are taken captive by him at his will.

ROMANS 15:1—We then that are strong ought to bear the infirmities of the weak, and not to please ourselves.

1 THESSALONIANS 5:12-18—(12) And we beseech you, brethren, to know them which labor among you, and are over you in the Lord, and admonish you; (13) and to esteem them very highly in love for their work's sake. And be at peace among yourselves. (14) Now we exhort you, brethren, warn them that are unruly, comfort the feebleminded, support the weak, be patient toward all men. (15) See that none render evil for evil unto any man; but ever follow that which is good, both among yourselves, and to all men. (16) Rejoice evermore. (17) Pray without ceasing. (18) In every thing give thanks: for this is the will of God in Christ Jesus concerning you.

1 CORINTHIANS 9:22—To the weak became I as weak, that I might gain the weak: I am made all things to all men, that I might by all means save some.

ROMANS 14:2 [a]
For one believeth that he may eat all things: another, who is weak, eateth herbs.

To "eat all things" isn't referring to the consumption of unclean animals. Contrary to Christian doctrine, TMH doesn't change, and at no time did He declare *all* animals clean. Swine, bunnies, and cobras were never considered food. I repeat, swine, bunnies, cobras, bats, warthogs, eels, frogs, geckos, turtles, rats, snails, armadillos, ducks, crocodiles, dogs, crabs, cats, crows, oysters, and anacondas were *never* considered food. This wasn't even up for debate during NT times. Only now has this issue surfaced. Therefore, the "all things" one believes he can eat are all 'lawful' things. This is referring to animals TMH always deemed **clean**.

Romans 14:2 is simply contrasting a clean meat diet vs. a diet of vegetables. Why was this an issue? Heathens were sacrificing animals to demons, and then serving the meat. And if they weren't doing that, they were casting spells over the food. Small wonder many of the faithful were vexed and afraid to eat anything. In fact, during the Greek captivity, this problem was a catalyst that led to the Maccabean revolt:

> **2 MACCABEES 5:27**—But Judas Maccabeus with nine others, or thereabout, withdrew himself into the wilderness, and lived in the mountains after the manner of beasts, with his company, who fed on herbs continually, lest they should be partakers of the pollution.

Hundreds of years later, the apostles were mindful to steer Israelite Gentiles new to the faith away from the idolatrous influences around them, influences they once gave into.

> **ACTS 15:19-21**—(19) Wherefore my sentence is, that we trouble not them, which from among the Gentiles are turned to God: (20) But that we write unto them, that they abstain from pollutions of idols, and from fornication, and from things strangled, and from blood. (21) For Moses of old time hath in every city them that preach him, being read in the synagogues every Sabbath day.

Some NT believers thought it best to be vegetarian because they couldn't be sure what wickedness was done to the meat. This was such a huge concern in the Corinthian assembly that Paul had to address it in an epistle:

> **1 CORINTHIANS 8:4-12**—(4) As concerning therefore the eating of those things that are offered in sacrifice unto idols, we know that an idol is nothing in the world, and that there is none other God but one. (5) For though there be that are called gods, whether in heaven or in earth, (as there be gods many, and lords many,) (6) But to us there is but one God,

the Father, of whom are all things, and we in him; and one Lord Jesus Christ, by whom are all things, and we by him. (7) <u>Howbeit there is not in every man that knowledge: for some with conscience of the idol unto this hour eat it as a thing offered unto an idol; and their conscience being weak is defiled.</u> (8) But meat commendeth us not to God: for neither, if we eat, are we the better; neither, if we eat not, are we the worse. (9) <u>But take heed lest by any means this liberty of yours become a stumbling block to them that are weak.</u> (10) <u>For if any man see thee which hast knowledge sit at meat in the idol's temple, shall not the conscience of him which is weak be emboldened to eat those things which are offered to idols;</u> (11) <u>And through thy knowledge shall the weak brother perish, for whom Christ died?</u> (12) <u>But when ye sin so against the brethren, and wound their weak conscience, ye sin against Christ.</u>

1 CORINTHIANS 10:27-28—(27) If any of them that believe not bid you to a feast, and ye be disposed to go; whatsoever is set before you, eat, asking no question for conscience sake. (28) But if any man say unto you, This is offered in sacrifice unto idols, eat not for his sake that shewed it, and for conscience sake: for the earth is the Lord's, and the fullness thereof.

A believer strong in the faith would have no problem eating what was put in front of him, <u>no questions asked</u>. His unflappable faith was bound with TMH, so his conscience would be clear. However, a weak brother or unbeliever might struggle with it. Hence this:

1 CORINTHIANS 10:23—All things are lawful for me, but all things are not expedient: all things are lawful for me, but all things edify not.

Paul is basically saying that while it may be okay to eat a meal of questionable origin, it wouldn't be wise to do so in the presence of a weaker brother. The stronger saint should not put stumbling blocks in the weaker saint's way. This is why he writes:

1 CORINTHIANS 9:22—To the weak became I as weak, that I might gain the weak: I am made all things to all men, that I might by all means save some.

Contemporary Israelites face this today. Say you're about to walk into an Indian restaurant and your weaker brother refuses to enter because of an idol in the window. It's best to accommodate his weaker conscience so as not to make him stumble. As believers we are to pray in faith that TMH will bless and clean what we ingest while we remain in exile since prophecy confirms we would eat defiled food while in captivity:

EZEKIEL 4:13—And the LORD said, Even thus shall the children of Israel eat their defiled bread among the Gentiles, whither I will drive them.

ROMANS 14:2 [b]
For one believeth that he may eat all things: another, who is weak, eateth herbs.

As outlined in *Romans 14:2* [a]'s commentary, the 'eat all things' reference isn't speaking about eating swine, shellfish, and other unclean foods, yet some like to use *1 Timothy 4:1-5* as proof that these foods are acceptable:

1 TIMOTHY 4:1-5—(1) Now the Spirit speaketh expressly, that in the latter times some shall depart from the faith, giving heed to seducing spirits, and doctrines of devils; (2) Speaking lies in hypocrisy; having their conscience seared with a hot iron; (3) Forbidding to marry, and commanding to abstain from meats, which God hath created to be received with thanksgiving of **them which believe and know the truth**. (4) For every creature of God is good, and nothing to be refused, if it be received with thanksgiving: (5) for it is sanctified by the word of God and prayer.

We must first ask, what is the truth?

JOHN 14:6—Jesus saith unto him, I am the way, the truth, and the life: no man cometh unto the Father, but by me.

Why is He the truth?

JOHN 1:1—In the beginning was the Word, and the Word was with God, and the Word was God.

The Messiah is literally the WORD of TMH in the flesh—the living, breathing, Torah, who came "in the volume of the book." *(Psalms 40:7; Hebrews 10:7)* The Torah is TMH's law.

What is the law?

PSALMS 119:142—Thy righteousness is an everlasting righteousness, and **thy law is the truth**.

If the Law is the truth everything in the Law is perfect. The Messiah being perfect fulfilled the law of sacrifice, which made the need for the blood of goats and bulls obsolete. But He did not do away with the whole Law. If He had, it would now be lawful to worship idols, murder people, and commit adultery. Those who know 'the truth,' understand that *they can eat all clean things* within TMH's law because the laws pertaining to clean and unclean foods still stand, just as the moral laws still stand.

QUESTION: But what about *1 Timothy 4:4*?

> **1 TIMOTHY 4:4-5**—(4) For every creature of God is good, and nothing to be refused, if it be received with thanksgiving: (5) for it is sanctified by the word of God and prayer."
>
> **ANSWER: Every creature of God is good and nothing is to be refused <u>within the law</u>—which we've just seen is <u>the truth</u>.**

We know this because of *1 Timothy 4:5*: <u>*"For it is **sanctified** by the word of God.*"</u> The **only** foods sanctified (or set apart) by TMH are foods He deemed clean *within* the Law. Everything else, AKA unclean animals, aren't even part of the equation because, again, they were never considered food.

ROMANS 14:3
Let not him that eateth despise him that eateth not; and let not him which eateth not judge him that eateth: for God hath received him.

ROMANS 15:1—We then that are strong ought to bear the infirmities of the weak, and not to please ourselves.

1 CORINTHIANS 8:1—Now as touching things offered unto idols, we know that we all have knowledge. Knowledge puffeth up, but charity edifieth.

1 CORINTHIANS 9:22—To the weak became I as weak, that I might gain the weak: I am made all things to all men, that I might by all means save some.

1 CORINTHIANS 10:23-25—(23) All things are lawful for me, but all things are not expedient: all things are lawful for me, but all things edify not. (24) Let no man seek his own, but every man another's wealth. (25) Whatsoever is sold in the shambles, that eat, asking no question for conscience sake.

SIRACH 14:2—Blessed is he whose conscience hath not condemned him, and who is not fallen from his hope in the Lord.

COLOSSIANS 2:16—Let no man therefore judge you in meat, or in drink, or in respect of an holyday, or of the new moon, or of the Sabbath days

TITUS 1:15—Unto the pure all things are pure: but unto them that are defiled and unbelieving is nothing pure; but even their mind and conscience is defiled.

ROMANS 14:4

Who art thou that judgest another man's servant? To his own master he standeth or falleth. Yea, he shall be holden up: for God is able to make him stand.

JAMES 4:11-12—(11) Speak not evil one of another, brethren. He that speaketh evil of [his] brother, and judgeth his brother, speaketh evil of the law, and judgeth the law: but if thou judge the law, thou art not a doer of the law, but a judge. (12) There is one lawgiver, who is able to save and to destroy: who art thou that judgest another?

MATTHEW 7:1—Judge not, that ye be not judged.

LUKE 6:37—Judge not, and ye shall not be judged: condemn not, and ye shall not be condemned: forgive, and ye shall be forgiven.

ROMANS 2:1—Therefore thou art inexcusable, O man, whosoever thou art that judgest: for wherein thou judgest another, thou condemnest thyself; for thou that judgest doest the same things.

ROMANS 14:5-6

(5) One man esteemeth one day above another: another esteemeth every day alike. Let every man be fully persuaded in his own mind. (6) He that regardeth the day, regardeth it unto the Lord; and he that regardeth not the day, to the Lord he doth not regard it. He that eateth, eateth to the Lord, for he giveth God thanks; and he that eateth not, to the Lord he eateth not, and giveth God thanks.

This delves into liberty in Messiah vs. the sacrificial law and its ordinances. Some brethren were still tied to these aspects within the Law, arguing about the sacrificial days and drink-offering portions of the Law. *(Numbers 28:7-10)* In other words, they were still offering sacrifices, while others enjoyed the liberty Messiah's sacrifice gave them. For example:

NUMBERS 28:7-10—(7) And the drink offering thereof shall be the fourth part of an hin for the one lamb: in the holy place shalt thou cause the strong wine to be poured unto the LORD for a drink offering. (8) And the other lamb shalt thou offer at even: as the meat offering of the morning, and as the drink offering thereof, thou shalt offer it, a sacrifice made by fire, of a sweet savor unto the LORD. (9) And on the Sabbath day two lambs of the first year without spot, and two tenth deals of flour for a meat offering, mingled with oil, and the drink offering thereof: (10) This is the burnt offering of every Sabbath, beside the continual burnt offering, and his drink offering. (11) And in the beginnings of your months ye shall offer a burnt offering unto the LORD; two young bullocks, and one ram, seven lambs of the first year without spot.

EZEKIEL 45:17—And it shall be the prince's part to give burnt offerings, and meat offerings, and drink offerings, in the feasts, and in the new moons, and in the sabbaths, in all solemnities of the house of Israel: he shall prepare the sin offering, and the meat offering, and the burnt offering, and the peace offerings, to make reconciliation for the house of Israel.

Messiah's sacrifice fulfilled the ordinances and offerings for sin and reconciliation. Therefore, in *Romans 14:5-6*, Paul continues his argument from *Romans 14:1* by reminding believers not to judge each other, but to be thoroughly convinced in their own mind about their stance.

COLOSSIANS 2:14-17—(14) Blotting out the handwriting of ordinances that was against us, which was contrary to us, and took it out of the way, nailing it to his cross (15) And having spoiled principalities and powers, he made a shew of them openly, triumphing over them in it. (16) Let no man therefore judge you in meat, or in drink, or in respect of an holyday, or of the new moon, or of the Sabbath days: (17) Which are a shadow of things to come; but the body is of Christ.

1 CORINTHIANS 10:31—Whether therefore ye eat, or drink, or whatsoever ye do, do all to the glory of God.

HEBREWS 9:6-10—(6) Now when these things were thus ordained, the priests went always into the first tabernacle, accomplishing the service of God. (7) But into the second went the high priest alone once every year, not without blood, which he offered for himself, and for the errors of the people: (8) The Holy Ghost this signifying, that the way into the holiest of all was not yet made manifest, while as the first tabernacle was yet standing: (9) which was a figure for the time then present, in which were offered both gifts and sacrifices, that could not make him that did the service perfect, as pertaining to the conscience; (10) Which stood only in meats and drinks, and divers washings, and carnal ordinances, imposed on them until the time of reformation.

HEBREWS 10:1-4—(1) For the law having a shadow of good things to come, and not the very image of the things, can never with those sacrifices which they offered year by year continually make the comers thereunto perfect. (2) For then would they not have ceased to be offered? Because that the worshippers once purged should have had no more conscience of sins. (3) But in those sacrifices there is a remembrance again made of sins every year. (4) For it is not possible that the blood of bulls and of goats should take away sins.

HEBREWS 10:9-11—(9) Then said he, Lo, I come to do thy will, O God. He taketh away the first, that he may establish the second. (10) By the which will we are sanctified through the offering of the body of Jesus Christ once for all. (11) And every priest standeth daily ministering and offering oftentimes the same sacrifices, which can never take away sins.

ROMANS 14:7-9

(7) **For none of us liveth to himself, and no man dieth to himself.** (8) **For whether we live, we live unto the Lord; and whether we die, we die unto the Lord: whether we live therefore, or die, we are the Lord's.** (9) **For to this end Christ both died, and rose, and revived, that he might be Lord both of the dead and living.**

ACTS 10:36, 42—(36) The word which God sent unto the children of Israel, preaching peace by Jesus Christ: (he is Lord of all:)...(42) And he commanded us to preach unto the people, and to testify that it is he which was ordained of God to be the Judge of quick and dead.

ROMANS 8:34—Who is he that condemneth? It is Christ that died, yea rather, that is risen again, who is even at the right hand of God, who also maketh intercession for us.

1 CORINTHIANS 6:19—What? know ye not that your body is the temple of the Holy Ghost which is in you, which ye have of God, and ye are not your own?

2 CORINTHIANS 5:14-15—(14) For the love of Christ constraineth us; because we thus judge, that if one died for all, then were all dead: (15) And that he died for all, that they which live should not henceforth live unto themselves, but unto him which died for them, and rose again.

GALATIANS 2:20—I am crucified with Christ: nevertheless I live; yet not I, but Christ liveth in me: and the life which I now live in the flesh I live by the faith of the Son of God, who loved me, and gave himself for me.

1 THESSALONIANS 5:10—Who died for us, that, whether we wake or sleep, we should live together with him.

1 PETER 4:2—That he no longer should live the rest of his time in the flesh to the lusts of men, but to the will of God.

REVELATION 1:18-19—(18) I am he that liveth, and was dead; and, behold, I am alive for evermore, Amen; and have the keys of hell and of death. (19) Write the things which thou hast seen, and the things which are, and the things which shall be hereafter;

ROMANS 14:10
But why dost thou judge thy brother? Or why dost thou set at nought thy brother? For we shall all stand before the judgment seat of Christ.

ROMANS 2:16—In the day when God shall judge the secrets of men by Jesus Christ according to my gospel.

MATTHEW 25:31-32—(31) When the Son of man shall come in his glory, and all the holy angels with him, then shall he sit upon the throne of his glory: (32) And before him shall be gathered all nations: and he shall separate them one from another, as a shepherd divideth his sheep from the goats:

2 CORINTHIANS 5:10—For we must all appear before the judgment seat of Christ; that every one may receive the things done in his body, according to that he hath done, whether it be good or bad.

ROMANS 14:11
For it is written, As I live, saith the Lord, every knee shall bow to me, and every tongue shall confess to God.

ISAIAH 45:23-24—(23) I have sworn by myself, the word is gone out of my mouth in righteousness, and shall not return, That unto me every knee shall bow, every tongue shall swear. (24) Surely, shall one say, in the LORD have I righteousness and strength: even to him shall men come; and all that are incensed against him shall be ashamed.

PHILIPPIANS 2:10-11—(10) That at the name of Jesus every knee should bow, of things in heaven, and things in earth, and things under the earth; (11) And that every tongue should confess that Jesus Christ is Lord, to the glory of God the Father.

REVELATION 5:13—And every creature which is in heaven, and on the earth, and under the earth, and such as are in the sea, and all that are in them, heard I saying, Blessing, and honour, and glory, and power, be unto him that sitteth upon the throne, and unto the Lamb forever and ever.

ROMANS 14:12
So then every one of us shall give account of himself to God.

MATTHEW 12:36-37—(36) But I say unto you, that every idle word that men shall speak, they shall give account thereof in the day of judgment.

(37) For by thy words thou shalt be justified, and by thy words thou shalt be condemned.

MATTHEW 16:27—For the Son of man shall come in the glory of his Father with his angels; and then he shall reward every man according to his works

1 PETER 4:5—Who shall give account to him that is ready to judge the quick and the dead.

2 CORINTHIANS 5:10—For we must all appear before the judgment seat of Christ; that every one may receive the things done in his body, according to that he hath done, whether it be good or bad.

HEBREWS 9:27-28—(27) And as it is appointed unto men once to die, but after this the judgment: (28) So Christ was once offered to bear the sins of many; and unto them that look for him shall he appear the second time without sin unto salvation.

EPHESIANS 6:7-8—(7) With good will doing service, as to the Lord, and not to men: (8) Knowing that whatsoever good thing any man doeth, the same shall he receive of the Lord, whether he be bond or free.

JOB 34:11—For the work of a man shall he render unto him, and cause every man to find according to his ways.

ECCLESIASTES 3:16-17—(16) And moreover I saw under the sun the place of judgment, that wickedness was there; and the place of righteousness, that iniquity was there. (17) I said in mine heart, God shall judge the righteous and the wicked: for there is a time there for every purpose and for every work.

ROMANS 14:13
Let us not therefore judge one another any more: but judge this rather, that no man put a stumbling block or an occasion to fall in his brother's way.

1 CORINTHIANS 8:3, 9-13—(3) But if any man love God, the same is known of him...(9) But take heed lest by any means this liberty of yours become a stumbling block to them that are weak. (10) For if any man see thee which hast knowledge sit at meat in the idol's temple, shall not the conscience of him which is weak be emboldened to eat those things which are offered to idols; (11) And through thy knowledge shall the weak brother perish, for whom Christ died? (12) But when ye sin so against the brethren, and wound their weak conscience, ye sin against Christ. (13)

Wherefore, if meat make my brother to offend, I will eat no flesh while the world standeth, lest I make my brother to offend.

1 CORINTHIANS 9:22—To the weak became I as weak, that I might gain the weak: I am made all things to all men, that I might by all means save some.

1 CORINTHIANS 10:32—Give none offence, neither to the Jews, nor to the Gentiles, nor to the church of God.

GALATIANS 6:1-2—(1) Brethren, if a man be overtaken in a fault, ye which are spiritual, restore such an one in the spirit of meekness; considering thyself, lest thou also be tempted. (2) Bear ye one another's burdens, and so fulfill the law of Christ.

PHILIPPIANS 2:2-4—(2) Fulfill ye my joy, that ye be likeminded, having the same love, being of one accord, of one mind. (3) Let nothing be done through strife or vainglory; but in lowliness of mind let each esteem other better than themselves. (4) Look not every man on his own things, but every man also on the things of others.

ROMANS 15:1—We then that are strong ought to bear the infirmities of the weak, and not to please ourselves.

DEUTERONOMY 15:7-11—(7) If there be among you a poor man of one of thy brethren within any of thy gates in thy land which the LORD thy God giveth thee, thou shalt not harden thine heart, nor shut thine hand from thy poor brother: (8) But thou shalt open thine hand wide unto him, and shalt surely lend him sufficient for his need, in that which he wanteth. (9) Beware that there be not a thought in thy wicked heart, saying, The seventh year, the year of release, is at hand; and thine eye be evil against thy poor brother, and thou givest him nought; and he cry unto the LORD against thee, and it be sin unto thee. (10) Thou shalt surely give him, and thine heart shall not be grieved when thou givest unto him: because that for this thing the LORD thy God shall bless thee in all thy works, and in all that thou puttest thine hand unto. (11) For the poor shall never cease out of the land: therefore I command thee, saying, Thou shalt open thine hand wide unto thy brother, to thy poor, and to thy needy, in thy land.

ROMANS 14:14
I know, and am persuaded by the Lord Jesus, that there is nothing unclean of itself: but to him that esteemeth any thing to be unclean, to him it is unclean.

TMH spent the entire books of *Leviticus* and *Deuteronomy* outlining right and wrong and clean and unclean things. So Paul isn't saying unclean things are clean. Remember the context which is outlined in *Romans 14:1-13*. As an expert in the law, he's speaking within the framework of a man's *conscience*. That what is clean doesn't become unclean *unless* it's a personal stumbling block for the individual.

1 CORINTHIANS 8:4-10—(4) As concerning therefore the eating of those things that are offered in sacrifice unto idols, we know that an idol is nothing in the world, and that there is none other God but one. (5) For though there be that are called gods, whether in heaven or in earth, as there be gods many, and lords many, (6) but to us there is but one God, the Father, of whom are all things, and we in him; and one Lord Jesus Christ, by whom are all things, and we by him. (7) Howbeit there is not in every man that knowledge: for some with conscience of the idol unto this hour eat it as a thing offered unto an idol; and their conscience being weak is defiled. (8) But meat commendeth us not to God: for neither, if we eat, are we the better; neither, if we eat not, are we the worse. (9) But take heed lest by any means this liberty of yours become a stumbling block to them that are weak. (10) For if any man see thee which hast knowledge sit at meat in the idol's temple, shall not the conscience of him which is weak be emboldened to eat those things which are offered to idols.

1 CORINTHIANS 10:23-28—(23) All things are lawful for me, but all things are not expedient: all things are lawful for me, but all things edify not. (24) Let no man seek his own, but every man another's wealth. (25) Whatsoever is sold in the shambles, that eat, asking no question for conscience sake: (26) For the earth is the Lord's, and the fullness thereof. (27) If any of them that believe not bid you to a feast, and ye be disposed to go; whatsoever is set before you, eat, asking no question for conscience sake. (28) But if any man say unto you, This is offered in sacrifice unto idols, eat not for his sake that shewed it, and for conscience sake: for the earth is the Lord's, and the fullness thereof

1 TIMOTHY 4:3-5—(3) Forbidding to marry, and commanding to abstain from meats, which God hath created to be received with thanksgiving of them which believe and know the truth. (4) For every creature of God is good, and nothing to be refused, if it be received with thanksgiving: (5) for it is sanctified by the word of God and prayer.

ROMANS 14:15-16

(15) But if thy brother be grieved with thy meat, now walkest thou not charitably. Destroy not him with thy meat, for whom Christ died. (16) Let not then your good be evil spoken of...

1 CORINTHIANS 6:12-13—(12) All things are lawful unto me, but all things are not expedient: all things are lawful for me, but I will not be brought under the power of any. (13) Meats for the belly, and the belly for meats: but God shall destroy both it and them. Now the body is not for fornication, but for the Lord; and the Lord for the body.

1 CORINTHIANS 8:7-13—(7) Howbeit there is not in every man that knowledge: for some with conscience of the idol unto this hour eat it as a thing offered unto an idol; and their conscience being weak is defiled. (8) But meat commendeth us not to God: for neither, if we eat, are we the better; neither, if we eat not, are we the worse. (9) But take heed lest by any means this liberty of yours become a stumbling block to them that are weak. (10) For if any man see thee which hast knowledge sit at meat in the idol's temple, shall not the conscience of him which is weak be emboldened to eat those things which are offered to idols; (11) And through thy knowledge shall the weak brother perish, for whom Christ died? (12) But when ye sin so against the brethren, and wound their weak conscience, ye sin against Christ (13) Wherefore, if meat make my brother to offend, I will eat no flesh while the world standeth, lest I make my brother to offend.

1 CORINTHIANS 13:4-7—(4) Charity suffereth long, and is kind; charity envieth not; charity vaunteth not itself, is not puffed up, (5) Doth not behave itself unseemly, seeketh not her own, is not easily provoked, thinketh no evil; (6) Rejoiceth not in iniquity, but rejoiceth in the truth; (7) Beareth all things, believeth all things, hopeth all things, endureth all things.

PHILIPPIANS 2:1-5—(1) If there be therefore any consolation in Christ, if any comfort of love, if any fellowship of the Spirit, if any bowels and mercies, (2) Fulfill ye my joy, that ye be likeminded, having the same love, being of one accord, of one mind. (3) Let nothing be done through strife or vainglory; but in lowliness of mind let each esteem other better than themselves. (4) Look not every man on his own things, but every man also on the things of others. (5) Let this mind be in you, which was also in Christ Jesus.

ROMANS 14:17-19

(17) **For the kingdom of God is not meat and drink; but righteousness, and peace, and joy in the Holy Ghost.** (18) **For he that in these things serveth Christ is acceptable to God, and approved of men.** (19) **Let us therefore follow after the things which make for peace, and things wherewith one may edify another.**

HEBREWS 12:14—Follow peace with all men, and holiness, without which no man shall see the Lord.

ROMANS 12:18—If it be possible, as much as lieth in you, live peaceably with all men.

ROMANS 15:2—Let every one of us please his neighbour for his good to edification.

1 CORINTHIANS 8:8—But meat commendeth us not to God: for neither, if we eat, are we the better; neither, if we eat not, are we the worse.

2 TIMOTHY 2:22—Flee also youthful lusts: but follow righteousness, faith, charity, peace, with them that call on the Lord out of a pure heart.

ROMANS 8:6—For to be carnally minded is death; but to be spiritually minded is life and peace.

ROMANS 14:20-21

(20) **For meat destroy not the work of God. All things indeed are pure; but it is evil for that man who eateth with offence.** (21) **It is good neither to eat flesh, nor to drink wine, nor any thing whereby thy brother stumbleth, or is offended, or is made weak.**

MATTHEW 15:11—Not that which goeth into the mouth defileth a man; but that which cometh out of the mouth, this defileth a man.

ROMANS 14:15—But if thy brother be grieved with thy meat, now walkest thou not charitably. Destroy not him with thy meat, for whom Christ died.

1 CORINTHIANS 8:9-13—(9) But take heed lest by any means this liberty of yours become a stumbling block to them that are weak. (10) For if any man see thee which hast knowledge sit at meat in the idol's temple, shall not the conscience of him which is weak be emboldened to eat those things which are offered to idols; (11) And through thy knowledge shall the weak brother perish, for whom Christ died? (12) But when ye sin so against the brethren, and wound their weak conscience, ye sin against Christ. (13) Wherefore, if meat make my brother to offend, I will eat no flesh while the world standeth, lest I make my brother to offend.

TITUS 1:15—Unto the pure all things are pure: but unto them that are defiled and unbelieving is nothing pure; but even their mind and conscience is defiled.

(For more information about meats, see Romans 14:2 [a] & [b] commentary, pgs. 370-373.)

ROMANS 14:22
Hast thou faith? Have it to thyself before God. Happy is he that condemneth not himself in that thing which he alloweth.

SIRACH 14:2—Blessed is he whose conscience hath not condemned him, and who is not fallen from his hope in the Lord.

1 JOHN 3:21—Beloved, if our heart condemn us not, then have we confidence toward God.

ROMANS 14:23
And he that doubteth is damned if he eat, because he eateth.

TITUS 1:15—Unto the pure all things are pure: but unto them that are defiled and unbelieving is nothing pure; but even their mind and conscience is defiled.

HEBREWS 11:6—But without faith it is impossible to please him: for he that cometh to God must believe that he is, and that he is a rewarder of them that diligently seek him.

ROMANS 15

ROMANS 15:1-2
(1) We then that are strong ought to bear the infirmities of the weak, and not to please ourselves. (2) Let every one of us please his neighbour for his good to edification.

1 CORINTHIANS 10:24, 33—(24) Let no man seek his own, but every man another's wealth...(33) Even as I please all men in all things, not seeking mine own profit, but the profit of many, that they may be saved.

1 CORINTHIANS 9:22—To the weak became I as weak, that I might gain the weak: I am made all things to all men, that I might by all means save some.

ROMANS 14:1—Him that is weak in the faith receive ye, but not to doubtful disputations.

ROMANS 14:19—Let us therefore follow after the things which make for peace, and things wherewith one may edify another.

GALATIANS 6:1-2—(1) Brethren, if a man be overtaken in a fault, ye which are spiritual, restore such an one in the spirit of meekness; considering thyself, lest thou also be tempted. (2) Bear ye one another's burdens, and so fulfill the law of Christ.

1 THESSALONIANS 5:14—Now we exhort you, brethren, warn them that are unruly, comfort the feebleminded, support the weak, be patient toward all men.

JOHN 13:5-17—(5) After that he poureth water into a bason, and began to wash the disciples' feet, and to wipe them with the towel wherewith he was girded. (6) Then cometh he to Simon Peter: and Peter saith unto him, Lord, dost thou wash my feet? (7) Jesus answered and said unto him, What I do thou knowest not now; but thou shalt know hereafter. (8) Peter saith unto him, Thou shalt never wash my feet. Jesus answered him, If I wash thee not, thou hast no part with me. (9) Simon Peter saith unto him, Lord, not my feet only, but also my hands and my head. (10) Jesus saith to him, He that is washed needeth not save to wash his feet, but is clean every whit: and ye are clean, but not all. (11) For he knew who should betray him; therefore said he, Ye are not all clean. (12) So after he had washed their feet, and had taken his garments, and was set down again, he said unto them, Know ye what I have done to you? (13) Ye call me Master and Lord: and ye say well; for so I am. (14) If I then, your Lord and

Master, have washed your feet; ye also ought to wash one another's feet. (15) For I have given you an example that ye should do as I have done to you. (16) Verily, verily, I say unto you, The servant is not greater than his lord; neither he that is sent greater than he that sent him. (17) If ye know these things, happy are ye if ye do them.

MATTHEW 23:11-12—(11) But he that is greatest among you shall be your servant. (12) And whosoever shall exalt himself shall be abased; and he that shall humble himself shall be exalted.

ROMANS 15:3
For even Christ pleased not himself; but, as it is written, The reproaches of them that reproached thee fell on me.

PSALMS 69:7-9—(7) Because for thy sake I have borne reproach; shame hath covered my face. (8) I am become a stranger unto my brethren, and an alien unto my mother's children. (9) For the zeal of thine house hath eaten me up; and the reproaches of them that reproached thee are fallen upon me.

2 CORINTHIANS 8:9—For ye know the grace of our Lord Jesus Christ, that, though he was rich, yet for your sakes he became poor, that ye through his poverty might be rich.

PHILIPPIANS 2:5-8—(5) Let this mind be in you, which was also in Christ Jesus: (6) Who, being in the form of God, thought it not robbery to be equal with God: (7) But made himself of no reputation, and took upon him the form of a servant, and was made in the likeness of men: (8) And being found in fashion as a man, he humbled himself, and became obedient unto death, even the death of the cross.

ISAIAH 53:3-10—(3) He is despised and rejected of men; a man of sorrows, and acquainted with grief: and we hid as it were our faces from him; he was despised, and we esteemed him not. (4) Surely he hath borne our griefs, and carried our sorrows: yet we did esteem him stricken, smitten of God, and afflicted. (5) But he was wounded for our transgressions, he was bruised for our iniquities: the chastisement of our peace was upon him; and with his stripes we are healed. (6) All we like sheep have gone astray; we have turned every one to his own way; and the LORD hath laid on him the iniquity of us all. (7) He was oppressed, and he was afflicted, yet he opened not his mouth: he is brought as a lamb to the slaughter, and as a sheep before her shearers is dumb, so he openeth not his mouth. (8) He was taken from prison and from judgment:

and who shall declare his generation? For he was cut off out of the land of the living: for the transgression of my people was he stricken. (9) And he made his grave with the wicked, and with the rich in his death; because he had done no violence, neither was any deceit in his mouth. (10) Yet it pleased the LORD to bruise him; he hath put him to grief: when thou shalt make his soul an offering for sin, he shall see his seed, he shall prolong his days, and the pleasure of the LORD shall prosper in his hand.

ROMANS 15:4
For whatsoever things were written aforetime were written for our learning, that we through patience and comfort of the scriptures might have hope.

2 TIMOTHY 3:16-17—(16) All scripture is given by inspiration of God, and is profitable for doctrine, for reproof, for correction, for instruction in righteousness: (17) That the man of God may be perfect, thoroughly furnished unto all good works.

1 CORINTHIANS 10:6, 11—(6) Now these things were our examples, to the intent we should not lust after evil things, as they also lusted...(11) Now all these things happened unto them for ensamples: and they are written for our admonition, upon whom the ends of the world are come.

ROMANS 4:20-24—(20) He staggered not at the promise of God through unbelief; but was strong in faith, giving glory to God; (21) And being fully persuaded that, what he had promised, he was able also to perform. (22) And therefore it was imputed to him for righteousness. (23) Now it was not written for his sake alone, that it was imputed to him; (24) But for us also, to whom it shall be imputed, if we believe on him that raised up Jesus our Lord from the dead.

1 CORINTHIANS 9:9-10—(9) For it is written in the law of Moses, Thou shalt not muzzle the mouth of the ox that treadeth out the corn. Doth God take care for oxen? (10) Or saith he it altogether for our sakes? For our sakes, no doubt, this is written: that he that ploweth should plow in hope; and that he that thresheth in hope should be partaker of his hope.

PSALMS 119:50—This is my comfort in my affliction: for thy word hath quickened me.

ROMANS 15:5-7

(5) Now the God of patience and consolation grant you to be likeminded one toward another according to Christ Jesus: (6) That ye may with one mind and one mouth glorify God, even the Father of our Lord Jesus Christ. (7) Wherefore receive ye one another, as Christ also received us to the glory of God.

ROMANS 12:16—Be of the same mind one toward another. Mind not high things, but condescend to men of low estate. Be not wise in your own conceits.

1 CORINTHIANS 1:10—Now I beseech you, brethren, by the name of our Lord Jesus Christ, that ye all speak the same thing, and that there be no divisions among you; but that ye be perfectly joined together in the same mind and in the same judgment.

2 CORINTHIANS 13:11—Finally, brethren, farewell. Be perfect, be of good comfort, be of one mind, live in peace; and the God of love and peace shall be with you

ROMANS 14:1-3—(1) Him that is weak in the faith receive ye, but not to doubtful disputations. (2) For one believeth that he may eat all things: another, who is weak, eateth herbs. (3) Let not him that eateth despise him that eateth not; and let not him which eateth not judge him that eateth: for God hath received him.

ACTS 4:24—And when they heard that, they lifted up their voice to God with one accord, and said, Lord, thou art God, which hast made heaven, and earth, and the sea, and all that in them is.

ROMANS 5:2—By whom also we have access by faith into this grace wherein we stand, and rejoice in hope of the glory of God.

ROMANS 15:8
Now I say that Jesus Christ was a minister of the circumcision for the truth of God, to confirm the promises made unto the fathers:

ROMANS 9:4-5—(4) Who are Israelites; to whom pertaineth the adoption, and the glory, and the covenants, and the giving of the law, and the service [of God], and the promises; (5) Whose are the fathers, and of whom as concerning the flesh Christ came, who is over all, God blessed for ever. Amen.

(For a complete breakdown of the "promises made unto the fathers, see the commentary for Romans 9:4 [f] on pg. 232.)

ROMANS 15:9
And that the Gentiles might glorify God for his mercy; as it is written, For this cause I will confess to thee among the Gentiles, and sing unto thy name.

Here Paul is quoting King David's psalm, which he composed after TMH delivered him from the hands of his enemies—non-Israelites as well as wicked brethren like King Saul. This song of praise and worship is recorded in 2 Samuel and the Psalms. King David is giving thanks for the unfailing mercy of TMH who delivered him from his many foes.

Prophetically speaking, David's psalms (and Paul's usage of this verse) highlights how Israelite Gentiles, who were scattered to the four corners, (Deuteronomy 32:26) would also praise and confess the TMH's unfailing mercy while they lived in exile in the lands of their enemies, amongst the Gentiles. (John 7:35) Therefore, 'amongst the Gentiles' are TMH's saints praising and confessing His glorious, unfailing mercy, which came via the new covenant, a contract made with the children of Israel (Jeremiah 31:31-33) for the forgiveness of sin (Jeremiah 31:34) through Messiah's sacrifice. (Matthew 1:21)

PSALMS 18:40-50—(40) Thou hast also given me the necks of mine enemies; that I might destroy them that hate me. (41) They cried, but there was none to save them: even unto the LORD, but he answered them not. (42) Then did I beat them small as the dust before the wind: I did cast them out as the dirt in the streets. (43) Thou hast delivered me from the strivings of the people; and thou hast made me the head of the heathen: a people whom I have not known shall serve me. (44) As soon as they hear of me, they shall obey me: the strangers shall submit themselves unto me. (45) The strangers shall fade away, and be afraid out of their close places. (46) The LORD liveth; and blessed be my rock; and let the God of my salvation be exalted. (47) It is God that avengeth me, and subdueth the people under me. (48) He delivereth me from mine enemies: yea, thou liftest me up above those that rise up against me: thou hast delivered me from the violent man. (49) Therefore will I give thanks unto thee, O LORD, among the heathen, and sing praises unto thy name. (50) Great deliverance giveth he to his king; and sheweth mercy to his anointed, to David, and to his seed for evermore.

2 SAMUEL 22:50—Therefore will I give thanks to thee. O Lord, among the Gentiles, and will sing to thy name.

COLOSSIANS 1:27—To whom God would make known what is the riches of the glory of this mystery among the Gentiles; which is Christ in you, the hope of glory.

(For a breakdown on the usage of "Gentiles" see The People Of Romans, pg. 53)

ROMANS 15:10
And again he saith, Rejoice, ye Gentiles, with his people.

In verse 10, Paul quotes *Deuteronomy 32:43*. Let's read it **very carefully, and in context**, starting at verse 26:

DEUTERONOMY 32:26-43—(26) <u>I said, I would scatter them into corners, I would make the remembrance of them to cease from among men</u>: (27) Were it not that I feared the wrath of the enemy, lest their adversaries should behave themselves strangely, and lest they should say, Our hand is high, and the LORD hath not done all this. (28) For they are a nation void of counsel, neither is there any understanding in them. (29) O that they were wise, that they understood this, that they would consider their latter end! (30) How should one chase a thousand, and two put ten thousand to flight, except their Rock had sold them, and the LORD had shut them up? (31) For their rock is not as our Rock, even our enemies themselves being judges. (32) For their vine is of the vine of Sodom, and of the fields of Gomorrah: their grapes are grapes of gall, their clusters are bitter: (33) their wine is the poison of dragons, and the cruel venom of asps. (34) Is not this laid up in store with me, and sealed up among my treasures? (35) To me belongeth vengeance, and recompence; their foot shall slide in due time: for the day of their calamity is at hand, and the things that shall come upon them make haste. (36) For the LORD shall judge his people, and repent himself for his servants, when he seeth that their power is gone, and there is none shut up, or left. (37) And he shall say, Where are their gods, their rock in whom they trusted, (38) which did eat the fat of their sacrifices, and drank the wine of their drink offerings? Let them rise up and help you, and be your protection. (39) See now that I, even I, am he, and there is no god with me: I kill, and I make alive; I wound, and I heal: neither is there any that can deliver out of my hand. (40) For I lift up my hand to heaven, and say, I live forever. (41) If I whet my glittering sword, and mine hand take hold on judgment; I will render vengeance to mine enemies, and will reward them that hate me. (42) I will make mine arrows drunk with blood, and my sword shall devour flesh; **<u>and that with the blood of the slain and of the captives, from the beginning of revenges upon the enemy. (43) Rejoice, O ye nations, with his people: for he will avenge the blood of his servants, and will render vengeance to his adversaries, and will be merciful unto his land, and to his people</u>**.

If Paul, in *Romans 15:10* were referring to non-Israelite Gentiles—calling on them to rejoice—why would he quote a scripture about TMH raining vengeance upon non-Israelite Gentiles? *Deuteronomy 32:43* outlines how TMH will take vengeance on the heathen not only because of their cruelty to His people, but also because they wickedly believe—to this day—that Israel's downfall was by their own power. TMH is making a case for non-Israelites to see past their pride—that one man can't chase a thousand men unless an almighty God had given them into his hand. In other words, the only reason non-Israelites were able to subject, oppress, kill, and manipulate the children of Israel is because TMH allowed it.

This is why TMH is vowing retribution in *Deuteronomy 32:43*. The heathen is destined to fall by TMH's hand, which is what is happening today. The God of Israel is taking vengeance on Israel's oppressors just as He promised in His word. *(Jeremiah 30:16-24)* So the scattered, who TMH cut off and said they were not His people *(Hosea 1:9)* will finally taste reconciliation and mercy.

EZEKIEL 37:18-23—(18) And when the children of thy people shall speak unto thee, saying, Wilt thou not shew us what thou meanest by these? (19) Say unto them, Thus saith the Lord GOD; Behold, I will take the stick of Joseph, which is in the hand of Ephraim, and the tribes of Israel his fellows, and will put them with him, even with the stick of Judah, and make them one stick, and they shall be one in mine hand. (20) And the sticks whereon thou writest shall be in thine hand before their eyes. (21) And say unto them, Thus saith the Lord GOD; Behold, I will take the children of Israel from among the heathen, whither they be gone, and will gather them on every side, and bring them into their own land: (22) And I will make them one nation in the land upon the mountains of Israel; and one king shall be king to them all: and they shall be no more two nations, neither shall they be divided into two kingdoms any more at all: (23) Neither shall they defile themselves any more with their idols, nor with their detestable things, nor with any of their transgressions: but I will save them out of all their dwelling places, wherein they have sinned, and will cleanse them: so shall they be my people, and I will be their God.

Because of this, the lost sheep will be called TMH's people again:

HOSEA 1:10—Yet the number of the children of Israel shall be as the sand of the sea, which cannot be measured nor numbered; and it shall come to pass, that in the place where it was said unto them, Ye are not my people, there it shall be said unto them, Ye are the sons of the living God.

These are the promises made to Israel and to the fathers, as recorded in *Isaiah 61* and *Luke* chapter 1. That TMH would deliver His people from their enemies and all who hate them—in essence, salvation to Israel. This is what compels the scattered to rejoice *with* His people because they will be saved from the lands of their captivity *(Jeremiah 30:9-11)* and reconciled/grafted in/reunited *(Romans 11:17-24)* with their brethren to become one tree, one nation.

ROMANS 15:11
And again, Praise the Lord, all ye Gentiles; and laud him, all ye people.

PSALMS 117:1-2—(1) O praise the LORD, all ye nations: praise him, all ye people. (2) For his merciful kindness is great toward us: and the truth of the LORD endureth forever. Praise ye the LORD.

PSALMS 67:1-7—(1) God be merciful unto us, and bless us; and cause his face to shine upon us; Selah. (2) That thy way may be known upon earth, thy saving health among all nations. (3) Let the people praise thee, O God; let all the people praise thee. (4) O let the nations be glad and sing for joy: for thou shalt judge the people righteously, and govern the nations upon earth. Selah. (5) Let the people praise thee, O God; let all the people praise thee. (6) Then shall the earth yield her increase; and God, even our own God, shall bless us. (7) God shall bless us; and all the ends of the earth shall fear him.

(For a breakdown on this use of 'Gentiles' in Romans 15:11, see the commentary on Romans 15:9 and Romans 15:10, pgs. 388-389)

ROMANS 15:12
And again, Esaias saith, There shall be a root of Jesse, and he that shall rise to reign over the Gentiles; in him shall the Gentiles trust.

Here, Paul is quoting *Isaiah 11:10*. The root of Jesse is Messiah, and the Gentiles who will trust Him are the scattered lost sheep of the house of Israel and Judah.

Here's the whole chapter *in context*:

ISAIAH 11:1-16—(1) <u>And there shall come forth a rod out of the stem of Jesse, and a Branch shall grow out of his roots</u>: (2) And the spirit of the LORD shall rest upon him, the spirit of wisdom and understanding, the spirit of counsel and might, the spirit of knowledge and of the fear of the LORD; (3) And shall make him of quick understanding in the fear of the LORD: and he shall not judge after the sight of his eyes, neither reprove after the hearing of his ears: (4) But with righteousness shall he judge the poor, and reprove with equity for the meek of the earth: and he shall smite the earth with the rod of his mouth, and with the breath of his lips shall he slay the wicked. (5) And righteousness shall be the girdle of his loins, and faithfulness the girdle of his reins. (6) The wolf also shall dwell with the lamb, and the leopard shall lie down with the kid; and the calf and the young lion and the fatling together; and a little child shall lead them. (7) And the cow and the bear shall feed; their young ones shall lie down together: and the lion shall eat straw like the ox. (8) And the sucking child shall play on the hole of the asp, and the weaned child shall put his hand on the cockatrice' den. (9) They shall not hurt nor destroy in all my holy mountain: for the earth shall be full of the knowledge of the LORD, as the waters cover the sea. (10) <u>And in that day there shall be a root of Jesse, which shall stand for an ensign of the people; to it shall the Gentiles seek: and his rest shall be glorious.</u> (11) And it shall come to pass in <u>that day, that the Lord shall set his hand again the second time to recover the remnant of his people, which shall be left, from Assyria, and from Egypt, and from Pathros, and from Cush, and from Elam, and from Shinar, and from Hamath, and from the islands of the sea.</u> (12) <u>And he shall set up an ensign for the nations, and shall assemble the outcasts of Israel, and gather together the dispersed of Judah from the four corners of the earth.</u> (13) <u>The envy also of Ephraim shall depart, and the adversaries of Judah shall be cut off: Ephraim shall not envy Judah, and Judah shall not vex Ephraim.</u> (14) <u>But they shall fly upon the shoulders of the Philistines toward the west; they shall spoil them of the east together: they shall lay their hand upon Edom and Moab; and the children of Ammon shall obey them.</u> (15) <u>And the LORD shall utterly destroy the tongue of the Egyptian sea; and with his mighty wind shall he shake his hand over the river, and shall smite it in the seven streams, and make men go over dryshod.</u> (16) <u>And there shall be an highway for the remnant of his people, which shall be left, from Assyria; like as it was to Israel in the day that he came up out of the land of Egypt.</u>

Paul quoted this scripture because it aligns with the point he began in the previous verses. That TMH's mercy would come to the Israelite Gentiles scattered abroad. That He would gather them from amongst the heathen nations where they were scattered, *(Ezekiel 34:13)* that they'd be reconciled as one nation instead of two *(Ezekiel 37:18-23)* and would find rest. *(Hebrews 4:1-11)*

For a breakdown on this use of 'Gentiles' in Romans 15:12, see the commentary on Romans 15:9 and Romans 15:10, pgs. 388-389)

ROMANS 15:13-14
(13) Now the God of hope fill you with all joy and peace in believing, that ye may abound in hope, through the power of the Holy Ghost. (14) And I myself also am persuaded of you, my brethren, that ye also are full of goodness, filled with all knowledge, able also to admonish one another.

ROMANS 12:12—Rejoicing in hope; patient in tribulation; continuing instant in prayer.

ROMANS 14:17—For the kingdom of God is not meat and drink; but righteousness, and peace, and joy in the Holy Ghost.

1 CORINTHIANS 1:5—That in every thing ye are enriched by him, in all utterance, and in all knowledge

1 JOHN 2:21—I have not written unto you because ye know not the truth, but because ye know it, and that no lie is of the truth.

JAMES 5:16—Confess your faults one to another, and pray one for another, that ye may be healed. The effectual fervent prayer of a righteous man availeth much

ROMANS 15:15
Nevertheless, brethren, I have written the more boldly unto you in some sort, as putting you in mind, because of the grace that is given to me of God,

ROMANS 1:5-6—(5) By whom we have received grace and apostleship, for obedience to the faith among all nations, for his name: (6) Among whom are ye also the called of Jesus Christ:

1 CORINTHIANS 9:2—If I be not an apostle unto others, yet doubtless I am to you: for the seal of mine apostleship are ye in the Lord.

ROMANS 15:31—That I may be delivered from them that do not believe in Judaea; and that my service which I have for Jerusalem may be accepted of the saints.

ACTS 13:1-3—(1) Now there were in the church that was at Antioch certain prophets and teachers; as Barnabas, and Simeon that was called Niger, and Lucius of Cyrene, and Manaen, which had been brought up with Herod the tetrarch, and Saul. (2) As they ministered to the Lord, and fasted, the Holy Ghost said, Separate me Barnabas and Saul for the work whereunto I have called them. (3) And when they had fasted and prayed, and laid their hands on them, they sent them away.

ROMANS 15:16 [a]
That I should be the minister of Jesus Christ to the Gentiles, ministering the gospel of God, that the offering up of the Gentiles might be acceptable, being sanctified by the Holy Ghost.

ROMANS 11:13—For I speak to you Gentiles, inasmuch as I am the apostle of the Gentiles, I magnify mine office.

GALATIANS 2:8—For he that wrought effectually in Peter to the apostleship of the circumcision, the same was mighty in me toward the Gentiles.

Let's look at *Acts 9:15* where Paul's calling is defined:

ACTS 9:15—But the Lord said unto him, Go thy way: for he is a chosen vessel unto me, to bear [*bastazó (βαστάζω)*] my name before the Gentiles, and kings, and the children of Israel.

STRONG'S #941: "bear"—*bastazó (βαστάζω)*
Definition: to take up, carry
Usage: (a) I carry, bear, (b) I carry (take) away

The same word *bastazó (βαστάζω)* is used in *Matthew 3:11:* "I indeed baptize you with water unto repentance: but he that cometh after me is mightier than I, whose shoes I am not worthy to bear"

Now, back to Acts 9:15: "*...to bear my name before the Gentiles...*"

STRONG'S #1799: "before"—enópios (ἐνώπιον)
Definition: in sight of, before
Usage: before the face of, in the presence of, in the eyes of

This word is also used in James 4:10: "Humble yourselves in the sight of the Lord, and he shall lift you up"

So, with these points in mind, Paul was called to stand in the presence of the nations, kings, and the children of Israel, bearing TMH's name.

ISAIAH 52:15—So shall he sprinkle many nations; the kings shall shut their mouths at him: for that which had not been told them shall they see; and that which they had not heard shall they consider.

What else do the scriptures say the Messiah and the apostle's mission would be? What *message* were they to deliver "*before the Gentiles, and kings, and the children of Israel*"?

That *message* would be the gospel of the kingdom:

LUKE 1:67-79—(67) And his father Zacharias was filled with the Holy Ghost, and prophesied, saying, (68) Blessed be the Lord God of Israel; for he hath visited and redeemed his people, (69) And hath raised up an horn of salvation for us in the house of his servant David; (70) As he spake by the mouth of his holy prophets, which have been since the world began: (71) That we should be saved from our enemies, and from the hand of all that hate us; (72) To perform the mercy promised to our fathers, and to remember his holy covenant; (73) The oath which he sware to our father Abraham, (74) That he would grant unto us, that we being delivered out of the hand of our enemies might serve him without fear, (75) In holiness and righteousness before him, all the days of our life. (76) And thou, child, shalt be called the prophet of the Highest: for thou shalt go before the face of the Lord to prepare his ways; (77) To give knowledge of salvation unto his people by the remission of their sins, (78) Through the tender mercy of our God; whereby the dayspring from on high hath visited us, (79) To give light to them that sit in darkness and in the shadow of death, to guide our feet into the way of peace. *(See also Isaiah 61)*

This gospel of the kingdom was hardly "good news" to the kings, queens, principalities, powers, non-Israelites, and wicked Israelites who loved this evil world. It meant the destruction of their kingdom, a kingdom built from the fall of the Israelites. It meant the beginning of the kingdom of TMH.

ADDITIONS TO ESTHER 10:5-11—(5) For I remember a dream which I saw concerning these matters, and nothing thereof hath failed. (6) A little fountain became a river, and there was light, and the sun, and much water: this river is Esther, whom the king married, and made queen: (7) And the two dragons are I and Aman. (8) And the nations were those that were assembled to destroy the name of the Jews: (9) And my nation is this Israel, which cried to God, and were saved: for the Lord hath saved his people, and the Lord hath delivered us from all those evils, and God hath wrought signs and great wonders, which have not been done among the Gentiles. (10) Therefore hath he made two lots, one for the people of God, and another for all the Gentiles. (11) And these two lots came at the hour, and time, and day of judgment, before God among all nations.

Considering all this, we must ask ourselves why would King Herod (an Edomite) try to murder the Messiah by killing all male Israelite children, newborns to two years old? *(Matthew 2:7-18)* Why did the Greeks paint over Israelite images with their own, *(1 Maccabees 3:46-50)* and demand TMH's people abandon His laws? *(1 Maccabees 1:41-42)* Why was Paul imprisoned *(Acts 28:16, 30; Ephesians 6:20)* and why were many of the apostles and disciples martyred? *(Matthew 24:9; Mark 10:39; John 21:18–19)* Why did the nations, even before all this, team up to destroy TMH's people from the beginning? *(Psalms 83)* Why were the Israelites enslaved, oppressed, and killed by non-Israelites worldwide? *(Deuteronomy 28:15-68)* AND why is this gospel of the kingdom being met with such strong opposition today?

Why? Because it's not the lollypops and unicorns gospel contemporary Christianity preaches. The true gospel of the kingdom is one where the first will be last and the last will be first. "For Esau is the end of the world, and Jacob is the beginning of it that followeth." *(2 Esdras 6:9)*

The coming of the kingdom of heaven means the end of non-Israelite Gentile rule. Therefore, again, this gospel was/is hardly good news to them. Yet it was Paul's main mission. As a representative of TMH, he went before kings, queens, and rulers of the lands that Israelite Gentiles were scattered. No, Paul was not sent to target non-Israelites. He was sent to the lost sheep of the House of Israel to give them beauty for ashes, *(Isaiah 61:3)* to tell them their God hadn't abandoned them, *(Isaiah 49:15-16)* and that they'd soon take their rightful place of rulership under the righteous lamb of God. *(Exodus 19:6, Revelation 1:6)*

> **ROMANS 9:4-5**—(4) Who are Israelites; to whom pertaineth the adoption, and the glory, and the covenants, and the giving of the law, and the service of God, and the promises; (5) whose are the fathers, and of whom as concerning the flesh Christ came, who is over all, God blessed for ever. Amen.

That said, I must reiterate that yes, the gospel of the kingdom was to the lost sheep of the house of Israel, however faithful, and sincere non-Israelites were always welcome to worship TMH. This is a fact of biblical history, going back to the mixed multitude out of Egypt, Rahab the prostitute, and the Gibeonites, etc. It was also true in the apostle's time and it is just as true today.

(To read more about non-Israelites within the Kingdom of TMH, see The Strangers Among Us, pg. 426.)

ROMANS 15:16 [b]
That I should be the minister of Jesus Christ to the Gentiles, ministering the gospel of God, that the offering up of the Gentiles might be acceptable, being sanctified by the Holy Ghost.

> **ISAIAH 66:20**—And they shall bring all your brethren for an offering unto the LORD out of all nations upon horses, and in chariots, and in litters, and upon mules, and upon swift beasts, to my holy mountain Jerusalem, saith the LORD, as the children of Israel bring an offering in a clean vessel into the house of the LORD.

> **ROMANS 8:28-30**—(28) And we know that all things work together for good to them that love God, to them who are the called according to his purpose. (29) For whom he did foreknow, he also did predestinate to be

conformed to the image of his Son, that he might be the firstborn among many brethren. (30) Moreover whom he did predestinate, them he also called: and whom he called, them he also justified: and whom he justified, them he also glorified.

ROMANS 9:4-5—(4) Who are Israelites; to whom pertaineth the adoption, and the glory, and the covenants, and the giving of the law, and the service of God, and the promises; (5) Whose are the fathers, and of whom as concerning the flesh Christ came, who is over all, God blessed for ever. Amen.

ROMANS 15:17-19

(17) **I have therefore whereof I may glory through Jesus Christ in those things which pertain to God.** (18) **For I will not dare to speak of any of those things which Christ hath not wrought by me, to make the Gentiles obedient, by word and deed,** (19) **Through mighty signs and wonders, by the power of the Spirit of God; so that from Jerusalem, and round about unto Illyricum, I have fully preached the gospel of Christ.**

ACTS 15:12—Then all the multitude kept silence, and gave audience to Barnabas and Paul, declaring what miracles and wonders God had wrought among the Gentiles by them.

ACTS 19:11—And God wrought special miracles by the hands of Paul

ACTS 21:19—And when he had saluted them, he declared particularly what things God had wrought among the Gentiles by his ministry.

GALATIANS 2:8—For he that wrought effectually in Peter to the apostleship of the circumcision, the same was mighty in me toward the Gentiles.

ROMANS 15:20-21

(20) **Yea, so have I strived to preach the gospel, not where Christ was named, lest I should build upon another man's foundation:** (21) **But as it is written, To whom he was not spoken of, they shall see: and they that have not heard shall understand.**

ISAIAH 52:6-15—(6) Therefore my people shall know my name: therefore they shall know in that day that I am he that doth speak: behold, it is I. (7) How beautiful upon the mountains are the feet of him that bringeth good tidings, that publisheth peace; that bringeth good tidings of good, that publisheth salvation; that saith unto Zion, Thy God reigneth! (8) Thy watchmen shall lift up the voice; with the voice together shall they sing: for they shall see eye to eye, when the LORD shall bring again Zion. (9) Break forth into joy, sing together, ye waste places of Jerusalem: for the LORD hath comforted his people, he hath redeemed Jerusalem. (10) The LORD hath made bare his holy arm in the eyes of all the nations; and all the ends of the earth shall see the salvation of our God. (11) Depart ye, depart ye, go ye out from thence, touch no unclean thing; go ye out of the midst of her; be ye clean, that bear the vessels of the LORD. (12) For ye shall not go out with haste, nor go by flight: for the LORD will go before you; and the God of Israel will be your rereward. (13) Behold, my servant shall deal prudently, he shall be exalted and extolled, and be very high. (14) As many were astonied at thee; his visage was so marred more than any man, and his form more than the sons of men: (15) So shall he sprinkle many nations; the kings shall shut their mouths at him: for that which had not been told them shall they see; and that which they had not heard shall they consider.

1 CORINTHIANS 3:10—According to the grace of God, which is given unto me, as a wise master builder, I have laid the foundation, and another buildeth thereon. But let every man take heed how he buildeth thereupon.

2 CORINTHIANS 10:13-16—(13) But we will not boast of things without our measure, but according to the measure of the rule which God hath distributed to us, a measure to reach even unto you. (14) For we stretch not ourselves beyond our measure, as though we reached not unto you: for we are come as far as to you also in preaching the gospel of Christ: (15) Not boasting of things without our measure, that is, of other men's labors; but having hope, when your faith is increased, that we shall be enlarged by you according to our rule abundantly, (16) To preach the gospel in the [regions] beyond you, and not to boast in another man's line of things made ready to our hand.

ROMANS 15:22-25

(22) For which cause also I have been much hindered from coming to you. (23) But now having no more place in these parts, and having a great desire these many years to come unto you; (24) Whensoever I take my journey into Spain, I will come to you: for I trust to see you in my journey, and to be brought on my way thitherward by you, if first I be somewhat filled with your company. (25) But now I go unto Jerusalem to minister unto the saints.

ROMANS 1:11-13—(11) For I long to see you, that I may impart unto you some spiritual gift, to the end ye may be established; (12) That is, that I may be comforted together with you by the mutual faith both of you and me. (13) Now I would not have you ignorant, brethren, that oftentimes I purposed to come unto you, (but was let hitherto,) that I might have some fruit among you also, even as among other Gentiles.

ACTS 15:3—And being brought on their way by the church, they passed through Phenice and Samaria, declaring the conversion of the Gentiles: and they caused great joy unto all the brethren.

ACTS 19:21—After these things were ended, Paul purposed in the spirit, when he had passed through Macedonia and Achaia, to go to Jerusalem, saying, After I have been there, I must also see Rome.

ACTS 20:3—And there abode three months. And when the Jews laid wait for him, as he was about to sail into Syria, he purposed to return through Macedonia.

ACTS 20:22—And now, behold, I go bound in the spirit unto Jerusalem, not knowing the things that shall befall me there.

ACTS 23:11—And the night following the Lord stood by him, and said, Be of good cheer, Paul: for as thou hast testified of me in Jerusalem, so must thou bear witness also at Rome.

1 THESSALONIANS 2:17-18—(17) But we, brethren, being taken from you for a short time in presence, not in heart, endeavored the more abundantly to see your face with great desire. (18) Wherefore we would have come unto you, even I Paul, once and again; but Satan hindered us.

ROMANS 15:26-29

(26) **For it hath pleased them of Macedonia and Achaia to make a certain contribution for the poor saints which are at Jerusalem.** (27) **It hath pleased them verily; and their debtors they are. For if the Gentiles have been made partakers of their spiritual things, their duty is also to minister unto them in carnal things.** (28) **When therefore I have performed this, and have sealed to them this fruit, I will come by you into Spain.** (29) **And I am sure that, when I come unto you, I shall come in the fullness of the blessing of the gospel of Christ.**

ACTS 24:17—Now after many years I came to bring alms to my nation, and offerings.

1 CORINTHIANS 9:11—If we have sown unto you spiritual things, is it a great thing if we shall reap your carnal things?

1 CORINTHIANS 16:1—Now concerning the collection for the saints, as I have given order to the churches of Galatia, even so do ye.

PHILIPPIANS 4:17—Not because I desire a gift: but I desire fruit that may abound to your account.

ROMANS 1:11-13—(11) For I long to see you, that I may impart unto you some spiritual gift, to the end ye may be established; (12) That is, that I may be comforted together with you by the mutual faith both of you and me. (13) Now I would not have you ignorant, brethren, that oftentimes I purposed to come unto you, (but was let hitherto,) that I might have some fruit among you also, even as among other Gentiles.

1 THESSALONIANS 1:7-8—(7) So that ye were ensamples to all that believe in Macedonia and Achaia. (8) For from you sounded out the word of the Lord not only in Macedonia and Achaia, but also in every place your faith to God-ward is spread abroad; so that we need not to speak any thing.

2 CORINTHIANS 11:10—As the truth of Christ is in me, no man shall stop me of this boasting in the regions of Achaia.

ROMANS 15:30-32

(30) Now I beseech you, brethren, for the Lord Jesus Christ's sake, and for the love of the Spirit, that ye strive together with me in your prayers to God for me; (31) That I may be delivered from them that do not believe in Judaea; and that my service which I have for Jerusalem may be accepted of the saints; (32) That I may come unto you with joy by the will of God, and may with you be refreshed. (33) Now the God of peace be with you all. Amen.

ACTS 18:21—But bade them farewell, saying, I must by all means keep this feast that cometh in Jerusalem: but I will return again unto you, if God will. And he sailed from Ephesus.

ACTS 20:22-23—(22) And now, behold, I go bound in the spirit unto Jerusalem, not knowing the things that shall befall me there: (23) Save that the Holy Ghost witnesseth in every city, saying that bonds and afflictions abide me.

ROMANS 1:10—Making request, if by any means now at length I might have a prosperous journey by the will of God to come unto you.

1 CORINTHIANS 16:18—For they have refreshed my spirit and yours: therefore acknowledge ye them that are such.

2 CORINTHIANS 1:10-11—(10) Who delivered us from so great a death, and doth deliver: in whom we trust that he will yet deliver us; (11) Ye also helping together by prayer for us, that for the gift bestowed upon us by the means of many persons thanks may be given by many on our behalf.

2 CORINTHIANS 8:4—Praying us with much intreaty that we would receive the gift, and take upon us the fellowship of the ministering to the saints.

COLOSSIANS 4:12—Epaphras, who is one of you, a servant of Christ, saluteth you, always laboring fervently for you in prayers, that ye may stand perfect and complete in all the will of God.

2 THESSALONIANS 3:2—And that we may be delivered from unreasonable and wicked men: for all men have not faith.

2 TIMOTHY 3:11—Persecutions, afflictions, which came unto me at Antioch, at Iconium, at Lystra; what persecutions I endured: but out of them all the Lord delivered me.

2 TIMOTHY 4:17—Notwithstanding the Lord stood with me, and strengthened me; that by me the preaching might be fully known, and that all the Gentiles might hear: and I was delivered out of the mouth of the lion.

ROMANS 16

ROMANS 16:1-4

(1) I commend unto you Phebe our sister, which is a servant of the church which is at Cenchrea: (2) That ye receive her in the Lord, as becometh saints, and that ye assist her in whatsoever business she hath need of you: for she hath been a succourer of many, and of myself also. (3) Greet <u>Priscilla and Aquila</u> my helpers in Christ Jesus: (4) Who have for my life laid down their own necks: unto whom not only I give thanks, but also all the churches of the Gentiles.

> **ACTS 18:2, 18**—(2) And found <u>a certain Jew named Aquila</u>, born in Pontus, lately come from Italy, <u>with his wife Priscilla</u>; (because that Claudius had commanded all Jews to depart from Rome:) and came unto them...(18) And Paul after this tarried there yet a good while, and then took his leave of the brethren, and sailed thence into Syria, and with him <u>Priscilla and Aquila</u>; having shorn his head in Cenchrea: for he had a vow.
>
> **ACTS 18:26**—And he began to speak boldly in the synagogue: whom when <u>Aquila and Priscilla had heard, they took him unto them, and expounded unto him the way of God more perfectly</u>.
>
> **1 CORINTHIANS 16:19**—The churches of Asia salute you. <u>Aquila and Priscilla</u> salute you much in the Lord, with the church that is in their house.
>
> **PHILIPPIANS 4:3**—And I entreat thee also, true yokefellow, help those women which labored with me in the gospel, with Clement also, and with other my fellow laborers, whose names are in the book of life.

(1 Corinthians 16:19; 2 Timothy 4:19)

ROMANS 16:5-9

(5) Likewise greet the <u>church that is in their house</u>. Salute my well-beloved Epaenetus, who <u>is the firstfruits of Achaia</u> unto Christ. (6) Greet Mary, who bestowed much labor on us. (7) Salute Andronicus and Junia, <u>my kinsmen</u>, and my fellow prisoners, who are of note among the <u>apostles</u>, who also

were in Christ before me. (8) Greet Amplias my beloved in the Lord. (9) Salute Urbane, our helper in Christ, and Stachys my beloved.

1 CORINTHIANS 16:15, 19—(15) I beseech you, brethren, (ye know the house of Stephanas, that it is the firstfruits of Achaia, and that they have addicted themselves to the ministry of the saints,)...(19) The churches of Asia salute you. Aquila and Priscilla salute you much in the Lord, with the church that is in their house.

ACTS 1:13, 26—(13) And when they were come in, they went up into an upper room, where abode both Peter, and James, and John, and Andrew, Philip, and Thomas, Bartholomew, and Matthew, James the son of Alphaeus, and Simon Zelotes, and Judas the brother of James...(26) And they gave forth their lots; and the lot fell upon Matthias; and he was numbered with the eleven apostles.

ROMANS 16:11, 21—(11) Salute Herodion my kinsman. Greet them that be of the household of Narcissus, which are in the Lord...(21) Timotheus my workfellow, and Lucius, and Jason, and Sosipater, my kinsmen, salute you.

ROMANS 16:10-16

(10) Salute Apelles approved in Christ. Salute them, which are of Aristobulus' household. (11) Salute Herodion my kinsman. Greet them that be of the household of Narcissus, which are in the Lord. (12) Salute Tryphena and Tryphosa, who labor in the Lord. Salute the beloved Persis, which labored much in the Lord. (13) Salute Rufus chosen in the Lord, and his mother and mine. (14) Salute Asyncritus, Phlegon, Hermas, Patrobas, Hermes, and the brethren, which are with them. (15) Salute Philologus, and Julia, Nereus, and his sister, and Olympas, and all the saints, which are with them. (16) Salute one another with an holy kiss. The churches of Christ salute you.

PSALMS 50:5—Gather my saints together unto me; those that have made a covenant with me by sacrifice.

PSALMS 148:14—He also exalteth the horn of his people, the praise of all His saints; even of the children of Israel, a people near unto Him. Praise ye the LORD.

WISDOM OF SOLOMON 4:15—This the people saw, and understood it not, neither laid they up this in their minds, That his grace and mercy is with his saints, and that he hath respect unto his chosen.

ROMANS 16:2—That ye receive her in the Lord, as becometh saints, and that ye assist her in whatsoever business she hath need of you: for she hath been a succourer of many, and of myself also.

MARK 15:21—And they compel one Simon a Cyrenian, who passed by, coming out of the country, the father of Alexander and Rufus, to bear his cross.

ROMANS 16:17
Now I beseech you, brethren, mark them which cause divisions and offences contrary to the doctrine which ye have learned; and avoid them.

2 THESSALONIANS 3:14—And if any man obey not our word by this epistle, note that man, and have no company with him, that he may be ashamed.

1 CORINTHIANS 3:3—For ye are yet carnal: for whereas there is among you envying, and strife, and divisions, are ye not carnal, and walk as men?

2 THESSALONIANS 3:6—Now we command you, brethren, in the name of our Lord Jesus Christ, that ye withdraw yourselves from every brother that walketh disorderly, and not after the tradition which he received of us.

TITUS 3:10—A man that is an heretic after the first and second admonition reject.

ROMANS 14:13—Let us not therefore judge one another any more: but judge this rather, that no man put a stumbling block or an occasion to fall in his brother's way.

ROMANS 16:18
For they that are such serve not our Lord Jesus Christ, but their own belly; and by good words and fair speeches deceive the hearts of the simple.

MATTHEW 7:15—Beware of false prophets. They come to you in sheep's clothing, but inwardly they are ravenous wolves.

PHILIPPIANS 3:17-19—(17) Brethren, be followers together of me, and mark them which walk so as ye have us for an ensample. (18) For many walk, of whom I have told you often, and now tell you even weeping, that they are the enemies of the cross of Christ: (19) Whose end is destruction, whose God is their belly, and whose glory is in their shame, who mind earthly things.

COLOSSIANS 2:4, 8—(4) And this I say, lest any man should beguile you with enticing words...(8) Beware lest any man spoil you through philosophy and vain deceit, after the tradition of men, after the rudiments of the world, and not after Christ.

2 TIMOTHY 3:6-9—(6) For of this sort are they which creep into houses, and lead captive silly women laden with sins, led away with divers lusts, (7) Ever learning, and never able to come to the knowledge of the truth. (8) Now as Jannes and Jambres withstood Moses, so do these also resist the truth: men of corrupt minds, reprobate concerning the faith. (9) But they shall proceed no further: for their folly shall be manifest unto all men, as theirs also was.

2 TIMOTHY 4:3—For the time will come when they will not endure sound doctrine; but after their own lusts shall they heap to themselves teachers, having itching ears...

2 PETER 2:1-3—(1) But there were false prophets also among the people, even as there shall be false teachers among you, who privily shall bring in damnable heresies, even denying the Lord that bought them, and bring upon themselves swift destruction. (2) And many shall follow their pernicious ways; by reason of whom the way of truth shall be evil spoken of. (3) And through covetousness shall they with feigned words make merchandise of you: whose judgment now of a long time lingereth not, and their damnation slumbereth not.

1 JOHN 4:1—Beloved, believe not every spirit, but try the spirits whether they are of God: because many false prophets are gone out into the world

2 JOHN 1:7—For many deceivers are entered into the world, who confess not that Jesus Christ is come in the flesh. This is a deceiver and an antichrist.

JUDE 1:4—For there are certain men crept in unawares, who were before of old ordained to this condemnation, ungodly men, turning the grace of our God into lasciviousness, and denying the only Lord God, and our Lord Jesus Christ.

(1 Kings 13:18-19; Jeremiah 14:14; 23:16; 29:8; 1 John 2:18, 26, 4:2)

ROMANS 16:19-20

(19) For your obedience is come abroad unto all men. I am glad therefore on your behalf: but yet I would have you wise unto that which is good, and simple concerning evil. (20) And the God of peace shall bruise Satan under your feet shortly. The grace of our Lord Jesus Christ be with you. Amen.

GENESIS 3:15—And I will put enmity between thee and the woman, and between thy seed and her seed; it shall bruise thy head, and thou shalt bruise his heel.

PSALMS 91:11-13—(11) For he shall give his angels charge over thee, to keep thee in all thy ways. (12) They shall bear thee up in their hands, lest thou dash thy foot against a stone. (13) Thou shalt tread upon the lion and adder: the young lion and the dragon shalt thou trample under feet.

LUKE 10:19—Behold, I give unto you power to tread on serpents and scorpions, and over all the power of the enemy: and nothing shall by any means hurt you.

ISAIAH 27:1—In that day the LORD with his sore and great and strong sword shall punish leviathan the piercing serpent, even leviathan that crooked serpent; and he shall slay the dragon that is in the sea

MATTHEW 10:16—Behold, I send you forth as sheep in the midst of wolves: be ye therefore wise as serpents, and harmless as doves.

PSALMS 74:14—Thou brakest the heads of leviathan in pieces, and gavest him to be meat to the people inhabiting the wilderness

REVELATION 20:1-3, 7-10—(1) And I saw an angel come down from heaven, having the key of the bottomless pit and a great chain in his hand. (2) And he laid hold on the dragon, that old serpent, which is the Devil, and Satan, and bound him a thousand years, (3) And cast him into the bottomless pit, and shut him up, and set a seal upon him, that he should deceive the nations no more, till the thousand years should be fulfilled: and after that he must be loosed a little season…(7) And when the thousand years are expired, Satan shall be loosed out of his prison, (8) And shall go out to deceive the nations which are in the four quarters of the earth, Gog and Magog, to gather them together to battle: the number of whom is as the sand of the sea. (9) And they went up on the breadth of the earth, and compassed the camp of the saints about, and the beloved city: and fire came down from God out of heaven, and devoured them. (10) And the devil that deceived them was cast into the lake of fire and brimstone, where the beast and the false prophet are, and shall be tormented day and night forever and ever.

1 CORINTHIANS 14:20—Brethren, be not children in understanding: howbeit in malice be ye children, but in understanding be men.

ROMANS 15:33—Now the God of peace be with you all. Amen.

1 CORINTHIANS 16:23—The grace of our Lord Jesus Christ be with you.

TARGUM JONATHAN/PALESTINE ON GENESIS III, pg. 166—And the Lord God brought the three unto judgment; and He said to the serpent, Because thou hast done this, cursed art thou of all the cattle, and of all the beasts of the field: upon thy belly thou shalt go, and thy feet shall be cut off, and thy skin thou shalt cast away once in seven years; and the poison of death shall be in thy mouth, and dust shalt thou eat all the days of thy life. And I will put enmity between thee and the woman, and between the seed of thy son, and the seed of her sons; and it shall be when the sons of the woman keep the commandments of the law, they will be prepared to smite thee upon thy head; but when they forsake the commandments of the law, thou wilt be ready to wound them in the heel. Nevertheless, for them there shall be a medicine, but for thee there shall be no medicine, and they shall make a remedy for the heel in the days of the King Meshiba.

TARGUM ONKELOS ON GENESIS III, pg. 41—And the Lord God said to the serpent, Because thou hast done this, more accursed art thou than all cattle, and then all the beasts of the field; upon thy belly shalt thou go, and the dust shalt thou eat all the days of thy life. And I will put enmity between thee and between the woman, and between thy son and here son. He will remember thee, what thou didst to them from the beginning, and thou shalt be observant unto him at the end.

ROMANS 16:21
Timotheus my workfellow, and Lucius, and Jason, and Sosipater, my kinsmen, salute you.

ACTS 13:1—Now there were in the church that was at Antioch certain prophets and teachers; as Barnabas, and Simeon that was called Niger, and Lucius of Cyrene, and Manaen, which had been brought up with Herod the tetrarch, and Saul.

ACTS 16:1—Then came he to Derbe and Lystra: and, behold, a certain disciple was there, named Timotheus, the son of a certain woman, which was a Jewess, and believed; but his father was a Greek.

ACTS 17:5-9—(5) But the Jews which believed not, moved with envy, took unto them certain lewd fellows of the baser sort, and gathered a company, and set all the city on an uproar, and assaulted the house of Jason, and sought to bring them out to the people. (6) And when they found them not, they drew Jason and certain brethren unto the rulers of the city, crying, These that have turned the world upside down are come hither also (7) Whom Jason hath received: and these all do contrary to the decrees of Caesar, saying that there is another king, one Jesus. (8) And they troubled the people and the rulers of the city, when they heard these things. (9) And when they had taken security of Jason, and of the other, they let them go.

ACTS 19:22—So he sent into Macedonia two of them that ministered unto him, Timotheus and Erastus; but he himself stayed in Asia for a season.

ACTS 20:4—And there accompanied him into Asia Sopater of Berea; and of the Thessalonians, Aristarchus and Secundus; and Gaius of Derbe, and Timotheus; and of Asia, Tychicus and Trophimus.

1 CORINTHIANS 4:17—For this cause have I sent unto you Timotheus, who is my beloved son, and faithful in the Lord, who shall bring you into remembrance of my ways which be in Christ, as I teach every where in every church.

1 CORINTHIANS 16:10—Now if Timotheus come, see that he may be with you without fear: for he worketh the work of the Lord, as I also do.

1 THESSALONIANS 3:2—But now when Timotheus came from you unto us, and brought us good tidings of your faith and charity, and that ye have good remembrance of us always, desiring greatly to see us, as we also to see you

(Acts 17:14, 15, 18:5, 20:4; 1 Corinthians 16:24; 2 Corinthians 1:19; Philippians 1:1, 2:19; Colossians 1:1; 1 Thessalonians 1:1; 3:2; 2 Thessalonians 1:1; 2 Timothy 4:22)

ROMANS 16:22-23

(22) **I Tertius, who wrote this epistle, salute you in the Lord.** (23) **Gaius mine host, and of the whole church, saluteth you. Erastus the chamberlain of the city saluteth you, and Quartus a brother.**

ACTS 19:22—So he sent into Macedonia two of them that ministered unto him, Timotheus and Erastus; but he himself stayed in Asia for a season.

ACTS 19:29—And the whole city was filled with confusion: and having caught Gaius and Aristarchus, men of Macedonia, Paul's companions in travel, they rushed with one accord into the theatre.

ACTS 20:4—And there accompanied him into Asia Sopater of Berea; and of the Thessalonians, Aristarchus and Secundus; and Gaius of Derbe, and Timotheus; and of Asia, Tychicus and Trophimus.

1 CORINTHIANS 1:14—I thank God that I baptized none of you, but Crispus and Gaius

(Acts 20:4; 3 John 1:1; 1 Corinthians 16:20; 2 Timothy 4:20)

ROMANS 16:24-25

(24) The grace of our Lord Jesus Christ be with you all. Amen. (25) Now to him that is of power to establish you according to my gospel, and the preaching of Jesus Christ, according to the revelation of the mystery, which was kept secret since the world began

ROMANS 2:16—In the day when God shall judge the secrets of men by Jesus Christ according to my gospel.

1 CORINTHIANS 2:7—But we speak the wisdom of God in a mystery, even the hidden wisdom, which God ordained before the world unto our glory.

EPHESIANS 1:9—Having made known unto us the mystery of his will, according to his good pleasure which he hath purposed in himself.

EPHESIANS 3:3-9—(3) How that by revelation he made known unto me the mystery; (as I wrote afore in few words, (4) Whereby, when ye read, ye may understand my knowledge in the mystery of Christ) (5) Which in other ages was not made known unto the sons of men, as it is now revealed unto his holy apostles and prophets by the Spirit; (6) That the Gentiles should be fellow heirs, and of the same body, and partakers of his promise in Christ by the gospel: (7) Whereof I was made a minister, according to the gift of the grace of God given unto me by the effectual working of his power. (8) Unto me, who am less than the least of all saints, is this grace given, that I should preach among the Gentiles the unsearchable riches of Christ; (9) And to make all men see what is the fellowship of the mystery, which from the beginning of the world hath been hid in God, who created all things by Jesus Christ.

COLOSSIANS 1:26-27—(26) Even the mystery which hath been hid from ages and from generations, but now is made manifest to his saints: (27) To whom God would make known what is the riches of the glory of this mystery among the Gentiles; which is Christ in you, the hope of glory.

COLOSSIANS 2:2—That their hearts might be comforted, being knit together in love, and unto all riches of the full assurance of understanding, to the acknowledgement of the mystery of God, and of the Father, and of Christ

COLOSSIANS 4:3—Withal praying also for us, that God would open unto us a door of utterance, to speak the mystery of Christ, for which I am also in bonds.

ROMANS 16:26
But now is made manifest, and by the scriptures of the prophets, according to the commandment of the everlasting God, made known to all nations for the obedience of faith:

ROMANS 1:2, 5—(2) Which he had promised afore by his prophets in the holy scriptures...(5) By whom we have received grace and apostleship, for obedience to the faith among all nations, for his name.

EPHESIANS 3:3-9—(3) How that by revelation he made known unto me the mystery; (as I wrote afore in few words, (4) Whereby, when ye read, ye may understand my knowledge in the mystery of Christ) (5) Which in other ages was not made known unto the sons of men, as it is now revealed unto his holy apostles and prophets by the Spirit; (6) That the Gentiles should be fellow heirs, and of the same body, and partakers of his promise in Christ by the gospel: (7) Whereof I was made a minister, according to the gift of the grace of God given unto me by the effectual working of his power. (8) Unto me, who am less than the least of all saints, is this grace given, that I should preach among the Gentiles the unsearchable riches of Christ; (9) And to make all [men] see what [is] the fellowship of the mystery, which from the beginning of the world hath been hid in God, who created all things by Jesus Christ.

ACTS 6:7—And the word of God increased; and the number of the disciples multiplied in Jerusalem greatly; and a great company of the priests were obedient to the faith.

ROMANS 16:27
To God only wise, be glory through Jesus Christ forever. Amen. (Written to the Romans from Corinthus, and sent by Phebe servant of the church at Cenchrea.)

1 CORINTHIANS 1:21, 24—(21) For after that in the wisdom of God the world by wisdom knew not God, it pleased God by the foolishness of preaching to save them that believe...(24) But unto them which are called, both Jews and Greeks, Christ the power of God, and the wisdom of God.

1 CORINTHIANS 2:7—But we speak the wisdom of God in a mystery, even the hidden wisdom, which God ordained before the world unto our glory

1 TIMOTHY 1:17—Now unto the King eternal, immortal, invisible, the only wise God, be honour and glory forever and ever. Amen.

JUDE 1:25—To the only wise God our Saviour, be glory and majesty, dominion and power, both now and ever. Amen.

APPENDIX 1: DEFINITIONS

> The secret things belong unto the LORD our God: but those things, which are revealed, belong unto us and to our children forever, that *we* may do all the words of this law.
> —Deuteronomy 29:29

Below you'll find a list of words used in *The Book of Romans* and/or precepts included with it. Definitions that contradict or don't fully pinpoint and/or define the intended meaning in scripture will include scriptural examples titled "Biblical Context," for clarity. For example, see below. In the definition for "Elect," Christians (as defined by contemporary Christianity and 'Replacement Theology") are *not* the Elect. That title belongs solely to the children of Israel. *(For "Greek," "Gentile," "Grecian," "Nation" etc....definition breakdowns, see The People of Romans, pg. 53)*

ELECT/CHOSEN

STRONG'S #G1588: "elect"—*eklektos* (ἐκλεκτός)
DEFINITION: select, by implication favorite
USAGE: chosen out, elect, choice, select, sometimes as subst: of those chosen out by God for the rendering of special service to Him (of the Hebrew race, particular Hebrews, the Messiah, ~~and the Christians~~).
BIBLICAL CONTEXT: "For Jacob my servant's sake, and Israel mine elect, I have even called thee by thy name: I have surnamed thee, though thou hast not known me." *(Isaiah 45:4)* | "Deliver Israel, your elect one; and those of the house of Jacob, your chosen one." *(Psalms 155:21)*

1 Peter 2:9

(**You**—Ὑμεῖς) (**however**—δὲ) (**[are] a race**—γένος) (**CHOSEN**—ἐκλεκτόν) (**a royal**—βασίλειον) (**priesthood**—ἱεράτευμα) (**a nation**—ἔθνος) (**holy**—ἅγιον) (**a people**—λαὸς) (**for [His]**—εἰς) (**possession**—περιποίησιν) (**so that**—ὅπως) (**the**—τὰς) (**excellencies**—ἀρετὰς) (**you may proclaim**—ἐξαγγείλητε) (**of the [One]**—τοῦ) (**out of**—ἐκ) (**darkness**—σκότους) (**you**—ὑμᾶς) (**having called**—καλέσαντος) (**to**—εἰς) (**the**—τὸ) (**marvelous**—θαυμαστὸν) (**of Him**—αὐτοῦ) (**light**—φῶς·)

See also: Exodus 4:22, 19:5; Deuteronomy 4:20, 7:7-8-14, 10:15, 14:2, 26:18-19, 28:1, 32:8-9; Psalms 50:5, 148:14; 2 Samuel 7:23-24; 1 Chronicles 17:21; Wisdom of Solomon 3:9, 4:15; Sirach 46:1, 47:22; Acts 13:17; 2 Baruch 48:20; Words of Gad the Seer 1:56;

FAITH

STRONG'S #G4102: "faith"—*pistis* (πίστις)
DEFINITION: faith, faithfulness
USAGE: faith, belief, trust, confidence; fidelity, faithfulness

GOSPEL

STRONG'S #G2098: "gospel"—*euaggelion* (εὐαγγέλιον)
DEFINITION: good news
USAGE: the good news of the coming of the Messiah, the gospel; the gen. after it expresses sometimes the giver (God), sometimes the subject (the Messiah, etc.), sometimes the human transmitter (an apostle).

BIBLICAL CONTEXT: "Blessed be the Lord God of Israel; for he hath visited and redeemed his people, and hath raised up an horn of salvation for us in the house of his servant David; as he spake by the mouth of his holy prophets, which have been since the world began: That we should be saved from our enemies, and from the hand of all that hate us; to perform the mercy promised to our fathers, and to remember his holy covenant; the oath which he sware to our father Abraham, that he would grant unto us, that we being delivered out of the hand of our enemies might serve him without fear, in holiness and righteousness before him, all the days of our life. And thou, child, shalt be called the prophet of the Highest: for thou shalt go before the face of the Lord to prepare his ways; to give knowledge of salvation unto his people by the remission of their sins" *(Luke 1:68-77)*

GRACE

STRONG'S #G5485: "grace"—*charis* (χάρις)
DEFINITION: graciousness (as gratifying), of manner or act (abstract or concrete; literal, figurative or spiritual; especially the divine influence upon the heart, and its reflection in the life; including gratitude):—acceptable, benefit, favor, gift, grace(-ious), joy, liberality, pleasure, thank(-s, -worthy).
USAGE: (a) grace, as a gift or blessing brought to man by Jesus Christ, (b) favor, (c) gratitude, thanks, (d) a favor, kindness.

HOLY

STRONG'S #G40: "holy"—*hagios* (ἅγιος)
DEFINITION: sacred (physically, pure, morally blameless or religious, ceremonially, consecrated):—(most) holy (one, thing), saint.
USAGE: set apart by (or for) God, holy, sacred

INIQUITY

STRONG'S #G439: "iniquity"—*anomos* (ἄνομος)
DEFINITION: lawless, without law
USAGE: wicked:—without law, lawless, transgressor, unlawful, wicked.

THAYER'S: 1. destitute of (the Mosaic) law: used of Gentiles, 1 Corinthians 9:21, (without any suggestion of 'iniquity'; just as in Additions to Esther 4:42, where ἄνομοι ἀπερίτμητοι and ἀλλότριοι are used together).
2. departing from the law, a violator of the law, lawless, wicked; (Vulg. iniquus; [also injustus]): Mark 15:28 [R L Tr brackets]; Luke 22:37; Acts 2:23 (so in Greek writings); opposed to ὁ δίκαιος, 1 Timothy 1:9; ὁ ἄνομος (κατ᾽ ἐξοχήν), he in whom all iniquity has as it were fixed its abode, 2 Thessalonians 2:8; ἀν. ἔργον, an unlawful deed, 2 Peter 2:8; free from law, not subject to law [Vulg. sine lege]: μὴ

STRONG'S #G4189: "iniquity"—*ponéria* (πονηρία)
DEFINITION: depravity, i.e. (specially), malice; plural (concretely) plots, sins- iniquity, wickedness.
USAGE: wickedness, iniquities

THAYER'S: πονηρία, πονηρίας, ἡ (πονηρός) (from Sophocles down), the Sept. for רֹעַ and רָעָה, depravity, iniquity, wickedness ((so A. V. almost uniformly)), malice: *Matthew 22:18; Luke 11:39; Romans 1:29; 1 Corinthians 5:8; Ephesians 6:12*; plural αἱ πονηρίαι (cf. Winers Grammar, § 27, 3; Buttmann, § 123, 2; R. V. wickednesses), evil purposes and desires, *Mark 7:22*; wicked ways (A. V. iniquities), *Acts 3:26*. (Synonym: see κακία, at the end.)

JUST

STRONG'S #G1342: "Just"— *dikaios* (δίκαιος)
DEFINITION: correct, righteous, by implication innocent
USAGE: just; especially, just in the eyes of God; righteous; **the elect**
THAYER'S DEFINITION: in a wide sense, upright, righteous, virtuous, **keeping the commands of God**.

LAW

STRONG'S #3551: "law"—*nomos* (νόμος)
DEFINITION: that which is assigned, usage, law
USAGE: usage, custom, law; in NT: of law in general, plur: of **divine laws**; of a force or influence impelling to action; of the Mosaic law; meton: of the books which contain the law, the Pentateuch, the Old Testament scriptures in general.

THAYER'S: νόμος, νόμου, ὁ (νέμω to divide, distribute, apportion), in secular authors from Hesiod down, anything established, anything received by usage, a custom, usage, law; in the Sept. very often for הָרוֹתּ, also for קֹח, תַּד, etc. In the N. T. a command, law; and 1. of any law whatsoever: διά ποίου νόμου; Romans 3:27; νόμος δικαιοσύνης, a law or rule producing a state approved of God, i. e. by the observance of which we are approved of God, Romans 9:31, cf. Meyer (see Weiss edition), Fritzsche, Philippi at the passage; a precept or injunction: κατά νόμον ἐντολῆς σαρκίνης, Hebrews 7:16; plural of the things prescribed by the divine will, Hebrews 8:10

LAWLESS

STRONG'S #G113: "lawless"—*athesmos* (ἄθεσμος)
DEFINITION: lawless, i.e. (by implication) criminal – wicked
USAGE: lawless, unrestrained, licentious
THAYER'S: ἄθεσμος, -όν, (θεσμός), lawless [A. V. wicked]; of one who breaks through the restraints of law and gratifies his lusts: *2 Peter 2:7; 2 Peter 3:17.* [Sept., Diodorus, Philo, Josephus, Plutarch.]

STRONG'S #G459: 'lawless'—*anomos* (ἄνομος)
DEFINITION: lawless, without law
USAGE: lawless, wicked, without law
THAYER'S: 1. destitute of (the Mosaic) law: used of Gentiles, *1 Corinthians 9:21*, without any suggestion of 'iniquity'; just as in Additions to Esther 4:42 [Esther 4:374:17u], where ἄνομοι ἀπερίτμητοι and ἀλλότριοι are used together). 2. departing from the law, a violator of the law, lawless, wicked; (Vulg.iniquus; (alsoinjustus)): *Mark 15:28* (R L Tr brackets); *Luke 22:37; Acts 2:23* (so in Greek writings); opposed to ὁ δίκαιος, *1 Timothy 1:9*; ὁ ἄνομος (κατ' ἐξοχήν), he in whom all iniquity has as it were fixed its abode, *2 Thessalonians 2:8*; ἀνόμοις ἔργοις, unlawful deeds, *2 Peter 2:8*; free from law, not subject to law (Vulg.sinelege): μή ὤν ἄνομος θεοῦ (Buttmann, 169 (147)) (Rec. θεῷ), *1 Corinthians 9:21*. (Very often in the Sept.) (Synonym: see ἀνομία, at the end.)

REDEEM

STRONG'S #H1350: "redeem"—*ga'al* (גָּאַל)
DEFINITION: to redeem, act as kinsman

BIBLICAL CONTEXT: "Wherefore say unto the children of Israel, I am the LORD, and I will bring you out from under the burdens of the Egyptians, and I will rid you out of their bondage, and I will redeem you with a stretched out arm, and with great judgments" *(Exodus 6:6)*

STRONG'S #G805. "redeem"—*Exagorazó* (ἐξαγοράζω)
DEFINITION: to buy up, ransom, to rescue from loss
USAGE: buy out, buy away from, ransom; mid: I purchase out, buy, redeem, choose

BIBLICAL CONTEXT: "But when the fullness of the time was come, God sent forth his Son, made of a woman, made under the law, to redeem them that were under the law, that we might receive the adoption of sons." *(Galatians 4:4-5)*

REDEMPTION

STRONG'S #G629: "redemption"—*apolytrōsis* (ἀπολύτρωσις)
DEFINITION: a release effected by payment of ransom
USAGE: release effected by payment of ransom; redemption, deliverance.

BIBLICAL CONTEXT "...in whom you also, having heard the word of the truth, the Good News of your salvation—in whom, having also believed, you were sealed with the Holy Spirit of promise, who is a pledge of our inheritance, to the redemption of God's own possession, to the praise of his glory." *(Ephesians 1:13-14)* | *"And when these things begin to come to pass, then look up, and lift up your heads; for your redemption draweth nigh"* *(Luke 21:28)*

RIGHTEOUS

STRONG'S #G1342: "righteous"—*dikaios* (δίκαιος)
DEFINITION: correct, righteous, by implication innocent
USAGE: just; especially, just in the eyes of God; righteous; **the elect**
THAYER'S DEFINITION: in a wide sense, upright, righteous, virtuous, keeping the commands of God.

SAINTS

STRONG'S #G40: "saints"—*hagios (ἅγιος)*
DEFINITION: sacred (physically, pure, morally blameless or religious, ceremonially, consecrated):—(most) holy (one, thing), saint.
USAGE: set apart by (or for) God, holy, sacred
BIBLICAL CONTEXT: "Gather my saints together unto me; those that have made a covenant with me by sacrifice." *(Psalms 50:5)* | "He also exalteth the horn of his people, the praise of all His saints; even of the children of Israel, a people near unto Him. Praise ye the LORD." *(Psalms 148:14)* | "This the people saw, and understood it not, neither laid they up this in their minds, That his grace and mercy is with his saints, and that he hath respect unto his chosen." *(Wisdom of Solomon 4:15)* | "Jesus the son a Nave was valiant in the wars, and was the successor of Moses in prophecies, who according to his name was made great for the saving of the elect of God, and taking vengeance of the enemies that rose up against them, that he might set Israel in their inheritance." *(Sirach 46:1)*

SALVATION

STRONG'S #H8668: "salvation"—*teshuah (תְּשׁוּעָה)*
DEFINITION: deliverance, help, safety, salvation, victory
BIBLICAL CONTEXT: "But Israel shall be saved in the LORD with an everlasting salvation: ye shall not be ashamed nor confounded world without end." *(Isaiah 45:17)* | "I bring near my righteousness; it shall not be far off, and my salvation shall not tarry: and I will place salvation in Zion for Israel my glory." *(Isaiah 46:13)*

STRONG'S #G4991: "salvation"—*sótéria (σωτηρία)*
DEFINITION: deliverance, salvation
USAGE: welfare, prosperity, deliverance, preservation, salvation, safety
BIBLICAL CONTEXT: "Blessed be the Lord God of Israel; for he hath visited and redeemed his people, and hath raised up an horn of salvation for us in the house of his servant David; as he spake by the mouth of his holy prophets, which have been since the world began: That we should be saved from our enemies, and from the hand of all that hate us; to perform the mercy promised to our fathers, and to remember his holy covenant; the oath which he sware to our father Abraham, that he would grant unto us, that we being delivered out of the hand of our enemies might serve him without fear, in holiness and righteousness before him, all the days of our life. And thou, child, shalt be called the prophet of the Highest: for thou shalt go before the face of the Lord to prepare his ways; to give knowledge of salvation unto his people by the remission of their sins" *(Luke 1:68-77)*

SAVE

STRONG'S #H3467: "save"—yasha (יָשַׁע)
DEFINITION: to deliver

BIBLICAL CONTEXT: "Alas! for that day is great, so that none is like it: it is even the time of Jacob's trouble; but he shall be saved out of it *(Jeremiah 30:7)*

BDB: 1 be liberated, saved (properly placed in freedom; compare for the figurative מֶרְחָב, הִרְחִיב), from external evils *Proverbs 28:18*, by God *Isaiah 30:15; Isaiah 45:22; Isaiah 64:4; Jeremiah 4:14; Jeremiah 8:20; Jeremiah 17:14; Jeremiah 23:6; Jeremiah 33:16; Psalms 80:4; Psalms 80:8; Psalms 80:20; Psalms 119:117;* with מִן, *Jeremiah 30:7;* מְאֹיְבִים *Numbers 10:9* (P), *2 Samuel 22:4 = Psalms 18:4*.

STRONG'S #G4982: "save"—sózó (σῴζω)
DEFINITION: to save
USAGE: save, heal, preserve, rescue

THAYER'S: to save, to keep safe and sound, to rescue from danger or destruction

BIBLICAL CONTEXT: "That we should be saved from our enemies, and from the hand of all that hate us" *(Luke1:71)*

SIN

STRONG'S G264: "sin"—hamartanó (ἁμαρτάνω)
DEFINITION: to miss the mark, do wrong, sin
USAGE: originally: I miss the mark, hence (a) I make a mistake, (b) I sin, commit a sin (against God); sometimes the idea of sinning against a fellow-creature is present.

BIBLICAL CONTEXT: "Whosoever committeth sin transgresseth also the law: for sin is the transgression of the law. *(1 John 3:4)*

APPENDIX 2: 'ENEMIES AND ALL THAT HATE US'

> And the LORD thy God will circumcise thine heart, and the heart of thy seed, to love the LORD thy God with all thine heart, and with all thy soul, that thou mayest live. And the LORD thy God will put all these curses upon thine enemies, and on them that hate thee, which persecuted thee.
> —Deuteronomy 30:6-7

If by chance you're reading this book, and you're a non-Israelite with a *perpetual* hatred for TMH's chosen people, *(Ezekiel 35:5-14)* this section is specifically about you:

Perpetual: (1) Continuing forever in future time; destined to continue or be continued through the ages; everlasting: as, a perpetual covenant; a perpetual statute. (2) Continuing or continued without intermission; uninterrupted; continuous; continual; as, a perpetual stream...

Just to be clear, TMH has an inherent order. He's first, Messiah's next, after that, His chosen people, and then the nations. Since TMH's children are the apple of His eye, *(Zechariah 2:7-9)* those who hate them shouldn't think to receive <u>*anything*</u> but curses from Him.

BTW, this hierarchy was set up at the very beginning with Abraham:

GENESIS 12:3—And I will bless them that bless thee, and curse him that curseth thee: and in thee shall all families of the earth be blessed.

GENESIS 22:17—That in blessing I will bless thee, and in multiplying I will multiply thy seed as the stars of the heaven, and as the sand which *is* upon the sea shore; and thy seed shall possess the gate of his enemies...

THE BOOK OF JUBILEES 18:15-16—(15) And he said: 'By Myself have I sworn, saith the Lord, because thou hast done this thing, and hast not withheld thy son, thy beloved son, from Me, that in blessing I will bless thee, and in multiplying I will multiply thy seed as the stars of heaven, and as the sand which is on the seashore. And thy seed shall inherit the cities of its enemies, (16) and in thy seed shall all nations of the earth be blessed; because thou hast obeyed My voice, and I have shown to all that thou art faithful unto Me in all that I have said unto thee: Go in peace.

TMH's confirmed these promises in the blessing Jacob/Israel received through Isaac. All these blessings applied directly to Jacob's bloodline, the children of Israel:

GENESIS 27:26-29—(26) And his father Isaac said unto him, Come near now, and kiss me, my son. (27) And he came near, and kissed him: and he smelled the smell of his raiment, and blessed him, and said, See, the smell of my son is as the smell of a field which the LORD hath blessed: (28) Therefore God give thee of the dew of heaven, and the fatness of the earth, and plenty of corn and wine: (29) Let people serve thee, and nations bow down to thee: be lord over thy brethren, and let thy mother's sons bow down to thee: cursed be every one that curseth thee, and blessed be he that blesseth thee.

SIRACH 44:21-22—(21) Therefore, he assured him by an oath, that he would bless the nations in his seed, and that he would multiply him as the dust of the earth, and exalt his need as the stars, and cause them to inherit from sea to sea, and from the river unto the utmost part of the land. (22) With Isaac did he establish likewise for Abraham his father's sake the blessing of all men, and the covenant, And made it rest upon the head of Jacob. He acknowledged him in his blessing, and gave him an heritage, and divided his portions; among the twelve tribes did he part them.

THE BOOK OF JUBILEES 26:17-24—(17) And Jacob went near to Isaac, his father, and he felt him and said: 'The voice is Jacob's voice, but the hands are the hands of Esau,' (18) and he discerned him not, because it was a dispensation from heaven to remove his power of perception and Isaac discerned not, for his hands were hairy as his brother Esau's, so that he blessed him. (19) And he said: 'Art thou my son Esau?' And he said: 'I am thy son': and he said, 'Bring near to me that I may eat of that which thou hast caught, my son, that my soul may bless thee.' (20) And he brought near to him, and he did eat, and he brought him wine and he drank. (21) And Isaac, his father, said unto him: 'Come near and kiss me, my son. (22) And he came near and kissed him. And he smelled the smell of his raiment, and he blessed him and said: 'Behold, the smell of my son is as the smell of a field, which the Lord hath blessed. (23) And may the Lord give thee of the dew of heaven and of the dew of the earth, and plenty of corn and oil: Let nations serve thee, and peoples bow down to thee. (24) Be lord over thy brethren, and let thy mother's sons bow down to thee; And may all the blessings wherewith the Lord hath blessed me and blessed Abraham, my father; Be imparted to thee and to thy seed forever: Cursed be he that curseth thee, and blessed be he that blesseth thee.

THE LADDER OF JACOB 1 (Rec 1)—...And as I looked, behold, the Angels of God ascending and descending thereon: but the Lord was set above it, and he called me, saying: Jacob, Jacob. And I said: Here am I, Lord; And he said to me: The land whereon thou sleepest I will give to thee and to thy seed after thee: and I multiply thy seed as the stars of heaven and as the sand of the sea; through thy seed shall all the earth be blessed, and they that dwell thereon, unto the last times, the years of the end. My blessing wherewith I have blessed thee shall pour out from thee unto the last generation. All in the east and the west shall be full of thy seed. *The Lost Apocrypha of the Old Testament, Their Titles And Fragments, pg. 96-97*

These passages show us just how blessings and curses flow from TMH through His people to the nations. Again, that's the hierarchy and it hasn't changed. TMH has always intended for His people to be above all others.

Why? Because He's God. He does whatever He wants.

EXODUS 4:22—And thou shalt say unto Pharaoh, Thus saith the LORD, Israel is my son, even my firstborn.

DEUTERONOMY 7:6, 14—(6) For thou art an holy people unto the LORD thy God: the LORD thy God hath chosen thee to be a special people unto himself, above all people that are upon the face of the earth...(14) Thou shalt be blessed above all people: there shall not be male or female barren among you, or among your cattle.

DEUTERONOMY 10:15—Only the LORD had a delight in thy fathers to love them, and he chose their seed after them, even you above all people, as it is this day.

DEUTERONOMY 14:2—For thou art an holy people unto the LORD thy God, and the LORD hath chosen thee to be a peculiar people unto himself, above all the nations that are upon the earth.

DEUTERONOMY 26:18-19—(18) And the LORD hath avouched thee this day to be his peculiar people, as he hath promised thee, and that thou shouldest keep all his commandments; (19) And to make thee high above all nations which he hath made, in praise, and in name, and in honour; and that thou mayest be an holy people unto the LORD thy God, as he hath spoken.

2 BARUCH 48:18-20—(18) Protect us in Your compassions, and in Your mercy help us. (19) Behold the little ones that are subject unto you, and save all that draw near unto you: and destroy not the hope of our people, and cut not short the times of our aid. (20) For this is the nation, which you have chosen, and these are the people, to whom you find no equal.

THE BOOK OF JUBILEES 16:18—For he should become the portion of the Most High, and all his seed had fallen into the possession of God, that it should be unto the Lord a people for (His) possession above all nations and that it should become a kingdom and priests and a holy nation.

In the Old Covenant, the Levites acted as priestly mediators between Israel and TMH. In the New Covenant, which TMH made, not with the nations, but with the children of Israel, the Israelite's mediator is the Messiah. Once the children of Israel are glorified in TMH, sealed, changed from death to life, having the Law written in our hearts, TMH's chosen will be kings and priests in the Kingdom of heaven.

JEREMIAH 31:33-34—(33) But this shall be the covenant that I will make with the house of Israel; After those days, saith the LORD, I will put my law in their inward parts, and write it in their hearts; and will be their God, and they shall be my people. (34) And they shall teach no more every man his neighbour, and every man his brother, saying, Know the LORD: for they shall all know me, from the least of them unto the greatest of them, saith the LORD: for I will forgive their iniquity, and I will remember their sin no more.

REVELATION 1:4-6—(4) John to the seven churches which are in Asia: Grace be unto you, and peace, from him which is, and which was, and which is to come; and from the seven Spirits which are before his throne; (5) And from Jesus Christ, who is the faithful witness, and the first begotten of the dead, and the prince of the kings of the earth. Unto him that loved us, and washed us from our sins in his own blood, (6) and hath made us kings and priests unto God and his Father; to him be glory and dominion forever and ever. Amen.

These scriptures apply to the children of Israel alone:

ROMANS 9:4-5—(4) Who are Israelites; to whom pertaineth the adoption, and the glory, and the covenants, and the giving of the law, and the service of God, and the promises; (5) Whose are the fathers, and of whom as concerning the flesh Christ came, who is over all, God blessed for ever. Amen.

TMH's people were chastised and humbled by the nations when we sinned against our God. However, according to scripture, TMH's people will be restored and *all nations* will be subject to them in the kingdom of heaven.

ISAIAH 60:10-12—(10) And the sons of strangers shall build up thy walls, and their kings shall minister unto thee: for in my wrath I smote thee, but in my favor have I had mercy on thee. (11) Therefore thy gates shall be open continually; they shall not be shut day nor night; that *men* may bring unto thee the forces of the Gentiles, and *that* their kings *may be* brought. (12) For the nation and kingdom that will not serve thee shall perish; yea, *those* nations shall be utterly wasted.

Therefore, how can a non-Israelite claim to truly love TMH God of Israel, yet hate His people, and then expect to be blessed?

They can't.

Matthew 25:31-34, 40-46—(31) When the Son of man shall come in his glory, and all the holy angels with him, then shall he sit upon the throne of his glory: (32) And before him shall be gathered all nations: and he shall separate them one from another, as a shepherd divideth his sheep from the goats: (33) And he shall set the sheep on his right hand, but the goats on the left. (34)Then shall the King say unto them on his right hand, Come, ye blessed of my Father, inherit the kingdom prepared for you from the foundation of the world:...(40)...**Inasmuch as ye have done it unto one of the least of these *my brethren*, ye have done it unto me**...(41) Then shall he say also unto them on the left hand, Depart from me, ye cursed, into everlasting fire, prepared for the devil and his angels: (42) For I was an hungred, and ye gave me no meat: I was thirsty, and ye gave me no drink: (43) I was a stranger, and ye took me not in: naked, and ye clothed me not: sick, and in prison, and ye visited me not. (44) Then shall they also answer him, saying, Lord, when saw we thee an hungred, or athirst, or a stranger, or naked, or sick, or in prison, and did not minister unto thee? (45) Then shall he answer them, saying, Verily I say unto you, Inasmuch as ye did it not to one of the least of these, ye did it not to me. (46) And these shall go away into everlasting punishment: but the righteous into life eternal.

This has been the case from the time Israel left Egypt and will be especially true once Israel is restored. Nothing can ever change what TMH has ordained. *This* among many other ways is how the nations will be humbled, by being forced to admit that the very people they've hated, murdered, and cursed for centuries, if not millenniums, are the people TMH has always loved.

ZECHARIAH 8:23—Thus saith the LORD of hosts; In those days it shall come to pass, that ten men shall take hold out of all languages of the nations, even shall take hold of the skirt of him that is a Jew, saying, We will go with you: for we have heard that God is with you.

REVELATION 3:9—Behold, I will make them of the synagogue of Satan, which say they are Jews, and are not, but do lie; behold, I will make them to come and worship before thy feet, and to know that I have loved thee.

This order is TMH's doing. For the last shall be first, and the first shall be last. Just how serious is TMH about punishing those who've hated and oppressed His people? The scriptures lay it out quite succinctly:

DEUTERONOMY 32:42-43—(42) I will make mine arrows drunk with blood, and my sword shall devour flesh; and that with the blood of the slain and of the captives, from the beginning of revenges upon the enemy. (43) Rejoice, O ye nations, with his people: for he will avenge the blood of his servants, and will render vengeance to his adversaries, and will be merciful unto his land, and to his people.

ISAIAH 51:22-23—(22) Thus saith thy Lord the LORD, and thy God [that] pleadeth the cause of his people, Behold, I have taken out of thine hand the cup of trembling, [even] the dregs of the cup of my fury; thou shalt no more drink it again: (23) But I will put it into the hand of them that afflict thee; which have said to thy soul, Bow down, that we may go over: and thou hast laid thy body as the ground, and as the street, to them that went over.

JEREMIAH 10:25—Pour out thy fury upon the heathen that know thee not, and upon the families that call not on thy name: for they have eaten up Jacob, and devoured him, and consumed him, and have made his habitation desolate.

JEREMIAH 30:16-20—(16) Therefore all they that devour thee shall be devoured; and all thine adversaries, every one of them, shall go into captivity; and they that spoil thee shall be a spoil, and all that prey upon thee will I give for a prey. (17) For I will restore health unto thee, and I will heal thee of thy wounds, saith the LORD; because they called thee an Outcast, saying, This is Zion, whom no man seeketh after. (18) Thus saith the LORD; Behold, I will bring again the captivity of Jacob's tents, and have mercy on his dwelling places; and the city shall be builded upon her own heap, and the palace shall remain after the manner thereof. (19) And out of them shall proceed thanksgiving and the voice of them that make merry: and I will multiply them, and they shall not be few; I will also glorify them, and they shall not be small. (20) Their children also shall be as aforetime, and their congregation shall be established before me, and I will punish all that oppress them.

JOEL 3:19-21—(19) Egypt shall be a desolation, and Edom shall be a desolate wilderness, for the violence [against] the children of Judah, because they have shed innocent blood in their land. (20) But Judah shall dwell forever, and Jerusalem from generation to generation. (21) For I will cleanse their blood [that] I have not cleansed: for the LORD dwelleth in Zion.

AMOS 1:11—Thus saith the LORD; For three transgressions of Edom, and for four, I will not turn away the punishment thereof; because he did pursue his brother with the sword, and did cast off all pity, and his anger did tear perpetually, and he kept his wrath forever.

OBADIAH 1:9-10—(9) And thy mighty [men], O Teman, shall be dismayed, to the end that every one of the mount of Esau may be cut off by slaughter. (10) For thy violence against thy brother Jacob shame shall cover thee, and thou shalt be cut off forever.

ZECHARIAH 2:8-9—(8) For thus saith the LORD of hosts; After the glory hath he sent me unto the nations which spoiled you: for he that toucheth you toucheth the apple of his eye. (9) For, behold, I will shake mine hand upon them, and they shall be a spoil to their servants: and ye shall know that the LORD of hosts hath sent me.

Just as Israelites can't get to TMH apart from our Messiah's finished work, non-Israelites can't receive blessings from the God of Israel apart from loving and honoring *His people*. So again, if you're a non-Israelite with a *perpetual* hatred for the children of Israel, TMH's curses are upon you.

REPENT

APPENDIX 3: THE STRANGERS AMONG US

> Love ye therefore the stranger: for ye were
> strangers in the land of Egypt.
> —Deuteronomy 10:19

Non-Israelites who love TMH and His people have *always* been welcome to worship and receive blessings from Him, and to cleave to Israel. This has been the case since forever. However, TMH's *Psalms 83* enemies weren't satisfied with His divine order and plans, so they created a non-Israelite 'grafting in' doctrine, albeit 'another gospel' that dissolves TMH's hierarchy, inheritance, and kingdom design.

In order for their counterfeit to work, they had to completely ignore OT precedence, prophecy and the historical record of the Apocrypha and Pseudepigrapha. This new gospel's *raison d'être* was designed to conceal true Israel's divine significance, TMH's promise of reconciliation, regathering and redemption, and Israel's God-ordained position. Let's look at prophecy:

GENESIS 12:3—And I will bless them that bless thee, and curse him that curseth thee: and in thee shall all families of the earth be blessed.

THE BOOK OF JUBILEES 18:15-16—(15) And he said: 'By Myself have I sworn, saith the Lord, because thou hast done this thing, and hast not withheld thy son, thy beloved son, from Me, that in blessing I will bless thee, and in multiplying I will multiply thy seed as the stars of heaven, and as the sand which is on the seashore. And thy seed shall inherit the cities of its enemies, (16) and in thy seed shall all nations of the earth be blessed; because thou hast obeyed My voice, and I have shown to all that thou art faithful unto Me in all that I have said unto thee: Go in peace.

GENESIS 22:17—That in blessing I will bless thee, and in multiplying I will multiply thy seed as the stars of the heaven, and as the sand which *is* upon the sea shore; and thy seed shall possess the gate of his enemies...

Galatians 3:16—Now to Abraham and his seed were the promises made. He saith not, And to seeds, as of many; but as of one, And to thy seed, which is Christ.

THE BOOK OF JUBILEES 15:30-32—(30) For Ishmael and his sons and his brothers and Esau, the Lord did not cause to approach Him, and he chose them not because they are the children of Abraham, because He knew them, but He chose Israel to be His people. (31) And He sanctified it, and gathered it from amongst all the children of men; for there are many nations and many peoples, and all are His, and over all hath He placed spirits in authority to lead them astray from Him. (32) But over Israel He did not appoint any angel or spirit, for He alone is their ruler, and He will preserve them and require them at the hand of His angels and his spirits, and at the hand of all His powers in order that He may preserve them and bless them, and that they may be His and He may be theirs from henceforth forever.

These scripts make several things abundantly clear. TMH established His order from the beginning. [1] The children of Israel were TMH people whom He placed above all others. [2] Nations were set up to be blessed and cursed according to their treatment of His people and their acknowledgment of His preeminence and power. Some early blessing examples include:

Egyptian Servants Of Pharaoh

During the plagues of Egypt, TMH offered mercy to those Egyptians who hearkened to His word. Because they feared Him, they listened to Moses' warning, and by doing so, they and their households were spared:

EXODUS 9:18-24—(18) Behold, to morrow about this time I will cause it to rain a very grievous hail, such as hath not been in Egypt since the foundation thereof even until now. (19) Send therefore now, and gather thy cattle, and all that thou hast in the field; for upon every man and beast which shall be found in the field, and shall not be brought home, the hail shall come down upon them, and they shall die. (20) He that feared the word of the LORD among the servants of Pharaoh made his servants and his cattle flee into the houses: (21) and he that regarded not the word of the LORD left his servants and his cattle in the field. (22) And the LORD said unto Moses, Stretch forth thine hand toward heaven, that there may be hail in all the land of Egypt, upon man, and upon beast, and upon every herb of the field, throughout the land of Egypt. (23) And Moses stretched forth his rod toward heaven: and the LORD sent thunder and hail, and the fire ran along upon the ground; and the LORD rained hail upon the land of Egypt. (24) So there was hail, and fire mingled with the hail, very grievous, such as there was none like it in all the land of Egypt since it became a nation.

TARGUM OF PALESTINE: "Behold, at this time tomorrow, I will cause to come down from the treasures of the heavens a mighty hail, the like of which hath never been in Mizraim since the day when men were settled upon it until now. But now send, gather together thy flocks, and all that thou hast in the field: for upon all men and cattle that are found in the field, and not gathered together within the house, will the hail come down, and they will die. Hiob, who reverenced the word of the Lord, among the servants of Pharaoh gathered together his servants and his flocks within the house. But Bileam, who did not set his heart upon the word of the Lord, left his servants and his flocks in the field. And the Lord said to Mosheh, Uplift thy hand towards the height of the heavens, and there shall be hail on all the land of Mizraim, upon men, and upon beasts, and upon every herb of the field in the land of Mizraim. And Mosheh lifted up his rod toward the height of the heavens, and the Lord gave forth thunders and hailstones with flaming fire upon the ground; the Lord made the hail descend upon the land of Mizraim. And there was hail, and fire darting among the hail with exceeding force: unto it had never been the like in all the land of Mizraim ever since it was a nation and a kingdom. And the hail smote in all the land of Mizraim whatsoever was in the field, of men and of cattle, and all the herbage of the field the hail smote, and every tree of the field it shattered and uprooted. Only in the land of Goshen, where the children of Israel were, there was no hail. *The Targums of Onkelos and Jonathan Ben Uzziel On The Pentateuch, Targum of Palestine (aka Targum Jonathan), On Exodus, chapter 9, pg. 467-468*

Here we see two things:

1. Just as the Israelites in Goshen remained untouched, TMH gave the Egyptians the option to receive mercy from the judgment (hail & fire) He was about to inflict upon the nation.

2. Believing Egyptians harkened to Moses' warning and their servants and livestock received mercy and were spared.

3. Those Egyptians who ignored Moses' warning died beneath TMH's hail and fire as did their livestock.

The Mixed Multitude

Some Egyptians who lived through the destruction of their homeland, were allowed to leave with and live among the children of Israel.

EXODUS 12:35-38, 43-49—(35) And the children of Israel did according to the word of Moses; and they borrowed of the Egyptians jewels of silver, and jewels of gold, and raiment: (36) And the LORD gave the people favor in the sight of the Egyptians, so that they lent unto them such things as they required. And they spoiled the Egyptians. (37) And the children of Israel journeyed from Rameses to Succoth, about six hundred thousand on foot that were men, beside children. (38) And a mixed multitude went up also with them; and flocks, and herds, even very much cattle...(43) And the LORD said unto Moses and Aaron, This is the ordinance of the Passover: There shall no stranger eat thereof: (44) But every man's servant that is bought for money, when thou hast circumcised him, then shall he eat thereof. (45) A foreigner and an hired servant shall not eat thereof. (46) In one house shall it be eaten; thou shalt not carry forth ought of the flesh abroad out of the house; neither shall ye break a bone thereof. (47) All the congregation of Israel shall keep it. (48) And when a stranger shall sojourn with thee, and will keep the Passover to the LORD, let all his males be circumcised, and then let him come near and keep it; and he shall be as one that is born in the land: for no uncircumcised person shall eat thereof. (49) One law shall be to him that is homeborn, and unto the stranger that sojourneth among you.

TARGUM OF ONKELOS—"And the children of Israel journeyed from Ramases to Succoth; about six hundred thousand men on foot besides children (or families); and a multitude of strangers also went up with them, and flocks and herds and very much cattle." *The Targums of Onkelos and Jonathan Ben Uzziel On The Pentateuch, Targum Of Onkelos, On Exodus, chapter 12, pg. 372*

DEUTERONOMY 10:17-19—(17) For the LORD your God is God of gods, and Lord of lords, a great God, a mighty, and a terrible, which regardeth not persons, nor taketh reward: (18) He doth execute the judgment of the fatherless and widow, and loveth the stranger, in giving him food and raiment. (19) Love ye therefore the stranger: for ye were strangers in the land of Egypt.

TARGUM OF ONKELOS—"And when the sojourner who sojourneth with thee will perform the pesach before the Lord, every male of his shall be circumcised and he may then approach and perform it; he shall be as one born in the land, but none uncircumcised shall eat of it. One law shall there be for the native and for the proselyte who sojourneth among you." *The Targums of Onkelos and Jonathan Ben Uzziel On The Pentateuch, Targum Of Onkelos, On Exodus, chapter 13, pg. 373 (See also Exodus 12:48-49)*

EXODUS 14:24-31—(24) And it came to pass, that in the morning watch the LORD looked unto the host of the Egyptians through the pillar of fire and of the cloud, and troubled the host of the Egyptians, (25) And took off their chariot wheels, that they drave them heavily: so that the Egyptians said, Let us flee from the face of Israel; for the LORD fighteth for them against the Egyptians. (26) And the LORD said unto Moses, Stretch out thine hand over the sea, that the waters may come again upon the Egyptians, upon their chariots, and upon their horsemen. (27) And Moses stretched forth his hand over the sea, and the sea returned to his strength when the morning appeared; and the Egyptians fled against it; and the LORD overthrew the Egyptians in the midst of the sea. (28) And the waters returned, and covered the chariots, and the horsemen, and all the host of Pharaoh that came into the sea after them; there remained not so much as one of them. (29) But the children of Israel walked upon dry land in the midst of the sea; and the waters were a wall unto them on their right hand, and on their left. (30) Thus the LORD saved Israel that day out of the hand of the Egyptians; and Israel saw the Egyptians dead upon the sea shore. (31) And Israel saw that great work which the LORD did upon the Egyptians: and the people feared the LORD, and believed the LORD, and his servant Moses.

These scriptures tell us several things:

1. Strangers feared TMH God and humbled themselves by cleaving to Israel.

2. Strangers were subject to TMH's laws.

3. TMH loved the strangers.

4. Israelites are commanded to love the stranger. And what is love? That we keep TMH's commandments. *(John 14:15; 2 John 1:6)* Strangers sojourning with Israel were considered neighbors and were therefore to be treated as such.

5. Strangers who cleaved to the children of Israel were delivered from destruction.

Rahab, The Harlot

Rahab and her entire family received mercy because of her righteous fear of our God. That fear showed belief and that belief translated into faith, which TMH accounted as righteousness. Her family must have been accounted as righteous too since they believed enough to shelter beneath the safety of her roof.

JOSHUA 2:3-14, 18-21—(3) And the king of Jericho sent unto Rahab, saying, Bring forth the men that are come to thee, which are entered into thine house: for they be come to search out all the country. (4) And the woman took the two men, and hid them, and said thus, There came men unto me, but I wist not whence they were: (5) And it came to pass about the time of shutting of the gate, when it was dark, that the men went out: whither the men went I wot not: pursue after them quickly; for ye shall overtake them. (6) But she had brought them up to the roof of the house, and hid them with the stalks of flax, which she had laid in order upon the roof...(8) And before they were laid down, she came up unto them upon the roof; (9) And she said unto the men, I know that the LORD hath given you the land, and that your terror is fallen upon us, and that all the inhabitants of the land faint because of you. (10) For we have heard how the LORD dried up the water of the Red sea for you, when ye came out of Egypt; and what ye did unto the two kings of the Amorites, that were on the other side Jordan, Sihon and Og, whom ye utterly destroyed. (11) And as soon as we had heard these things, our hearts did melt, neither did there remain any more courage in any man, because of you: for the LORD your God, he is God in heaven above, and in earth beneath. (12) Now therefore, I pray you, swear unto me by the LORD, since I have shewed you kindness, that ye will also shew kindness unto my father's house, and give me a true token: (13) And that ye will save alive my father, and my mother, and my brethren, and my sisters, and all that they have, and deliver our lives from death. (14) And the men answered her, Our life for yours, if ye utter not this our business. And it shall be, when the LORD hath given us the land, that we will deal kindly and truly with thee...(18) Behold, when we come into the land, thou shalt bind this line of scarlet thread in the window which thou didst let us down by: and thou shalt bring thy father, and thy mother, and thy brethren, and all thy father's household, home unto thee. (19) And it shall be, that whosoever shall go out of the doors of thy house into the street, his blood shall be upon his head, and we will be guiltless: and whosoever shall be with thee in the house, his blood shall be on our head, if any hand be upon him. (20) And if thou utter this our business, then we will be quit of thine oath which thou hast made us to swear. (21) And she said, According unto your words, so be it. And she sent them away, and they departed: and she bound the scarlet line in the window.

JOSHUA 6:16-25—(16) And it came to pass at the seventh time, when the priests blew with the trumpets, Joshua said unto the people, Shout; for the LORD hath given you the city. (17) And the city shall be accursed, even it, and all that are therein, to the LORD: only Rahab the harlot shall live, she and all that are with her in the house, because she hid the messengers that we sent. (18) And ye, in any wise keep yourselves from the accursed thing, lest ye make yourselves accursed, when ye take of the accursed thing, and make the camp of Israel a curse, and trouble it. (19) But all the silver, and gold, and vessels of brass and iron, are consecrated unto the LORD: they shall come into the treasury of the LORD. (20) So the people shouted when the priests blew with the trumpets: and it came to pass, when the people heard the sound of the trumpet, and the people shouted with a great shout, that the wall fell down flat, so that the people went up into the city, every man straight before him, and they took the city. (21) And they utterly destroyed all that was in the city, both man and woman, young and old, and ox, and sheep, and ass, with the edge of the sword. (22) But Joshua had said unto the two men that had spied out the country, Go into the harlot's house, and bring out thence the woman, and all that she hath, as ye sware unto her. (23) And the young men that were spies went in, and brought out Rahab, and her father, and her mother, and her brethren, and all that she had; and they brought out all her kindred, and left them without the camp of Israel. (24) And they burnt the city with fire, and all that was therein: only the silver, and the gold, and the vessels of brass and of iron, they put into the treasury of the house of the LORD. (25) And Joshua saved Rahab the harlot alive, and her father's household, and all that she had; and she dwelleth in Israel even unto this day; because she hid the messengers, which Joshua sent to spy out Jericho.

HEBREWS 11:31—By faith the harlot Rahab perished not with them that believed not, when she had received the spies with peace.

Three things stand out here:

1. Rahab blessed the children of Israel by hiding them to save their lives because she feared TMH God of Israel.

2. Rahab and her family were then blessed with mercy and deliverance from wrath and destruction because of the blessing she bestowed upon TMH's people.

3. Rahab is a shining example of a non-Israelite who was justified by faith.

The Gibeonites

The Gibeonites joined with Israel via covenant and became servants, (water carriers to be exact). When the Canaanites saw that the Gibeonites had joined with Israel, they sought to attack them, however, since Israel had made a covenant with the Gibeonites, Israel protected them and the Canaanites relented. However, King Saul broke covenant and slayed the Gibeonites, and as a punishment to Israel, TMH sent a famine in the land during Saul's successor, King David's reign:

2 SAMUEL 21:1-9—(1) Then there was a famine in the days of David three years, year after year; and David enquired of the LORD. And the LORD answered, It is for Saul, and for his bloody house, because he slew the Gibeonites. (2) And the king called the Gibeonites, and said unto them; (now the Gibeonites were not of the children of Israel, but of the remnant of the Amorites; and the children of Israel had sworn unto them: and Saul sought to slay them in his zeal to the children of Israel and Judah.) (3) Wherefore David said unto the Gibeonites, What shall I do for you? and wherewith shall I make the atonement, that ye may bless the inheritance of the LORD? (4) And the Gibeonites said unto him, We will have no silver nor gold of Saul, nor of his house; neither for us shalt thou kill any man in Israel. And he said, What ye shall say, that will I do for you. (5) And they answered the king, The man that consumed us, and that devised against us that we should be destroyed from remaining in any of the coasts of Israel, (6) Let seven men of his sons be delivered unto us, and we will hang them up unto the LORD in Gibeah of Saul, whom the LORD did choose. And the king said, I will give them. (7) But the king spared Mephibosheth, the son of Jonathan the son of Saul, because of the LORD'S oath that was between them, between David and Jonathan the son of Saul. (8) But the king took the two sons of Rizpah the daughter of Aiah, whom she bare unto Saul, Armoni and Mephibosheth; and the five sons of Michal the daughter of Saul, whom she brought up for Adriel the son of Barzillai the Meholathite: (9) And he delivered them into the hands of the Gibeonites, and they hanged them in the hill before the LORD: and they fell all seven together, and were put to death in the days of harvest, in the first days, in the beginning of barley harvest.

Three points we shouldn't miss:

1. Israel fought for and delivered loyal non-Israelites.

2. TMH is not a respecter of persons. What's wrong is wrong.

3. Unrighteousness against non-Israelites was never tolerated in Israel.

The Syro-Phoenician Woman

Here's another example of a non-Israelite exercising faith in TMH via Messiah and receiving mercy and healing:

MARK 7:24-30—(24) From there He arose and went to the region of Tyre and Sidon. And He entered a house and wanted no one to know it, but He could not be hidden. (25) For a woman whose young daughter had an unclean spirit heard about Him, and she came and fell at His feet. (26) The woman was a Greek, Syro-Phoenician by birth, and she kept asking Him to cast the demon out of her daughter. (27) But Jesus said to her, "Let the children be filled first, for it is not good to take the children's bread and throw it to the little dogs." (28) And she answered and said to Him, "Yes, Lord, yet even the little dogs under the table eat from the children's crumbs." (29) Then He said to her, "For this saying go your way; the demon has gone out of your daughter." (30) And when she had come to her house, she found the demon gone out, and her daughter lying on the bed.

From this we can glean 3 things:

1. Messiah reminded her of the order when he said, "It is not good to take the children's bread and throw it to the little dogs." In other words, the children of Israel are first.

2. She acknowledges this in her answer, "Yes, Lord, yet even the little dogs under the table eat from the children's crumbs."

3. Because of her faith she received mercy. Messiah blessed her by healing her daughter.

If we analyze all these examples, several things become clear: repentant non-Israelites who acknowledge and respect the God of Israel and His people can and will receive healing, mercy, blessings, and deliverance from wrath. Again, TMH has _always_ accepted and loved the stranger who _truly_ fears and honors Him _and_ respects His people.

GENESIS 27:28-29—(28) Therefore God give thee of the dew of heaven, and the fatness of the earth, and plenty of corn and wine: (29) Let people serve thee, and nations bow down to thee: be lord over thy brethren, and let thy mother's sons bow down to thee: cursed _be_ every one that curseth thee, and blessed _be_ he that blesseth thee.

ISAIAH 56:6-8—(6) Also the sons of the stranger, that join themselves to the LORD, to serve him, and to love the name of the LORD, to be his servants, every one that keepeth the sabbath from polluting it, and taketh hold of my covenant; (7) Even them will I bring to my holy mountain, and make them joyful in my house of prayer: their burnt offerings and their sacrifices shall be accepted upon mine altar; for mine house shall be called an house of prayer for all people. (8) The Lord GOD which gathereth the outcasts of Israel saith, Yet will I gather others to him, beside those that are gathered unto him.

EZEKIEL 44:9—Thus saith the Lord GOD; No stranger, uncircumcised in heart, nor uncircumcised in flesh, shall enter into my sanctuary, of any stranger that is among the children of Israel.

1 KINGS 8:41-43—(41) Moreover concerning a stranger, that is not of thy people Israel, but cometh out of a far country for thy name's sake; (42) For they shall hear of thy great name, and of thy strong hand, and of thy stretched out arm;) when he shall come and pray toward this house; (43) Hear thou in heaven thy dwelling place, and do according to all that the stranger calleth to thee for: that all people of the earth may know thy name, to fear thee, as do thy people Israel; and that they may know that this house, which I have builded, is called by thy name.

LEVITICUS 23:22—And when ye reap the harvest of your land, thou shalt not make clean riddance of the corners of thy field when thou reapest, neither shalt thou gather any gleaning of thy harvest: thou shalt leave them unto the poor, and to the stranger: I am the LORD your God.

That said, as pointed out earlier, the children of Israel were called to be above all nations and to rule in TMH's kingdom:

ROMANS 9:4-5—(4) Who are Israelites; to whom pertaineth the adoption, and the glory, and the covenants, and the giving of the law, and the service of God, and the promises; (5) whose are the fathers, and of whom as concerning the flesh Christ came, who is over all, God blessed for ever. Amen.

Because of this divine election the nations will cleave and be subject to the Israelites in the Kingdom of TMH. This is a promise from our God to us. We shall inherit the kingdom and the nations, in righteousness.

ISAIAH 14:1-4—(1) For the LORD will have mercy on Jacob, and will yet choose Israel, and set them in their own land: and the strangers shall be joined with them, and they shall cleave to the house of Jacob. (2) And the people shall take them, and bring them to their place: and the house of Israel shall possess them in the land of the LORD for servants and handmaids: and they shall take them captives, whose captives they were; and they shall rule over their oppressors. (3) And it shall come to pass in the day that the LORD shall give thee rest from thy sorrow, and from thy fear, and from the hard bondage wherein thou wast made to serve, (4) That thou shalt take up this proverb against the king of Babylon, and say, How hath the oppressor ceased! The golden city ceased!

ISAIAH 54:2-3—(2) Enlarge the place of thy tent, and let them stretch forth the curtains of thine habitations: spare not, lengthen thy cords, and strengthen thy stakes; (3) For thou shalt break forth on the right hand and on the left; and thy seed shall inherit the Gentiles, and make the desolate cities to be inhabited.

2 BARUCH 72:4-6—(4) Every nation, which knows not Israel and has not trodden down the seed of Jacob, shall indeed be spared. (5) And this because some out of every nation shall be subjected to your people. (6) But all those who have ruled over you, or have known you, shall be given up to the sword.

ISAIAH 49:22-23—(22) Thus saith the Lord GOD, Behold, I will lift up mine hand to the Gentiles, and set up my standard to the people: and they shall bring thy sons in *their* arms, and thy daughters shall be carried upon *their* shoulders. (23) And kings shall be thy nursing fathers, and their queens thy nursing mothers: they shall bow down to thee with *their* face toward the earth, and lick up the dust of thy feet; and thou shalt know that I *am* the LORD: for they shall not be ashamed that wait for me.

ZECHARIAH 8:23—Thus saith the LORD of hosts; In those days it shall come to pass, that ten men shall take hold out of all languages of the nations, even shall take hold of the skirt of him that is a Jew, saying, We will go with you: for we have heard that God is with you.

AMOS 9:11-12—(11) In that day will I raise up the tabernacle of David that is fallen, and close up the breaches thereof; and I will raise up his ruins, and I will build it as in the days of old: (12) That they may possess the remnant of Edom, and of all the heathen, which are called by my name, saith the LORD that doeth this.

ISAIAH 45:14—Thus saith the LORD, The labor of Egypt, and merchandise of Ethiopia and of the Sabeans, men of stature, shall come over unto thee, and they shall be thine: they shall come after thee; in chains they shall come over, and they shall fall down unto thee, they shall make supplication unto thee, saying, Surely God is in thee; and there is none else, there is no God.

MICAH 4:2—And many nations shall come, and say, Come, and let us go up to the mountain of the LORD, and to the house of the God of Jacob; and he will teach us of his ways, and we will walk in his paths: for the law shall go forth of Zion, and the word of the LORD from Jerusalem.

ISAIAH 2:3—And many people shall go and say, Come ye, and let us go up to the mountain of the LORD, to the house of the God of Jacob; and he will teach us of his ways, and we will walk in his paths: for out of Zion shall go forth the law, and the word of the LORD from Jerusalem.

ISAIAH 60:2-5—(2) For, behold, the darkness shall cover the earth, and gross darkness the people: but the LORD shall arise upon thee, and his glory shall be seen upon thee. (3) And the Gentiles shall come to thy light, and kings to the brightness of thy rising. (4) Lift up thine eyes round about, and see: all they gather themselves together, they come to thee: thy sons shall come from far, and thy daughters shall be nursed at thy side. (5) Then thou shalt see, and flow together, and thine heart shall fear, and be enlarged; because the abundance of the sea shall be converted unto thee, the forces of the Gentiles shall come unto thee.

ISAIAH 60:10-12—(10) And the sons of strangers shall build up thy walls, and their kings shall minister unto thee: for in my wrath I smote thee, but in my favor have I had mercy on thee. (11) Therefore thy gates shall be open continually; they shall not be shut day nor night; that *men* may bring unto thee the forces of the Gentiles, and *that* their kings *may be* brought. (12) For the nation and kingdom that will not serve thee shall perish; yea, *those* nations shall be utterly wasted.

ISAIAH 60:16—Thou shalt also suck the milk of the Gentiles, and shalt suck the breast of kings: and thou shalt know that I the LORD *am* thy Saviour and thy Redeemer, the mighty One of Jacob.

ISAIAH 61-1-9—(1) The Spirit of the Lord GOD *is* upon me; because the LORD hath anointed me to preach good tidings unto the meek; he hath sent me to bind up the brokenhearted, to proclaim liberty to the captives, and the opening of the prison to *them that are* bound; (2) To proclaim the acceptable year of the LORD, and the day of vengeance of our God; to comfort all that mourn; (3) To appoint unto them that mourn in Zion, to give unto them beauty for ashes, the oil of joy for mourning, the garment of praise for the spirit of heaviness; that they might be called trees of righteousness, the planting of the LORD, that he might be glorified. (4) And they shall build the old wastes, they shall raise up the former desolations, and they shall repair the waste cities, the desolations of many generations. (5) And strangers shall stand and feed your flocks, and the sons of the alien *shall be* your plowmen and your vinedressers. (6) But ye shall be named the Priests of the LORD: *men* shall call you the Ministers of our God: ye shall eat the riches of the Gentiles, and in their glory shall ye boast yourselves. (7) For your shame *ye shall have* double; and *for* confusion they shall rejoice in their portion: therefore in their land they shall possess the double: everlasting joy shall be unto them. (8) For I the LORD love judgment, I hate robbery for burnt offering; and I will direct their work in truth, and I will make an everlasting covenant with them. (9) And their seed shall be known among the Gentiles, and their offspring among the people: all that see them shall acknowledge them that they *are* the seed, which the LORD hath blessed.

If you're a sincere, repentant non-Israelite, may TMH's truth and light shine upon you and your house. *(Zechariah 8:23, Isaiah 2:2-3)* May He shield you from the wrath to come. *(Genesis 12:1-3, Isaiah 14:21-11, Jeremiah 51:59, Ezekiel 35:5-15, Zechariah 2:7-9, Revelation 18:20)* And may He use you to bless and aid His people. *(Genesis 12:3, 27:28-29; Isaiah 60:10-12)*

BIBLIOGRAPHY

BIBLES
American King James Version
American Standard Version
Berean Study Bible
Brenton Septuagint Translation
Christian Standard Bible
Darby Bible Translation
Douay-Rheims Bible
English Revised Version
Good News Translation
God's Word Translation
Holman Christian Standard Bible
International Standard Version
JPS Tanakh
Jubilee Bible 2000
King James Bible
1611 King James Bible w/Apocrypha
King James 2000 Bible
New American Standard Bible
New American Standard 1977
Net Bible
New Heart English Bible
Northern Kingdom
New King James Version
Webster's Bible Translation
World English Bible
Young's Literal Translation

PSEUDEPIGRAPHA AND OTHER TEXTS

The Book Of Jubilees
The Ladder Of Jacob
2 Baruch
The Targums of Onkelos and Jonathan Ben Uzziel On The Pentateuch With The Fragments Of The Jerusalem Targum: From The Chaldee, J.W. Etheridge, M.A.

DICTIONARIES, ENCYCLOPEDIAS & LEXICONS

Zondervan's Compact Bible Dictionary

A Greek-English Lexicon of the New Testament and Other Early Christian Literature, Walter Bauer
The Century Dictionary and Cyclopedia
Strong's Exhaustive Concordance, James Strong, S.T.D., LL.D.
Thayer's Greek–English Lexicon of the New Testament, Joseph Henry Thayer
The Brown-Driver-Briggs Hebrew-English Lexicon, Francis Brown, R. Driver, and Charles Briggs

REFERENCE/HISTORICAL
Antiquities of the Jews, Flavius Josephus
For A Sign And A Wonder, Leah Yehudah

www.ingramcontent.com/pod-product-compliance
Lightning Source LLC
Chambersburg PA
CBHW071225290426
44108CB00013B/1291